HISTORY

—OF—

LINCOLN COUNTY, MISSOURI

FROM THE EARLIEST TIME TO THE PRESENT.

INCLUDING A DEPARTMENT DEVOTED TO THE PRESERVATION OF SUNDRY
PERSONAL, BUSINESS, PROFESSIONAL AND PRIVATE RECORDS;
BESIDES A VALUABLE FUND OF NOTES, ORIGINAL
OBSERVATIONS, ETC., ETC.

ILLUSTRATED

CHICAGO:
THE GOODSPEED PUBLISHING CO.
1888.

This volume was reproduced from
An 1970 edition located in the
Publisher's private library,
Greenville, South Carolina

All rights reserved. No part of this publication
may be reproduced, stored in a retrieval system,
transmitted in any form, posted on to the web
in any form or by any means without the
prior written permission of the publisher.

Please direct all correspondence and orders to:

www.southernhistoricalpress.com
or
SOUTHERN HISTORICAL PRESS, Inc.
PO BOX 1267
375 West Broad Street
Greenville, SC   29601
southernhistoricalpress@gmail.com

Originally published: Chicago 1888
Reprinted by:
Southern Historical Press, Inc.
Greenville, SC
New Material Copyright 2018
Southern Historical Press, Inc.
ISBN #0-89308-908-7
All rights Reserved.
Printed in the United States of America

LINCOLN COUNTY.

CHAPTER I.

LOCATION, TOPOGRAPHY, GEOLOGY, ETC.

Lincoln County, Mo., is located in the east central part of the State, and occupies portions of Townships 48, 49, 50 and 51 north, and Ranges 1, 2 and 3 east and west of the fifth principal meridian. It is bounded on the north by Pike County, on the east by the Mississippi River which separates it from Calhoun County in Illinois, on the south by St. Charles and Warren Counties, and on the west by Montgomery County, and has an area of 620 square miles or 396,148 acres. The 39th degree of north latitude passes through its center, and its isothermal line is 56, which passes through the mouth of the Potomac River, giving the same mean degree of temperature as that point on the Atlantic coast, which is intersected by the 38th degree of latitude.

TOPOGRAPHY.

The topography presents some striking features. Along the Mississippi River is a bottom prairie averaging about three miles, or perhaps a little more, in width. This is bounded on the west by rock bluffs which vary from 50 to 200 feet in elevation. In some places the bluffs are marked for considerable distances with a perpendicular wall of limestone rock varying from a few feet to 100 feet in height. These bluffs are cut in several places by narrow valleys through which flow the streams that lie east of the dividing ridge. This main ridge is nearly parallel with the Mississippi River, and from eight to twelve miles distant and from three to ten miles from the *Cuivre River on its west. The eastern half of the county has an uneven surface with ridges

---
* Pronounced Quiver.

rising in places more than a hundred feet above the adjacent valleys, generally parallel to the dividing ridge, and in the northeast is a ridge of knobs running north and south, and from 300 to 400 feet high. From many points the landscape scenery is very beautiful. The western half of the county is mostly high rolling prairie, cut through in several places with the streams tributary to the Cuivre. The prairie land comprises from one-fourth to one-third of the area of the county, the balance being timbered. To the lover of romance and beautiful and changeable scenery the eastern portion of the county is preferable, but for agricultural purposes and good roads for driving, the western portion far surpasses. One may travel from Auburn to Whiteside, thence to Louisville, thence to Olney, and thence by way of Millwood to Silex, and be all the way in an excellent agricultural country with a gently rolling surface, with the exception of a few valleys on the route with some broken land along their margins. There is also some quite level country lying between Troy and the western boundary of the county.

STREAMS.

The county is drained on the east by the Mississippi and some of its tributaries, the principal ones being Bryant's, Big Sandy, McLean's and Bob's Creeks, and the Cuivre River, which forms a portion of the southern boundary of the county. All that part of the county lying west of the dividing ridge before mentioned is drained by the Cuivre and its tributaries. This river is formed by the flowing together of Sulphur Fork, Sandy Fork, and other small streams in the northwestern corner of the county, in Waverly Township. It then flows in a southerly direction to the mouth of Big Creek at the southern boundary of the county, and thence north of east on a very tortuous line on the county boundary to the Mississippi. The tributaries of the Cuivre on the east, or rather the northeast side, are Mill Creek, Fork Branch, Sugar Creek and other small streams, and the principal tributaries on the opposite side are Null Creek, Lead Creek, West Cuivre, Spring, Crooked and Big Creeks. The latter has many tributaries and is the principal drainage for Clark Township. From the point where it crosses the fifth principal meridian to its confluence with the Cuivre it forms the southern boundary of the county. Upon the whole the county is well drained, especially the uplands, but the river bottoms are subject to frequent overflows. In June last the Mississippi bottom previously described was overflowed in some places all the way from the river to the bluffs, and in other places from the river to points from a quarter to a half mile from the bluffs. From all of this overflowed territory the cattle grazing thereon had to be driven to the uplands for safety and allowed to consume the grass in the meadows, thus occasioning a scarcity of hay for the season in that part of the county. The bottoms along the Cuivre were also overflowed, and thousands of acres of corn along this and the Mississippi were "scalded out" by the long standing of the water.

The smaller streams are not subject to much overflow, and the bottom lands along the Mississippi and Cuivre can be saved from overflow by proper levees which, in the course of time, will be constructed. By observing the course of the water courses it will be seen that the county has a general trend toward the south and southeast. There are many valuable springs of water adjacent to the streams, the most noted one of which is the "public spring" in the city of Troy. By these springs the first settlers built their cabins, but as the country developed they abandoned the springs in many instances, built their new residences on the arid uplands, where they made cisterns to hold rain-water for family use. There are also many wells in the county, as water is easily obtained at a convenient depth by digging, but cistern water is almost universally preferred for family use. Stock water in abundance is obtained from the streams and artificial ponds, which are supplied with water by the rain fall.

Before the settlement of the county, and for a number of years afterward, the water in nearly all of the streams flowed constantly throughout the year, and in several places grist and saw mills were erected on sites where the water power was sufficient to run them. Since the face of the country has been changed by clearing and cultivating it the constant supply of water, especially in the smaller streams, has ceased, and during the summer season they become dry with the exception of standing pools of water here and there, while in the wet seasons they frequently overflow their banks. In many places on the high prairies, before the land was cultivated, and while it was covered with the native grasses, there were beautiful pools or ponds of clear water which never went dry, and which were stocked with fish; but after the original sods were broken, and the tall native grasses became extinct, these pools became dry, and their beds are now under cultivation.

The Cuivre River was first navigated by steamboats in the summer of 1844, when the "Bee," a small stern-wheel boat of seventy-five tons burthen, went up as far as the mouth of Big Creek. Soon after, during the high water in June, the "Pearl," of 125 tons, passed over the dam half a mile beyond Moscow, and returned. During that summer the back water from the Mississippi extended over the mill-dam at Moscow. Since that time and before the building of the St. Louis, Keokuk & Northwestern Railway, steamboats, for several months nearly every summer, plied up the Cuivre to the mouth of Big Creek.

TIMBER.

The timbers comprise all the serviceable woods except pine and poplar. Lincoln is the best timbered county in North Missouri. In it are found oak, walnut, cherry, ash, maple, birch, hickory, linden, cottonwood, sycamore, locust, elm, pecan, hackberry, mulberry, willow, coffeetree, cedar, catalpa, ironwood, dogwood, hornbeam, box-elder, sassafras, persimmon and some others, showing an excellent variety for domestic, farm and manufacturing purposes. Of the eighteen species of oak found in this State more than a dozen are here; of hickory, six; locust, maple, sycamore and elm, three each; walnut, two, and so on. This list embraces all that is required in nearly the whole range of manufactures, including, as it does, an admirable variety of hard, soft and finishing woods, and the supply may be said to be practically inexhaustible.

The walnut, however, of large size, has been mostly exhausted. The sycamore, elm, soft maple, linden, hackberry, birch and willow grow principally on the bottoms along the streams. The walnuts, cherry, ash, hickory, cottonwood, locust, cedar, dogwood, hornbeam and some other varieties grow principally on the hill sides bordering the valleys, and some of the more level uplands are covered mostly with oak and hickory. The oak in some variety is found in all places where the timber grows. All the timber of the county, though some of it attains to a great thickness, has a short and more or less scrubby growth. In length it will not compare with that of the Eastern States.

The great bulk of timber suitable for lumber that has been cut from the forests of Lincoln county, has been shipped out of it in the shape of "saw logs," instead of in the shape of lumber. Thousands upon thousands of walnut, sycamore, oak and other valuable timbers have been floated from the Cuivre and its tributaries to the Mississippi, and thence rafted to market in the cities below. The first raft of logs taken out of the Cuivre was by Lewis Castleman and Harrison Munday, in 1828, started half a mile above Chain of Rock. This afterward grew to be a great industry and is still continued, and yet the supply is not exhausted, except as to walnut.

When the county was first settled there was no underbrush or small timber such as now exists. The timbered lands were open, the trees standing so far apart that the hunters could see the deer at distances from one to five hundred yards. The entire surface of the country was then covered with a rank growth of vegetation, consisting of the native grasses and wild flowers, which gave to the landscape, especially in the timbered lands, a much more beautiful appearance than it now has. Annually, after this rank growth of vegetation became frosted, dead and dry, the Indians set fire to it, and burned it from the entire surface of the country. This they did to destroy the places of concealment for the wild game, the better to enable them to secure their prey. This burning of the decaying vegetation destroyed the germs or sprouts, and thus prevented the growth of young timber. This practice was continued a few years after the first settlers located, and it was sometimes with the greatest difficulty that they saved their buildings and fences from being consumed. When the grasses were set on fire the long line of blaze, the flames of which encircled the tree tops, swept over the country with great rapidity and produced a sound like the roaring of distant thunder. When this annual burning ceased, the germs of underbrush and young timber began to grow, and the surface of the timbered lands, where they have not been cleared, are now covered with a dense growth of young timber and bushes. The supply of this young or "second growth timber," as it is sometimes called, is so abundant that it is believed that there is as much wood in the country as when first settled, though the acreage of timbered land is much less. The young timber is scarcely yet large enough for lumber, but much of it will do for rails.

ECONOMICAL GEOLOGY.

The minerals of Lincoln County are almost entirely undeveloped. In the southwest part of the county coal is found to the thickness of twenty-seven feet, the layers containing cannel, bituminous and block coals. An analysis of cannel coal from this mine by the chemist of the State Geological Board, exhibits: water 1.15, volatile matter 41.25, fixed carbon 49.60, ash 8. Several shafts have been sunk, but owing to want of transportation facilities, only enough coal has been mined to supply local demand. A good quality of coal is also found in the southeastern part of the county. Iron ore, mostly the red hematite, exists in many places, though no attempt has been made to utilize it, and its supply is a matter of conjecture. It is of excellent quality, as its analysis shows: insoluble siliceous matter 4.10, peroxide of iron 92.32, and the per cent of metallic iron 66.72. Abundant and excellent building stone is obtained in nearly every neighborhood of the county. Over a large area of the northern and northeastern parts Trenton limestone is found in layers from ten to twenty-five inches thick. It is light yellowish gray or drab in color, fine crystalline, very hard and compact, with smooth conchoidal fracture and susceptible of a fine polish, in many cases resembling a marble. In the southeast is the St. Louis limestone, hard, fine crystalline, and of a light blue and drab color. Over the remainder of the county are the Encrinital and Archimides limestones. The latter is fine crystalline, firm in texture, and bluish-gray in color. The sills and cap-stones of the county jail are of this kind. Of the Encrinital the coarse gray and buff colored is well adapted for ordinary masonry, as seen in the basement story of the Planters Hotel in Troy, while the purer white crystalline makes a handsome and durable ornamental building stone. Fire rock is plentifully obtained from the impure magnesian beds of the Hudson limestone in the northeastern parts of the county. Superior lime can be made in every section of the county. There are many beds of nearly pure carbonate of lime in the varieties of limestone mentioned above. In several places is found a hydraulic limestone of from four to six feet thick. It is capable of making a fair article of hydraulic cement, as its analysis shows : silica 21.35, peroxide of iron 1.79, lime 42.14, magnesia 0.66, carbonic acid 34.14. These limestones are not used except to supply local demand. Good fire clay is found with most of the coal beds. Good potter's clay exists in several places ; also white clay suitable for whitewash. None of these clays are utilized. For several years a potter's kiln was run, turning out excellent ware, but its owner went off during the war, and no one conversant with the business has since visited the spot. In several places are immense deposits of the very finest glass sand. The analysis is : silica 99.55, alumina 0.33, iron, a trace, lime 0.08, water 0.015. Want of facilities for transportation prevents the working of the beds.

CAVES.

There are several small caves in the county occurring in the upper beds of the Trenton limestone, which are often very cavernous. On Sulphur Fork of Cuivre, in Waverly Township, there is a cave and Natural Bridge, to which parties often resort for pleasure. This is among the most interesting features of Lincoln County. It is situated on the old J. S. Wilson farm—Section 15, Township 51, Range 2, west. At this point the right bank of Sandy Fork, with a north and south trend, raises an abrupt limestone cliff, and then slopes westward to a hollow. The Natural Bridge, as it is called, connects this hollow and the creek. This archway is in length about 125 feet, and has an average width of some twelve feet, though its walls are quite irregular. Toward the center the walls, all at once, contract, thus cutting the bridge into two rooms, leaving just space for a man to pass from one to the other. The ceiling of the rooms is apparently one large, flat rock, extending the entire 125 feet. The first room is entered by a large sink in the hollow, some fifteen feet deep, which brings one to the floor of the room. This part of the opening has a height of twenty-two feet. Passing over this rocky and slightly declining floor to the second room, there is a sudden precipitation of the floor of about sixteen feet, making the height of this department thirty-eight feet. The bridge is inaccessible from the east, as it opens immediately into the creek. On the creek side and some yards below the bridge, is a large hole, 10x12 feet high, in the rocky wall, which may be reached by climbing over stone and washed-out debris. Soon after entering the passage divides. The left hand divide gradually diminishes till it terminates some seventy feet back; the right hand divide, starting with a width of ten feet, and a height of seven feet, reduces its height to about three and one-half feet, when it suddenly expands to its former height and opens into the southeast upper corner of the second room of the bridge, where one may contemplate the pleasure of falling a distance of thirty-five feet.

At the W. B. Sitton place, near Louisville, is a mild chalybeate spring. A brown deposit is found in the adjacent wells. On Bryant's Creek, near the Mississippi River bottoms, are several springs of similar character, and sulphur springs exist along the Cuivre.

SOIL.

The soil of Lincoln County is varied in kind and quality. In quality it ranges from poor to extremely rich. Yet while none is too rich for careful and thorough cultivation not to pay largely. over slovenly tilling, so none is too poor to make fair return for labor judiciously bestowed. The prairie soil is tolerably uniform; none of it can be called poor. A small proportion of the prairie land is what is called crow-foot land, the best upland prairie soil known. It has sufficient sand for the water to drain off rapidly in wet weather, and enough of clay, lime, magnesia and humus to retain moisture. Four-fifths of the prairie is of the kind known as resin weed land, possessing less sand and more clay than the crow-foot land, and like it based upon siliceous marl, which insures, with proper cultivation, practically unlimited durability. While inferior in quality and scope to the crow-foot land, it is of great fertility, and in favorable seasons and with proper cultivation will produce from fifty to seventy-five bushels of corn, forty to sixty bushels of oats, twenty-five to thirty-five bushels of wheat and two to three tons of grass per acre; with the average season and the various grades of tillage in vogue among our farmers, good, fair to middling and bad, the general averages will reach about half the above estimates. The bottom prairies have a very rich and inexhaustible soil. Lying mostly on the Mississippi River, by reason of its occasional overflow, which has occurred about every ten years, and of insufficient drainage, most of these lands are yet uncultivated. The difference in the soils of prairie and timbered lands of the same formation in this county has been nearly obliterated in the process of cultivation, and in a few years the limits of the prairies cannot be told by the characteristics of its soil. The timbered lands in this county comprise the kinds known as hackberry lands, elm lands, hickory lands, white oak lands and post oak lands. The first two are contiguous and interspersed and contain very superior soil, growing in great luxuriance corn, wheat, oats, barley, tobacco and all kinds of fruit. The hickory lands are next in grade, with a soil more clayey and not so deep, subsoil more impervious and the underlying marls containing less sand and lime and more clay. It responds generously to good culture, and is easily rendered durable. It is adapted to corn, wheat and other cereals, tobacco and the grasses; blue grass, will grow on it spontaneously and luxuriantly. This kind in this county has an area about equal to that of hackberry and elm lands combined. White oak lands occupy a relatively large area in this county. The surface soil is not so rich as that of the hickory lands, but the subsoil is quite as good, and the underlying marls not so clayey and impervious. It produces good corn, fair timothy, very fine sorghum and the best wheat and tobacco in America. It is well adapted to all kinds of fruits, especially peaches and grapes. Post oak lands comprise a smaller area in this county. The soil is similar to that of white oak lands, with rather less lime and sand. Its productions are also similar. Another variety of soil is the magnesian limestone, occupying the slopes, hillsides and narrow valleys of the northeastern parts of the county. It is rich in lime, magnesia and humus, producing corn, the cereals and all kinds of fruits.

MOUNDS.

Ages ago, so far in the dim, shadowy past that neither they nor their history can be traced, those mysterious beings called Mound Builders were here and occupied the country for a season, leaving behind them their sepulchral mounds, their fragments of pottery, their stone axes, and their flint arrow points and lance heads. It is out of place to discuss here the mooted question whether or not the Mound Builders were a distinct race; it is enough to say that their mounds and their relics are here.

At Old Monroe, just north of the railroad bridge across the Cuivre on the level surface of the valley, stood three circular mounds in the form of a triangle, each being from five to six rods in diameter, and from eight to ten feet in height at their centers. One of them was wholly removed in excavating the railroad bed, and the others partially removed. In one of those only partially removed a human skull, a knife and a bracelet or pair of bracelets were found. The latter were made of silver. The two mounds partially removed by the railroad company are astride of the west line of the right of way, and recently the public authorities have hauled away and deposited on the highways all that part of these mounds extending outside of the line of the railroad right of way, leaving a perpendicular wall of earth from the general level to the top of the mounds. From this it plainly appears that the mounds were constructed by some human agency, the earth all being of the same kind, and apparently composed mostly of surface soil from the surrounding country. The centers of these two mounds and the north and south escarpments are still standing. About sixty rods west thereof, on an elevated ridge, stands a larger and higher mound, to the northward of which are a number of smaller mounds at regular intervals along the top of the same ridge. None of these have been explored. These Old Monroe mounds have an appearance clearly distinguishable from that of natural formations. Other mounds supposed to be the work of the Mound Builders are found on the lands of Mr. Lindsey in Township 49 north, Range 2 east. A row of four mounds stands north and south on lands of Alfred Johnson, being the southeast quarter of the northwest quarter of Section 27, Township 51 north, Range 2 west. The largest mound stands at the north end of the row, and from that to the other end they grow less in regular proportion. They are located about 100 yards from a bluff containing the same kind of rock of which they are partially composed. On the field where the mounds are located no rock is exposed, consequently it is presumed that the rock used in their construction was carried from the bluff.

It is the generally accepted belief among archæologists that the Mound Builders were here before the red or modern Indians, and built the mounds; that the red Indians never made flint arrow and lance points or pottery, and did not build mounds, but that they picked up and employed the arrow-points, and often buried their dead in the mounds which they found ready built when they came into the country. It is certain that two kinds of bones are often found in the mounds—one kind presumably those of the Mound Builders, buried hundreds of years ago, nearly decayed, the other, perhaps those of modern Indians buried more recently, and usually well preserved. Who were before the Mound Builders is not known, but after them came the red Indians, who, for years and perhaps centuries, danced and hunted over the surface of this county, fished in its streams, drank from its clear, sweet springs, and wooed their dusky sweethearts in its bosky dells. By-and-by came the white man, stealthily and timidly at first, and profuse in sweet words and fair promises to the original tenants, and after a while with more boldness, assumption and aggression.

CHAPTER II.

INDIAN AFFAIRS AND WAR OF 1812.

In connection with the early settlement of Lincoln County, Dr. Mudd, in his history in the county atlas, gives an extensive account of the conduct of the "wild men of the forest," from which the following has been largely obtained.

There were many settlements of the Sac and Fox Indians within the limits of the county at that time, and the district watered by the two Cuivres and Big and Peruque Creeks was one of the favorite hunting grounds of the two tribes, whose head quarters were in the Rock River country in Illinois. Black Hawk, or Ma-ka-tai-me-she-kia-kiak, the name by which he was known among his people, one of the most celebrated braves that ever lived, frequented this county, first on the hunt, and afterward on the bloody trail of war. He was popular with the whites, and liked their company; he was particularly fond of attending the dancing parties of that day and took his place in the quadrille with infinite zest. He had a partiality for strong drink, and much of his leisure time was spent at the still-houses which were then considered the vanguard of civilization. He lived for some time with Adam Zumwalt, whose capacious larder, the generous and free hospitality of himself and wife, his four daughters, Elizabeth, Rachel, Mary, and Catharine, pretty, lively, and ever ready for the dance; his four sons, John, Andrew, Jonathan and Solomon, vigorous, full of life and spirit, and excelling as hunters, and last but not least, the two still-houses near by, all combined to render this a most agreeable home for Black Hawk, when resting from the excitement and fatigue of the chase. He was often very drunk; but in all his intercourse with the whites, drunk or sober, his bearing was gentle and dignified, characteristic of his kindness of disposition and greatness of intellect. Black Hawk was perhaps more friendly toward the white people than any other Indian, certainly more so than the most of them; but he was not a chief, and it was about twenty-five years afterward, when he had nearly reached his sixtieth year, and his eminent wisdom in council recognized far and near, before he had much to do in shaping the policy of his tribe.*

The attitude of the Indians was exceedingly threatening and dangerous toward the first settlers of Lincoln County. From the first, they and the whites regarded each other with more or less suspicion. The Indians would sometimes drive off horses, kill stock and fire into the houses of the settlers. On one occasion they shot at two of Maj. Clark's children in the door, and one of the balls came within six inches of the mark, and at another time shot and killed a horse in his stable. Maj. Clark (more extended mention of whom appears in Chapter III) had long before learned to be cautious and wary in his dealings with the savages, the result of his frontier campaigns in Kentucky. While returning from Kentucky the second time, in 1800, bringing with him his black girl, and within a short distance from home, he camped one night with three Indians. Everything passed off quietly until next morning, when one of the Indians wanted to trade rifles with the Major, *nolens volens*. The Major let the Indian's gun fall, held on to his own with a strong grasp, and by a sudden twist loosened the hold of the would-be trader. Springing out of the reach of the Indian's knife, should he attempt to use one, he put himself in an attitude of defense, and cast a look of defiance at the red men, whose eyes fell before his keen glance. He then left without further ceremony than to keep a close watch on their movements as long as he was in sight of them. In speaking of this incident afterward, the Major said that he made up his mind that his bones should bleach on that camp ground before he gave up his gun. At his settlement in this county it was his invariable custom to place his gun and butcher-knife at the head of his bed every night, and to have the ax brought into the house. In the morning he would reconnoiter some distance from the house in every direction to see if any of the redskins were lurking in the bush. This vigilance was the more necessary on account of his isolated situation. Sometimes

---

*It is possible here that Dr. Mudd has unintentionally attributed in a measure to Black Hawk the character of Keokuk, chief of the Foxes, for it is well known that the latter was always, and especially during a period including the Black Hawk War, very friendly with the whites, while Black Hawk was hostile. Keokuk was also very fond of whisky and exceedingly fond of all manner of sporting. It is claimed by citizens of the extreme northeast part of this State, who personally knew Black Hawk before and after his war of 1812, that he was not a dissipated man. However, it may be true that the character assigned him by Dr. Mudd was correct at the time alluded to—that is before the War of 1812.

for the space of six weeks he saw not a white face outside of his own family. The Indians called Maj. Clark the "man with the big hands," and often threatened to kill him because he spoiled their hunting grounds. The Major never believed, however, that they really intended to kill him, because they had so many opportunities. Their object was rather to intimidate the whites, and to prevent by that means a further encroachment on their territory.

MASSACRE OF McHUGH'S CHILDREN.

Except the massacre of the McHugh children, there is no authentic account of any murders of any white persons by the Indians, prior to the breaking out of the War of 1812. Doubtless some were perpetrated, as some of the descendants of the pioneers remember to have heard the facts so stated; but names and circumstances are alike forgotten. In 1804 William McHugh sent his sons James, William and Jesse, to hunt the horses, which they found about a mile from home, up Sandy Creek. On their return they fell in with Frederick Dixon, a famous Indian scout. The two older boys were each riding a horse, and Jesse, a lad of ten or twelve, got up behind Dixon. At the ford of Sandy Creek, a short distance below where the bluff from Cap-au-Gris to New Hope now crosses the stream, they were fired upon by the Indians, who were concealed behind a large sycamore. The two oldest boys were instantly killed. Dixon's horse made a spring up the bank, breaking the girth and throwing the riders to the ground. They sprang to their feet and fled for their lives. Jesse McHugh could not keep up with Dixon, and he kept crying out, "Oh, Mr. Dixon, don't leave me! Don't leave me!" In spite of his piteous appeals for help, and his own strong sympathy for the unhappy youth, Dixon kept on, knowing that to do otherwise would be but a useless sacrifice of his life, as he was entirely unarmed. He said that he should never forget the agonizing shrieks of the poor little fellow, mingled with the demoniac yells of the savages as they cleft his skull with their tomahawks. Dixon was pursued to McHugh's fence. The three boys were buried in one grave, on a high point of land near the place of their murder, on the north side of the creek, and between where the old trail ran and the present bluff road. John Lindsey helped to bury them, placing split puncheons around them for a coffin, and then cut their initials on a white oak tree, and his own on another, the two standing on either side of the grave. These trees, with the marks nearly grown over, have been seen by persons now living in the vicinity, but they have disappeared. Capt. Stonebreaker cut the last remaining one for a saw log some thirty years ago. The bluff road at this point is a part of the first public road laid off in this county. It was located in the early part of the War of 1812 as a military road from Fort Howard in this county to Fort Madison, on the Mississippi River, in Iowa.

The Indians claimed that the massacre of the McHugh boys was done out of revenge for a difficulty with some white men a short time previous, in which three dogs belonging to the Indians were killed. The murdering party numbered only four or five, and is supposed to have been under the command of Black Hawk himself. Black Hawk, in his "Life," written at his own dictation, says nothing about this; but many rangers who had taken part in the War of 1812, and who read Black Hawk's life when it was written in 1833, claimed that the narrative was not strictly true in several matters to their own knowledge, but was rather an apology than a correct history, Black Hawk having committed many acts of which his natural nobility of character was ashamed. The impression that Black Hawk commanded the party referred to, has this authority: a brother of the murdered boys lived many years afterward near the Iowa River in the country frequented by the Sacs, and it came to his ears that Black Hawk on several occasions boasted of being concerned in this particular exploit. On the whole, the weight of testimony is against the probability of Black Hawk's participation in the affair. McHugh declared his determination to ascertain the truth of the matter, and if Black Hawk was really concerned in the murder of his brothers, to avenge their blood by shedding his. It is scarcely probable that he failed to satisfy himself. There is also strong reason to believe that Black Hawk was then at home in the Sac village.

At this time the Sacs held a council and sent Quash-qua-me, Pa-she-pa-ho, Ou-che-qua-ka, and Ha-she-quar-hi-qua, four of their principal civil chiefs, to St. Louis, to ransom a captive who was in prison for killing a white man. This they expected to do by paying a sufficient sum of money to satisfy the relatives of the murdered man, thus "covering up the blood," according to their own custom. This delegation was gone long enough to excite the apprehensions of the tribe. It finally returned with many presents, and told that a treaty for land had been signed; that the prisoner was let out of prison, when he started to run and was shot dead, and that great quantities of the white men's fire-water had been drunk. The result of this embassy was not at all satisfactory to the tribe. The inference is a reasonable one that these four Indians, realizing that they had failed in the purpose for which they were sent, and that they had exceeded their instructions in consequence of their prolonged sprees, during which they were outwitted by the whites, were determined on some specific act of revenge, and that they were the men who perpetrated the bloody massacre.

THE WAR OF 1812—FORTS ERECTED.

The apprehensions of the early settlers as to the Indian attitude were greatly increased by the intelligence of the declaration of war between this country and Great Britain. The exposed condition of the inhabitants would invite the hostile attention of the five or six tribes, who considered this county and adjacent territory as their hunting ground. It was expected that these would make common cause with the British. The declaration was made by Congress on the 12th of June, 1812; and when it became known, the people lost no time in providing for the defense of their homes. Stockade forts were built at convenient points. Maj. Clark, with the assistance of two hired men, built a stockade at his residence, and it was called Clark's Fort. It took six weeks to complete it, the three working every day except two Sundays. When done the Major put up 7,000 pounds of pork to cure, with other provisions for the use of those families that would seek shelter within its walls after being driven from their homes. A large stockade was built at Troy, and called Woods' Fort. It was built on the lands of Deacon Joseph Cottle and Zadock Woods, and took in the spring. Stout's Fort was built on Fort Branch, near Auburn. A large stockade was built on what is now called the Tinbrook place, and known before that as the Samuel Bailey place. * * * It stood on the bluff north of the intersection of the bluff road with that leading from Chain of Rocks to Cap au Gris, and not far back of the Cave Spring where until recently stood the house erected by Samuel Bailey. This was called Fort Howard, in honor of Benjamin Howard, who was governor of this Territory, but resigned November 29, 1812, to engage in the war as brigadier-general. At the time of his appointment as governor, September 19, 1810, he was member of Congress from Kentucky. He was an efficient military officer. He died at St. Louis September 18, 1814. During the war he made one or two visits to the fort. He complimented the people for having made the best selection and built the best fort in his district. He was a large, fine looking man, and wore a buckskin coat or hunting shirt plentifully adorned with fringe.

VOLUNTEERS.

As far as known, most of the rangers who volunteered from this county served in the companies of Capt. Christopher Clark of this county, and of Capt. (afterward colonel) Daniel W. Boone, Capt. Nathan Boone, and Capt James Callaway, the last a grandson, and the other two sons of Daniel Boone, all of St. Charles County. A few were under Capt. Craig, who was killed in this county, but where he came from is not known. Lieutenant (afterward General and President) Taylor, of the regular army, had his headquarters at Woods' Fort, and under his command were quite a number of the citizens of this county, including Zadock Woods, the Cottles and Collards; but whether it was the last year of the war, or just after the war ended, it is not now known. David Bailey, Jonathan Riggs and John McNair, all of this county, were lieutenants in active service. Before the war ended Bailey was promoted to the command of a company, with the rank of captain. Riggs was a man of undaunted courage, but of cool judgment. He was frequently intrusted with the command, and on many occasions his sagacity and knowledge of Indian methods of warfare saved the lives of his men. McNair, son of Robert McNair and nephew to Gov. McNair, was a good soldier, and a brave but rash man. He saw a good deal of service in Illinois. He was killed in a skirmish opposite Cap-au-Gris. The campaign of the Lincoln County Rangers extended from the Missouri River to past the Iowa line, principally in the vicinity of the Mississippi River.

ATTACK BY BLACK HAWK.

In the latter part of the year 1812 Black Hawk was commissioned brigadier-general in the British army, and wished to descend at once upon these settlements; but Gen. Proctor would not consent until after the second unsuccessful siege of Fort Meigs, which ended in July, 1813. Black Hawk then came down, as he says, with thirty braves; but the rangers of that day said that he had a much larger force. His avowed purpose was to avenge the death of his adopted son, whom he said was killed by the whites. He divided his force, and he and a party landing near Cap-au-Gris, came across the bottom, and reached the bluff in the vicinity of McLane's Creek; the other party ascended Cuivre and made a feint on Fort Howard. Benjamin Allen, Francis Riffle, Frederick Dixon, Roswell Durgee, John Lindsey and William McHugh went up to Lindsey Lick, a place since owned by Joel Crenshaw and John Averall, under the escort of five rangers, among whom was James Bowles, to sow turnips. It was the custom in those troublous times to keep the families in the forts, while the men would go out under a guard to work in the fields cultivating and gathering crops. The party, not fearing any immediate danger, was somewhat scattered. Dixon and Durgee were riding on one horse along a path, on the side of which Black Hawk and another Indian were concealed. When they got within reach the Indians fired, mortally wounding Durgee. The horse jumped, and both men fell to the ground. Black Hawk started in pursuit of Dixon, who arose and ran. The latter ran over a pile of new rails, when, as he was about to be overtaken, he picked up a stout stick and turned to defend himself. As he did so Black Hawk saw his face. He says in his Life, "I knew him. He had been at Quash-qua-me's village, to learn his people how to plow. We looked upon him as a good man. I did not wish to kill him, and pursued him no further."

In the meantime the ranger Bowles was killed. Before the alarm had been given, the boys, Edwin Allen, Chauncy Durgee, John Ewing, and John McLane were bathing in the creek. When the firing began Benjamin Allen galloped up, took his son Edward on the horse, and telling the other boys to hide, rode off. The little fellows lost no time in hurrying out of the water, and finding on the bank a large hollow log, crawled into it. Black Hawk, in turning from the pursuit of Dixon, heard the noise and sprang upon the log. Chauncy Durgee afterward said that he looked through a knot-hole and saw the Indian, who seemed to be looking him right in the eye, but that he turned off without discovering them.

Black Hawk said that he saw the boys, but thought of his own boys at home, and let them escape. Dixon soon recovered his horse, and found Durgee and attempted to help him mount, but the latter being severely wounded and scalped, had partially lost the use of his reason, and could not be made to comprehend what was desired of him. Finally he took hold of the horse's tail, and Dixon made him understand that he was to hold fast and travel as rapidly as he could. After going about a hundred yards his hold relaxed and he fell back. Dixon being hard pressed made his escape. Black Hawk and his companions came across Durgee. He says, "The latter was staggering like a drunken man all covered with blood. This was the most terrible sight I had ever seen. I told my comrades to kill him to put out of his misery; I could not look at him."

FIGHT NEAR FORT HOWARD.

Not long after the foregoing incident a rise took place in the Mississippi River, and the back water came up from Cuivre along the bluff. A party from Fort Howard went out in three skiffs for some purpose. They had not gone far before they were fired upon by a party of Black Hawk's band, and seven men killed, among whom was George Burnes, son of James Burnes, who settled on Sandy Creek, as already mentioned. The survivors put back, and the Indians rejoined Black Hawk. The latter expected an attack and formed his men in line, himself standing boldly in front. This was scarcely done before the rangers, who had heard the firing from the fort, were seen advancing with great impetuosity, led by Capt. Craig. Black Hawk took deliberate aim and fired, and Capt. Craig fell dead from his horse. The rangers never halted, but fired as they advanced and killed five of the bloodthirsty savages. Then, without taking time to reload, the Indians retreated into a sink-hole, the bottom of which was covered with bushes, which afforded protection from the fire of the rangers. They also dug holes with their knives in the sides of the depression, which gave them a pretty safe shelter. A desultory firing from both sides was kept up for some time. William McCormick, one of the rangers, declared that he was going to kill an Indian, and that he would shoot him in the mouth. He carried out the boast exactly, he and several others going up to the edge of the sink-hole for that purpose. The others fired without effect. The fire was returned, killing Lieut. Spears on the brink and mortally wounding McCormick.

Black Hawk thus continues the narrative: "Some of my warriors commenced singing their death-songs. I heard the whites talking and called to them to come out and fight. I did not like my situation, and wished the matter settled. I soon heard chopping and knocking; I could not imagine what they were doing. Soon after they ran up wheels with a battery on it, and fired down without hurting any of us. I called to them again, and told them if they were brave men to come down and fight us. They gave up the siege and returned to the fort about dusk. There were eighteen in this trap with me. We all got out safe, and found one white man dead on the edge of the sink-hole. They could not remove him for fear of our fire. We scalped him and placed our dead man upon him. We could not have left him in a better situation than on an enemy." The "battery" was a keg of powder, to which was attached a fuse, and placed on the fore wheels of a wagon. This was run up to the brink, and intended to be pushed down into the midst of the Indians, but it exploded prematurely. The abandonment of the siege, which had continued from early in the day, was the result of a false alarm. This sink-hole was not a great distance from the fort, and is only a few yards from the Chain of Rocks and Cap-au-Gris road. Near by is a large spring, known to this day as the Black Hawk Spring. When the rangers returned to the fort, some of them brought the head of one of the fallen savages and stuck it upon a pole. Being without an officer, and in need of re-enforcements, they sent for Capt. Whiteside, who came the next day and had the pole taken down and the head buried. Black Hawk and his party abandoned their canoes and returned to Iowa by land, taking with them only two scalps, those of Durgee and Lieut. Spears. The body of the Lieutenant was found where he fell, with the dead Indian sitting astride it.

MASSACRE OF THE O'NEAL FAMILY.

Chauncey Durgee, one of the boys who hid in the log as before mentioned, moved to Canton, in this State, and died some years ago. John Ewing, who was one of his companions in the log, was a son of William Ewing, who, when his wife died, divided out his children, giving the youngest, Willie, a boy not quite two years old, to Mrs. O'Neal, whose husband had moved a few years before to a place three miles above Clarksville. At the beginning of the war O'Neal and his neighbors were engaged in building a stockade, where Clarksville now stands. On returning home in the evening O'Neal saw the hogs dragging some object down the path, quite a distance from the cabin. It was the body of his eldest daughter, seventeen years of age. The whole family, consisting of his wife and nine children, and the Ewing boy, had been massacred. Most of the bodies were found in the yard. Hanging over the fire was a large kettle, which Mrs. O'Neal had been using to heat water for washing. In this kettle O'Neal's youngest child, a mere infant, was thrown alive and literally roasted. Willie Ewing had been thrown on the fire, beneath the kettle, where his body was found partially consumed. This horrible butchery was perpetrated by a band of Pottawattomies. The next year this tribe made peace with the Americans after the defeat at Malden. Many of them were in the habit of visiting Fort Clark, at Peoria, Ill., while going on their hunting excursions down the Sangamon. One of the band, who visited the fort frequently, became very friendly, and loved to talk of his exploits during the time his tribe was at war with the whites. In one of his talks he told of having led the party that massacred the O'Neal family, and how, when scalping one of the boys, the victim grinned in the agonies of death.

This came to the ears of Lieut. John McNair, who lived in Troy before he enlisted, but was then in Fort Clark. McNair said, "The next time I see him I'll make *him* grin." The next day the Indian came back. McNair was asleep at the time. When he awoke he was told that the Indian had just gone. Inquiring the way, he gave immediate pursuit. He got almost upon the Indian before each saw the other. From the manner of his pursuer, the Indian saw that the matter was one of life or death, and prepared himself for defense. McNair got the first shot, and sent a ball crashing through the skull of the savage. Near the close of the war, Lieut. McNair was stationed at Cap-au-Gris, where Capt. Musick had command. A force of Indians came down on the Illinois side. Hearing of this the Lieutenant took six men and crossed over to reconnoiter, against the advice and caution of Frederick Dixon, who was familiar with the ways of the savages. They had not proceeded far from the river when four of their number were killed and McNair severely wounded. He and the other two men, Burnside and Webber, made for the skiff. The Indians reaching the boat first, sunk it. The white men plunged into the river, and the Indians after them. Webber being overtaken, plunged his hunting knife so deep into the breast of his pursuer that he could not withdraw it. He and Burnside reached a drift, where they were rescued by Dixon, David Lamaster and Thomas McNair, John's brother. Lieut. McNair was never afterward seen.

A JOKE WITH SAD RESULTS.

A party of rangers going from Fort Howard to Madison, on the bluff road, camped one night at a house on Hurricane Creek that had been lately abandoned. They found some provisions and a barrel of honey beer, of which they partook freely. The next morning, after marching a mile or more, the party concluded they must have some more beer, and sent about a dozen men back to get it, agreeing at the same time to march slowly, so as to be easily overtaken. As soon as the men started back, the onward party decided to have some fun, and to this end they deployed themselves in an ambush in such a manner as to make as large a show of strength as possible, intending to give their comrades a good scare when they returned with the beer, and then laugh at them. The result was not according to programme—the scare being changed to the other side. Presently the dozen rangers were seen coming along the road, happy in the possession of their beer and anticipating no danger. Their friends in ambush, at the proper moment, fired their guns in the air, raised the Indian yell, and kept up scattering volleys. The surprised men fell back with some disorder, which was keenly relished by their comrades in ambush. They rallied, and believing that they were attacked by concealed Indians, advanced and poured a well directed volley into the bush from whence came the heaviest firing. The command came out sharp and clear, "Load, boys, and let the red devils have it again." And again the leaden hail rattled through the brush. The fun had now lost all its charm. Several of the originators of it had been wounded, though not seriously, and they realized that they were in imminent danger. The other party was so intent upon the work of self-defense that all the shouting and hallooing could not make them understand the real situation. Finally some of the party in the bush rushed into the midst of the others and explained the affair. The wounded men were cared for, the beer was drank, and every man pledged himself not to engage in a practical joke of that kind again during his life. Pain and sadness took the place of the anticipated laugh.

DEATH OF LYNN AND KEIGHTLEY.

William Lynn, who lived where Brown's addition to Troy is situated, was a ranger, and at one time on duty at Fort Howard. He was fond of his dram and used to keep his bottle hid out. One day he took his usual walk to enjoy his bottle and was in the act of drinking, when he was shot and killed by the Indians. Abraham Keightley, of St. Charles County, while hunting his horses, crossed Cuivre at White's Bar, about a mile above Chain of Rocks, and when a few yards from the river, on the land between Maj. H. Anderson and Francis Freise, was killed by the savages. His son, who died near Troy a few years ago, preserved his vest which showed the mark of the fatal bullet. Samuel Groshong, son of Jeremiah Groshong, was wounded in the shoulder, which caused a paralysis of the arm that lasted for several years. This occurred near Moscow, which vicinity was greatly infested by the Indians. After this five men were detailed from Clark's Fort to guard Groshong's mill. Among these was Peter Pugh, who used to declare that he would die before he would run from the Indians. He was a very pleasant and agreeable man, had been in several engagements and possessed an excellent reputation for courage. How well he kept his vow will be seen further on.

EXPEDITION TO RELIEVE PRAIRIE DU CHIEN.

The disastrous attempt to relieve Prairie du Chien, was made early in the spring of 1814. The expedition consisted of three flat boats of soldiers, forty-two regulars under Lieut. Campbell, and sixty-five rangers, mostly from this county, under the command of Lieuts. Riggs and Rector, and one or two boats loaded with provisions. At the rapids Campbell's boat grounded, and the other two passed on. Black Hawk attacked Campbell's boat, set it on fire and killed several of the men. Seeing this the other two boats put back, Riggs' getting aground and being delayed nearly an hour. Rector ran his boat alongside of Campbell's and took off the men. The Indians attacked them with great fury, causing considerable confusion among the soldiers, rendering their fire ineffectual, and preventing a proper management of the boat. Riggs, after getting his boat off, concealed most of his men, handled his boat as if he were panic stricken, but managed to get it between the rest of the force and the Indians. The latter poured several volleys into it, to which Riggs paid no attention, but keeping up the show of utter demoralization, ran his boat toward the shore where the Indians stood. As soon as it touched, the savages rushed pell-mell for it, anticipating an easy triumph, but they found it a hornet's nest. Riggs saw his opportunity. At his orders the men rose and delivered a volley that sent the savages flying from the scene of battle. This diversion allowed the other boats time to recover, and they proceeded with all dispatch down the river. Lieut. Riggs hoisted sail and followed them, without having lost a man. The expedition returned to Cap-au-Gris. Two or three from Lincoln County were killed in this action, one of them being Peter Harpole, who was killed in Campbell's boat. The total loss was twelve killed and between twenty and thirty wounded. Black Hawk, in speaking of the conduct of Lieut. Riggs, says: "I had a good opinion of this war chief; he managed so much better than the others. It would give me pleasure to shake him by the hand."

DEATH OF M'COY, PUGH AND M'NAIR.

In April, 1814, Joseph McCoy, Sr., and his nephew, Joseph McCoy, Jr., and James McCoy, the first two being commonly known respectively as Big Joe and Little Joe, the latter a son-in-law of Maj. Christopher Clark, were sent from Fort Howard to find the whereabouts of the Indians. They went to Sulphur Lick, a spring strongly impregnated with sulphur, iron, salt and other minerals. It is situated about a quarter of a mile east of North Cuivre, and a mile and a half north of the Riggs Ford, on Section 3, Township 49, Range 1 west. The place had been settled some time before the war, a cabin built, and a small patch of ground cleared around the spring, but at this time it had been abandoned. The mineral water made the spring a favorable resort for deer. On this occasion no Indians were seen, and the scouts concluded to take a hunt. They unsaddled their horses and turned them in the old field to graze. Big Joe was not very well; he lay down in the lap of a fallen tree and went to sleep. James McCoy had killed a deer, and was at the spring washing out his gun. The Indians fired on him, wounding him in the thigh, and ran him about 300 yards, where they overtook and killed him. Big Joe awoke at the sound of the firing, but could not get a good chance to shoot, as the Indians were running about through the woods. Presently he was discovered, and as the savages closed in on him, he made a run for life. He was the fleetest footed and most active of all the rangers. A big Indian, swift footed and active, soon distanced his fellows, and held McCoy a tight race for a mile or so. A large oak had been felled, and the branches lay directly in the path. Without swerving in the least, Big Joe made a terrific spring and leaped entirely over the tree top. The Indian stopped in amazement: "Whoop! Heap big jump! Me no follow!" McCoy's speed never slackened until he had gone several miles.

Little Joe was standing on the bank of the Lick Branch about a quarter of a mile below the spring when his brother was killed. He went up to the old field, caught and saddled his horse, and, finding the coast clear, went in the direction of the fort, leading the other two horses. He sent word to Maj. Clark. There were only two men in the fort besides the Major, Isaac White (who had both thumbs shot off a short time previous while in the act of firing, in a skirmish below Cap-au-Gris, where the rangers were driven back by the superior force) and David McNair. Maj. Clark collected eight men and gave pursuit. He followed the Indians some distance up North Cuivre to a point where they separated. It is said there were twenty-seven of the savages. Some time after this Peter Pugh and Robert McNair, the latter being a mere boy, and a brother to Lieut. John McNair, went to the same lick to hunt horses. The Indians attacked them and killed both. They might have easily escaped by a timely retreat, but Pugh dismounted, put his gun across his horse, and fought until he died. He killed four Indians. The savages, in revenge for his bloody work, hacked his body to pieces, and scattered it over the field. The remains were collected and buried with the body of young McNair on the bank of the lick stream.*

DEFEAT AND DEATH OF CAPT. CALLAWAY.

In March, 1815, Capt. James Callaway, with a body of rangers from Woods' Fort, was encamped on Loutre Island, in what is now Montgomery County. One night the Indians made a sudden dash into the camp and captured about thirty horses. The next day, being the ninth of the month, the Captain divided his men, leaving one detachment on guard, and with the other started in pursuit of the depredators. After following the Indian trail some twelve miles or more, Loutre Creek was crossed, and the

---

*Thus far the history of the War of 1812, pertaining to Lincoln County, has been principally copied, with some changes in the language, from Dr. Mudd's account of it as given in the county atlas. Quotation marks have been omitted because of the changes of the language, which have been made to adapt it to the present.

horses were discovered tied close together, but not an Indian was visible. Capt. Callaway proposed to advance and secure them at once; but Lieut. Riggs, who was with the command, objected to this for fear of being led into a trap, and volunteered to make a reconnoissance. This being agreed to, he rode entirely around the horses, examined the ground, and returned without seeing an Indian. Being now satisfied that the enemy was not concealed within range of the horses, the command advanced and secured them, and turned about to go back to camp. The whole affair looked very suspicious; Riggs advised returning by another route, but the Captain refused to act upon this advice, and started back on the same route on which he went out. Loutre Creek was re-crossed, and the trail was followed down its banks and under the bluffs for several hundred yards. In this narrow defile a murderous fire was received from the concealed Indians. The rangers were thrown into confusion and disorder, from which the Captain, by his coolness and bravery, soon extracted them and made a desperate resistance; but their courage and desperate fighting were unavailing. The Captain and a large number of his men were killed. The command now devolved upon Lieut. Riggs, who, with the remnant of the command, cut his way out and returned to camp. The next day a party of rangers went out from the fort and buried the dead. The scene of their mangled forms was appalling.

Woods' Fort.—During the war twenty-five or thirty families took refuge in this fort. Among the men the following names have been preserved: Jacob Null and his son, John, Joseph Cottle, Joseph Collard and his son Elijah, Alambe and Job Williams, —— McNair, a blacksmith, Zadock Woods and a man named Paris. These names have been preserved through the memory of John Null, who was then a boy. He remembered the Paris family on account of a fight between Mrs. Paris and another woman at the spring. This fight caused a considerable sensation in the fort.

During the War of 1812 many skirmishes with the Indians, and other incidents took place, which have been lost to history. No doubt but that many others, not herein mentioned, were killed. The sufferings of the early settlers during that period, from hunger and other privations, not to mention the anguish and grief of the friends of the slain, can now scarcely be imagined. The hardy pioneers labored hard, and fought their way in the midst of savages, to subdue the wilderness and make homes for their children and the succeeding generations. Their memory should be revered by all.

CHAPTER III.

EARLY SETTLEMENT.

The history of Lincoln County properly dates from the beginning of the nineteenth century, when Maj. Christopher Clark erected his cabin, and became the first permanent settler within its limits. About five years previous, a few persons located on Spanish grants in the eastern part of the county, adjacent to the Mississippi and Cuivre Rivers. These were mostly French trappers and hunters, whose residences were only temporary. These settlements came to nought, and in a very few years every single grant was held by a non-resident owner. Hon. Tully R. Cornick, in an address before the first agricultural and mechanical fair ever held in the county, October 4, 1856, estimated that at the commencement of the present century less than forty acres of land had ever been put in cultivation in the county.

THE FIRST SETTLERS.

Maj. Clark was born in Lincoln County, N. C., in the year 1766. His father, James Clark by name, was a native of Ireland, and his mother, Catharine Horine, of Scotland. They first settled in Winchester, Va. They had six sons: Alexander, William, James, Christopher, John and David. Alexander, James and John remained in North Carolina. William was killed by the Indians in Kentucky. David visited Missouri in 1811. Returning to his native State he married Margaret Douglass, by whom he had one son, William, who was afterward well known all over this county. The family of David came to this State in

1823, and settled on the Wright City road, three miles south of Troy. He died many years ago. He was greatly respected for his honest and upright character, and was for many years a justice of the peace. Christopher Clark settled in Lincoln County, Ky., in the year 1788. He married Elizabeth Adams, by whom he had six children: James, Sarah, Catharine, David, Hannah and Elizabeth. He served as lieutenant in a company of volunteers, guarding the frontiers of Kentucky, and also during a campaign up the Wabash River in 1790. He came to Missouri in 1799, bringing with him his horses and cattle. On this occasion he came on a prospecting tour as far north as the present site of Troy, where was then situated a small Indian village, the wigwams being placed in a kind of circle around the spring. The following year he brought his family in a pirogue, or large keel-boat, down the Kentucky and Ohio, and up the Mississippi and Missouri Rivers, and landed at St. Charles. He settled at what is now known as Gilmore Springs, on the Wabash Railroad. A few days after his arrival his wife died. He immediately returned to Kentucky, and purchased a black girl to do the housework in his new home, where he resided about a year. In April, 1801, he moved into the limits of this county, being the first white man to cross Big Creek with a wagon, and built his cabin within a few feet of the present residence of Frederick Wing, Esq., three and a half miles southeast of Troy, on the St. Charles road. This was the first permanent settlement in the state north of the present limits of St. Charles County. At that time his nearest neighbor was Anthony Keller, who lived on the south bank of Big Creek, four miles off; after that the nearest settlement was made at Flint Hill.

Maj. Clark, in 1804, married his second wife, Hetty Calvert, of Virginia, by whom he had three children: Ralph H. F., Julia, and William Calvert. He died in 1841. He was a man of sterling honesty and of good solid judgment, and ever retained the confidence of his fellow citizens. During the last twenty years of his life, he was frequently solicited to run for office, but invariably refused. Of his children, James served one year as orderly sergeant under Capt. Nathan Boone, the youngest son of Daniel Boone, and was once severely wounded. David served one year under Capt. James Callaway, who was a grandson of Daniel Boone. He went to Texas with his brother James, in 1826, and was killed in battle in 1838. Sarah married Col. Alambe Williams, and went with him to Texas in 1831, where they both died many years ago. Catharine married Capt. Joseph McCoy, and went to Texas in 1824, where her husband died a few years afterward. She was living when last heard from. Hannah died single in 1820. Elizabeth married Jesse Cox, and lived and died in this county. Ralph was born while his mother was on a visit to Green's Bottom, in St. Charles County, in 1804. He married Mary Murphy, of Kentucky, by whom he had two children. She died in 1839, and he afterward married Mary Atkinson, also of Kentucky, by whom he had eight children. He served many years as justice of the peace, while residing at the old homestead in this county. In 1858 he moved to Martinsburg in Audrain County. Julia married Valentine J. Peers, who was sheriff of this county from 1836 to 1838. Mr. Peers died in St. Louis. William died on his way to California in 1850. James died in Texas. McCoy and Williams each served a year under Capt. Daniel M. Boone, and a year under Capt. Callaway, during the War of 1812.

Soon after the settlement of Maj. Clark came Jeremiah Groshong, a native of Pennsylvania, who had lived a few years in St. Charles County, near the Missouri River. He settled half a mile northeast of Clark's, on the land known as the Castleman or Herndon place. He built a stone house on this farm, raised a family of nine children, was a prominent citizen, and took an active part in the organization of the county. In 1836, he and his family, excepting his son Jacob, moved to Wisconsin, where both he and his wife died—he at the age of eighty-six years. Jacob was born in October, 1800, a few months before his father settled in this county. About the year 1843, he settled on a farm four miles from Chain of Rocks on the Troy road, and lived there till his death at a very advanced age. At the time of his death he had been a resident of the county longer than any other person, and was doubtless the only person within its limits who had been a subject of Spain and France, and a citizen of the District of Louisiana, the Territory of Louisiana, the Territory of Missouri and the State of Missouri, without a material change of his place of residence. Alexander McLane came from Kentucky in 1801, and settled on the Stuart place, on the bluff, four miles from Cap-au-Gris. He took his negroes, dammed the creek which was afterward named for him, and built a grist-mill on the spot where the stream cuts through the bluff. The buhrs were quarried in the vicinity, and dressed by himself and slaves. This was the first water-power mill built in the county. Next came the families of Zadock Woods and Joseph Cottle, from Woodstock, Vermont, who settled in Troy in 1802. With Mr. Woods came his mother and his two brothers, James and Martin, who settled at the same time near Old Monroe. Mrs. Woods died in this county at a very advanced age. The three brothers went to Texas in an early day, where Zadock and some of his sons were killed fighting for the independence of the Lone Star Republic. They were each possessed of considerable means. Zadock was a stone-mason, and built the first stone-chimney in Hurricane Township.

Ira Cottle, nicknamed "Muxey," came from Vermont in 1799, and settled at Old Monroe, in this county, in 1802. His father, Warren Cottle, settled in St. Charles County, and was afterward a soldier in the War of 1812. Ira Cottle married his cousin, Suby Cottle, and after her death he married the widow of John Ewing. During the trouble with the Indians he, unlike the other settlers, would not retire into the fort, but remained at home. In 1820 he was the richest man in the county, and paid taxes on 1,000 acres of land. He built the house since occupied by Mrs. Henry Hemmersmeyer, as a store and dwelling, which is one of the finest brick blocks erected in the county, and, at the time it was built, the largest. He died in 1843.

Francis Riffle, born in Virginia, October 14, 1781, came to this county from Kentucky, where he was reared, and settled on the ridge below McLane's Creek, in 1803. He died in this county, May 22, 1858.

William McHugh, whose three sons were murdered by the Indians, was of Scotch ancestry. In 1803 he settled on Sandy Creek, on the farm since owned by Burt J. Cocke. He died a few years after the War of 1812. He and his wife were buried on the banks of Sandy Creek, about 200 yards north of the site of their cabin. The male line of his family is extinct, except probably a grandson, John McHugh, who was living some years ago on the Des Moines River, in Iowa. Col. David Bailey, the first sheriff of Lincoln County, and who afterward occupied many official positions, came here from Vermont in 1803. He was a captain of rangers in the War of 1812. His death occurred in 1864. John Lindsay, from Maine, settled on Sandy Creek in 1803. He possessed an excellent education, was deputy county clerk in 1820, county court justice from 1825 to 1828, and served several years as a justice of the peace. He died in the winter of 1833-34, having survived his two children. His widow went to Wisconsin. James Burnes, about the same time, settled on Sandy Creek, a quarter of a mile above the scene of the McHugh massacre. Roswell Durgee, also, about the same time, settled at the mouth of Durgee Hollow, on the David T. Killam place. The same year, 1803, Frederick Dixon settled in Monroe Township. He married Elizabeth, daughter of James Burnes, and lived here many years after the War of 1812, and died in Iowa.

John Riffle, son-in-law of Alexander McLane, settled in Lincoln County in 1804. His daughter, Mrs. Nancy Daniels, was with her parents in Fort Howard during the War of 1812, and, being nearly grown, became very familiar with the events of the time, and carried them distinctly in her memory to old age. Benjamin Allen, of Woodstock, Vt., came to St. Louis in 1804, and removed, a few years before the War of 1812, to the Tinbrook place, near Monroe. After the War he settled on Hurricane Creek, where he died about the year 1840. He was a prominent citizen, and served many years as a justice of the peace. Ezekiel Downing, an Irishman, and cousin to Gov. McNair, came about the same time. He established the first tanyard in Lincoln County. It was on the Capt. Wehde place. He was stepfather to Freeland Rose, Esq. About this time came John and William Ewing. They were not closely related, if at all. The former settled near the Mississippi River, not far from the line dividing Townships 49 and 50, north. He possessed considerable property. He died about 1819-20. Col. Ira Cottle administered on this estate, and married his widow. William Ewing settled farther down, probably between Sandy and Bob's Creeks. His wife died in 1811, and he then divided out his children and had no settled home thereafter. His youngest child, named after himself, was killed in the O'Neal massacre. Jacob Null came from Cocke County, Tenn., and settled in St. Charles County in 1808. The following year he moved to what is now Lincoln County, and settled on the Jackson farm three miles west of Troy. He afterward moved to a farm one mile south of Troy, where he died in 1819. He was a great bee hunter, and spent much of his time hunting bees on Honey Creek, and in the forks of Cuivre River, and was so successful that the name of the stream was changed to Null's Creek. His brother John, and the latter's son, Jacob Jr., came to the county the same year (1809). The Nulls, like most of their neighbors, left their farms, and abode in Woods' Fort, during the War of 1812-15. They took an active part in the defense of the settlement, and also in the organization of the county.

Several other families settled in the vicinity of Troy before the War of 1812, but the exact dates cannot now be ascertained, nor can all their names be recollected. The following were among them: John and Joseph Hunter, the former being the father of the late John M. Hunter, of New Hope. He settled near West Cuivre, five miles northwest of Troy. Robert McNair, a blacksmith, of Irish parentage, born in Pennsylvania, and brother to Gov. McNair, settled in Troy. After the war he moved to near Auburn and subsequently to Hurricane Township, where he died. Elijah Collard and his father, Joseph Collard, settled in the county in 1811, as did Alambe and Job Williams, Maj. Robert Jameson and his son, George W. The latter, subsequently, in 1817, settled on a farm two and a half miles east of Millwood, and was the first settler in the forks of Cuivre. David Porter came from Tennessee and settled on Big Creek in 1810.

As soon as the Indians ceased their hostilities, at the close of the War of 1812-15, the settlers retired from the forts to their respective homes. Some of them, who had only settled temporarily, now selected their permanent homes and moved thereon. Those who became permanent settlers in the vicinity of Auburn, in 1815 or 1816, were James S. Lewis, David Meracle, Daniel Draper, Joseph Howdeshell, Samuel and James Gibson, James Clark, Joseph McCoy, Lawrence B. Sitton, Robert McNair, Thacker Vivion and Ezekiel Downing. Some of these, as has already been noted, settled in the county before the war. Levi Brown, from Tennessee, settled in 1815 or 1816, and James Porter, from the same State, in 1817. Freeland Rose from Kentucky, settled in 1817, and remained here until his death, April 27, 1885. William Miller, with his family, left North Carolina in November, 1817, and arrived at Clark's Fort, now the Frederick Wing place, June 5, 1818. About this time, and perhaps earlier, James Wilson came from South Carolina and settled on the farm now owned by James Riley, three miles northeast of Auburn. Both of these old settlers are still living—the latter at Auburn, at the age of ninety-four years—the former on his farm near Moscow. Walton Perkins came to this county with his father in 1818, and settled on the farm known as the old "Bickel place," about two miles south of Troy. In 1820 he visited the land office at St. Louis, to make a payment on his father's land. In the fall of 1817 Philip Sitton settled in the forks of Cuivre. He was born in North Carolina in 1772, and died in this county in 1861. John Hudson, born in Washington County, Ga., in 1796, came to this county in the fall of 1818, and with him came Jarot Ingram and James Owens. The latter settled on what is known as the Daniel Kempler place, and Ingram on a place cornering thereto and lying just over the line in Pike County. At this time John R. Gililland was living near the present Sulphur Lick Church, and William Trail on the road where his widow, "Aunt Sallie Trail," now lives, on the road between Troy and Millwood. Capt. Thomas Hammond and his brother, Slade, had also settled in that vicinity. A man named Lowe lived on the Brice H. Wommack farm, and another, named Barnett, lived on the old Beard place near Louisville. The last named settlers, commencing with Philip Sitton, together with George W. Jameson, who has been noted as the first settler in the forks of Cuivre, and a man who lived near the mouth of Lead Creek, were probably all the people living in the northwest part of the county, not including the Auburn settlement, in 1818.

At this time, Mr. Hudson observed that Indian wigwams were very thick; and after selecting a place on which to locate, he returned to Georgia, married his sweetheart, and, in June, 1819, moved to this county, bringing with him his parents and three brothers. In the interim nearly all the Indians had gone; Col. Meredith Cox had settled at Louisville, and Mr. Moore, father of Fountain Moore, had settled on the Dr. McFarland place. These, with other parties mentioned above, helped Mr. Hudson build his cabin, where he located, in what is now Nineveh Township. There was then no settlement west of him until Grand Prairie was reached, forty miles distant. He settled a quarter of a mile north of Lead Creek and half a mile west of the head of Null Creek. On the ridge between these creeks was the trail road leading to Troy. Samuel Gladney, born July 9, 1789, in South Carolina, settled near the site of Auburn in 1820. He died August 9, 1875, having been a citizen of the county fifty-five years.

In 1826 Charles Hoss came from Kentucky and settled near Louisville. He died at Truxton, December 26, 1879. The same year Samuel Howell settled about four miles northeast of Troy. In an interview published in the *Herald* in 1876 Mr. Howell stated that when he settled his neighbors were Armstrong Kennedy, John Hunter, Thomas East, John Wilson, Lemon and William Barker, brothers, an old man named Jennings, who soon left the county, and one Hatfield, who also left. These, with Kennedy, lived near Cuivre River, and each had hunted up a spring of water near which to build. Beyond these settlements there were none on the north nearer than the Auburn settlement, on the northwest, those of George W. Jameson and others, and further to the west, the Hudson settlement. Mr. Howell could not remember of any settlements west of Hudson's in 1826. By this time, however, the eastern and southern parts of the county had become much more thickly settled.

In 1828 Stephen A. Stephens, born in Virginia February 6, 1790, came to Lincoln County and settled near Millwood. He says that the grass where Millwood now stands was then tall enough to hide a man on horseback. Daniel Draper was then living in Auburn; and shortly afterward Andrew Cochran and his brother kept a store at Fort Spring, just south of Auburn. The same year Henry Watts, from Tennessee, settled near the site of Elsberry. William Uptegrove, born in North Carolina, October 11, 1785, settled at Louisville November 8, 1829, on the place since owned by Ben. R. Williams, near the old bridge ford of North Cuivre. To Mr. Uptegrove this seemed to be a perfect paradise. The soil was fertile to a wonderful degree, to him who had been used to the red hills and flint stones of North Carolina. Cochran's store at Fort Spring, near Auburn, was then the best one in that part of the county, and had the most custom. James Beck, of South Carolina, and his wife settled in Lincoln County at an early day. He died in 1839, and his widow died December 18, 1879, at the age of eighty-nine. John Britton, a prominent citizen of the county, was born in Virginia, March 12, 1796, came to this county in 1841, remained over forty years, and died at the house of his son, J. R. Britton, in Rock Hill, Mo., March 22, 1882. He was a soldier in the War of 1812, and was engaged at the White House, below Alexandria, on the Potomac, and had the satisfaction of firing seven shots at the British.

SURVIVORS OF THE REVOLUTION.

Among the early settlers of Lincoln County were a number of the survivors of the Revolutionary War, and the following can be mentioned: Noah Rector, Isaac Hudson, John Chambers, John Barco and Alembe Williams. Noah Rector died near Millwood about the year 1849, at the age of one hundred and two years. Isaac Hudson was born in North Carolina, and after the war lived in Washington County, Ga., until 1799; he then went to South Carolina, and in 1804 moved to that part of Logan that is now included in Simpson County, Ky.; in June, 1819, he came with his wife and four sons, John, Thomas, William and Charles, to this county, and settled in what is now Nineveh Township. He died many years ago at an advanced age. He was a blacksmith and farmer, and was much respected for his strict honesty. John Chambers was born in 1740. In 1778 he enlisted in Capt. Alexander Cummins' company of the Fourteenth Virginia Regiment, and was in the battle of Monmouth. He died in Clark Township in 1844 or 1845. John Barco was born in 1744;

enlisted May 24, 1877, in Camden County, N. C., as a drummer in Capt. Dempsey Gregory's company of the Tenth North Carolina Infantry, Col. Shepherd commanding; was at Valley Forge and West Point; in 1779 was sent to Charleston with his command and assigned to Gen. Lincoln; surrendered with the other forces to the British, May 12, 1780, and put on board a prison-ship where he remained five months. A short time after exchange he was mustered out of service at Richmond, Va. Alambe Williams was born in 1757; he enlisted from Guilford County, N. C., June 10, 1781, in Capt. Moore's company of the First North Carolina Infantry, commanded by Maj. Armstrong. He was afterward in Capt. Michael Randolph's company in Col. Henry Lee's legion. He was present in several battles, and at the storming of several forts. He received his discharge from Gen. Nathaniel Green.

PIONEER TAXPAYERS IN 1821.

The taxpayers in Lincoln County in 1821, as shown on the tax-list of that year, it being the earliest one preserved among the records, are as follows: [This probably is a complete list of the heads of the pioneer families at that time, as they should appear on the list. Their names are classified, as indicated by the lands described opposite them, in each of their four municipal Townships.]

In Monroe Township, comprising the southeast quarter of the county, there were David Bailey, Samuel Bailey, Ira Cottle, Almond Cottle, Zachariah Callaway, Ezekiel Downing, Abijah M. Highsmith, David Lard, John Lindsey, Otis Peck, James E. Paddock, Thomas Riffle, Joseph Russell, Barnabas Thornhill, James Turnbull, James Woods, Martin Woods, Allen Woolfolk and A. C. Woolfolk.

In Bedford Township, comprising the southwest quarter of the county, there were John Armstrong, Thomas Armstrong, Seth Allen, Frederick Avery, Jeremiah Beck, John Bell, John Barker, William Brown, Sr., William Brown, Jr., John Black, Emanuel Block, Gabriel Brown, Levi Brown, Benjamin Blanton, Thompson Blanton, David Boyd, John Brunk, John Cannon, Lambert Collier, James Collard, Elijah Collard, Christopher

Clark, William Cannon, James Chambers, Joseph Cottle, Sherman Cottle, Stephen Cottle, Lee F. T. Cottle, Benjamin Cottle, Isaac Cottle, Andrew Cottle, Samuel Cannon, Benjamin Croce, James Duncan, Cary K. Duncan, William S. Duncan, John S. Duncan, Samuel L. Davis, David Erwin, Terah B. Farnsworth, Rufus Fullerton, John Geiger, Samuel Groshong, Jacob Groshong, Thomas Gammon, George Guinn, Thomas A. Guinn, William Guinn, Malcolm Henry, Sr., Malcolm Henry, Jr., John Hunter, Joseph Hunter, Horace Harding, Allen Jameson, Armstrong Kennedy, David Keller, Joseph King, James Knox, Sr., James Knox, Jr., David W. McFarland, Thomas Mann, Jonathan D. Morris, Hiram Millsap, John Null, David Pressley, Jehu Piles, John Parkinson, Philander Powers, Elisha Perkins, Nathan Ramy, Bethuel Riggs, Jonathan Riggs, Shapley Ross, Mervin Ross, William H. Robinson, John M. Seymour, James Stanley, John Shrum, John Thurman, John Talbolt, Winslow Turner, Sr., Winslow Turner, Jr., Miles Turner, Elias Turner, John Ward, John Waggoner, Alambe Williams, Levin Williams, Thomas Williams, John Williams, Morgan Wright, Zadock Woods, G. W. Zimmerman, Conrad Yater, Peter Yater, and J. M. Zimmerman.

In Union Township, comprising the northwest quarter of the county, there were Hugh Barnett, John Cantriel, James Cantriel, Meredith Cox, John Cox, Adam Coose, Daniel Draper, Richard Fenton, James Galloway, Sr., James Galloway, Jr., William N. Galloway, John Gililland, Mathias Gililland, Samuel Gibson, James Gibson, Isaac Hudson, John Hudson, Thomas Hudson, Brice Hammock, Martin Hammock, Thomas Hammond, William Harris, Joseph Howdeshell, John Howdeshell, Robert Jameson, Sr., Robert Jameson, Jr., George W. Jameson, Samuel Lewis, James Lewis, Robert McNair, Joseph McCoy, David Merikle, Thomas Merikle, Quinten Moore, Thomas Moore, William Moore, David Porter, Samuel Smiley, Joseph Sitton, Sr., Joseph Sitton, Jr., Philip Sitton, William Sitton, Lawrence B. Sitton, Guian Sitton, James Shaw, William Trail, Nicholas Wells and Josiah Wilson.

In Hurricane Township, comprising the northeast quarter of the county, there were the following: Benjamin Allen, Reuben

Abbott, Benjamin Barton, Thomas Barton, William Burnes, Jonathan Cottle, Ezekiel Downing, David Diggs, John Ezell, Samuel Gladney, John Galloway, Peter Galloway, Sr., Peter Galloway, Jr., Samuel Galloway, William Galloway, William Hammock, Elijah Myers, John Sapp, Jesse Sitton, Jehu L. Sitton, James Sconce, Samuel Sconce, George Turnbaugh, Daniel VanBurklon, Edward Wyatt, David Wilson and Francis Withington.

The following had no description attached to their lands, and consequently it cannot be determined in which township they resided: Sylvanus Allison, Elijah Barton, Charles Broadwater, William Beatty, Joseph Barnett, James Cannon, John Cox, James Downing, John H. Downing, Silas Davis, James Early, Walter Emory, John Griffith, Andrew Gilbert, Benjamin Highsmith, William Highsmith, Lovell Harrison, William Harley, George Harley, Martin Harley, James Harley, Henry Howdeshell, Alexander Hill, Jesse Low, Andrew Love, Andrew Miller, David McCoy, William McCoy, William McLean, Reuben Nowell, Bennet Palmer, Andrew Patterson, William O. Ross, Moses Rainey, Return Strong, Samuel Sargent, Samuel Shaw, Samuel Smith, Andrew Smith, George W. Smith, Charles Stewart, Thomas Spillman, John Turnbaugh, William Talbert, Peter Teague, Isaac Thurman, Joseph Thurman, Kesiah Woods, John Walker, Jacob Williamson, Thomas Wells, Severn Wallace, James Wilson, and John Wilson. Of all these it is believed that none are now living in the county. This list, together with the widows and the estates of deceased persons, made the number of 276 taxpayers.

MEETING FRIENDLY INDIANS.

About three years after Samuel Howell settled in the county, he went, with a small party, down the Mississippi for a week's hunt. They camped about a hundred yards from the river bank. In the afternoon of the first day, a fine buck was killed not far from the camp. The next morning, after his comrades had been gone some time, Mr. Howell took his rifle and walked down the river about half a mile. Approaching the bank and looking toward the opposite shore, he saw an Indian push his boat out and step into it. For several minutes he remained motionless, as if listening. He appeared to be of powerful build. Presently the canoe shot swiftly and noiselessly up the river, closely hugging the shore, as if to screen itself in the shadows of the overhanging bushes. At a point opposite the camp it turned and made directly for the western shore. Mr. Howell rapidly returned to camp, and a few minutes later the Indian landed and walked up the bank. He was entirely unarmed, but strode on without showing by his countenance whether he meant friendship or not. Stepping up, he grasped Mr. Howell's hand, and grunted "How do?" which was probably all the English he knew. The next thing he snatched the rifle with an exhibition of rough cordiality, but smiled complacently as he examined every part of it. Mr. Howell was not sure but that his smiles meant mischief, and to use his own expression, never felt so "spotted" before, nor since. The examination ended with apparent satisfaction, the Indian made signs, by taking aim, imitating the noise of the discharge of the piece, going through the antics of a wounded deer, then pointing to the deer skin and the spot where the deer had been killed, to show that he had been a witness on the occasion. He then handed back the rifle and examined, with many nods and smiles, the other paraphernalia of the camp. Mr. Howell invited the Indian to eat of the venison steak, but he declined, made several unintelligible signs, shook hands and departed the way he came.

Shortly after this, Mr. Howell was with another hunting party on the Mississippi, near the mouth of the Cuivre. Riding out one day, they came to an Indian tent, at the door of which sat a venerable looking old warrior. Inside was an old squaw engaged in cooking, and a young one, who sat some distance off on a mat of deer skins. Squire Howell thought she was the handsomest woman he ever saw. He and the other hunters could not keep their eyes from her face. Their admiring glances annoyed her; an angry fire gleamed in her beautiful eyes. Her evident displeasure producing no effect, she covered her face and head with one of the skins and remained covered while the interview lasted. The old squaw gave each visitor a piece of jerked venison, at the same time pouring a little salt into the palm of each one's hand. Politeness compelled them to eat, but their politeness was never put to a severer test. The venison was hard dried in the sun and none of the sweetest. The old warrior related in broken English, aided by signs, how the Indians caught great numbers of deer by driving them into the overflowed bottoms.

THE PIONEER'S CABIN.

This oft-mentioned habitation was always made of logs, sometimes hewed on two sides, and sometimes not hewed at all. When hewed, the logs were put up with the flat surfaces on the inside and outside of the building. The cracks were filled with "chinking," and this was daubed over with mud. The form of the cabin was always an oblong square, with a huge fire-place in one end. The fire-place was set back in a crib composed of logs, with the face even with the inner wall. This crib was heavily lined with stone and mortar, built up on a hearth made of flat stones. On top of the stone and mortar lining was made a stick and mud chimney, the latter always being entirely on the outside of the building, and extending a little above the comb of the roof. The cabin was only one story in height, and was covered with clap-boards resting on poles running the long way of the building, and weighted down with other poles. One or two small openings were cut out for windows, in which greased paper, when it could be had, was often substituted for glass. The floor was made of puncheons, prepared wholly with an ax, and laid down on "sleepers." The door was made of light puncheons or heavy clap-boards fastened together with pins and hung on wooden hinges. This is a fair description of the completed "pioneer's cabin." All the tools required in building it were the ax, broad-ax-frow and auger. Many such a cabin was built without the use of a nail.

Those adventurous pioneers who settled miles in advance of any settlement had to construct their cabins alone, with the assistance of their families, unless men advanced from the settlement to help them, but those who settled where a few had gone before were more fortunate. The early settlers were so anxious to have others join them that they would go sometimes twenty miles to help a new comer build his cabin. All the pioneer had to do was to drive to the place selected for his home, unhitch his team, go into camp, as he had often done on his journey, then saddle a horse and ride around to his nearest neighbors, and send them for further ones, notifying them of his arrival and when and where to meet to erect his cabin. All who possibly could would be on hand at the "house raising;" the trees would be felled, the logs and poles prepared, the clap-boards riven, and the building erected, ready for occupancy in a single day. The putting in of the puncheon floor, the making and hanging of the door, the chinking and daubing of the cracks, was usually left for the new comer to do at his leisure; and not unfrequently this finishing of the house was postponed until a truck patch was cleared and planted, and sometimes not until cold weather made it a necessity, the pioneer, meanwhile, occupying all his time in extending his "clearing." If a man wanted two rooms erected, he was considered aristocratic, and could not get that spontaneous assistance that one of more moderate desires might command. However, the additional room would be raised if extra inducements were offered, such as a "frolic" and an abundance of whisky. This latter article was always on hand at a "house raising," and was usually as free as water, the price of it being 25 cents per gallon. Mr. Howell relates that before raising his cabin, he went to Troy, and for 50 cents, all the money he had, he purchased two gallons of whisky of superior quality, then went to Armstrong Kennedy and bought a hog, promising to pay for it by breaking flax. With these and other provisions, he managed to supply the wants of those who so kindly helped to erect his cabin. The log house is yet a common thing in Lincoln County; but in many places east of this it has become extinct, and is remembered only as a thing of the past.

PIONEER WEDDINGS.

The first marriage record for Lincoln County begins with November 1825, a quarter of a century after the first settler erected his cabin. During this period, as a matter of course, a number of the children of the early settlers had intermarried, but no public records of their nuptials have been preserved. A pioneer wedding in this "western wild" could not compare in point of elegance and style with one of these days, for there were lacking the paraphernalia of display, the pomp and circumstances of the present day. No artistic cards of invitation were then sent out, but a general invitation was given orally to the few scattered pioneers, who would go many miles to attend such an occasion. In those days but few fine clothes were worn, especially by the young people who were reared, or partially reared, west of the Mississippi. After the "best suits" brought here by the pioneers were worn out, all had to content themselves with homespun clothing. A "Sunday suit" was nothing more than a new "every day suit."

The bridal trousseau did not consist of the most costly apparel —the finest silk dress, the most stylish and latest fashioned head gear, and the whole adorned with costly beads and jewelry, and the outfit of the bridegroom was not made of the finest broadcloth, nor did the silk hat form a part thereof. The bride was neatly attired in a plain homespun dress, all her apparel corresponding, and was admired for her beauty, not for that of her dress. The bridegroom was also attired in homespun goods, and the marriage was as fortunate and felicitous, and the wedding as joyous, as any at the present day. The wedding feast did not embrace so great a variety of eatables, champagne and wine, and dessert of ice-cream, strawberries, oranges etc., but the food consisted of the wholesome necessaries, and all were merry with the gay festivities of a humble wedding on the frontier of civilization. In those days there were not so many amusements as now exist, and a wedding was quite a rare thing. The guests being isolated and somewhat lonely would eagerly assemble and participate in the festivities of the day, which often consisted of athletic sports, and a dance on the puncheon floor, after the wedding-feast was over.

The wedding feast was always worthy of the name. The champagne and claret were good old Kentucky and Missouri whisky, clear and pure as mountain dew, unadulterated by mercenary 'rectifiers,' untouched and untaxed by gauger and government. There were venison steaks and roasts, turkey, grouse, nectar-like maple-syrup and other edibles, toothsome and elegant.

The first marriage recorded in Lincoln County, but not the

first occurring, was that of John English to Catharine Davis, solemnized August 3, 1825, by Thompson Blanton, a justice of the peace. The next was Richard Wommack to Cinthy Smiley, daughter of Maj. Samuel Smiley, solemnized August 18, 1825, by William Hammock, justice of the peace. Then followed Ephraim Cannon and Dorothy Hunter, November 20, by Rev. David Hubbard. Because of their brevity and peculiar wording the following certificates are given in full.

LINCOLN COUNTY, UNION TOWNSHIP, } STATE OF MISSOURI. }

Joined in wedlock John Jimerson and Polly Gillerland agreeable to request, they both being of full age to act for themselves. Given under my hand and seal, this 12th day of November, 1825. THOMAS HAMMONDS, J. P.

John Gilleland and Elizabeth Pressley was married to each other December 25, 1825. In witness whereof I hereunto set my hand and seal.
DAVID HUBBARD. [Seal]
an ordained minister.

Married on the 25th day of December, 1825, Mr. Hary Oakley to Mrs. Susanna Willson, both of lawful age and citizens of Union Township, County of Lincoln and State of Missouri. DANIEL DRAPER, J. P.

I do certify that on the 13th day of October in the year 1825, I Cellebrated the Rite of Mattrimony between Abraham Evans and Linney Shrum, both of lawful age. PHILIP SITTON.

LINCOLN COUNTY, } MISSOURI. }

I do hereby certify that Thomas Hampton and Sarah Hatfield was married to each other on March the fourth, 1827. DAVID HUBBARD.

I certify that I joined in Wedlock, Francis Henry and Judith Perkins, March 17, 1829. D. BAINBRIDGE, Ordained Preacher of the Gospel.

The marriages recorded for 1826 are: Samuel G. Sitton and Rebecky Porter, February 23, by Jesse Sitton; Edwin Allen and Jane Wade, May 6, by Benjamin Allen, justice of the peace; Eli Hubbard and Kesiah Cannon, July 23, by Rev. David Hubbard; Samuel Sapp and Millinde Sapp, July 27, by Benjamin Allen, justice of the peace; Thomas Edwards and Mrs. Voughn, July 12, by Samuel Smiley, justice of the peace; Thomas Hopkins and Lydia Beck, October 22, by Rev. David Hubbard; William Humes and Issabellah Howard, November 2, by John Lindsey, justice of the peace; William B. Sitton and Polly Ingram, December 21, by Jesse Sitton.

While some officers and ministers joined the happy aspirants in wedlock, Rev. Hubbard always married them "to each other." The spelling of the names and words in these certificates is given as they appear on record, though some of them are evidently incorrect. For want of space, the list of early marriages cannot be further continued.

OLD SETTLERS' RE-UNION AT ELSBERRY.

In compliance with previous arrangements, a re-union of old settlers of Lincoln County was held at Elsberry, in August, 1882. A stand was erected for the use of the speakers, and a platform or floor for the use of those who wished to "trip the light fantastic toe." It is presumed, however, that the old settlers did not indulge much in the latter exercise, but were, no doubt, amused to see their children and grandchildren engaged in it. The music was furnished by the Prairieville Band. The dinner was served after the old barbecue style; two beeves, twenty-seven sheep and several hogs were dressed and roasted for the occasion, besides an abundant supply of bread, pyramids of cake, lemonade and other good things in proportion. The tables were spread in a leafy grove, and from them the multitude of people fed, from the gray-haired and venerable pioneer, down to the little child in its mother's arms. Speeches of a miscellaneous character, full of rehearsals and reminiscences of "ye olden time," were delivered by Col. N. B. Minor, and D. A. Ball, of Louisiana; Judge Thomas, J. C. Fagg and T. J. Forgey of St. Louis; Hon. H. S. Parker of Troy, and others. Many old settlers were present, and the meeting was claimed to be the largest ever held in the county up to that time.

> Should auld acquaintance be forgot,
> And never brought to mind?
> Should auld acquaintance be forgot,
> And days o' lang syne?

OLD SETTLERS' ORGANIZATION IN TROY.

On Saturday, June —, 1883, a number of old settlers of Lincoln County assembled in Troy, and organized an Old Settlers' Association, with the following as officers: Capt. William Miller, president; W. T. Thurmond, secretary; H. F. Childers, corresponding secretary; vice-presidents: Dr. M. H. McFarland,

Bedford Township; Judge Henry T. Mudd, Millwood Township; John Downing, Nineveh Township; O. N. Coffee, Waverly Township; Judge Alex. Wilson, Union Township; Duncan Ellis, Hurricane Township; Jonathan Crume, Snow Hill Township; B. F. Roberts, Burr Oak Township; Judge Charles Martin, Monroe Township; I. B. Lynn, Clark Township; Alex. Kennedy, Prairie Township.

The meeting then adjourned to June 23d, at which time a much larger number assembled. On motion, a committee on programme and general arrangements was appointed, as follows: T. J. Nalley, John M. Ellis, Capt. Colbert, Dr. McFarland and A. V. McKee. A committee on invitations, consisting of one from each township and the editors of the local newspapers, was then appointed as follows: J. M. Wilson, of Clark; J. A. Elmore, of Prairie; Judge Shaw, of Nineveh; James Wilson, of Waverly; Judge H. T. Mudd, of Millwood; Isaac Ellis, of Union; Robert Elsberry, of Hurricane; Elijah Myers, of Snow Hill; Frank Withington, of Burr Oak; William Lindsay, of Monroe; and Jordan Witt, of Bedford; J. W. Powell, of the Elsberry *Advance;* H. F. Child, of the *Free Press;* and W. T. Thurmond, of *The Herald.*

The following were then appointed as a finance committee: Frederick Wing, W. T. Powell, H. M. Brown, Jeff. Wray, T. K. Nichols, Ben. Elliott, Rufus Hall, P. G. Shelton, John W. Wilson, Levi J. Garrett, W. A. Woodson, W. T. Thurmond and H. W. Perkins. The committee of arrangements met subsequently, and among their deliberations extended a special invitation to the following named non-residents, some of whom had formerly been residents of the county, to attend the re-union at Troy, on the 31st day of August following, viz.: Judges Gilchrist Porter, Thomas J. C. Fagg, N. P. Minor, Elijah Robinson, Hon. A. H. Buckner, Col. J. E. Hutton, Hon. Charles E. Peers, Hon. D. P. Dyer, Hon. James A. Rollins, Hon. James O. Broadhead, J. S. Besser, of Texas, Seneca W. Hammock, and Hon. J. B. Henderson.

Accordingly, at the appointed time, August 31, 1883, the people assembled in Troy and made a memorable day in the history of Lincoln County. The day was splendid in its bright sunshine. H. W. Perkins, marshal of the day, at the request of President Miller, called the meeting to order at 11 o'clock, A. M. Prayer was offered by Rev. T. J. McDonald. The choir sang "Auld Lang Syne," and was followed by music by the Winfield Band. The address of welcome was then delivered by Dr. J. W. Welch, who reminded the people that many had settled in this county long before the first steamship crossed the ocean, and before railroads and telegraphs had been constructed. The next speaker was Judge N. P. Minor, of Bowling Green, who contrasted the educational advantages then enjoyed by the youth, with those of his boyhood days, when he had to walk six miles to school, following hog paths through gigantic grass, infested with ticks and snakes. The meeting then adjourned for dinner, and the immense mass of people separated into groups about the tables and on the lawn, and ate and related the trials, hardships and pleasures of pioneer life with general satisfaction. The first exercise after dinner was the "May Pole" dance by little girls and boys of Troy, A. S. Buchanan skillfully touching the violin and calling. Charles E. Peers was the next orator, and gave an interesting history of the courts and county officials, interspersed with amusing anecdotes. Col. D. P. Dyer then appeared upon the stand. His venerable mother, ninety-two years old, was seated near him. His was an acceptable speech for the occasion, full of paternal feeling, with allusions to his school experience, under John M. Ellis as teacher, and many other amusing incidents of early times.

Hon. Jeptha Wells, in behalf of the young men of Troy, then presented a silver cup to the lady who had lived the longest in Lincoln County. Mrs. Nancy Daniels, who had lived in the county from her birth in 1804, was the happy recipient. A silver cup was then presented by O. F. Busswell, of the Laclede Hotel, to the gentleman who had lived longest in the county. This was received by John S. Null, aged nearly seventy-seven years, who settled here in 1808. L. R. Downing, of the Clarksville *Sentinel*, in behalf of Thomas P. Miller, proprietor of the St. James Hotel, St. Louis, presented a silver cup to the mother of the largest number of children. This present fell to Mrs. Frances Williams, aged fifty-six, and the mother of sixteen children. She had resided in the county forty-nine years.

The decorations of the town on this occasion are worthy of especial mention. On the courthouse majestically waved a mammoth flag thirteen by thirty feet, and in the windows were ninety-seven smaller ones. Over the door was this. "1819—Welcome—1883." The Farmers' and Mechanics' Bank presented a handsome appearance, with its magnificent new vault and time-lock safe which cost $1,300—its "1873—Welcome—1883," and the life-size pictures of President Walton Perkins and his wife. The Laclede had shady green oaks in front, and posts festooned handsomely. The Planters House was similarly decorated, and above the door were the suggestive words, "Come Again." At the Laclede Hotel stables was a hanging card, decorated with green leaves, running thus: "We'll feed the old horse as well as the old man." Over the postoffice door were the letters "O. S. R." On an ornamental card, in front of J. J. Cheely's, were the words, "We'll smoke to the health of the old settlers." The word "Welcome" in evergreen, was very handsomely arranged in the door of James A. Jackson. Joseph Hart had swinging, a decorated card with this inserted: "Hearty Welcome. Established in 1858. Oldest merchant in Troy." "Troy *Herald*," in evergreen, was suspended across the street in front of the office, and "Welcome" in evergreens over windows of the front wall, and several mottoes in the entrance. Chenewn & Hutchinson's drug store had over the door a deer head with two stalks of corn crossed under the chin, just under an arch of green oak, and at the top of it the word "Welcome." Bragg Brothers had "Welcome" displayed in large letters on the front wall, and an oat stack in their front, with the sign "Grain Wanted," and on a card: "To the old settlers: May you live long and prosper, and be happy and jolly in your old age, which is a certain boon, if you buy your goods of Bragg Brothers." R. A. Trail's saloon had green oaks in front and huge ears of green corn suspended around the awning, suggestive of corn juice. Sturgeon & Co. had, in front, "Welcome, Old Settlers." Alexandria & McNalley, milliners, had "Welcome" handsomely displayed in their show window. *Free Press* had "Welcome" in large gilt letters suspended across the street. "Eureka" in large red letters was suspended from M. Sedlacek's saddlery establishment. H. Havercamp, A.

F. Winn & Co., T. W. Withrow, Bragg & Kabler, A. Kuhne, Henry Bros., I. W. Clark and others had green oaks in front and almost all the stores were profusely decorated with flags. A shooting contest was held at the fair ground, and was enjoyed by both old and young. The number of people at the re-union was estimated at from 6,000 to 8,000.

SECOND RE-UNION AT TROY.

A preliminary meeting of the Old Settlers' Association was held at the courthouse in Troy, on the evening of July 7, 1886. Committees were appointed, and instructed to make arrangements for accommodating 10,000 people, on the occasion of the Old Settlers' Reunion, to be held at Troy, on the third day of August following. When the day came, the weather was pleasant, and an immense crowd of people assembled to participate in the festivities of the occasion. By some, the number of people assembled was considered greater than the number at the first re-union three years before. The meeting was called to order at 11 o'clock A. M., by President William Miller, and prayer was offered by Rev. I. A. M. Thompson. The address of welcome was then delivered by W. T. Thurmond. Prof. M. S. Goodman, of the *Pike County Democrat*, was then introduced to the audience, and after a short speech the meeting adjourned for dinner. After dinner, Dr. Cook, president of the LaGrange College, was introduced to the re-assembled audience. He addressed the people in an able and instructive manner, and was followed by Rev. Thompson, who gave an interesting talk of "ye olden time." The next speaker was Hon. Charles E. Peers, who spoke of the changes since his boyhood days. The music furnished for the occasion, by the Eolia Band, was excellent. The town was decorated similarly as it was on the occasion of the first re-union, and all seemed well pleased with the exercises of the day.

LETTER FROM JOHN H. BROWN, OF TEXAS.

After the last re-union a letter from John H. Brown, of Texas, referring to early settlers of this county, was published in one of the Troy papers. Omitting the introductory part, it reads as follows:

"Though not a native of Lincoln, I was born in Pike, within a mile of the line, and about two and a half miles north of Louisville, and knew in childhood an equal number of persons in each county. It is a singular fact that Pike County furnished but three of the early settlers in Texas, viz.: Arthur Burnes, Josiah Wilbarger and my father, Capt. Henry S. Brown, while Lincoln furnished a large number. It occurs to me that a few facts on this subject will be interesting to many old 'Lincolnians.' My parents lived in the Missouri Point, in St. Charles County, from 1808 to 1819–20, when they removed to Pike. In 1824 my father entered Texas from New Orleans, as an Indian and Mexican trader. Returning home in the winter of 1826–27, his description of Texas, to his old friends in St. Charles and Lincoln, created a lively interest, and determined many to emigrate. He returned to Texas in the beginning of 1828. About the same time Wilbarger, after marrying Miss Barker, of Lincoln, came with the Barker family. In 1833 he was wounded, scalped and left for dead by Indians, but recovered, lived twelve years and died wealthy. One of his sons was killed by Indians about 1851.

"Of citizens of Lincoln who came to Texas from 1827 to about 1833 may be named James, a son of Capt. Christopher Clark, an excellent man, who reared a large family and died, at an advanced age, since the Civil War; Alum B. Williams, whose wife was a daughter of Capt. Clark; Job Williams, his brother, both with large families, Mrs. Turner, their sister, also having a large family; Samuel Highsmith, then single, who became a gallant soldier and died in 1849; the Cottle family, of whom George W. became one of the 182 martyrs of the Alamo, March 6, 1836; Andrew Kent, from St. Charles, was another martyr, and we have a county named for each. The numerous family of McCoy, all good Indian fighters, came from Lincoln—Daniel, Joseph, 'Devil' John and others. The wife of Joseph was another daughter of Capt. Clark. 'Devil' John, who killed a fellow-soldier near Stout's Fort, in Lincoln, after the War of 1815, drifted into Arkansas, and entered Texas, several years before any of the others. He had quite a history, and was a clever man unless excited by liquor. The Collards, also quite numerous, were from Lincoln. David Clark, a son of Capt. Christopher, came later, and was killed by Indians in 1837. In that same year, in the wilderness, in the extreme northeast corner of the State, young McFarland and Turner, en route to Texas from Troy, were murdered by two robbers, father and son, both of whom were hung. Thacker Vivion, from about Auburn, came from Arkansas at a late day, but had a son killed by the Indians in 1848. From 1830 to 1834, Samuel Gibson and two of his sons, George and 'Big' Jim, from near Auburn, made several trips to Texas, but only the latter finally remained. He, 'Big Jim,' was a gallant soldier in my father's company, in the bloody battle of Velogeo, June 26, 1832. From St. Charles, in those days, came several families of the Zumwalt stock, representatives from the families of Baldridge, Burkett or Burgett, etc.

"Among late comers from Lincoln, were John S. Besser, Shapley P. Ross and others, besides additional kinsmen of the families first named. Taken altogether, enough is shown to form a kindly tie between Lincoln County and Texas, which has been strengthened by occasional recruits down to this time, covering a period of sixty years. I have omitted, strangely enough, for they were lifetime friends, the married daughters of Mrs. Riggs, near Troy, Mrs. James Shaw and Mrs. N. C. Raymond, all now dead, and their brother, Sam Riggs. These hasty reflections, the work of a moment, might be extended, but might also be wearisome."

HARDSHIPS, DISADVANTAGES, ETC.

As is common in all newly settled countries, the early settlers of Lincoln County labored under many disadvantages, being deprived of highways and bridges, saw and grist-mills, postoffices, blacksmith, and other mechanical shops, and the conveniences and luxuries that their posterity now enjoy; yet, with all, they had some luxuries. They had choice venison, wild turkeys and wild honey, in great abundance, and with their "hoe cake" to sop in the meat gravy, or swim in the honey, they had food fit for a king. Wild game was then so plentiful, and so easily obtained, that the first settlers supplied their families with all the wild meat they could consume, and so many hollow trees in the forest were filled with wild honey, that that article was also easily obtained in great abundance. The price of grain and all kinds of farm produce was then so low, and the markets so distant, that there was no inducement for raising a surplus. Consequently many of the early settlers were content, after having cleared a few acres on which to raise corn to make meal for their families, and to feed their horses, to raise a home supply of vegetables, and a patch of flax, which they manufactured into clothing. Spinning-wheels and the loom were then common articles of household furniture. A little cotton was also raised, and all cloth for wearing apparel, such as cotton, linsey, jeans, flax-cloth, etc., was manufactured and made into clothing at home. Buttons were made out of wood or other hard substances, and covered with the same kind of cloth as that of which the garment was made.

Uncle Walton Perkins, before his death, published some reminiscences, in which he said: "The women thought they were dressed in the height of fashion when arrayed in fancy plaid linsey; and we men were regular dudes in our own estimation when dressed in a new suit of flashing blue homespun jeans, trimmed in brass buttons." Then of the amusements incident to those days, he said: "We had our log-rollings, our puncheon-floor dances, our game hunts, and lastly, our corn shuckings. The latter was a popular pastime. We would gather at a neighbor's, and the first thing would be to choose captains. Then the captains would 'throw heads or tails,' to decide who should have first choice of men; the choosing would then continue until all were chosen, and—well, if corn-shucks ever flew, it was then." Add to these amusements, the "quiltings" and the "apple cuttings," "corn shellings," etc., and the reader can have an idea of the life of the pioneer settlers.

Samuel Howell, an old settler of 1826, wrote that in 1828 corn was worth 15 cents per bushel, wheat 30 cents, bacon $1\frac{1}{2}$ cents per pound, best horses $30 to $40, best cows $5 to $7, all in trade. All money that then came into the county was horded up and taken to the land-office to pay for lands that had been entered. Stock required but little feeding the grass and mast being sufficient for their support. The mast was so plentiful that in many places it could be scooped up with shovels. It would so fill up the ruts or wagon tracks that in driving over the roads the wheels kept up a continual popping of the acorns.

One of the sources through which the early settlers obtained merchandise was the following: Wagons would come up from St. Louis at stated times, filled with such goods as the people needed. These goods would be exchanged for game and peltry. When it was known that a wagon had arrived in a neighborhood, the settlers would turn out with their rifles, and in a short time have it filled with deer, turkeys, etc.

A BEAR HUNT.

On one occasion, Eli Perkins, brother of Walton Perkins, while looking for deer in the neighborhood of the present poor house, saw a big buck cross the road. He fired at him, and in another instant he discovered a big black bear approaching him with savage intent. His gun being empty he reloaded and started on the retreat. The bear gave chase, and for some time it was a pretty tight race, but the bear finally stopped and returned to the woods. Walton Perkins went to Troy the next morning and mustered up a few boys, and together they set out for the bear. On entering the woods where Eli last saw Bruin, they soon discovered a bear's nest containing a dead cub, and three young bears about the size of a grown raccoon near by, and took after them. They retreated a short distance, and then took refuge in a tall oak tree. The boys then held a council to determine who should climb the tree, and shake the bears down. The task fell to Walton. It was not a pleasant job, as the cubs showed fight, and Walton was not certain whether he should get the bears or they him. He finally succeeded in shaking them down, and when they reached the ground, his associates pounced upon them, captured two and let the other one escape. Zadock Woods and Walton Perkins took possession of the bears. Walton's hung himself soon after, and the other lived to be grown. When the boys were enjoying the sport of capturing the cubs, the old bear was not around, otherwise this narrative might have been different.

NATIVE ANIMALS AND WILD FOWLS.

A hundred years ago, ere the "pale faces" came, the land

now enclosed within the boundaries of Lincoln County was a vast solitude, over which the native animals prowled, and the wild fowls sported, unmolested save by the Indian's arrow. The native species of animals were the buffalo, bear, elk, deer, wolf, lynx, catamount, panther, wildcat, raccoon, opossum, fox, woodchuck, skunk, rabbit, squirrel, etc., and of the wild fowls, there were geese, swans, turkeys, ducks, quails, and an almost innumerable variety of beautiful birds that filled the "native wilds" with the music of their songs. Ere the close of the last century, the buffaloes, scenting the approach of civilization, moved westward, and abandoned their pastures to the white man's plow. The other animals, seemingly, were not thus disposed to give up their native haunts, but remained until nearly all the larger kinds became extinct, in consequence of their destruction by the new possessors of the soil. The few that were not destroyed retired to the unsettled and undisturbed forests and prairies, that lay in advance of the onward march of civilization.

At the beginning of the settlement of the county the bears were not very numerous, and consequently not very troublesome to the settlers. They were fond of pigs, however, and not a few of these domestic animals were sacrificed to gratify Bruin's appetite. Being large animals, they could not well hide from the early settlers, whose combined efforts soon put a stop to their depredations, and caused them to become extinct in an early day. The elk were likewise scarce and soon disappeared. From the antlers found by early settlers, it is evident that very large animals of that species once existed here. Deer were very numerous—so numerous that herds containing as many as fifty each were frequently seen. Many of the first settlers supplied their families with all the venison they could consume, and for a long time only 25 cents could be realized for a "saddle of venison." A "saddle" consisted of the hind-quarters or hams, the balance of the carcass being usually thrown away. As the settlers increased in numbers, the deer decreased—venison became more of a rarity, and the animals were hunted, chased and killed until they finally became extinct. In the fall of 1862, William Watts, of the northeastern part of the county, killed fourteen deer, and never saw any afterward. It is believed that they became extinct during the war period.

The wolves were also very numerous, very destructive, and a greater source of annoyance to the early settlers than any other of the wild animals. They would destroy all the hogs, pigs especially, sheep and calves that they could get, and would sometimes devour grown cattle. Many a pioneer saved his first milch cow from destruction by these hungry and ferocious animals, by allowing her to feed around his cabin under the observance of his family during the day, and confining her at night in a tight log pen with a tight pole covering. They were the most destructive to sheep, and the only way that these domestic animals could be raised, while the wolves were numerous, was by confining them in tight pens at night. The wolves generally went in "packs" or "gangs," and at night kept up a continual howling around the pioneer's cabin. In 1829 the county court offered 50 cents each for wolf scalps, and in 1830 it offered 50 cents each for wolf scalps under six months old and $1 for those six months old or over. [Unless the officers knew just how to tell when a wolf was six months old by an examination of its scalp, it is most likely that Lincoln County paid $1 each for many scalps not quite six months old.] Bounties for wolf scalps have always continued to be paid. In the early days wolf scalps were legal tender for paying taxes. Being very destructive, and not good for food or anything at all, the wolves were hunted and killed with a view to their extermination; and were so substantially exterminated that they ceased to be troublesome years ago, and now one is seldom ever heard of. The lynxes, catamounts, panthers and wildcats, all savage and destructive animals, have shared the fate of the wolves. Of these, probably the wildcats were the most numerous. All these latter animals belong to the feline race, and, like the wolves, are destructive and worthless.

The raccoons and opossums have also been numerous, and remain in considerable numbers yet. They have been extensively captured and used by the colored people as articles of food. The woodchucks still remain in limited numbers, and are also sometimes used for food. Foxes, as remarks an old settler, have been as plentiful as poultry is now. They are very destructive to poultry, and on this account have been chased and hunted for their extermination, but being so sly and cunning, they still remain in sufficient numbers to be quite annoying. Skunks (polecats) have been numerous, and still remain in sufficient quantities. Though their odor is not pleasant, they have one redeeming quality, their skins are valuable for ladies' muffs, etc. The innocent rabbits, that eat the cabbage and bark the fruit trees, and the nimble squirrels, have always been and are yet abundant, though not so numerous as formerly. These little animals are used for food by all classes.

After the county was settled, and as long as game was plentiful, the people had their "Christmas frolics" during the holidays. That is, large numbers of men would assemble at certain points, well armed for the chase, and well supplied with horns for signals, and would extend a circular line around a certain tract of country, then commence blowing the horns and contracting the line, and thus drive the animals toward the center. In this way all kinds of animals would be corralled on a small spot of ground, and finding themselves surrounded, would attempt their escape through the closed up line of sportsmen. Then came the fun; many animals would be killed in attempting to pass through the line, and many would escape. Upon the settlement of the county, and for many years thereafter, the wild fowls, especially turkeys, were very numerous, but latterly all have become scarce. Most of the species of native birds still remain.

CHAPTER IV.

ORGANIZATION OF THE COUNTY, COURTS, ETC.

The county of Lincoln was organized in accordance with an act of the Legislature of the Territory of Missouri passed December 14, 1818, and a subsequent act passed on the 23d day of the same month. To the first settler of the county was reserved the honor of securing its establishment, and of selecting its name. In the Territorial Legislature which convened at St. Louis in December, 1818, being the fifth session after the creation of the Territory, the organization of several new counties was discussed. Maj. Christopher Clark, who was a member from St. Charles County, living in that portion out of which Lincoln was carved, proposed the creation of the new county, with the boundaries corresponding very nearly to the present lines. The project met with favorable consideration, and a bill providing for the organization of the county was prepared, a blank space being left for the insertion of its name. Several names were proposed and discussed.

Maj. Clark arose to address the assembly, a duty he seldom attempted in that body. He was not a fluent speaker and was not accustomed to speaking in public. He was a man of excellent sense and judgment, and possessed clear and vigorous ideas upon every subject that engaged his attention, which he could always express in his plain, homely, yet terse and forcible manner. With the peculiarities of a rude frontier education, that read more of the beauty and grandeur of wild nature than of books, he united all those finer qualities of head and heart that under other circumstances develop into the cultured and polished gentleman. His stern and inflexible principles of personal integrity and honesty, which ever shaped his rule of conduct, never warped his mind into any puritanical bias, but charity and forbearance toward every human creature were as natural to him as his own unbounded generosity and hospitality. These qualities made him a quiet, unobtrusive, industrious and valuable member of the Legislature, and they were as fully recognized and appreciated by his fellow members, as by his fellow citizens at home. His stalwart and powerful form, his dignified and courteous bearing, and the courage that upheld him on the battle-field and in the peril of the wilderness, and that shown unmistakably in the gleam of his bright eye, always secured him the attentive ear of the entire Assembly. On this occasion, his manner was earnest, and yet without any exhibition of that egotism his words might suggest. His purpose was evident; he gave a personal reason for the motion he was about to offer. He said: "Mr. Speaker, I was the first man to drive a wagon across Big Creek, the boundary of the proposed new county, and the first permanent white settler within its limits. I was born, sir, in *Link-horn* County,

N. C. I lived for many years in *Link-horn* County, in old Kaintuck. I wish to live, the remainder of my days, and die in *Link-horn* County, in Missouri; and I move, therefore, that the blank in the bill be filled with the name of *Link-horn*." The motion was carried unanimously, and the clerk, not adopting the frontier parlance of the Major, wrote "Lincoln" in the blank space of the bill. This was on the 14th day of December, 1818. On the 8th, Jefferson County had been created, and on the 11th, Franklin and Wayne. In 1813 Washington County had been established, and in 1816 the county of Howard. Thus Lincoln was the sixth county established by the Territorial Legislature, not counting the county of Arkansas, set off during the session of 1813-14, and afterward formed into a separate State. The following is a copy of the caption of the record of proceedings of the first term of court held in Lincoln County, as provided by the acts creating it:

COUNTY COURT PROCEEDINGS.—FIRST TERM.

TERRITORY OF MISSOURI, } Northwestern Circuit, April Term, 1819.
LINCOLN COUNTY.

Be it remembered that on this fifth day of April, one thousand eight hundred and nineteen, at the house of Zadock Woods, in said county and Territory, being the time and place directed by the several acts of the Legislature of said Territory, the first entitled "An act for establishing the county of Lincoln," passed the 14th of December, 1818, and the other entitled "An act fixing the times and places for holding superior and circuit courts, and for other purposes," passed the 23d day of December, 1818.

David Todd appeared and produced a commission appointing him judge of the Northwestern Circuit in said territory, which was read openly and is in the following words:

FREDERICK BATES, SECRETARY OF THE TERRITORY OF MISSOURI, AND EXERCISING THE GOVERNMENT THEREOF.

To all who shall see these presents, Greeting:—Know ye, that reposing special trust and confidence in the integrity, abilities and diligence of David Todd, I do appoint him judge of the courts of the Northwestern Circuit, composed of the counties of Cooper, Howard, Montgomery, Lincoln and Pike, and empower him to discharge the duties of said office according to law. To have and to hold the said office with all the powers, privileges and emoluments to the same of right appertaining, from and after the first day of February next.

In testimony whereof, I have hereunto affixed the seal of the Territory. Given under my hand at St. Louis the first day of January, in the year of our Lord, one thousand eight hundred and nineteen, and of the independence of the United States, the forty-third.

[SEAL.] (Signed,) FREDERICK BATES.

Upon the back of Judge Todd's commission was endorsed his oath of office, as taken before Squire Augustus Storrs, of Howard County. After the reading of his commission, the Judge took his seat, and proclamation being made by David Bailey, sheriff, the first court was opened and constituted for Lincoln County. John Ruland then appeared, and produced the following commission appointing him clerk of the court, to-wit:

WILLIAM CLARK, GOVERNOR OF THE TERRITORY OF MISSOURI AND COMMANDER-IN-CHIEF OF THE MILITIA THEREOF.

To all who shall see these presents, Greeting:—Know ye, that whereas the Hon. David Todd, judge of the Northwestern Circuit, has appointed John Ruland, Clerk of the circuit court for the county of Lincoln, I do hereby commission the said John Ruland clerk of the circuit court of Lincoln County, and empower him to discharge the duties of said office according to law. To have and to hold the said office with all the powers, privileges and emoluments to the same of right appertaining.

In testimony whereof, I have caused the seal of the Territory to be affixed. Given under my hand at St. Louis, the first day of April, in the year of our Lord, one thousand eight hundred and nineteen, and of the independence of the United States the forty-third. (Signed,) WILLIAM CLARK.

FIRST OFFICIALS.

John Ruland, the clerk thus commissioned, then filed his bond in the sum of $3,000, with Samuel Wells and Nathan Heald, of St. Charles County, as sureties, and took the oath and assumed the duties of his office. David Bailey then produced his commission as sheriff of Lincoln County, it having been executed January 1, 1819, by Frederick Bates, then acting Governor, and executed his official bond to the satisfaction of the court, with Ira Cottle and James White as sureties. He then took the oath of his office, and assumed the duties thereof. This completed the organization of the first court held in Lincoln County, the first business of which was the selection and empaneling of the first grand jury.—Joseph Cottle, foreman; John Null, Prospect K. Robbins, Samuel H. Lewis, Thacker Vivion, Job Williams, Alambe Williams, Jr., Jeremiah Groshong, John Bell, Jacob Null, Sr., John Hunter, Elijah Collard, William Harrell, Jacob Null, Jr., Isaac Cannon, Hiram Millsaps, Alambe Williams, Sr., and Zachariah Callaway. Being duly sworn and charged, this jury retired to their room, and after "inquiring in and for the body of the county," returned without making any presentments, and were discharged.

The commissioners, David Bailey, James White, Daniel Draper, Hugh Cummins and Abraham Kennedy, appointed by the Legislature in the act creating the County of Lincoln, to select a site, and to locate the county-seat thereof, then appeared and filed their official bond in the sum of $15,000, with Jonathan Riggs, Hugh Barnett, Zadock Woods, Ira Cottle and Allen B. Wilson as sureties. The bond was approved by the court, and the commissioners qualified to perform their duties. This ended the business of the first day of the court. The following day the court ordered the clerk to apply to the clerk of St. Charles County, for certified copies of all orders establishing public roads within the boundaries of Lincoln County, and all orders appointing overseers of roads, who were then in office, and a transcript of all orders, and the original papers pertaining to roads not fully established in the territory of Lincoln County.

FORMATION OF TOWNSHIPS.

The court then divided the county into four parts, and ordered that all that part lying east of the fifth principal meridian, and south of the township line, between townships forty-nine and fifty north, should constitute one municipal township to be called and known by the name of Monroe; and all that part lying west of the fifth principal meridian, and south of the above named township line, should constitute a municipal township to be called and known by the name of Bedford; all that part lying west of the fifth principal meridian, and north of Bedford Township, to constitute a municipal township to be called and known by the name of Union; and that all that part lying east of Union and north of Monroe, should constitute a municipal township to be called and known by the name of Hurricane.

APPOINTMENTS.

Judges were then appointed to hold elections in the several townships, at the places designated as follows: Prospect K. Robbins, James Duncan and Joseph Oldham, for Monroe

Township, at the house of Prospect K. Robbins; Elijah Collard, Benjamin Blanton and Alambe Williams, Jr., for Bedford Township, at the house of Zadock Woods (Troy); Robert Jameson, Philip Sitton and Samuel Gibson, for Union Township, at the house of Samuel Gibson; Benjamin Allen, John Ewing, and Jesse Sitton, for Hurricane Township, at the house of Benjamin Allen.

Constables for the several townships were then appointed as follows: James Woods, for Monroe; Lee F. T. Cottle, for Bedford; Thacker Vivion, for Union; and Allen Turnbaugh, for Hurricane. They were all required to execute bonds in the sum of $1,000 each, with approved security, before assuming the duties of their offices. The court then recommended Joseph Cottle to the Governor, as a suitable person to be commissioned surveyor of the county, and Samuel Bailey was appointed deputy sheriff. This completed the organization of the county, and the court adjourned "to term in course."

The first justices of the peace in the county, appointed by the Governor, were Benjamin Cottle and James Duncan, for Bedford Township; Daniel Draper, for Union; Benjamin Allen, for Hurricane; and Prospect K. Robbins, for Monroe.

FIRST ELECTION.

The elections provided for, as above mentioned, were held August 2d, following the organization of the county, and was for a delegate to Congress; Samuel Hammond and John Scott being the opposing candidates. For some reason, no election was held in Hurricane Township. In Monroe Township nine votes were cast for Samuel Hammond, in Bedford five for John Scott and forty-eight for Hammond, and in Union, twelve for Hammond, making a total of seventy-four votes cast in the county at its first election, and of these Hammond received sixty-nine and Scott five. The latter, however, was elected, notwithstanding the large majority against him in Lincoln. He was then the incumbent of the office, having been first elected in 1816, from which time he held it until Missouri was admitted as a State, and then served three terms as a member of Congress, retiring in 1827.

SECOND TERM OF COURT.

The second term of the court was held at the same place as before, beginning on Monday, August 2, 1819. A number of petitions for the location of public roads, the particulars of which are given under the head of "Highways," were presented and considered. Joseph Cottle produced his commission as surveyor of Lincoln County, and filed his bond as such in the sum of $2,000, with Elijah Collard as surety. David Bailey, sheriff, then filed two bonds with Joseph Cottle and Benajah English as sureties—one for the sum of $1,000, conditioned for the collection of the county tax, and the other for the sum of $1,500, conditioned for the collection and payment of all moneys for Territorial purposes. In fixing the penal sum of bonds it seems strange that the court should require $2,000 in the surveyor's bond, when no moneys went into his hands except his own fees, while only $2,500 was required in the bond of the sheriff, the general collector of the taxes. Christopher Clark, David Lord and Almond Cottle were each granted a license to keep tavern in the county, upon payment of a fee imposed by law, which was $10 per year. The grand jury at this term made a number of presentments, all of which will be considered elsewhere, excepting one in which they expressed their disapprobation of the attempt then recently made in Congress to impose certain restrictions in the constitution of Missouri, preparatory to its admission into the Union. This presentment reads as follows: "The grand jurors for the body of the county of Lincoln, Missouri Territory, beg leave to represent to the honorable court that they consider it their privilege, as well as their bounden duty, to take notice of all acts, whether of a public or private nature, calculated to deprive them and their fellow citizens of any of the privileges and immunities which as Republican freemen they have an unalienable right to exercise and enjoy. They therefore present that the restrictions attempted to be imposed upon the Missouri Territory, by the Congress of the United States, at the last session, in the formation of her State constitution, is unconstitutional and unprecedented, bearing the stamp of oppression heretofore unknown to and perfectly inconsistent with the principles upon which our happy Government is founded. They consider the formation of a State constitution the most solemn and important duty which freemen are ever called upon to perform, and in its performance they ought to enjoy the full exercise of unshackled and unrestricted volition. They much regret that the necessity has occurred which imperatively demands an expression of their feelings and sentiments, and trust that, when the question of the admission of the Missouri Territory into the Union of the States shall again be agitated in Congress, the true, genuine and Republican spirit of the constitution will be consulted and have its due influence unimpeded by mistaken notions of philanthropy, or the direful genius of usurpation." Signed by Isaac Thurman, Jacob Null, Reuben Noel, John Castleman, Allen Jameson, Abraham Kennedy, Christopher Clark, William Howdeshell, J. D. Morris, Jacob Null, Sr., Sherman Cottle, John Null, Jesse Cox, William Harle, Nathan Ramsey, John A. Spencer, Zachariah Callaway, Thomas Hampton, Benjamin Crose, Jeremiah Groshong, Miles Turner and Samuel Groshong.

The "restrictions" referred to in the foregoing consisted of a clause which the anti-slavery members of Congress insisted in having incorporated into the constitution of Missouri, to prohibit slavery, before they were willing to vote for its admission into the Union. Great political excitement then prevailed throughout the country, which finally culminated in the "Missouri Compromise," and the admission of Missouri as a State. [See State History on this subject.] These grand jurors, being representative men of the county, showed by the foregoing expressions how zealously the people of Lincoln County, in its infancy, protected what they believed to be their "sacred rights," and how strenuously they favored State sovereignty.

COUNTY SEAT.

In April, 1819, Ira Cottle, Almond Cottle and Nathaniel Simonds offered to donate to the county a tract of land containing fifty acres, at the town of Monroe, as a site for the seat of justice. The commissioners previously named, who were appointed by the act creating the county of Lincoln to select and fix upon a site for the seat of justice thereof, and to superintend the building of a courthouse and jail, accepted this offer and assisted in laying out the land into town lots, with appropriate streets, and procured title for the same from the donors by a deed dated April 29, 1819. They then proceeded to sell lots, and began to accumulate funds for the purpose of defraying the expenses of erecting public buildings. During that summer they caused to be erected a jail at Monroe, and in December following they reported to the court that they had selected and fixed upon a site for the seat of justice, at the town of Monroe, and that a sufficient jail had been erected thereon. The court then ordered that the courts within the county be thereafter held at the town of Monroe. In obedience to this order the next term of the court was held at Monroe, commencing on Monday, April 3, 1820; and there the courts continued to be held while the seat of justice remained at that place.

THE FIRST COUNTY COURT.

When Lincoln County was organized, there were no separate county courts in the Territory of Missouri; but the circuit court was given jurisdiction over all county and probate business, in addition to the business over which circuit courts usually have jurisdiction. Consequently, up to the time that county courts were established by law, the county and probate business was all transacted in the circuit court. The law providing for the formation of county courts was passed by the first session of the Legislature of the State of Missouri, even though the State had not at that time formally been admitted into the Union of States. The first term of the county court of Lincoln County was opened by Justices Ira Cottle and Jonathan Riggs, two of the persons commissioned by Gov. Alexander McNair for that purpose, and the following is a copy of the caption of the record of their proceedings at the first term.

STATE OF MISSOURI, }
LINCOLN COUNTY. } ss;

Be it remembered that on this 15th day of January, one thousand eight hundred and twenty-one, at the town of Monroe, in said county of Lincoln, being the time and place directed for holding the first county court in said county, by an act of the Legislature of said State of Missouri, passed at their session at St. Louis, November 28, A. D. 1820, entitled, "An Act establishing circuit and county courts."

David Bailey, sheriff, was also present, and constituted one of the officers of the court. The first action of the court was the appointment of Bennett Palmer as county court clerk. Constables were then appointed as follows: William S. Duncan and James Collard, for Bedford Township; David Bailey, for Monroe; and Edwin Allen, for Hurricane. David Bailey was also appointed collector of the State and county taxes, and Samuel Bailey was appointed assessor of the taxable property in the county. An order was then made for a transcript of the records of all business recorded in the office of the clerk of the circuit court, pertaining to county business, and the pay of the justices of the court was fixed at $2 per day. After transacting some other business, the court adjourned. At the following April term of the court, John Geiger appeared and produced his commission from the Governor, as one of the county court justices, and took his seat with the other members of the court.

REMOVAL OF THE COUNTY SEAT.

It is very evident that the commissioners who selected Monroe as the place for the seat of justice did not take into consideration the extent of the territory included within the boundaries of the county, else they surely would not have located the county seat clear to one corner. It was certainly a very inconsistent act, and was soon so regarded by the people. The only reason apparently that can be given why they seated Monroe, was because it was then in the most thickly settled portion of the county. In regard to the county seat and its removal from Monroe, and incidents connected therewith, Dr. Joseph A. Mudd, formerly of Troy, has given, in his brief but valuable history of the county, the following interesting account:

"The selection of Monroe as the county seat was never satisfactory to the people of the county. By reference to the session acts of the Legislature for 1822, will be found an act, Chapter 38, providing for its removal from that point. In the preamble it is set forth that 'the inhabitants of this county suffer great hardships and inconvenience, occasioned by their seat of justice having been located at Monroe, which is situated in the southeast corner of the county, and that a good majority of the citizens had presented a petition to the General Assembly, for the passage of a law for the removal of said seat of justice to the center, or some eligible spot not exceeding three miles from the center.' The Legislature therefore appointed Robert Gay, of Pike, Francis Howell, Sr., of St. Charles, and William Lamme, of Montgomery, commissioners, and empowered them with full authority to select a suitable site in accordance with the petition. The courts were to be continued at Monroe until the erection of a court house and jail at the new county seat. The Legislature also appointed Andrew Miller, Samuel Gibson and Thompson Blanton, all of this county, commissioners of the courthouse and jail to be erected, and empowered them or a majority of them to purchase or receive as a donation such lot or parcel of land, not less than fifty nor more than two hundred acres, as the first named commissioners should have fixed upon for the site of the public buildings referred to, and 'to take and receive to them and their successors in office, for the use of the county, from the person or persons of whom they may receive a donation or make a purchase of land as aforesaid, a warranty deed, in fee simple,' which should be made a trust for the county. And the last above-named commissioners should lay off the same into squares or lots, and dispose of or sell the same, and perform and fulfill the same duties as set forth in the provisions of the act establishing the county. The commissioners were required to take the usual oath and to give bond. It was further specified that any lots or lands remaining unsold by the commissioners should be by them released to the Governor of the State in trust for the county. This act was approved January 2, 1822. At the February term of the county court, Philip Sitton was appointed commissioner in place of Samuel Gibson, resigned, and William H. Robinson, of Bedford Township, in lieu of Thompson Blanton, also resigned. The court, at the August term, allowed the accounts of the first named commissioners, as follows: William Lamme, $12; Francis Howell and Robert Gay, each $10; James Duncan, a magistrate, for administering the oath to them, $31\frac{1}{4}$ cents.

"The last term held in Monroe was in November, 1822. No mention is made on the records of any compliance with the terms of the legislative act before the removal of the county seat; but on the first Monday in February, 1823, the county court convened at Alexandria, the point selected by the commissioners as the new county seat. The books and papers had been sent up the previous Saturday, and deposited in the only dwelling house of the place. This was a hewed-log building, one and a half story, with one window containing twelve lights of 8x10 glass, clap-board roof, floor and door of rough planks cut by a whip-saw, and a wood and mud chimney with stone back, capable of holding a six-foot log. A small room adjoining was used as a kitchen. This was quite a stylish and comfortable residence for the frontiers of Missouri in that day, and it was with no little pride that the good lady of the house surrendered the 'best room' for the use of the court, and retired to the kitchen. The room thus placed at the disposal of the county officials was large enough to accommodate them and some twenty spectators.

"Ira Cottle, Benjamin Cottle and John Geiger were the county justices; Gen. Jonathan Riggs the sheriff, and Francis Parker, clerk. The business of the court proceeded leisurely enough until an hour or two before noon, when it began to be whispered about that the kind lady of the house, who, it was plain to be seen, was in a delicate condition, had reached such a crisis as might compel the court and all attendants to leave at any moment, and without ceremony. The wheels of the car of justice moved faster from that hour. The cases that could not be dispatched in a few minutes each were continued over, and the crowd rapidly melted away. There was one case, however, that could neither be continued, on account of the persistent demands of the plaintiff, nor hurried through, because of the obstinate resistance of the defendant. The president of the court, Col. Ira Cottle, was the administrator of the estate of John Ewing, deceased, and William R. Gilbert, of Pike County, was guardian of Ewing's children. Gilbert desired to have Cottle ruled to give additional security in the sum of $2,000. This was the issue in controversy. Gilbert's lawyer was the late Ezra Hunt, afterward circuit attorney, and still later circuit judge of this circuit, who had ridden some forty miles from home, and did not intend to return without having the case settled. It was reached about night, when all, save the officers of the court and the lawyer, had gone. The court had been engaged incessantly, and endeavoring with the greatest diligence and exertion in furthering its work since the first note of warning was sounded, and it is to be presumed that its members were in anything but an equable state of mind. The evidence in this particular case was all of record. During its examination the respective parties became unusually excited. The Judge, forgetful of the dignity of his station, poured out the vials of his wrath upon the devoted head of the lawyer. The latter was not slow to retort in kind, and for several hours the trial was nothing else than a war of words, and these of the sharpest and most abusive character. Finally, about 11 o'clock, the disputants quieted down, and the case was submitted to the other judges, who, in a few minutes, decided in favor of the demand of the guardian's attorney.

"The court was now ready for adjournment, and the question was, to when should it adjourn? A motion was made to adjourn to the next court in course, when one of the members suggested that it would be about proper to adjourn till after midnight, then call the court and adjourn over to next term. This would show another day's session, and allow the judges to draw each $2 more and the sheriff $1.50. This latter course was agreed on, the officers of the court being satisfied that they had performed two days' service in one. In the interim the clerk was making up the records, the justices were lounging about, and Judge Hunt was trying to sleep, stretched on his back on the floor, with his head resting on the hearth. A pack of hungry wolves in the woods near by were making the night hideous with their howling, and the inmates of the court room, having fasted from early breakfast, and feeling acutely the gnawings of empty stomachs, would involuntarily compare the condition of the hungry pack inside with that of the hungry pack outside. Presently the cause just tried came up in the mind of Col. Cottle, and he began venting his spleen upon his adversary. He was a large man, of fine appearance, rather inclined to be boisterous in manner, and very profuse in the use of oaths. Judge Hunt was a much smaller man, but fully as irascible as his opponent. He replied in language thickly sprinkled with epithets more vigorous than polite or pious, and was about to rise from his position, as if to engage in something stronger than words. Luckily for the peace of the household on that interesting occasion, he happened to cast his eye up the chimney to where, about six feet above the hearth, hung a fine venison ham. All controversy was forgotten as he sprang like a famished tiger up the capacious jaws of the chimney, and brought down the prize in triumph. The anger of Col. Cottle was instantly changed into smiles, and in the place of oaths and epithets all was friendliness and joviality. The meat was well cured and really delicious. The hungry crowd never before had venison that tasted so sweetly. The repast was scarcely finished when sounds from the kitchen indicated the near advent of a new comer into the world. Court was hastily called and adjourned over to that in course, and all present left at once, accompanying Gen. Riggs to his hospitable home on Cuivre. Less than two hours afterward the family of the patriotic lady was increased by the addition of a daughter."

"At a special term held November 19, 1825, John Lindsey, Thompson Blanton, Jonathan Cottle and Benjamin Cottle, justices on the bench, the county commissioners for the courthouse and jail, Sitton, Miller and Robinson, appeared and made a final settlement. They produced a deed of relinquishment to the county for all such lands and lots as remained in their hands as commissioners in trust for the county. An examination of their accounts showed that at the two sales of town lots on April 11, and May 24, 1822, for the purpose of raising money to be appropriated to building a courthouse and jail, the sum of $887.25 was realized; and at the sale of October 1, 1824, $33.50, making a total of $920.75. To their credit was placed $380, paid by them for building a jail, and $448.50 for building a court house; for recording papers, $5; for chain carriers, $4, making a total of $846.50, and leaving on hand $74.25. This amount was divided equally, and turned over to the commissioners as part of their salary of $48 each, and for the remainder they received warrants."

SECOND REMOVAL OF THE COUNTY SEAT.

The county seat did not remain long at Alexandria until a

majority of the citizens of the county became dissatisfied with its location, being situated as it was on a ridge of land inaccessible to water. Accordingly, on the 5th day of August, 1828, during the sitting of the county court, with Justices James Duncan and John Lindsey on the bench, Joshua N. Robbins and Emanuel Block presented a petition signed by a lawful number of the taxable inhabitants of the county, namely, more than three-fifths thereof, praying for a removal of the county seat from Alexandria, to the town of Troy. Thereupon the Court appointed Felix Scott, of the county of St. Charles, Thomas Kerr, of the county of Pike, Richard Wright, Philip Glover and George Clay, of the county of Montgomery, commissioners to select a site whereon to locate the seat of justice of the county of Lincoln, and authorized them to meet at the house of Andrew Monroe,* in the town of Troy, on the 15th day of September following, to begin the performance of the duties assigned them. Notice of this meeting was given, as per orders of the Court, by the sheriff, who posted advertisements in ten of the most public places in the county. The commissioners met at the time and place appointed, and selected Troy as the site for the seat of justice, and on the 24th day of the same month they procured title by deed from George Collier and wife, donors, for two blocks of land, the first consisting of Lots 158, 159, 180 and 181, according to Collier's addition to the original plat of the town of Troy, and the other block of the same size lying west of, and adjoining the former. The consideration expressed in the deed was $1, and the promise that the courthouse should be erected on the first described block, and the jail on the other. The report of the proceedings of the commissioners was presented to, and approved by the judge of the circuit court, and a copy thereof, together with the judge's approval, was transmitted to the county court at its November term, 1828, whereupon an election was ordered to be held in the several townships of the county, on Monday, the 8th day of December following, to take the sense of the electors, as to the selection made by the commissioners. The election was accordingly held, and on Thursday following, James Duncan, Henry Watts and Joseph H. Allen, county court justices, held a

---

*This was Father Monroe, the famous Methodist preacher, who was then keeping a hotel in Troy.

special session to examine the poll books and count the votes. They found that a majority of the "free white male taxable resident land and householders" of the county had voted for the place selected, and that the number of votes cast in favor of the selection was 211, and only two against it. Thereupon the Court 'considered the seat of justice of Lincoln County removed to the place selected in the town of Troy, agreeable to the provisions of the statute in such cases made and provided.'

Then on motion of Alfred W. Carr, it was ordered by the Court that the citizens of Troy should be permitted to remove the jail and furniture belonging to the county, at Alexandria, to the town of Troy, and to erect the jail on the ground deeded to the county by George Collier and wife for that purpose; provided that the citizens of Troy should, at their own expense, put up the jail on the new premises, in every way in as good order as where it then stood. Alfred W. Carr was then appointed commissioner of the new seat of justice, and as such filed his official bond, and qualified accordingly. On the 3d day of January following he reported to the Court that a convenient courthouse and jail at Troy was then in readiness for use. Whereupon it was ordered that thereafter the courts of the county should be held in the courthouse at Troy, and the clerk was ordered to notify the Hon. Beverly Tucker, judge of the circuit court, of such removal of the seat of justice. The last session of the county court held in Alexandria, was on January 3, 1829, and the first one held in Troy was on Monday, February 9, 1829. The county seat, after much controversy, was now permanently located at the old place formerly known as Woods' Fort, and subsequently as Troy, the place where the county was organized, and where the first courts were held before a site was chosen for the county seat; and here it has remained ever since, and in all probability will continue to remain for generations to come. At the February term, 1829, the court ordered Commissioner Carr to sell "the old barn situated on the county property at Troy," also the courthouse at Alexandria, and the old jail at Monroe, also certain lots in Troy, on the first Monday of May following. These lots had been donated to the county by different persons, on consideration of the location of the county seat at Troy.

HIGHWAYS.

At the second term of the Lincoln County Circuit Court, commencing on Monday, August 2, 1819, a petition signed by a number of the inhabitants of Monroe Township, praying for a road to be laid out "from Moscow to St. Louis," and another one "leading from Big Creek to the south end of Mill street in the town of Moscow," were presented by John Geiger; and Barney Thornhill, William Howdeshell, Abraham Kennedy, Jacob Groshong, Sr., and Lambert Collier were appointed commissioners to review and mark out the proposed roads "on the nearest and most practicable route, and to the greatest ease and convenience of the inhabitants, and as little as may be to the prejudice of any person or persons, and report on the same next term." Another petition signed by a number of the inhabitants of Bedford Township, praying for a road "from Monroe to Woods' Fort (now Troy), and thence to the west line of the county, in a direction to the seat of justice of Howard County," was presented by Joseph Cottle, whereupon E. Collard, Samuel Gibson, Joseph McCoy, and Prospect K. Robbins were appointed commissioners to view and mark out the proposed road, with the same restrictions as enjoined on the first commissioners appointed. Another petition, praying for a road "from Woods' Fort to the north line of St. Charles County in a direction to St. Charles, and from Woods' Fort to the south line of Pike County in a direction to the seat of justice of said county, was presented by S. H. Lewis and Joseph Cottle, and the Court appointed David Porter, Samuel Gibson, Abraham Kennedy, E. Collard and David Bailey as commissioners to mark and lay it out. Another petition signed by a number of the inhabitants of the county, praying for a road to be established from Woods' Fort, on the most direct and practicable route, to the northern boundary of the county, in the direction of the mills on Salt River, and to pass by the habitations of Alambe Williams, Sr., Thomas Hammond and Col. Cox's Ford on North Cuivre, was presented by Benjamin Crose and Alambe Williams; whereupon the court appointed John Hunter, Zachariah Callaway, Hugh Barnett and Elijah Collard as commissioners to view and mark out the proposed road.

Afterward, at the December term following, the court being

then in session at Monroe, the new county-seat, a petition signed by a number of the inhabitants of Monroe Township, praying for a road to be established from the town of Monroe to Joseph Howdeshell's residence in Hurricane Township, and from there on the nearest and best route to intersect the Salt River road, was presented by David Bailey; and James Lewis, Samuel Gibson and Ira Cottle were appointed commissioners to view and mark out the same. At this time the following named persons were appointed by the Court to lay off and divide the roads in the several Townships and to allot lands to the several overseers, viz.: Benjamin Cottle, for Bedford Township; Prospect K. Robbins and James Duncan, for Monroe Township; Benjamin Allen, for Hurricane Township; and Daniel Draper, for Union Township. Subsequently, at the August term of the court in 1829, a petition signed by certain inhabitants of the county, praying for a road to be established from Monroe to Troy (Woods' Fort), was presented by John Geiger. William Baty, Morgan Wright, Abraham Kennedy, Andrew Miller and Stephen Cottle were appointed to mark and lay it out. Another petition was presented by Benjamin Cottle, signed by himself and others, praying for a road to be established from Monroe to the western boundary of the county, the route to commence "at the dwelling house of Moses Oldham, thence to cross the Cuivre at the Yankee Ford, and entering the town of Troy at the east end of Monroe Street," and thence to its termination. Christopher Clark, Jonathan Riggs and David Bailey were appointed to mark and lay it out, under the usual instructions pertaining to the ease and convenience of the people.

The foregoing proposed roads were all established upon reports of the commissioners appointed, and were the first highways established in Lincoln County after its organization. A few, however, had previously been located while the territory formed a part of St. Charles County. The county court being now established (January 15, 1821) assumed jurisdiction over the highways, and all unfinished business in the circuit pertaining thereto was transferred to this new tribunal. At the second term of the county court, held in April, 1821, a license was granted to Bennett Palmer for the sum of $2, authorizing him "to keep a ferry across the River aux Cuivre, opposite the town of Monroe." This is the first record of a license granted to run a ferry in Lincoln County. The following January, Jonathan Riggs, for the sum of $2, was granted a license "to keep a ferry across the River aux Cuivre at his residence," on the road from Troy to Auburn. His license was renewed annually for many years, and in February, 1829, as shown by the record of the court, he was authorized to charge the following rates of ferriage: Footman, 12½ cents; man and horse, 18½ cents; horse and dearborn, 25 cents; wagon and two horses, 37½ cents; wagon and three horses, 50 cents; wagon and four horses, 75 cents; cattle, grown, per head, 12½ cents. When the water was over the banks, he was allowed to charge for a man and horse, 25 cents, and to increase other ferriage in the same proportion. This crossing is still called Riggs' Ferry or Riggs' Ford.

INTERNAL IMPROVEMENT, ROAD AND CANAL FUND, ETC.

In 1847 Lincoln County received from the State $181.95 of the internal improvement fund, and the following year the further sum of $1,315. In November, 1848, Samuel James was paid from this fund the sum of $1,471.27, for building a bridge across North Cuivre; and the same year William Crouch was paid $1,495 out of a fund known as the "three per cent fund," for building the bridge across the Cuivre, at Moscow. Further sums of the internal improvement fund were received by the county, as follows: 1849, $626.95; 1850, $1,550.50. In 1852 Edward J. Peers received of this fund $280 for building a bridge across Spring Creek. In 1844 the condition of the road and canal funds belonging to the county was as follows:

Amount, including interest	$9,556 63
Deduct interest	1,697 73
Leaves principal on hand	$7,858 90

In 1846 the condition of these funds was:

Amount, including interest	$10,544 15
Interest deducted	1,813 43
Principal on hand	$8,730 72

From 1844 to 1846 $1,111.91 of these funds were expended and lost. In November, 1846, the following amounts were paid out on bridges then in process of construction: Moscow Slough, $165; King's Lake, $140; Main Cuivre, $1,020; West Cuivre, $995; Lower Big Slough, $200; Big Creek, $425. These funds were so expended from time to time that in May, 1853, only $1,228.20 remained, and that balance was exhausted soon after.

PUBLIC BUILDINGS.

The first public building erected in Lincoln County was the jail, which was constructed at Monroe in the summer of 1819. No courthouse was erected there, probably because it was too evident from the start the seat of justice would not long remain there. The records do not state in whose house the courts were held at Monroe while it was the county seat, but in December, 1819, Benjamin Cottle was allowed $16 " for the use of his house for court." From this it may be inferred that the courts were held in the house of Mr. Cottle while the seat of justice remained at Monroe. Perhaps they were held part of the time in the houses of other citizens. A small jail made of squared logs and a small frame courthouse were erected at Alexandria, when the county seat was moved to that place. In May, 1829, after the seat of justice was moved to Troy, the Court ordered that sealed proposals for the construction of a new courthouse should be received. Afterward, at the August term of that year, the sealed proposals were examined and it was found that David Bailey and Jesse Harrison were the lowest and only bidders, the amount proposed by each of them being $1,500 for building the court-house, which, according to the specifications, was to be a two-story brick building forty feet square. The Court, exercising its preference, awarded the contract to David Bailey, who erected the building and had it ready for occupancy in 1830. Immediately after Troy became the seat of justice, the citizens of the place moved the log jail from Alexandria to Troy and re-built it on the lot where the present jail stands. Alfred W. Carr was the commissioner who superintended the erection of the first public buildings at Troy.

THE JAIL.

In February, 1839, the Court appropriated $3,000 for the building of a new jail, and in August following plans and specifications were adopted for a two-story brick jail 24x48 feet in size, to contain "four rooms, with a passage of six feet across the width of the building, separating the dwelling rooms from the prison rooms," and to be covered with shingles, etc. John Chandler was appointed jail commissioner, and the contract for building the jail was awarded to John A. Woolfolk for the sum of $3,350, and in November, 1840, it was received completed from the hands of the contractor. John Chandler was allowed $75 for his services as superintendent. The present courthouse was built in 1870, by Edwards & Griffith, at a cost of $27,447.50. At a special term of the county court, November 10, 1870, Judge E. N. Bonfils, the commissioner, reported it completed according to contract, and it was accepted by the Court. It is a substantial brick structure, two stories in height, and sets upon a stone foundation. Its form is that of a T, with the top of the letter facing Main Street. The first story contains a hall with stairs to the second story, the office of the county clerk, the offices of the circuit court clerk and recorder in one room, two fire-proof vaults for the public records, the county court room and the office of the probate judge. The second story contains a hall, sheriff's and collector's offices in one room, the circuit court room, and a jury room. All rooms are large and commodious, and the building is constructed according to modern architecture. The present jail, which is also a substantial brick and iron structure, consisting of the jail proper and the jailer's residence combined, was built and finished in 1876, on the site of the former jail, by P. J. Pauly & Bro., of St. Louis, at a cost of $7,500. Col. T. G. Hutt was the commissioner.

POOR ASYLUM AND FARM.

In November, 1865, the Court appointed Richard Wommack commissioner to select a proper site for a county poorhouse, and authorized him to advertise for proposals for a tract of land not exceeding 160 acres, and to purchase the land he might select, and agree to pay one-half of the purchase price in cash and to issue bonds bearing 10 per cent interest for the other half, payable in one year after date. The Court reserved the right, however, to confirm or reject such purchase. In February following, the commissioner not being ready to report, the above order was renewed and further time given. At the May term, 1866, Commissioner Wommack reported that in response to advertising as ordered he had received six offers of farms, three of which he deemed entirely unsuitable, and that the other three consisted of a farm of 157 acres, lying two miles north of Troy, owned by Charles W. Parker, the price of which was $2,000, and a farm of 160 acres, owned by Joseph H. Withrow, in Township 49, Range 1 west, the price of which was $20 per acre, and another farm of 160 acres, owned by Francis C. Cake, the price of which was also $20 per acre. The Court, after approving the report and discharging the commissioner, viewed and examined the three farms offered, and decided that the one offered by Mr. Cake should be purchased on the terms expressed in the foregoing order. Whereupon Francis C. Cake presented to the court a deed, executed by himself and wife, conveying to Lincoln County, for the sum of $3,200, the southwest quarter of Section 2, in Township 48 north, Range 1 west, containing 160 acres, it being the farm selected. This deed was accepted by the Court and placed on record.

The Court then appointed J. B. Miller and James M. McLellan commissioners to prepare plans and specifications for the building of a poor asylum, and in July following Francis C. Cake was appointed to receive sealed bids for building the same. In August following the Court accepted the proposals of Ezekiel B. Adams, John R. Kendall and James H. Green, and entered into a contract with Messrs. Adams and Kendall for furnishing the materials and building the stone and brick work and plastering the poor house, according to the plans and specifications then on file, for the sum of $5,600. The contractors afterward gave bond to the satisfaction of the Court, conditioned for the faithful performance of their part of the contract. The Court also entered into a contract with James H. Green, who engaged to furnish the material and do the wood and carpenter work and painting of the building for the sum of $4,200, and afterward filed his bond to the satisfaction of the Court, conditioned for the faithful execution of his part of the contract. Afterward, on January 3, 1868, J. B. Miller, who had been appointed to superintend the building of the poorhouse, reported that Adams and Kendall had completed their part of the work according to contract. Accordingly the work was accepted from their hands, and the balance due them on the contract ordered allowed. The Court then appropriated $525 for the purpose of procuring furniture for the poorhouse, and appointed Francis C. Cake agent to purchase it. In February following Mr. Cake reported that he had purchased the furniture for $399.30, and thus saved $125.70 of the amount appropriated.

On the 28th day of November, 1868, Supt. Miller reported to the Court, recommending that certain deductions, amounting in the aggregate to $1,055, should be made from the amount agreed to be paid to James H. Green for failures to perform his part of the work according to contract. The Court approved the report and withheld the balance claimed by the contractor. Consequently, in April following, Green brought suit against the county, in the circuit court, and asked for judgment in his favor for the $1,055 claimed by him to be remaining due. The suit was brought by Henry Quigly, plaintiff's attorney, and A. V. McKee became the attorney for the county. The case was continued until April, 1870, when it was tried before a jury, who rendered a verdict in favor of the plaintiff for $699.91, whereupon judgment was entered accordingly. In May following the county court allowed the plaintiff, James H. Green, the sum of $702.91, being the amount of his judgment and costs. The first superintendent of the poor farm was Henry G. Bickel, who agreed with the Court to furnish to the county the services of himself and wife in managing the farm and taking care of the paupers for twelve months, commencing October 1, 1870, for the sum of $650. He was succeeded by James W. Brown, who took charge of the farm and the paupers December 1, 1871, and has continued to superintend it ever since. The first year he received for the services of himself and wife the sum of $400, and since then his annual salary has been sometimes greater and sometimes less than that amount.

MUNICIPAL TOWNSHIPS.

The organization of Monroe, Bedford, Union and Hurricane, the four original municipal townships, has been given. The first change in township boundary lines was made in April, 1820, when that part of Monroe lying between the Cuivre, Big Creek and the fifth principal meridian was cut off by order of the Court and added to Bedford. Afterward, from time to time, new townships were formed, with names, dates and boundaries as follows:

Waverly.—November 7, 1825, on petition of Gabriel P. Nash, Caleb McFarland, Marcus H. McFarland, Meredith Cox, James F. Moore and twenty other citizens of Union Township: Commencing at the northwest corner of Township 51, Range 2 west, and running to the southwest corner of Section 6, Township 50, and Range 2 west; thence east to the southeast corner of Section 1, Township 50, Range 2 west; thence north to the northeast corner of Section 1, Township 51, Range 2 west; thence west to the place of beginning The new township thus formed contained twenty-eight taxable inhabitants. The house of Meredith Cox was named as the place for holding elections, and Meredith Cox, Nicholas Wells and Hugh Barnett were appointed judges of elections. Henry Watts and Caleb McFarland were recommended to the Governor for appointment as justices of the peace. In August, 1826, that part of Union Township situated south of Waverly, being Township 50 north, and Ranges 2 and 3 west, was attached to Waverly.

Clark.—February 9, 1826, on petition of Christopher Clark, Cary K. Duncan, Morgan Wright, Malcom Henry, Jr., and twenty-six other citizens of Bedford Township, as follows: All that part of Bedford Township as is situated south of the line dividing Townships 48 and 49 north. The new municipal township thus formed contained eighty-eight taxable inhabitants. The elections were ordered to be held at the house of Christopher Clark and Thompson Blanton; David Clark, Sr., and Morgan Wright were appointed judges thereof. David Clark, Sr., Cary K. Duncan and Seymore Davis were recommended to the Governor for appointment as justices of the peace. In November, 1827, the line between Waverly and Union Townships was changed so as to enlarge the latter.

Prairie.—August 17, 1848, on petition of a large number of citizens: Commencing at the northwest corner of Section 4, Township 49 north, Range 3 west; running thence south on the county line four miles, to the southwest corner of Section 21, Township 49 north, Range 3 west; thence east on the Warren County line four miles to the southwest corner of Section 19, Township 49 north, Range 2 west; thence south on said Warren County line four miles to the southwest corner of Section 7, Township 48 north, Range 2 west; thence east three miles to the southeast corner of Section 9, Township 48 north, Range 2 west; thence north eleven miles to the northeast corner of Section 21, Township 50 north, Range 2 west, to the Waverly Township line; thence west on the Waverly Township line three miles to the Montgomery County line, at the northwest corner of Section 19, Township 50, north, Range 2 west; thence south on said Montgomery County line three miles to the southwest corner of Section 31, Township 50 north, Range 2 west; thence west on said Montgomery County line four miles to the place of beginning. The elections were ordered to be held at the house of Thomas Gammon, and Robert B. Allen, Isaac Cannon and Malen Spyres were appointed judges thereof.

Millwood.—May 31, 1856, on petition of Henry T. Mudd, Richard Wommack, Hilary P. Mudd, George I. Dyer, James S. Wilson, William C. Sands, Horatio C. Clare and eighty-four others: Commencing at the northeast corner of Township 50 north, Range 2 west; thence west to the northeast corner of Section 6; thence south to the southeast corner of Section 18, Township 50 north, Range 2 west; thence west to the county line; thence south to the southwest corner of Section 28, Township 50 north, Range 3 west; thence east to the southeast corner of Section 25; thence south to the township line dividing Townships 49 and 50 north; thence east with said township line until it reaches the north fork of Cuivre River, and making it (the river) the boundary until it reaches the east line of Section 1, Township 50 north, Range 2 west; thence north to the place of beginning. The elections were ordered to be held at the town of Millwood.

Nineveh.—August 12, 1872, on petition of William W. Shaw,

Owen C. Robinson, Joseph L. Duncan, James C. Ellmore, John C. Wells, John C. Williams and forty-four others: Beginning at the northwest corner of Section 33, Township 50 north, Range 3 west; thence north on the county line to the northwest corner of Section 4, Township 50 north, Range 3 west; thence east on the township line between Townships 50 and 51 north, to the northeast corner of Section 6, Township 50 north, Range 2 west; thence south on the section lines to the middle of the channel of West Cuivre River in Section 7, Township 49 north, Range 2 west; thence up the main channel of said river to the north line of Section 33, Township 50 north, Range 3 west; thence west on said line to the place of beginning. The town of Nineveh, since Olney, was made the place for holding the elections.

Burr Oak.—May 11, 1875, on petition of David Allen, Henry H. Morris, Charles L. Alloway, Henry L. Luck and 155 others: Beginning on the range line between Ranges 1 and 2 east, at the center line of Section 7, Township 50 north, Range 2 east; thence south on the range line to the southwest corner of Section 7 Township 49 north, Range 2 east; thence east on section lines to the west line of Survey No. 376; thence north on said line to the south line of Survey No. 1789; thence easterly on said line and section line to the range line between Ranges 2 and 3 east; thence ast on the line of Sections 1 and 12 and the line of Duey and Dalton to the east line of Lincoln County, in the Mississippi River; thence up said river to the north line of Survey 1678; thence west on said line to the section line of Sections 1 and 12, Township 50 north, Range 2 east, and on said line to the east line of Survey No. 1724; thence north on said line to the line between Reid and Withington; thence west on their lines to the west line of said survey; thence north on said west line to the center line of Section 9, Township 50 north, Range 2 east; thence west on said line to the place of beginning. It was then ordered that the village of Burr Oak should be the place for holding elections in the new township thus formed.

Snow Hill.—May 11, 1875, on petition of Joel B. Cunningham, William J. Dryden and others: Beginning on the fifth principal meridian at the center of Section 18,* Township 50 north,

---

*This should have read " at the center line," or more properly " at the west quarter post of Section 18," as that was the point intended.

Range 1 east; thence east to the west line of Survey No. 1680; thence on the west and south line of said survey to the center of Section 17, Township 50 north, Range 1 east; thence east to the range line of 1 and 2 east; thence south on said range line to the center line of Section 13, Township 49 north, Range 1 east; thence west to Cuivre River at the center line of Section 18, Township 49 north, Range 1 east; thence up Cuivre River to the fifth principal meridian; thence up said meridian to the place of beginning. The village of Dryden was designated as the place for holding elections.

Change between Nineveh and Prairie.—In August, 1884, on petition of H. H. Jones, John E. Mosley and thirty-seven other citizens, the county court ordered "that West Cuivre River be made the north boundary line of Prairie, and the south boundary line of Nineveh Townships; that is, that all of Prairie Township lying north of Cuivre River, be transferred to Nineveh Township." With the exception of this latter change, the municipal townships of the county are correctly shown on the county atlas, published by Edwards Bros., in 1878. In looking at the map, care should be taken to include that part of Prairie shown to lie north of the Cuivre, with Nineveh.

THE PUBLIC LANDS AND INDIAN TREATIES.

The manner by which the United States obtained title from France to the territory of which Lincoln County forms a part has been given in the State Department of this work; but how the title was obtained from the Indians, who claimed it by right of possesion, remains to be told. At the earliest period known, Northeast Missouri was claimed by the Missouri tribe of Indians, called by Father Marquette, the first white man who saw them, the "Ou-Messouret," and by other early French chroniclers, the "We-Messouret" nation. They claimed, at one time, all of the country between the Missouri and Des Moines Rivers. The first treaty between the United States and the Indians, resulting in the extinguishment of the Indian title to this region, was made at St. Louis, November 3, 1804, between the head chiefs and representatives of the Sacs and Foxes, and William Henry Harrison, governor of the Indiana Territory and of the District of Louisiana, superintendent of Indian affairs and of the said territory and district, and commissioner plenipotentiary of the United States. The chiefs representing the Indians were Layouvois (or Laiyuwa), Pashepaho (the "Gigger" or Fish Spearer), Quashquame (the Jumping Fish), Outchquaha (or Sun Fish), and Hashequaxhiqua (or the Bear).

The treaty was a lengthy one, consisting of twelve articles, in the first of which the United States received the Sac and Fox tribes into friendship and protection, and the tribes agreed to consider themselves "under the protection of the United States and no other power." Article 2 prescribed the general boundary line between the United States and the said Indian tribes, as follows:

Beginning at a point on the Missouri River, opposite to the mouth of the Gasconade River; thence on a direct course so as to strike the River Jeffreon (Fabius) at a distance of thirty miles from its mouth, and down said Jeffreon to the Mississippi; thence up the Mississippi to the mouth of the Ouisconsing (Wisconsin) River, and up the same to a point which shall be thirty miles in a direct line from the mouth of said river; thence by a direct line to a point where the Fox River, a branch of the Illinois, leaves the small lake called Sakaegan; thence down the Fox River to the Illinois, and down the same to the Mississippi. And the said tribes, for and in consideration of the friendship and protection of the United States, of goods of the value of $2,234.50, which they now deliver, and of the annuity hereinafter stipulated to be paid, do hereby cede and relinquish to the United States all the lands included within the above described boundary.

The annuity mentioned was to consist of $1,000 worth of goods, "suited to the circumstances of the Indians," to be delivered yearly to the tribes at St. Louis, or some other convenient point on the Mississippi; $600 worth for the Sacs, and $400 worth for the Foxes. It was also stipulated that the tribes should take an equivalent amount of the annuity in domestic animals, implements of husbandry, and other utensils. The tribes agreed to never sell any of their lands to any power but the United States. The other provisions of this treaty are not sufficiently important to be considered here. It was fairly observed, with the exceptions of some Indian depredations noted elsewhere in this work, until the breaking out of the War of 1812, when nearly all of the Sacs joined the British and fought against the United States.

After the War of 1812 it became necessary to make another treaty with the Sacs. This treaty was signed at St. Louis, September 13, 1815, by Gov. William Clark, Ninian Edwards and Auguste Chouteau, commissioners of the United States, and certain chiefs and warriors of a branch of the Sacs, designated as "a certain portion of the Sac Nation of Indians, residing on the Missouri River." This was the loyal portion of the tribe which had separated from the hostiles. Its leading representatives who signed the treaty were the ever faithful Quashquame, Shamaga (the Lance), Kataka (the Sturgeon), Neshota (the Twin), Wesaka (the Devil), Catchemackeseo (the Big Eagle) and Chekaqua (He-who-stands-by-the-tree). This treaty was a re-establishment of that of November 3, 1804. The next day, September 14, a similar treaty was made with the Foxes by the same commissioners.

Black Hawk and the others of his tribe who had joined the British during the war were at this time on Rock River, in Wisconsin. They were invited to come down and sign the treaty, but were afraid the United States would seize them and punish them for their faithlessness and bloody crimes. They could not be induced to come in and treat until the spring of 1816, when, on the 13th of May, a treaty was signed between "certain chiefs and warriors of the Sacs of Rock River and adjacent country," and Gov. William Clark, Ninian Edwards and Auguste Chouteau, the latter the commissioners of the United States. This, too, was a renewal of the treaty of 1804, and the Sacs of Rock River were amnestied, and placed upon the same footing they stood on before the war. As signed to this treaty, Black Hawk's name is translated "Black Sparrow Hawk." At this time he was but a sub-chief, by no means a "head-chief," and it may be that he was merely a warrior. The other Indians who signed this treaty were Anowart (the Speaker), Namawenane (the Sturgeon Man), Matchequawa (the Bad Axe), Sakeeto (the Thunder-that-frightens), Cashupwa (the Swan-whose-wings-crack-as-he-flies), and sixteen others. It will be seen by the terms of the treaty of 1804 that the whole of

Lincoln County lies within the boundary of the tract of land to which the United States then obtained title from the Indians. These treaties were made with the Indians simply to pacify and keep them quiet, not because the Government really recognized any title to these lands in the savages.

CHAPTER V.

LAND GRANTS, RAILROADS, ETC.

The first lands in what is now Lincoln County, to which individual titles were obtained, are certain tracts known as Spanish grants or surveys. Under Spanish rule, the Government, in order to encourage settlement, allowed individuals to select and survey unoccupied tracts of land of varying size wherever they chose to settle, and then gave them a grant or right to hold the same as individual property. The Spanish Government also granted large, and often very large tracts, to certain individuals, for services rendered the Government. Very few, if any, of the grantees of the Spanish grants became actual settlers. Perhaps a few obtained grants for the purpose of settlement, and a few made temporary settlements prior to 1800, and prior to the permanent settlements heretofore mentioned. It seems, however, that nearly all these grants in Lincoln County were made to persons who obtained them for speculative purposes and not for settlement. When the United States acquired title and took possession of this territory, these Spanish grants were the only lands to which individuals could obtain title, and they only by purchase from the original grantees or their assigns. When the territory was ceded by Spain to France, it was upon condition that individuals holding title to lands under the Spanish Government should be protected in their rights; and when France ceded the territory to the United States, the same stipulations were made. Consequently the United States respected these titles, and afterward, upon a proper showing of evidence of title, the lands were confirmed by Congress to the original grantees or their legal assignees.

The following shows to whom nearly all of these lands were confirmed, as certified to the county April 8, 1858, by A. W. Rush, registrar of the Palmyra land office:

TOWN 48 NORTH, RANGE 1 EAST.

Jeremiah Groshong, Survey* 1791, 640 acres; Christopher Clark, Survey 389, 462.36 acres; William Dunn or legal representatives, Survey 6256, 5,322.12 acres; Mackay Wherry, Survey 1733, 340.28 acres; Richard Taylor, Survey 950, 640 acres; James Morrison, Survey 969, 640 acres; James Lewis, Survey 1642, 340.24 acres; Charles Dehault De Lassus, Survey 3034, 11,011.38 acres. The latter was confirmed by Congress July 4, 1856.

TOWN 48 NORTH, RANGE 2 EAST.

Squire Boone, Survey 60, 595.45 acres; Arthur Burns, 640 acres; Ira Cottle and William Hays, Survey 524, 510.41 acres; Nathaniel Simonds, Survey 1795, 640 acres; Isaac Cottle, Survey 755, 640 acres; William Farnsworth, Survey 754, 640 acres; James McKay or legal representatives, Survey 3035, 14,176.95 acres. The latter, and others of smaller size, were confirmed by act of Congress of July 4, 1856. From Survey No. 3035, Section 16 (the school section) and the interfering parts of Surveys 60, 754, 1788 and 1795 were excluded at the time of confirmation.

TOWN 48 NORTH, RANGE 3 EAST.

Francis Roy, Survey 1650, 680.55 acres; Toussant Cerre, Survey 1654, 850.69 acres; Bernard Pratte and Joseph Beauchemin, Survey 1687, 1,361.11 acres. These three grants lie on the Mississippi.

TOWN 49 NORTH, RANGE 1 EAST.

This township contains a large part of Survey No. 3034 confirmed to Charles Dehault De Lassus, as mentioned in Town 48 north, Range 1 east, and also parts of Surveys 1648, 1805, 1645 and 1791.

TOWN 49 NORTH, RANGE 2 EAST.

John Campbell, Survey 747, 825.85 acres; Julius Emmons,

---

* On the public records the Spanish grants are all called "surveys."

Survey 1789, 640 acres; Jacob Kostetter, Survey 736, 640 acres; Alex. McLeans, Survey 742, 640 acres; Arthur Burns, Survey 1816, 680.55 acres; Robert Burns, Survey 306, 510.41 acres; Jonathan Cottle, Survey 885, 640 acres; James W. Cochran, Survey 1742, 680.55 acres.

TOWN 49 NORTH, RANGE 3 EAST.

Paul LaCroix, Survey 1756, 1,361.11 acres; Joseph Roy, Survey 1653, 680.55 acres; Louis Roy, Survey 1651, 680.55 acres; Baptiste Roy, Survey 1652, 680.55 acres; Francis Roy, Survey 1650, 680.55 acres.

TOWN 50 NORTH, RANGE 1 EAST.

James Rankin and Peter Primo, Survey 1681, 680.55 acres; Charles Bissonette, Survey 1682, 680.55 acres; Joseph Bissonette, Survey 1683, 680.55 acres; Paul Primo, Survey 1680, 680.55 acres; Gabriel Zenon Soulard and James Gaston Soulard, Survey 1674, 1,361.11 acres.

TOWN 50 NORTH, RANGE 2 EAST.

Louis Labeaume and children, Survey 1824, 3,572.91 acres; Claibourne Rhodes, Survey 1642, 510.41 acres; George Spencer, Survey 1718, 510.41 acres; Antoine Smith, Survey 1732, 1,020.83 acres; William Ewing, Survey 425, 640.56 acres; James Burns, Survey 823, 510.41 acres; John Bassy and legal representatives, Survey 3269, 1,361.11 acres. In this township are parts of other surveys lying mostly in township 50, Range 3 east.

TOWN 50 NORTH, RANGE 3 EAST.

Louis Brazeau, Survey 1679, 680.56 acres; Joseph Brazeau, Survey 1678, 680.56 acres; Pierre Dumond, Survey 1693, 1,361.11 acres; Auguste Chouteau, Survey 1748, 680.56 acres; Daniel Clark, Survey 1716, 680.56 acres; Louis Guitard, Survey 1718, 1,361.11 acres. All in this township and range lie on the Mississippi.

TOWN 51 NORTH, RANGE 1 EAST.

Mary Philip Le Duc, Survey 1683, 6,002.50 acres; Auguste Chouteau, Survey 1819, 3,402.78 acres; Aristides Auguste

Chouteau, Survey 1743, 6,002.50 acres; Louis Lelille, Survey 3227, 2,126.73 acres. All these except the latter extend into other townships.

TOWN 51 NORTH, RANGE 2 EAST.

William Ramsey, Survey 3100, 636.42 acres; Joseph Brazeau, Survey 1737, 6002.50 acres; William McHugh, Sr., Survey 3010, 640 acres; Peter Chouteau, Survey 1706, 6,002.50 acres; William Palmer, Survey 1760, 850 acres; Didier Marehand, Survey 1820, 680.55 acres; M. P. Le Duc, Survey 1676, 680.55 acres.

TOWN 48 NORTH, RANGE 1 WEST.

In Township 48 north, Range 1 west, there are only three small grants, and in Range 2 west, none. In Township 49 north, Range 1 west, there are several small grants, and in Range 2 west, only one—No. 1751, containing 680.55 acres, confirmed to James Green, Jr.; and in Range 3 west, none.

TOWN 50 NORTH, RANGE 1 WEST.

Pierre Chouteau, Survey 1745, 1,701.40 acres; Paul Chouteau, Survey 1744, 1,701.40. In Ranges 2 and 3 west in this township, none.

TOWN 51 NORTH, RANGE 1 WEST.

This congressional township is nearly all taken up with Spanish grants, which were confirmed to Mary P. Le Duc and other non-residents.

TOWN 51 NORTH, RANGE 2 WEST.

In this township, and extending into Pike and Montgomery Counties, lies Survey 3016, containing 8,506.94 acres. By decision of the supreme court, January term, 1836, it was confirmed to Julie Soulard, widow of James G. Soulard, and other heirs of Antoine Soulard. Survey 1812 containing 1,361.11 acres was confirmed to Vienve Rigôche.

Many of the foregoing surveys extend into one or more townships, but the greater portion lie in the townships where mentioned. Many of the early settlers purchased portions of these lands and settled thereon. All those who settled on the public lands of the United States could not obtain titles until after the Government surveys were made, and a land office established for the sale of the lands. Meanwhile, the pioneer settlers exercised the right of pre-emption; that is, they selected their lands, settled thereon, improved the same, and waited to enjoy the preference which the law gave them to purchase when the lands came into market.

THE PUBLIC SURVEYS.

The Government survey of the public lands in Lincoln County was taken about the year 1819, being mostly made by Col. Daniel M. Boone, a son of the famous hunter and adventurer, Daniel Boone, formerly of Kentucky. A land office was established at St. Louis, and afterward it was moved to Palmyra. As soon as the land office was established, the settlers who had pre-empted their lands hastened thereto and formally entered them, paid the Government price, $1.25 per acre, and received patent deeds for the same. The Spanish grants, as may be seen by reference to the county map, were never surveyed with any regard to east and west or north and south lines. They were governed by the irregular shape in which the best lands were found, and also by the course of the streams. The rectangular system formulated and adopted by the United States for surveying the public lands was not then in use, especially not by the Spaniards, under whose government the grants were made. When the surveys were made by the United States surveyors, the Spanish grants or surveys had to be regarded, and could not be interfered with. Consequently, when the line of a Government survey struck the line of one of these former surveys or grants, it had to close thereon, and be extended from the opposite side of the survey.

PRINCIPAL MERIDIANS.

The first principal meridian governing the surveys of public lands according to the rectangular system, whereby the lands are surveyed into townships, ranges and sections, is the State line between the States of Ohio and Indiana. The second principal meridian runs through the central part of Indiana, a few miles west of the city of Indianapolis. The third principal meridian runs through the central part of Illinois, about eight miles west of the city of Bloomington. The fourth principal meridian lies in the western part of Illinois, and extends from the Illinois River, near Beardstown, north to the Mississippi, on which it closes. The fifth principal meridian lies in the eastern parts of the States of Arkansas and Missouri, and passes through the center of Lincoln County, Mo., a little over a mile east of Troy, and closes on the Mississippi a few miles above Clarksville, in Pike County. Hence the lands in this county were in ranges both east and west. Other principal meridians governing the public surveys lie west of this State and number consecutively.

BASE LINES.

The base lines are run across the meridian at right angles in the southern part of the territory to be surveyed from them; thus the base line which governs the surveys in connection with the fifth principal meridian lies in the State of Arkansas, 126 miles south of the southern boundary of Missouri, and 282 miles south of the extreme southern boundary of Lincoln County. The last mentioned base and meridian lines govern the public surveys in both Arkansas and Missouri.

PUBLIC LANDS.

The public lands have been classified under the heads of Congress lands, school lands, swamp and overflowed lands, etc.

The first covers the great bulk of lands sold and conveyed by the general Government, through its land offices, to individual purchasers. The second consists of the sixteenth section (or its equivalent) in each congressional township throughout the State, all of which was donated by Congress to the State for educational purposes. (Further mention of the school lands is made in connection with the public schools.) An act of Congress passed September 28, 1850, to enable all the States of the Union to construct the necessary drains and levees to reclaim the swamp and overflowed lands therein, made unfit thereby for cultivation, and which remained unsold at the passage of the act, granted all lands belonging to that class to the respective States in which they were situated. The act also provided that these lands should be selected and conveyed to the several States by the Secretary of the Interior, and that the proceeds from the sale of the lands should be applied exclusively, as far as necessary, to reclaim them by means of levees and drains. In making the selection of the swamp and overflowed lands in Missouri, it seems that the people or the authorities of Lincoln County, whose business it was to look after her interest, thought the county contained no lands coming under that head. It was supposed that the act only applied to swamp lands, and not to other land subject to occasional overflow. In consequence of this strict construction of the law, and neglect of the proper officers to attend to the business, no swamp or overflowed lands were ever selected in Lincoln County. It is true that the Spanish grants covered a large percentage of this class of lands, but it is also true that there are thousands of acres of land in the county, such as the lands subject to overflow along the Cuivre and other streams, that were not covered with the Spanish grants, all of which might have been selected under the Swamp Land Act. These lands, after being selected and conveyed to the State, were transferred by the State to the counties, with instructions to the county court to appoint a swamp land commissioner to carry out the congressional act in regard to reclaiming the lands, with the additional proviso that whatever surplus of funds remained after the necessary levees and drains were constructed, should be appropriated at the option of the county court for other purposes, or made to constitute a permanent school fund. But as stated, Lincoln County acquired none of its swamps or overflowed lands, and consequently obtained no funds from that source.

The failure seems to have been the result of neglect, as evidenced by an order made by the county court, September 2, 1871, of which the following is a copy: "The Court appoints Eugene N. Bonfils agent for Lincoln County, Mo., to make an investigation into any interest which said county may have in any swamp or overflowed lands within said county, and take such steps as may be necessary to protect the interest of the county, and to ascertain and report to the Court what swamp or overflowed lands are within said county, or any proceeds thereof, to which the county might be entitled by reason of either State or National legislation."

The record does not show that Mr. Bonfils made any report of his investigation. It is presumed, however, that he made an oral report that the "day of grace had been sinned away," in accordance with the facts previously stated. It is proper to state here that Col. Thomas G. Hutt is entitled to the credit of calling the attention of the county court to this matter, he then representing the county in the State Legislature. Many counties in Missouri derived over $10,000 permanent school fund from the sale of swamp and overflowed lands.

RAILROADS.

The St. Louis, Keokuk & Northwestern Railroad was completed through Lincoln County in 1879. It enters the county from the south at Old Monroe, on the Cuivre River, and runs thence in a northerly direction, along and at the foot of the bluffs on the west side of the Mississippi bottoms, and at an average distance from the river of about three miles, and leaves the county at a point about one and a half miles east of the northwest corner of Township 51 north, Range 2 east. Its length within the county is 20.88 miles. It is valued for taxation at $148,483.

The St. Louis & Hannibal Railroad was finished through Lincoln County in May, 1882, and the first great excursion from Troy was to Sells Brothers' show at Hannibal, May 2—round trip $2. It enters the county from the south, near the mouth of Big Creek, and runs up the valley of the Cuivre in a northwesterly direction to the town of Silex, and there it leaves the valley, and bears northeastwardly, and leaves the county near the center of the north line of Township 51 north, Range 1 west. It has many curves occasioned by the hilly surface of the country through which it passes, and its length within the county is 33.04 miles. It is assessed for taxation at $136,883. The combined length of these two railroads is 53.92 miles, and their combined assessed value is $285,366. According to the present tax levies these two railroads will pay in the County of Lincoln for the year 1888 about $5,400 in taxes, and thus help the people, in a measure, to liquidate their bonded indebtedness. Of course the tax will be for all purposes. Along these railroads and elsewhere in the county, the Western Union Telegraph Company has eighty-five miles of its line, which is assessed for taxation at $7,500.

RAILROAD BONDS.

On the 21st day of December, 1866, the county court (then being composed of Justices Milton L. Lovell, Samuel T. Ingram and James Willson), upon petition of numerous citizens of the county, made an order appropriating $100,000 for the purpose of taking stock in the St. Louis & Keokuk Railroad, provided that it be located within one-half mile of the courthouse in Troy. At the same time Maj. Alex. H. Martin was appointed agent for the county, to confer with the directors of the railroad company in securing the location of their road, and to order the bonds of the county, bearing interest not to exceed 6 per cent., to be issued at such times and in such sums as he might think proper, and to sell the same to the best advantage of the county, and, in general, to do and perform all necessary things for the interest of the county in the premises. This order, upon the petition of a large number of citizens, filed January 7, 1867, was afterward rescinded.

On the 13th day of August, 1868, the county court, then being composed of Justices M. L. Lovell, S. R. Moxley and S. T. Ingram, ordered that Lincoln County subscribe $300,000 to the capital stock of the St. Louis & Keokuk Railroad Company, and that county bonds for that amount should be issued. The bonds were to run ten years from the date of issue, at the rate of 10 per cent per annum, the interest to be paid semi-annually. This subscription was made on the condition that the railroad should commence on the North Missouri Railroad, at or near Dardenne, thence to cross the Cuivre at or near Chain of Rocks, and thence to re-cross the Cuivre at or near Moscow, and pass up the west side of the river within one-half of a mile from the courthouse in Troy, and thence northwardly, passing near Auburn, or between Auburn and New Hope, on the most eligible ground to the Pike County line. And for the purpose of carrying this order into effect, the Court again appointed Maj. A. H. Martin as agent for the county, with like powers as were given him on his former appointment. By order of the court, this appropriation of $300,000 was made in lieu of the appropriation of the $100,000 made December 21, 1866. At the February term, of 1869, the county court set out in a preamble the alleged failure of Josiah Fogg, president of the St. Louis & Keokuk Railroad Company, to act in good faith with the county in carrying out and complying with the provisions set forth in the foregoing order, upon which the $300,000 in stock was subscribed, and thereupon asked him to resign his office "and thereby remove the only obstacle apparent to the court to the speedy completion of the road."

Afterward, at the following May term of the county court, Alex. H. Martin reported that at the meeting of the directors of the railroad company, held in St. Louis on the third day of that month, for the purpose of selecting judges of the election for directors of said road for the ensuing year, a majority of the judges selected were inimical to the best interests of Lincoln County, and that it appeared that large quantities of bogus stock had been subscribed to the road, with the view of controlling the *bona fide* stock taken therein by this and Pike Counties; and that with the determination of protecting the interests of the county, he refused to subscribe the stock ordered by the Court to be taken, and withdrew from the meeting, and refused longer to co-operate with the board of directors. Meanwhile a communication was received from President Fogg, which seems to have satisfied the Court that they had misapprehended his motives, and that he was acting in good faith with the county. On the 17th day of February, 1870, the Court ordered that all the powers and authority previously conferred upon Maj. A. H. Martin as agent of the county "concerning stock in the St. Louis & Keokuk Railroad Company" be revoked and withdrawn. Five days later the following entry, showing the subsequent action of the court, was made upon the record of its proceedings:

"In the matter of the St. Louis & Keokuk Railroad Company. WHEREAS, It is the opinion of the county court that the inhabitants of this county have not been sufficiently guarded in the appropriation of $300,000 heretofore made to the capital stock of the St. Louis & Keokuk Railroad Company; and, WHEREAS, The county court is advised that said company are willing that all proper and just safeguards should be thrown around the subscription aforesaid, it is therefore ordered, adjudged and decreed that in lieu of all subscriptions of every nature, kind and character whatever, made by the county court of this county to said railroad company, the sum of $300,000 in bonds of said county of Lincoln, State of Missouri, be, and the same is hereby subscribed to the capital stock of the St. Louis & Keokuk Railroad Company, subject to the following express conditions, reservations and stipulations, viz.:

"First. That the subscription be received by said company in lieu of all subscriptions of every kind whatsoever heretofore made by said county of Lincoln to said company.

"Second. That said railroad shall be permanently located, built and operated on the following line, viz.: Beginning at the North Missouri Railroad, thence to within one-half of a mile of the courthouse in Troy, in said county, thence to the northern line of Lincoln County, State of Missouri.

"Third. That a good and sufficient depot for passengers and freight shall be built and permanently maintained within one half of a mile of the courthouse in Troy, in said county.

"Fourth. That said subscription herein made may be paid to said company, or the duly accredited agent thereof, in the bonds of the county of Lincoln, State of Missouri; said bonds payable ten years after the dates thereof; to be dated on the day of delivery to said company or its agent; to bear interest from date at the rate of 10 per cent per annum; interest payable semi-annually, with coupons attached for said interest; principal and interest may be paid at the National Bank of the State of Missouri in current funds, and that said bonds shall be received by said railroad company at par.

"Fifth. That the work on said railroad shall be commenced and prosecuted continuously from a point on the Northern Missouri Railroad to the northern line of Lincoln County, Mo., on the established line of said St. Louis & Keokuk Railroad; and the said bonds shall not be issued, nor the said subscription paid in any manner whatsoever, except in proportion as the work on said line is actually done; and all of said subscription of $300,000 shall be expended within the limits of said county of Lincoln. *Provided*, That a sufficient sum may be used out of said $300,000 by said company to make necessary surveys of said railroad through said county of Lincoln.

"Sixth. That said bonds shall be delivered to said company only upon estimates of work actually done in said county, which work shall have been received by said company; said estimates shall be sworn to by the chief engineer of said railroad, and filed with the agent of said county. Should said estimates appear to be too high, said agent shall call to his aid a competent engineer, and said engineers shall make another estimate of the work done, and in case they disagree, a third engineer shall be called in by them, and the report of two of them shall be conclusive upon all parties.

"Seventh. That said company shall never charge for transportation of freight or passengers on said railroad to or from any point in said county, more than 10 per cent above regular rates from the *termini* of said railroad—distance to be in all cases the ratio of charges.

"Eighth. That said company shall accept this order within sixty days from this date, by a resolution of their board of directors, entering the same upon their records, and by delivering to the clerk of this court a duly authenticated copy of said resolutions of acceptance.

"Ninth. That upon the acceptance of this order by said company in the manner herein required, it is ordered that the agent of said county of Lincoln make subscription to the capital stock of said St. Louis & Keokuk Railroad Company, in the name of the county of Lincoln, in the sum of $300,000, conditioned as herein specified.

"*It is further ordered by the Court*, That David T. Waddy be, and he is hereby appointed agent for the county of Lincoln, to represent the interests of said county, and contract with said company for the due performance of the conditions herein, and in general to do and perform all acts, duties, offices and services, to protect the rights of said county in the premises, subject, however, to the approval of the county court of said county, and subject to removal at the will of said court. *Ordered further*, That the clerk of this court furnish a certified copy of the foregoing to the president of the board of directors of said company.

[Signed.] "Milton S. Lovell,
"A. K. Willson,
"S. T. Ingram.
} Justices of Lincoln County Court, Mo."

On the 30th day of May following, R. T. Gladney presented to the Court petitions signed by 278 citizens of the county, praying the Court to rescind the order subscribing stock to this railroad. These petitions were ordered to be placed on file. The next day Walter Perkins and six other directors of the railroad company appeared and notified the Court that the company did not accept the conditions of the order made by the Court at the last February term, as required by Section 8, thereof. At a special term of the county court, held June 21, 1870, the following entry was made upon the record of its proceedings:

"In the matter of the St. Louis & Keokuk Railroad: It is hereby ordered that the order of this court, made on the 13th day of August, 1868, be amended as follows, viz.:

"First. That David T. Waddy, of Troy, be and he is hereby appointed agent for Lincoln County.

"Second. That the bonds of the county for the subscription of $300,000 to the capital stock of the St. Louis & Keokuk Railroad Company, made August 13, 1868, be issued and duly signed by the presiding justice of the county court, and bearing date 21st day of June, 1870, and attested by the clerk thereof, with the seal of the court, and be placed in the hands of the said agent.

"Third. That the said bonds be paid by the agent of the county to the said company, in sums of not less than $10,000, upon estimates for work done, or materials supplied for the building of the road through Lincoln County; said estimates to be approved by any first-class engineer, if so required by the agent of said county. And for the purpose of defraying cost of instrumental surveys through Lincoln County, the agent of the county is hereby authorized and directed to pay to said company the sum of $3,000 in bonds of this county—part of the said subscription of $300,000—immediately on the completion of the said instrumental surveys through Lincoln County. *Provided,*

That the said surveys through Lincoln County be commenced within twenty days after notice in writing is given to the president of the company, by the clerk of the county court, that the aforesaid bonds are placed in the hands of the said agent, duly signed and attested as aforesaid.

"Fourth. That all past due coupons for interest on said bonds be cut off before delivery of the bonds to said company; and that the said past due coupons be returned to the county court for cancellation; and upon each and every delivery of bonds to said company, the said company shall deliver to the agent of said county, fully paid certificates of stock in amount equal to the bonds.

"Fifth. That a good and sufficient freight and passenger depot shall be built and maintained by said company, within one-half of a mile of the courthouse in Troy, at a cost of not less than $2,000.

"Sixth. That when the St. Louis & Keokuk Railroad is graded, tied and bridged through Lincoln County, as aforesaid, any surplus that may remain of said subscription of $300,000 may be expended in grading, or in superstructure of said road between Lincoln County and the North Missouri Railroad.

"Seventh. The said St. Louis & Keokuk Railroad Company are hereby authorized to commence their road at or near Wentzville, or at or near Gilmore Springs, on said North Missouri Railroad, thence to within one-half of a mile of the courthouse in Troy in this county, thence to the northern line of Lincoln County, State of Missouri.

"Eighth. The foregoing bonds shall be payable in ten years from the first day of July, 1870, and shall bear interest from the first day of July, 1870, at the rate of 10 per cent per annum, payable semi-annually on the first days of January and July, with coupons attached. The said bonds to be numbered from one to six hundred, and each bond shall be for the sum of $500."

The record of this order was signed by Levi Bickel, A. K. Willson and S. T. Ingram, justices of the county court.

At the August term, 1870, the court ordered David T. Waddy, agent, to pay over to Josiah Fogg, president of the railroad company, $3,000 in bonds, for the instrumental survey of the road made through Lincoln County, and to receive certificates of paid-up stock for the same amount. In compliance with this and other orders, Dr. Waddy reported to the court on February 13, 1871, that he had paid out in Lincoln County bonds the following amounts:

For instrumental survey	$ 3,000
For work done as per estimate of November 15, 1870	12,000
For work done as per estimate of November 18, 1870	2,500
For work done as per estimate of January 15, 1871	12,500
Total amount paid out	$30,000

being bonds from one to sixty-nine inclusive.

The report, which was further itemized, showing full compliance with instructions regarding past-due interest coupons, certificates of stock, etc., was approved by the court. In May following, Dr. Waddy reported to the court that he had paid out bonds from 60 to 112 inclusive, amounting to $26,000, on estimates of work done in the months of February, March and April. He also presented to the court 540 certificates of paid-up stock, which, with twenty certificates previously presented, made 560 shares of paid-up stock of $100 each. On the 14th of August following, John C. Downing presented a petition, signed by 1,520 citizens of the county, praying the court to remove Dr. D. T. Waddy from his office as agent for the county in relation to the St. Louis & Keokuk Railroad, and to appoint G. G. Wilson as his successor, with certain instructions set forth in the petition. The matter was continued until the next day, when Henry Quigley presented a remonstrance signed by 1,348 citizens of the county, praying the court not to remove Dr. Waddy from his office as such agent. Both petition and remonstrance were continued until the 18th, when the court, after hearing addresses of both parties, and after having duly considered the matter, were "unanimously of the opinion that they could not grant the prayer of said petition, without gross injustice to, and an unwarranted impeachment of the business capacity and moral integrity of said D. T. Waddy," and therefore ordered that the petition be respectfully dismissed.

On the 2d of September, 1871, Dr. Waddy reported that he

had paid to S. R. Woolfolk, who had succeeded Josiah Fogg as president of the railroad company mentioned, the further sum of $10,500 in bonds of the county, on estimates of work done on the proposed railroad, for the months of April, May and June of that year; and on the 17th day of November following, he reported that he had paid in county bonds to President Woolfolk the further sum of $55,000 on estimates of work done in the months of August, September and October. The work continued to progress, and at the February term, 1872, the court ordered Francis C. Cake to purchase twenty-four railroad bonds already issued to the company, and ordered that $10,200 be appropriated out of the railroad fund for that purpose. Accordingly, on the 16th day of May following, Mr. Cake reported, among other things, that he had purchased the twenty-four bonds as ordered, for the $10,200 appropriated. These bonds and coupons thereto attached were then returned to the court properly cancelled. He purchased the bonds for $425 each, and reported that the market price, at date of his report, was $450—the face of the bonds being $500 each. At the same time Dr. Waddy reported that he had paid to the president of the railroad company, on three different estimates of work done, the further sum of $52,500 in county bonds; and that the total number of bonds paid out thus far was 348, amounting to $174,000. And for the last amount paid out he presented to the court 340 shares of paid-up stock, and a receipt for 185 shares to be issued at the next meeting of the board of directors. This report, together with Dr. Waddy's resignation, then offered, was accepted by the court. James L. McLellan, of Troy, was then appointed agent of the county in relation to the railroad business. It was then ordered that Section 7 of the amended order of the court, made June 22, 1870, be further amended, as follows:

"SEC. 7. The said St. Louis & Keokuk Railroad Company are hereby authorized to commence their road at a suitable point on the North Missouri Railroad, thence by the mouth of Big Creek, in Lincoln County, thence within one-half mile of the courthouse in Troy, this county, thence on the present located route to the northern line of Lincoln County, State of Missouri."

On the next day the court caused the following entry to be made upon the record of its proceedings:

"In the matter of the St. Louis & Keokuk Railroad, WHEREAS, the Missouri & Iowa Railway Construction Company is endeavoring to obtain sufficient capital to insure the completion of the St. Louis & Keokuk Railroad, and WHEREAS, objections are urged by capitalists to the manner in which the stock of said railroad company is scattered; and WHEREAS, it seems necessary in order to secure the building of said road, to remove every obstacle so far as can be reasonably done. Now, therefore, in consideration of the premises and of one dollar in hand paid by the said Missouri & Iowa Railway Construction Company, the receipt of which is hereby acknowledged, we hereby agree that if said Construction Company takes the contract for building said railroad, and prosecutes the same in good faith, and shall have the track laid on said road through the County of Lincoln within one year from the 1st day of April, 1872, then and in that case said Construction Company shall have the right to purchase, for the sum of one hundred dollars, the three thousand shares of said railroad company's stock subscribed and to be paid by said Lincoln County; and we hereby agree to assign and deliver the said stock to the said Construction Company at any time on the receipt of the said sum of one hundred dollars, after the track is laid as aforesaid through the County of Lincoln, *Provided*, the said track is so laid within one year from April 1, 1872. Otherwise this agreement is to be void and of none effect.

"A. R. WILLSON, *J. L. C. C.*

"I sign the above and foregoing obligation with the express understanding that if it is in conflict with any existing laws, the same is to be void and I exempt from all liability.

"S. T. INGRAM,
"*Presiding Justice of Lincoln County Court.*
"D. T. WADDY,
"*Agent Lincoln County.*

"Troy, Mo., April 8, 1872."

This contract was made, as may be observed from its date, by the individual members of the court when they were not in session.

On the 15th of August, 1872, James M. McLellan, in his first report as county agent, stated that he received from the hands of his predecessor, Dr. Waddy, county railroad bonds Nos. 349 to 600 inclusive, and that he had paid to the railroad company, on estimates for work done in the county, bonds 349 to 428 inclusive, amounting to $40,000. He also presented to the Court certificates for 585 shares of paid-up stock, 185 of these certificates being due as per last report of Dr. Waddy. The county now had paid out 428 of her bonds, amounting to $214,000, and held 2,140 certificates of paid-up stock. On the 16th of November following, James M. McLellan reported that since making his last report, he had paid to the railroad company, on estimates of work done, ninety bonds, amounting to $45,000, and received 450 certificates of stock therefor. In February, 1873, the county court made the following entry on the record of its proceedings: "In view of the great scarcity of money, and the extreme high price of iron during the last half of the year 1872, the time for the completion of the road as mentioned in the foregoing agreement (that of April 8, 1872), is hereby extended to December 1, 1873.

[Signed.]
" A. R. WILLSON, *P. J. L. C. C.*
" HENRY T. MUDD, *J. L. C. C.*
" JAMES M. MCLELLAN, *Agent
of Lincoln County, Mo.*

" Troy, Mo., February 13, 1873."

At this term Agent McLellan reported that on December 28, 1872, he paid President Woolfolk twenty-two bonds, numbered 519 to 540 inclusive, making $11,000, and received for same 110 shares of stock; and on the 17th day of May following he reported that on the 2d day of that month he had paid the further sum of $12,500, being bonds 541 to 565 inclusive, and received 125 shares of stock; and in August following, he reported that during the last quarter he paid fifteen bonds more, amounting to $7,500. At the November term, 1873, the county court, upon application of the directors of the railroad company, extended the time for the completion of the road to December 1, 1874. On the 15th day of November, 1873, James M. McLellan made his final report, stating that he had paid out bonds 587 to 600 inclusive, being all the balance of bonds in his hands, and returned certificates for 175 shares of stock, making in all 3,000 shares of paid-up stock then held by the county. This report was approved and the agent discharged. The original 600 bonds for the subscription of the $300,000 to the capital stock of the company had now all been issued; and on the 1st day of January, 1874, as shown by the records, there was still outstanding, of this bonded debt, the sum of $270,000. On this the interest accumulated rapidly, and the taxes annually levied and collected to pay it began to grow burdensome to the people, especially as the railroad was not yet completed. Three years more passed away; the interest on the bonds rolled up in semi-annual installments, and the taxes which continued to be levied and collected still oppressed the taxpayers. Consequently on the 29th day of September, 1876, Charles U. Porter and Alexander Mudd presented to the county court, then in special session, the following petition, signed by about 2,000 taxpayers:

"*To the Honorable County Court of Lincoln County, Missouri:*

"We, the undersigned citizens and taxpayers of the above named State and county, fully recognizing our condition, and appreciating the responsibility of our action, but believing as we do that we are aggrieved by the action of the county court of said county at the August term, 1868, by which said court appropriated the sum of three hundred thousand dollars ($300,000) to a corporation known as the St. Louis & Keokuk Railroad Company, and issued the bonds of the county for the payment of the same, and believing that the action of the court was without authority of law, and hence void, and further believing in the sacred rights of petitioners for the redress of grievances,

"We, therefore, the undersigned citizens and taxpayers as aforesaid, do most earnestly and respectfully pray the court as follows:

"First. To cancel or revoke the order made by the court at the May term for 1876, by which a tax of 60 cents on the $100 was levied on the taxpayers of the county, to pay the interest on the bonds issued as aforesaid, and also order the collector of this county not to collect the same.

"Second. To make no further orders or provisions for the

collection of either the principal or interest of any of said bonds.

"Third. To make no appropriations or provisions for the payment of the January interest on said bonds.

"Fourth. That the court will, when any action or actions are brought, or proceedings instituted to enforce the payment of either principal or interest on said bonds, employ suitable counsel to aid in resisting the payment of the same in any court in which any such action may be tried, and, in fine, that the court will resist the payment of said bonds and interest by all means known to the law. And for the same your petitioners will ever pray."

The consideration of this petition was continued until the following day, when the court took action thereon, and made the following entry on the record of its proceedings:

"And now the petition of Charles U. Porter, Alexander Mudd and others, coming on to be heard, and the court being fully advised of the premises contained in said petition, it is hereby ordered by the court that the first prayer of said petition, viz.: praying for the expunging of the levy of six mills for railroad purposes, upon the tax books of the present year, which was made by this court at the May term thereof for 1876, be and the same is hereby rejected. And further that the court grant the prayer of said petitioners, relating to the payment of the January interest of 1877 on the railroad bonds, and that the treasurer be ordered not to pay the same; and that hereafter no money shall be paid for either principal or interest until the question of the legality of said bonds is finally and fully settled in the courts."

As soon as the payment of interest ceased, the holders of the bonds, or a number of them, brought suit in the United States Circuit Court, for the Eastern District of Missouri, to enforce its collection. Afterward, on the 16th day of January, 1877, the committee for the foregoing petition, and their attorney, A. V. McKee, and also the objectors to the petition, by their attorney, R. H. Norton, appeared before the court, and all matters pertaining to the litigation of the bonds being set forth by the contending parties, the court appointed A. V. McKee, on behalf of the petitioners, and R. H. Norton, on behalf of the objectors, to prepare a statement of facts pertaining to and connected with the issuing of the Lincoln County bonds to the St. Louis & Keokuk Railroad Company, and to submit the same to an able lawyer of their selection for his written opinion as to the validity of the bonds. In April, following, Messrs. McKee and Norton presented to the Court their statement of facts, prepared as directed, together with the written opinion of Hon. A. W. Lamb, of Hannibal, Mo., who held the bonds to be valid, and advised the county to make preparations to pay them. Then came the committee of taxpayers by their spokesman, Charles U. Porter, and presented a series of resolutions relating to the matter. The consideration of the written opinion and these resolutions was laid over to the second day of the following May term. At the appointed time the matter was taken up, whereupon R. H. Norton presented a petition signed by 251 other citizens and taxpayers of the county, praying the Court to "require of those persons still desiring to litigate the bonds to give to the county a good and sufficient bond of indemnity against all costs of suit and damages resulting to the county by reason of said litigation." The Court refused to grant the prayer of this petition, and rescinded their former order that the opinion of the attorney employed by Messrs. McKee and Norton should be final.

Afterward, at the June adjourned term, the Court chose Henry A. Cunningham, of St. Louis, as attorney for the county, to protect its interest in the litigation of the bonds, and appointed George T. Dunn to enter into a contract with him. The contract was afterward reduced to writing and placed on file. By its terms Cunningham was to have a retaining fee of $500, and five per cent on all he might save the county by reason of the litigations, if a test case should be taken to the supreme court of the United States, but upon the bringing of various suits by the bondholders, he was to have $1,000 as a retainer, and five per per cent on the amount saved to the county. Various suits, however, were brought and judgments obtained against the county, and on the 12th of November, 1878, Messrs. Overall and Judson, attorneys for certain bondholders, appeared before the county court and demanded that warrants be drawn on the treasurer of Lincoln County in favor of their clients for judgments obtained in the United States Circuit Court for the Eastern District of Missouri, as follows: To Henry C. McPike for $5,380.80; Joseph W. Douglass, $11,368.81; E. K. Thornton, $1,062.64, Vespasian Warner, $6,371.56; Elisha Foote, $3,189; and John W. Ritnour, $1,670.56. This court refused to draw the warrants as demanded. Afterward, on the 29th of April, 1879, the above mentioned court issued a writ of peremptory mandamus commanding the county court to forthwith make and deliver to each of these judgment creditors warrants on the county treasurer to pay their judgments, interest and costs; and if there was not enough money in the treasury subject to the payment thereof, they should forthwith proceed to levy and cause to be collected, at the same time taxes were collected for State and county purposes, a special tax sufficient to fully pay and discharge the same.

In obedience to this writ, the Court, finding no money in the treasury subject to the payment of said judgments, ordered Josiah Creech, prosecuting attorney, to petition the circuit court, or the judge thereof in vacation, for orders to make the special tax levy as set out in the writ of mandamus. Soon thereafter, June 12, 1879, the Court ordered Mr. Creech to call a mass meeting of the citizens of the county, to assemble at Troy on Monday, June 23, following, to consider the subject of compromising the railroad bonds. The meeting was held accordingly and the following resolution was adopted:

"*Resolved*, That it is the wish of this convention that the county court and the attorneys thereof, Henry A. Cunningham and Josiah Creech, act as commissioners to confer with the bondholders, and submit to them a proposition for a compromise on a basis of one-half their claims on all bonds held by innocent parties; said proposition to be for the period of from date."

This proposition, on being presented to the bondholders, was rejected. On the 6th of September following the cases of Henry C. McPike, Joseph M. Douglass and Vespasian Warner against the county of Lincoln having been appealed to the supreme court of the United States, the court ordered that warrants on the county treasury be issued to Elisha Foote, John W. Ritnour and E. K. Thornton, respectively, for the amount of their judgments, interest and costs, up to that date; their cases not having been appealed. Other suits were brought by the bondholders, and judgments rendered in their favor. In the cases appealed to the supreme court of the United States, the judgments of the lower court were confirmed; and on the 12th of June, 1882, Morrison R. Waite, chief justice of the supreme court of the United States, issued writs of mandamus on the county court ordering the judges thereof to issue and cause to be delivered to each of the relators, Henry C. McPike, Joseph M. Douglass and Vespasian Warner, a warrant on the county treasurer to forthwith pay the amount of their judgments, interest and costs. And in case there was not enough funds available for that purpose, to levy and cause to be collected, at the same time State and county taxes were collected, a special tax sufficient to pay all balances remaining due.

On the 19th day of August, following, the court, in obedience to the foregoing writs, issued warrants on the county treasurer in favor of the judgment creditors for the amounts due them respectively. The amount of money then in the treasury, available for the purpose, was paid to them in proportion to the amount of their respective claims, and for the balances remaining due, and for other claims of the bondholders which the county might be compelled to pay, a special tax of one per cent was levied upon all of the taxable property thereof. Another case brought by Frederick Kniderkoper, of Pennsylvania, one of the bondholders, was appealed to the supreme court of the United States, where judgment in his favor was confirmed, a writ of mandamus issued, and compliance therewith made by the county court.

REFUNDING THE BONDS.

At the February term, 1883, the county court, upon a petition signed by 106 taxpayers of the county, ordered that the proposition of the bondholders, made by their attorney, John H. Overall, to compromise and fund all judgments and bonds in litigation at 85 cents on the dollar, and all bonds not in litigation at 75 cents on the dollar, be submitted to the qualified voters of the county at a special election to be held on Tuesday, April 24, 1883, at the usual voting places. According to the proposition, the refunding bonds were to run twenty years from date, but to be payable at the option of the county at any time after five years, and to bear interest at the rate of 6 per cent per annum. There were then $255,000 of the old 10 per cent bonds outstanding, and the accrued interest thereon was about $190,000, making a total of the bonded indebtedness of about $445,000. The election was held as ordered, and when the returns were canvassed it was found that 1,126 votes had been cast in favor of the proposition to compromise and fund the old debt with new bonds, and 819 votes against it. Accordingly, on the first day of May, 1883, the court, for the purpose of carrying out the agreement and proposition to compromise, ordered that there be issued bonds of said county of Lincoln in the sum and to the amount of $365,000, which bonds should be issued in denominations as follows: that is to say, 300 of said bonds to be of the denomination of $1,000 each, and to be numbered from 1 to 300 inclusive; 105 of said bonds to be of the denomination of $500 each, and to be numbered from 1 to 105 inclusive; and 125 of said bonds to be of the denomination of $100 each, and to be numbered from 1 to 125 inclusive; that said funding bonds and coupons thereon be issued as aforesaid and bear date May 1, 1883, in accordance with said proposition to fund and compromise, and be made payable to bearer, and to be payable twenty years from the said May 1, 1883, and bear interest from date at the rate of 6 per cent per annum, payable on the first day of February of each year, with negotiable interest coupons thereto annexed and attached, and that said bonds and interest coupons be made payable to the bearer thereof, at the Third National Bank of St. Louis, Mo. The bonds were to be signed and executed by the presiding judge of the court, and attested by the signature of the clerk thereof, and the seal of the court. They were ordered also to be made redeemable at the pleasure of the court, after five years from date of their issue. G. G. Wilson and Japtha Wells were appointed financial agents of the county to carry out the provisions of the foregoing order and compromise.

At the same term of court Messrs. Wilson and Wells reported that they had issued and paid out new funding bonds to the amount of $286,619.17, on judgments and old bonds taken up to the amount of $339,167.15, whereby the county was saved by reason of the compromise the sum of $52,547.98. On the 17th of August following the agents reported that they had refunded the sum of $41,395.67 of old bonds for $31,003.73, and thus saved the county the further sum of $10,391.94. Other outstanding bonds of the original issue were subsequently refunded, and further sums saved to the county. On March 4, 1884, the Court ordered that the 3,000 shares of the capital stock held by the county in the St. Louis & Keokuk Railroad should be sold to the highest bidder for cash at public auction at the door of the courthouse in Troy on Monday, April 7, 1884. The stock was offered accordingly and bid in by the county for $225, as per sheriff's report dated April 11, following. The county still holds the stock. On the 19th day of February, 1887, the Court, upon examination, found that refunding 6 per cent bonds to the amount of $365,000 had been issued and registered in the office of the auditor of State, and had all been put in circulation in refunding old bonds, and that the amount was not sufficient to refund all, and thereupon ordered W. A. Woodson, agent, to forthwith register in the State auditor's office additional bonds to the amount of $10,000, being Nos. 106 to 125, inclusive, of the denomination of $500 each, in order to compromise and refund the remaining outstanding 10 per cent bonds, which amounted to $7,000, thus making the total of the 6 per cent. bonds issued amount to $372,000.

Subsequently, efforts were made to refund the bonds at 5 per cent interest, and the following entries and orders of the county court, made and spread upon its record, on the 15th day of May, 1888, will show with what result:

"WHEREAS, The outstanding funding bonds of this county, bearing 6 per cent interest, are now by the terms of said bonds and the orders of the court, subject to call and payment, and

"WHEREAS, This court has satisfied itself that the bonded indebtedness can be refunded in bonds bearing a lower rate of interest, and

"WHEREAS, Lincoln County has heretofore compromised and refunded its bonds and indebtedness under an act of the General Assembly of the State of Missouri, entitled 'An act entitled an act to enable counties, cities, townships and towns to fund all or any part of their bonded debt and unpaid subscriptions to the capital stock of any railroad company, after first submitting the same to a vote of the qualified voters thereof, and to create a sinking fund for the payment of such funded indebtedness, and repealing certain acts, approved March 27, 1875, April 12, 1877, and April 14, 1877, and all other acts and parts of acts inconsistent with this act.' Approved May 16, 1879.

"*Now, Therefore,* For the purpose of refunding three hundred and twenty-five thousand dollars of said bonded indebtedness, under and by virtue of the provisions of an act of the General Assembly of the State of Missouri entitled 'An act to provide for the funding of county and township bonds," approved March 30, 1887, it is now here ordered by the court that bonds be issued by Lincoln County to the amount of three hundred and twenty-five thousand ($325,000) dollars, to be designated Lincoln County Funding Bonds, and to be dated May 15, A. D. 1888, and made payable twenty years after June 1, A. D. 1888. One hundred and twenty-five thousand dollars of said bonds shall be redeemable at the option of said Lincoln County, on the first day of February, in any year after five years from the date thereof, and one hundred thousand dollars of said bonds shall be redeemable at the option of said Lincoln County on the first day of February, in any year after ten years from the date thereof, and one hundred thousand dollars of said bonds shall be redeemable at the option of said Lincoln County, on the first day of February in any year after fifteen years from the date thereof; notice, however, of the intention of said county to redeem any of the said bonds shall be given by publishing for at least four weeks prior to the day set for redemption, in some weekly newspaper of general circulation, published in the city of New York, a call for any of said bonds which the said county intends to redeem; said call shall state the place of payment, the serial numbers of the bonds called and the day of payment, and that after said mentioned day the interest thereon shall cease. Said funding bonds shall bear interest at the rate of 5 per cent per annum, payable on the first day of February in each year, with negotiable interest coupons thereto attached. Both the principal and interest thereof shall be payable in lawful money of the United States, at the National Bank of Commerce, in the city and State of New York, and shall be signed and executed in the name and on behalf of said county, by the presiding justice of this court, attested by the signature of its clerk and under the seal thereof.

"The said coupons annexed to said bonds shall be signed by said presiding justice and said clerk, by having their respective names engraved thereon, which said signatures so engraved shall have the same force and effect, and be as binding on said county as though the same were written by them. A copy of this order shall be printed on the backs of said funding bonds, and shall be referred to in the bodies of said bonds, and shall be considered a part thereof. Said funding bonds shall be issued in the denomination of $1,000 each, shall be numbered from 100 to 325, and all of said bonds and coupons shall be made payable to the bearer thereof, and shall be registered as provided by law and have the certificate thereof duly appearing on each.

"And it is further ordered by this court that Lincoln County hereby contracts and binds itself to the holders of said Lincoln County funding bonds to be issued as aforesaid, that it, through its county court, shall and will provide a sinking fund in the express manner provided by law for the gradual retirement of all said bonds, by levying in and after the year 1888 an annual tax sufficient therefor on all the taxable property in said county, which fund shall be used for the purpose of said funding bonds, and for no other purpose whatever.

"And it is further ordered by this court that Lincoln County binds itself to levy and collect, in the express manner now provided by law, in and after the year 1888, a sufficient amount on each dollar of the taxable property in said county to pay the interest upon all the bonds issued as aforesaid."

In accordance with the foregoing order, the refunding bonds to the amount of $325,000 have been issued. In addition to this, there remains outstanding of the 6 per cent bonds issued May 1, 1883, the sum of $35,300, thus making the total bonded indebtedness of the county in July, 1888, the sum total of $360,300. The bonds of the $35,300 are payable on call, and for that reason were not refunded. They could not be refunded at five per cent and be made payable in less than five years, so to enable the county to call and pay a portion of them annually, they were left as originally issued. The Court anticipates the payment in full of the $35,000 during the next five years.

BEDFORD TOWNSHIP SUBSCRIPTION.

On the 19th day of January, 1875, Hon. R. H. Norton presented to the court a petition, signed by S. R. Woolfolk, William Frazier and thirty-eight other citizens of Bedford Township, praying for a special election to be held for the purpose of ascertaining whether or not the qualified voters of the township were willing to subscribe the sum of $55,000 to the capital stock of the St. Louis & Keokuk Railroad Company, provided that the company complete their road from the St. Louis, Kansas City & Northwestern Railroad to Troy, Mo., so as to give continuous connection by rail to St. Louis, on or before October 1, 1875, and that the principal machine and repair shops of the road be located and built within eighty rods of the station grounds at Troy, and that one building of said shops be erected on or before the time last mentioned. In compliance with the foregoing, the Court ordered that an election be held at Bedford Township at the courthouse in Troy, on Saturday, February 20, 1875, for the purpose of submitting and deciding the question set forth in the petition. The election was held accordingly, and on the 9th of March following, the returns were canvassed, and it was found that of the whole number of votes cast (558), 373 were in favor of the proposition to subscribe the stock mentioned in the petition, and 185 against it. Thereupon the Court appointed Walton Perkins agent for the Township of Bedford, and ordered that 110 bonds, of $500 each, be signed and issued by the president and clerk of the court, dated March 9, 1875, and to be due and payable October 1, 1885; the interest coupons to be paid at the office of the county treasurer on the first day of April and October of each year, the interest not to commence until October 1, 1875. The bonds for the full amount of $55,000 were prepared accordingly, but in consequence of the failure of the railroad company to accept the subscription on the terms offered, they were, on the 9th day of August following, destroyed by fire in the presence of the Court, clerk, sheriff, agent and others. Had this project succeeded, it would have been a good thing for the town of Troy—that is, if the shops had been located here and continued to be operated.

CLARKSVILLE & WESTERN RAILROAD.

On the 8th day of May, 1871, F. G. Gilmer and twenty-eight other citizens of Hurricane Township filed a petition with the county court setting forth that they desired, as a township, to subscribe $75,000 to the capital stock of the Clarksville & Western Railroad Company, on certain conditions set out in the petition, and that only 5 per cent of the stock subscribed should be paid until after the proposed railroad should be completed from Louisiana, in Pike County, to St. Charles, in St. Charles County. Thereupon the Court ordered that an election should be held in said township at the office of Dr. J. W. Welch, in the town of New Hope, on Tuesday May 23, 1871, for the purpose of submitting the question of subscribing the amount of stock as prayed for in the petition to the qualified voters thereof. The same day Jonathan W. Crume and thirty-one other citizens of Monroe Township presented a petition to the county court setting forth that they desired that township to subscribe the sum of $50,000 to the capital stock of the same railroad company on like conditions as set forth in the petition from Hurricane Township. Thereupon the Court ordered that an election should be held in said township at the house of Dr. Talbott, in Chantilla, on Tuesday, May 23, 1871, for the purpose of submitting the question of subscribing such stock to the qualified electors thereof.

Accordingly, these elections were held, and upon canvassing the votes, it was found that in Hurricane Township 140 votes were cast in favor of, and 166 against subscribing the proposed $75,000 to the capital stock of the railroad company, and that in Monroe Township 31 votes were cast in favor of, and 206 against making the proposed subscription of $50,000.

Afterward, at a special term of the county court, held June 14, 1871, John C. Downing and F. G. Gilmer presented the petition of 336 citizens of Hurricane Township, containing the same prayer as that of the one presented to the court on the 8th day of May preceding. Upon this petition the Court ordered another election to be held for the same purpose as aforesaid, at the office of Dr. J. W. Welch, in the town of New Hope, on Thursday, June 29, 1871. This election was also held, and upon counting the votes it was found that 181 electors voted for the subscription, and only 79 against it. This proposed railroad was never built, and consequently no bonds were issued, and Hurricane Township was thus fortunately saved from the great burden that a majority of the voters proposed to place upon her.

CHAPTER VI.

TAXATION, FINANCES, POPULATION, ETC.

As all governments must have revenue to defray expenses and keep the machinery of governmemt in running order, it was found necessary at the second term of the circuit court of Lincoln County, which was held in August, 1819, and which had jurisdiction over all county business, to provide for the raising of a county revenue. For this purpose it was ordered "that there be levied and collected by the sheriff, for the year 1819, the following taxes: On each horse, mare, mule or ass, above three years old, 25 cents; on all neat cattle above three years old, $6\frac{1}{4}$ cents; for every stud-horse the sum for which he stands the season; on each and every negro or mulatto slave between the ages of sixteen and forty-five years, 50 cents; on each billiard table, $25; on each able-bodied man of twenty-one years old and upward, not being possessed of property of the value of $200, 50 cents; on water, grist and saw mills, horse mills, tan yards and distilleries, in actual operation, 40 cents on every $100 of their valuation."

At the third term of the court, in December, 1819, the first accounts ever presented against the county were allowed, among which were the following: To commissioners of the county seat, David Bailey, $51.25; James White, $35; Daniel Draper, Hugh Cummins and Abraham Kennedy, each $37.50; John Ruland, clerk, $51.68; David Bailey, sheriff, $100.19; Peyton R. Hayden, deputy circuit attorney, $20; William Christy, Jr., for copy of record, $6.12½; account for seal, screw press, etc., $33.50; Benjamin Cottle, for use of his house for court, $16. Other accounts were allowed at this term, so that the aggregate amount was $459.24. The county revenue collected up to this term of court, for the year 1819, was $175.66, as appeared by the report of Sheriff Bailey. One dollar of this revenue was a fine which had been imposed upon Zadock Woods for committing an assault and battery.

By comparing the figures it will be seen that the amount of expenses allowed far exceeded the whole amount of revenue collected. The tax levies for 1820 were made at the August term of the court for that year, and were the same as for 1819. In 1821, the number of taxpayers in the county, as shown by the tax list of that year, including the widows and the estates of deceased persons, was 276. "The tax averaged a fraction over 95 cents each, and ranged from 2½ cents to $12.41¼, the latter being the amount paid by Shapleigh Ross, the largest taxpayer in the county. He was assessed with 504 acres of land, on which stood a grist and saw mill (in Moscow), thirty-nine town lots, seventeen slaves, twelve horses, eighteen cattle, and one watch, valued in the aggregate at $9,860. Ross was also the largest slave holder. Meredith Cox had ten, Malcom Henry, Sr., had eight; after these the largest number was five. There were 242 slaves and one free black in the county. There were 466 horses, and 845 cattle; no other property than mentioned above was listed. Besides Ross' mill, Ira and Almond Cottle owned a mill on Cuivre, point not stated, valued at $1,400; Joseph Cottle had a horse mill in Troy, valued at $400; and Meredith Cox had a horse mill where Louisville now stands, valued at $200. Maj. Christopher Clark had a distillery valued at $600, and Jacob Groshong had one valued at $200. Ezekiel Dunning had a tanyard valued at $100. The non-resident tax list numbered forty-seven taxpayers, of whom Auguste Chouteau paid the largest tax, $48.40, on 25,256 acres of land, valued at $39,128. The non-residents list included the names of Thacker Vivion, Nathaniel Simonds, John Ruland, George Collier and others, who had been residents, and some of whom were again residents thereafter." [Extract from Dr. Mudd's history.]

David Bailey, the first collector of Lincoln County, served from its organization in 1819 until 1823. Afterward, at the February term of the county court in 1826, an examination of his accounts for the years 1819 and 1820 was made, whereby it appeared to the court that a balance of $419.56, the items of which were set out, was due and payable from him to the county. Bailey denied the claim and refused to pay it, claiming as he did that he did not owe it. At the following August term of the court the president thereof was ordered to issue an order to the county treasurer to collect the amount. Not succeeding in collecting it, the case of "The County of Lincoln vs. David Bailey" was brought in the circuit court of the county in November, 1826, for the above-mentioned amount of money. The case was tried before a jury, who rendered a verdict "that the county receive nothing for her bill," and thus the defendant was exonerated from the charge.

In 1830 the county tax was equal to one-half of the amount charged for State purposes, and in February, 1831, Walter Wright, the tax collector, made a full report of the receipts of county revenue for 1830. This report shows that he received from direct taxation $603.77, and on account of licenses granted to merchants, inn-keepers, keepers of dram shops and the like, $159.45, making a total of $763.22 as county revenue. On this amount he was allowed a commission of $51.17 as collector. The taxable property of Lincoln County and the taxes charged thereon for the year 1832, as shown by the tax list of that year, which is still preserved, is as follows: Number of acres of land charged to resident owners, 48,277, valued at $148,356; number of town lots, 234, valued at $20,562; number of slaves, 723, valued at $185,064; number of horses, 1,263, valued at $41,401; number of cattle, 1,980, valued at $17,819. Total value of property of resident owners, $415,803. The amount of taxes charged thereon for State purposes was $1,018.86, and for county purposes, $765.95. The whole number of acres charged to both resident and non-resident owners was 94,288, valued at $232,246; town lots, 236, valued at $20,662. These items, together with the value of the slaves and other personal property, made the total value of taxables amount to $499,093. On this amount there was charged $1,159.34 for State, and $871.32 for county purposes, making a total of $2,030.66. The heaviest taxpayers in Lincoln County in 1832 and the amount of taxes paid by each were as follows: William Boon, $11.80; Thompson Blanton, $13.51; David Bailey, $19.12; Meredith Cox, $21.63; Henry B. Sanford, $11.67; Benjamin Vance, $14.47; A. C. & N. Woolfolk, $18.72; Peter Chouteau, Sr., a non-resident, paid or was charged $32.08 on a valuation of $11,000. He was then the largest taxpayer in the county.

SLAVE HOLDERS.

Following is a list of slave holders in the county in 1832, who owned six or more slaves, with the number owned annexed to each name: Harrison D. Allen, 6; Thompson Blanton, 14; Lewis Castleman, 6; Jesse Cooper, 7; David Clark, 6; Meredith Cox, 15; John Dudley, 9; Richard Fenton, 6; John Forkner, 6; Samuel Findley, 7; Joseph W. Gibson, 6; Malcom Henry, 6; Wiley Hines, 10; John M. Hopkins, 6; Milton L. Love, 6; Elijah Myers, 9; John McQueen, 11; Caleb McFarland, 6; Mervin Ross, 7; Thomas Revier, 6; Gabriel Reeds, 7; Peter Shelton, estate, 6; Robert Stewart, 9; Thomas Stallard, 6; Samuel Smiley, 7; Henry B. Sanford, 7; Fulton Thompson, 6; Barnabas Thornhill, 7; Benjamin Vance, 12; A. C. & N. Woolfolk, 16; Jefferson Wright, 7. The other slave holders, holding five or less, were too numerous to mention here.

As time passed on the county became more thickly settled, property increased in value, and with the increased public improvements, a larger amount of revenue became necessary. The total amount of county revenue collected for the year 1840, as shown by the collector's report for that year, was $1,609.95. The taxable property of Lincoln County, for the year 1850, as shown by the tax books, was as follows: Total number of acres of land assessed, 273,371, valued at $539,487; value of town lots, $24,013; number of slaves, 1,811, valued at $454,365; other personal property, $125,970; mills, stills and tanyards, $31,433; other property, $736,585; total value of taxable property, $1,191,853. On this amount there was charged for State tax, $2,903.23, and for county tax, $2,177.43, making a total of taxes charged $5,080.66

The following is a list of the heaviest taxpayers of Lincoln County, in 1850, with the amount of tax paid annexed to their names, viz.: James Baird, $19.41; Talbot Bragg, $23.24; James Clark, $24.00; Andrew Cochran, $35.18; Duncan Ellis, $20.76; James Finley, $23.23; Elizabeth Lewis, $33.43; Fountain Meriwether, $22.68; William Overall, $20.83; James Stallard, $23.07; Charles Sydnor, $26.64; John W. Sydnor, $29.51; William Sydnor, $23.30; Thomas G. Hutt, $35.21; Richard Wright, $19.01; Woolfolk estate, $22.44; G. W. Zimmerman, $22.07.

The slave holders of 1850, owning ten or more slaves each, with the number owned annexed to their names, were as follows: Joel Blanks, 13; Talbot Bragg, 18; James Clark, 16; Andrew Cochran, 20; Duncan Ellis, 10; Joseph Gibson, 13; Francis Harvey, 11; M. L. Lovell, 20; Thomas H. Lewis, 18; Elizabeth Lewis, 25; Raleigh Mayes, 10; Fountain Meriwether, 21; Charles W. Martin, 14; Charles D. Morris, 10; Geo. D. Meriwether, 18; Nancy McFarland, 10; M. H. McFarland, 15; James F. Moore, 12; David W. McFarland, 13; Ira T. Nelson, 11; R. C. Prewit, 12; W. N. Reynolds, 16; Gabriel Reeds, 10; Kenchean Robinson, 11; M. H. Ross, 10; John H. Ricks, 11; Meacon Shelton, 11; Charles Sydnor, 19; William Seaton, 10; William Sydnor, 20; Thomas G. Hutt, 28; Fulton, 10; Nat. Williams, 11; William Watts, 10; Richard Wright, 15; Woolfolk estate, 17; G. W. Zimmerman, 14.

RECEIPTS AND EXPENDITURES.

The receipts and expenditures of county revenue for the fiscal year ending May 1, 1851, were as follows:

Receipts from taxation	$2,198 43
Receipts from fines imposed	89 00
Receipts from land tax sales	8 20
Military fund from State	175 58
Total receipts	$2,470 81
Expenditures for all purposes	1,795 94
Balance on hand	$674 87

The receipts and expenditures of county revenue for the fiscal year ending May 1, 1861, as shown by the report of the treasurer to the county court, were as follows:

HISTORY OF LINCOLN COUNTY. 321

Total receipts from all sources.....................$5,072 14
Total expenditures............................... 6,159 53
Expenditures in excess of receipts for the year........ 1,087 39

There was charged on the tax duplicates of 1860, $7,125.62 for State tax, $3,149.01 for State sinking fund, and $526.53 for State asylum fund, making a total of $10,801.16, of the several State taxes. After deducting delinquencies and commissions for collecting, these funds received cash as follows: State tax, $6,159.07; State sinking fund, $2,744.73; State asylum fund, $456.20; total $9,360. The amount of taxable property in the county in 1860 cannot be conveniently given for the reason that the tax books do not show the aggregate amount.

LAST YEAR OF SLAVERY.

In 1862, the last year previous to the issuing of that great edict known as the "Emancipation Proclamation," the number of slaves assessed for the taxation in Lincoln County was 2,564, and the following is a list of the slave holders then owning twelve or more slaves, with the number owned annexed to their names: David and Henry Bailey, 15; Ruce Bourland, 14; Andrew Cochran, 15; Thompson Cox, 23; O. N. Coffee, 14; Duncan Ellis, 15; John C. Carter, 85; F. G. Gilmer, 12; Mrs. Belinda Harvey, 15; Augustus Harvey, 16; Thomas G. Hutt, 24; Joseph M. Heady, 18; Thomas M. Lewis, 22; M. L. Lovell, 13; Raleigh Mayes, 14; M. H. McFarland, 26; Thomas S. McGinnis, 16; Samuel C. W. Motley, 16; Lloyd B. Magruder, 19; Charles W. Martin, 15; Mrs. A. W. Meriwether, 20; George D. Meriwether, 42; Elizabeth Prewitt, 12; John Pollard, 14; Abner Rodgers, 12; James Reid, Sr., 16; John W. Sydnor, 13; David Steward, 14; James Stallard, 19; James D. Shelton, 15; John Strethen, Sr., 17; John South, 26; R. M. and A. W. Vance, 14; William Whiteside, 12; George W. Zimmerman, 15.

This list is given for the purpose of showing who the largest slave holders were at that time. Supposing the average value of each of the 2,564 slaves, listed for taxation in 1862, to have been $600, which is thought to be a fair estimate, it follows that the loss of property to the county, by reason of the abolition of slavery, was $1,538,400. This loss, however, was soon regained in the enhanced value of property, after the Civil War closed.

TAXABLE PROPERTY IN 1870.

The abstract of taxable property in Lincoln County for the year 1870 shows the following:

Number of town lots, 1,538, valued at	$ 133,890
Number of acres, 394,205, valued at	2,593,920
Total value of real property	$2,727,810
Horses, 5,593, valued at	284,990
Mules and asses, 1,173, valued at	59,860
Neat cattle, 11,548, valued at	181,470
Sheep, 22,840, valued at	57,710
Hogs, 19,001, valued at	24,690
All other property, valued at	497,400
Total value of personal property	$1,106,120
Total value of taxable property	3,833,930

The same abstract shows that there were 310 full, and 217 fractional sections of land, and seventy-five Spanish surveys taxed in the county, and 360 acres not taxable. The receipts of county revenue for 1870, as shown by the treasurer's report filed in February, 1871, were $9,336.94, and the expenditures for the same time, $4,143.70, leaving a balance on hand of $5,193.24.

TAXABLE PROPERTY IN 1880.

For many years last past, the real estate of the county has been assessed on two separate books, one containing all the land east of the fifth principal meridian, and the other all lying west thereof, and the personal property has been assessed on another book. The abstract of values of taxable property for 1880 is as follows:

Land Book East	$1,285,060
Land Book West	1,409,220
Total value of real estate	$2,694,280
Total value of personal property	1,168,160
Total value of taxable property	$3,862,440

By comparison it will be seen that the increased assessed value of the taxable property of the county for the ten years from 1870 to 1880 only amounted to $28,510. It is to be presumed, however, that the real or actual increase was much greater than that amount. Valuations for taxation are very uncertain, and vary greatly in amount from time to time on the same piece of property. The taxes charged on the foregoing valuation for the year 1880 were as follows: State tax, $7,724.88; State interest tax, $7,724.88; county tax, $11,587.32; road tax, $3,862.44; making a total of $30,899.52. This amount does not include any school tax.

TAXABLE PROPERTY IN 1888.

The assessed valuation of the taxable property in Lincoln County for the present year, 1888, is as follows:

Land Book East	$1,399,240
Land Book West	1,495,000
Total value of real estate	$2,894,240
Total value of personal property	1,476,590
Value of merchandise on merchants' book	146,610
St. Louis, Keokuk & Northwestern Ry. 20.88 miles	148,483
St. Louis & Hannibal Ry. 33.04 miles	136,883
Western Union Telegraph Lines, 85 miles	7,500
Total assessed value of taxable property	$4,800,306

By comparison it will be observed that the increase in the assessed value of the real estate of Lincoln County from 1880 to 1888 was $199,960, and of the personal property, $298,430, making a total of $498,390 of the increased value in eight years. At the present writing the taxes for 1888 have not been completed; but the levy for State and county purposes amounts to $1.50 on each $100 of taxable property. This levy on the whole amount of taxable property, as given above, will produce $72,004.59 for State and county purposes. In addition to this amount the school tax levies, which average about 40 cents on each $100, will produce the further sum of $19,201.22 (or thereabout), making $91,205.81 as the grand total of taxes that will be charged on the tax books of the county for the year 1888. This latter amount will be about double the amount of taxes charged for all purposes in 1880, but it must be borne in mind that 60 cents of the county levy for 1888 (which will produce $28,801.83) is to raise revenue to pay whatever becomes due on the railroad bonded indebtedness. No railroad tax was charged in 1880.

POPULATION OF LINCOLN COUNTY.

The population of Lincoln County, including both white and black, as given by the several census reports of the United States, beginning with the year 1820, is as follows: 1820, 1,662; 1830, 4,059; 1840, 7,449; 1850, 9,428; 1860, 14,210; 1870, 15,960; 1880, 17,426.

With the natural increase, together with the increased immigration occasioned by the building up of several railroad towns since 1880, it is safe to estimate the population of the county in 1888 at 20,000. In 1860 there were 2,863 colored persons in the county; but according to the tax lists there were only 2,564 in 1862, the last year that they were enrolled for taxation. In 1870 the colored population was 1,987, and in 1880 it was 2,146. The decrease in the decade covering the war period was 873, and the increase in the next decade was 159.

CHAPTER VII.

AGRICULTURE, HORTICULTURE AND LIVE STOCK.

The principal agricultural products of Lincoln County are Indian corn, wheat, oats, hay, potatoes and tobacco. In an early day cotton was extensively raised, but its cultivation has since been entirely abandoned. The productions are varied, though not so much as a better development of resources and a higher cultivation would demand. All the grains and grasses are distributed over the county, but in some cases with unequal results. In the eastern and southeastern parts of the county, comprising about half its area, wheat is the prominent crop. Its quality is unsurpassed, being fully equal to the best raised in the State, which is recognized as producing the finest wheat in the world. The yield has been known to reach forty to forty-five bushels per acre, but only in the most favorable seasons and with the best of cultivation, the average usually being less than half that amount. The soil throughout the county is rich in wheat producing principles, and with proper fertilization, subsoiling and underdraining, it can be made to yield from thirty to forty bushels per acre in most all seasons. The preparation of soils by underdrainage has as yet been scarcely thought of in Lincoln County. Corn and oats are produced in great abundance. It would be difficult to find a soil better adapted to either of these cereals. The soil is also well adapted to the growing of the grasses, especially timothy, which is the best known grass for hay. Clover also succeeds well, but it is not extensively grown. Hungarian grass and millet grow well all over the county. Barley and buckwheat also yield well, but are not extensively sown.

Broom corn yields abundantly in every part of the county, but, except in a few localities, no attention has been paid to it. Tobacco is advantageously grown on the timbered lands. The golden leaf of the white oak and post oak ridges is of the very finest quality, and is in great demand for wrappers. In the great tobacco fair of St. Louis, in 1869, Lincoln County tobacco took the first premium, nearly every State in the Union being represented. Sorghum is grown in every part of the county; the uplands producing less but of a finer quality. The small mills in the different localities manufacture the cane into molasses with success varying according to skill employed. The syrups from some of these mills will rival in color and flavor the finest silver drips. The consumption of sorghum, in this county, is fast superseding that of foreign syrups. As yet scarcely any has been exported, but its manufacture is destined to become a profitable industry.

The soil is also well adapted to the raising of all kinds of garden vegetables. Potatoes of the best quality are easily grown, but as yet they have not been extensively grown for the market, the farmers being content to grow them only for home consumption.

FRUIT CULTURE.

To the experienced fruit raiser Lincoln County offers a most inviting field. Nearly every kind of marketable fruit can be raised here with great profit to the careful cultivator. Nowhere do strawberries, raspberries, blackberries, gooseberries or currants grow more plentifully or attain greater excellence of flavor.

Cherries grow extremely well, but the trees are not so long-lived as in Eastern States, nor do they reach the same size. Peaches, pears, plums and apricots do very well, but the great crop is the apple. The yield is good and flavor excellent. The average yield of well-kept trees is about ten barrels, though much larger yields are frequently seen. But little has been done as yet in the line of fruit culture, but it is not very uncommon for the farmer to receive a larger profit from his small orchard than from the remainder of his farm, showing what might be accomplished in this direction. The following kinds of winter apples, when grown here with any care, are of special fine flavor: Rawle's Janet, Northern Spy, Winesap, Rhode Island Greening, Baldwin, Stark, Bellflower, Ben Davis, Willowtwig, Pennsylvania Redstreak, Newton Pippin, Golden Pippin, Roman Beauty, Prior Red, Vandever, etc.

GRAPES AND WINES.

It is well known that for excellence in grapes and wines Missouri cannot be surpassed by any other State or country in the world. This fact is principally due to the success of the grapes producing clarets, Burgundies, sherries and other choice red wines, such as Norton's Virginia, Cynthiana, Neosho, Hermann, etc. The wine made from the Cynthiana grape grown in this State took the first premium in Vienna as the best red wine of all nations. There is another class of grapes and wine, namely, the Elvira, Taylor, Amber, etc., producing hocks and white wines, in which Missouri, while not excelling those grown elsewhere, can equal them, even rivaling the famous Johannisbergs and Riesslings. The stocks of both these classes, when grown in this State, are phylloxera proof, and vast quantities have, on this account, been shipped to France and California. But little attention has been paid to grape-growing in Lincoln County, but the success of the many small vineyards demonstrates the fact that it is equal to the very best for grape-culture, and wine has been made here that competent judges have pronounced superior to the best Rhine wines. There are thousands of acres in this county admirably adapted to the culture of red and white wine-producing grapes.

HISTORY OF LINCOLN COUNTY. 327

PRODUCTIONS.

According to the United States census for 1880, there were 2,441 farms in Lincoln County, with 194,311 acres of improved land. The value of the farms, including the lands, fences and buildings, was $4,243,837. The farm implements and machinery were valued at $211,759. The value of the live stock was $1,024,403. The estimated value of all farm productions for 1879 was $1,038,095. These are the latest reliable statistics, and he who lives to compare these figures with those of the forthcoming census of 1890, will find "food for reflection." He will find that a wonderful improvement will have been made during the decade of the eighties. The following is a list of the amounts of vegetable productions of Lincoln County for the year 1879, as given by the census of 1880: Indian corn, 1,563,356 bushels; wheat, 428,119 bushels; oats, 319,008 bushels; rye, 2,749 bushels; potatoes, 15,782 bushels; sweet potatoes, 837 bushels; hay, 2,458 tons; tobacco, 308,090 pounds; value of orchard products, $17,158.

According to the same census, Lincoln was an average county, in the 115 counties of the State, in the production of Indian corn, far above the average in the production of oats, the seventeenth county in the production of wheat, and the eleventh in the production of tobacco. This is certainly a very good showing—that Lincoln County is far above the average in the leading agricultural products.

Also, by the census of 1880, Lincoln County was shown to have 7,128 horses, 1,667 mules and asses, twenty-two working oxen, 6,686 milch cows, 13,997 other cattle, 14,957 sheep and 53,366 hogs. The production of wool was 90,133 pounds, and of butter 278,347 pounds. As compared with all the counties of the State, Lincoln was on an average in the production of horses, mules and asses, and above the average in regard to cattle, sheep and butter—the thirtieth in the production of hogs, and the same in the production of wool.

CLIMATE.

The climate of Lincoln County is mild and pleasant. The average temperature is the same as that of a degree further south on the Atlantic coast; but being nearly in the center of the continent, there are not experienced the sudden changes common to the Atlantic States. There are none of the tornadoes that rage over the States north and west. Drouths are very uncommon; the rainfall is generally sufficient and well distributed. These statements are proved by the State weather statistics for the past years. The average rainfall was: winter, seven inches; spring, twelve; summer, thirteen; autumn, nine; total, forty-one. The average number of rainy days was ninety-two, the extremes being sixty-eight and one hundred and fifteen. The winter rainfall includes melted snow, of which the average was two and one-third inches. The atmospheric pressure is more uniform than in any State of the same, or more northern latitude, between the Rocky Mountains and the Atlantic Ocean; this is particularly the case in the summer, thus insuring the greatest possible benefits of the usual rainfall to the growing crops. As regards health, this county is fully up to the average in the State, which statistics prove one of the healthiest in the union. There is very little malaria; typhoid fever is extremely rare, and consumption is almost unknown as originating here.

AGRICULTURAL SOCIETY.

An Agricultural and Mechanical Society was organized in 1855. Its officers were Maj. George W. Huston, president; Dr. F. G. Gilmer, vice-president; S. R. Woolfolk, treasurer; C. W. Parker, corresponding secretary; and A. V. McKee, recording secretary. The directors were Talbot Bragg, Sr., Gen. David Stewart, Joel Blanks, Raleigh Mayes, Tully R. Cornick, Jesse Orear, Joseph M. Heady, George W. Porter, Col. David Bailey, and Andrew Cochran. The society temporarily fitted a fair ground north of where the public schoolhouse now stands, and there held its first annual exhibition, commencing October 1, 1856. The following year it held another exhibition and some time thereafter dissolved. From that time forward up to 1879 the county had no agricultural and mechanical society.

LINCOLN COUNTY AGRICULTURAL AND MECHANICAL FAIR ASSOCIATION.

This association is a joint-stock company. It was organized

with a subscribed capital of $3,500 divided into shares of $10 each. The first exhibition was held in the fall of 1879, on the lot near the public school building known as the boarding house property. On the 3d day of August, 1880, the association purchased of John B. Gordon and wife a tract of land adjoining Troy on the east, consisting of sixty-four acres, and known as the Cottle place. Forty-four acres were afterward sold off, leaving the twenty which are now enclosed as the fair ground. Articles of the association were filed with the Secretary of State, whereupon a charter dated October 2, 1882, was granted. The first fair was held at the present fair ground in 1880, and exhibitions have since been annually given. The association has only been moderately successful, owing to the rains that have taken place at the time of holding the fairs. The grounds are enclosed with a tight board fence, and contain an amphitheatre capable of seating about 1,000 persons, an art hall, office, band stand, sheds and stalls for live stock, and a race track. The present officers are William Moore, president; Alex. Miller, vice-president; Robert Shelton, secretary; and W. H. Perkins, treasurer. The board of directors consists of one member from each municipal township of the county.

STOCK LAW.

At the August term, 1887, of the county court of Lincoln County, a petition for restraining certain domestic animals from running at large, was presented, and the following is a copy of the record of the proceedings of the court in relation thereto, made on the 9th day of that month:

"*In the Matter of the Stock Law of Lincoln County, Missouri:*

"Now at this day comes William H. Long, Joseph Jones and 285 others, who are householders of said county, and file their petition praying this court to submit to the qualified voters of said county the question of enforcing in said county the provisions of an act, passed by the General Assembly of the State of Missouri, to restrain domestic animals from running at large, approved May 27, 1883, in so far as said act is applicable to swine, sheep and goats, and asking this court to call a special election for the purpose of submitting said question. And it appearing to the satisfaction of the court that said petition is in conformity with Section 8 of said act, and contains more than one hundred of the resident householders of said county, it is ordered that a special election be held in said county, at the usual voting precincts thereof, on Saturday, the 10th day of September, 1887, so that the question of enforcing the provisions of said act against swine, sheep and goats from running at large may be submitted to the qualified voters of the county of Lincoln. There shall be written or printed on each ballot voted at this election either of the following sentences: 'For enforcing the law restraining swine, sheep and goats from running at large.' 'Against enforcing the law restraining swine, sheep or goats from running at large.'

"And at such election the voting, making returns thereof, and casting up the result, shall be governed in all respects by the law applicable to general elections for State and county purposes. And it is further ordered by the court that a copy of this order be inserted in some newspaper published in the county for three consecutive weeks, the last insertion of which shall be at least ten days before the day of said election. And that the sheriff of this county post up copies of this order in three of the most public places in each township in the county, at least twenty days before the day of said election."

The required notices of the election were given, and it was accordingly held at the appointed time, and the following table shows the number of votes cast for and against enforcing the law in regard to allowing the stock to run at large:

VOTING PRECINCT.	Votes for enforcing the law.	Votes against enforcing the law.
Chain of Rocks	66	28
Chantilla	46	29
Winfield	62	70
Burr Oak Valley	42	123
Brussells	20	101
New Hope	69	53
Elsberry	99	125
Smith's Schoolhouse	25	19
Auburn	35	44
Louisville	95	84
Olney	106	34

HISTORY OF LINCOLN COUNTY. 331

VOTING PRECINCT.	Votes for enforcing the law.	Votes against enforcing the law.
Millwood	73	70
Truxton	76	49
Linn's Mill	16	66
Hubbard's Schoolhouse	98	28
Troy	205	101
Richardson's Mill	13	52
Whiteside	58	40
Silex	41	76
Total	1245	1192

This gave a majority of fifty-three votes in favor of enforcing the law. Notice of the result of the election was published by the clerk of the court, as required by law, and in due time the law for restraining swine, sheep and goats from running at large was enforced.

CHAPTER VIII.

COUNTY OFFICERS.

The following is a list of officers of Lincoln County from its organization down to the present year, 1888.

STATE SENATORS.

Of those who lived in the county and represented the Senatorial District in the Legislature: Carry K. Duncan was elected in 1824; Hans Smith, 1834; Henry Watts, 1838; James Finley, 1840; M. H. McFarland, 1856; Thomas G. Hutt, 1880. All of these served four years, except Henry Watts, who died in office, and James Finley, who filled the unexpired term.

REPRESENTATIVES.

Christopher Clark, 1818–20; * Morgan Wright, 1820–22; Philip Sitton, 1822–24; John Ruland, 1824–26; Philip Sitton, 1826–28; Elijah Collard, 1828–30; Hans Smith, 1830–34; Henry

* See organization of county.

Watts and John S. Besser, 1834–36; Henry Watts and Richard H. Woolfolk, 1836–38; George W. Hutson and Enoch Emerson, 1838–40; Hans Smith and Carty Wells, 1840–42; George W. Hutson, 1842–44; James Finley, 1844–46; David Stewart, 1846–48; Richard Wommack, 1848–50; Charles U. Porter and Alexander Reed,* 1850–51; Charles U. Porter and Tully R. Cornick, 1851–52; James H. Britton and Increase Adams, 1852–54; James H. Britton and M. H. McFarland, 1854–56; Richard Wommack and John Snethen, 1856–58; Richard Wommack, 1858–60; James W. Welch, 1860–62; Richard Wommack, 1862–64; Joseph W. Sitton, 1864–66; Richard Wommack, 1866–68; Richard Gladney, 1868–70; Thomas G. Hutt, 1870–72; E. B. Hull, 1872–74; William H. Priest, 1874–76; W. E. Brown, 1876–78; Alexander Mudd, 1878–80; Howard S. Parker, 1880–84; George T. Dunn, 1884–88.

MEMBERS OF CONSTITUTIONAL CONVENTIONS.

Malcolm Henry, Sr., in 1820, when the original constitution, on the admission of the State into the Federal Union, was prepared and adopted; 1845, Thomas W. Hutt, of Lincoln County, and Edwin D. Bevitt, of St. Charles, Democrats, ran against Charles Wheeler, of Lincoln, and J. D. Coalter, of St. Charles, Whigs. The latter gentlemen were elected, but the constitution they helped to frame, was, on submission to the people, rejected; 1864, Alexander H. Martin; 1875, A. V. McKee. The constitution then framed was ratified by the people, and has since been the organic law of the State.

REPRESENTATIVES IN CONGRESS.

Prior to 1848 the representatives in Congress for the State of Missouri were elected at large. The first elections for congressmen by districts were held in 1848, and since that time Lincoln County has been represented in Congress, as follows: William V. N. Bay, 1848–50; Gilchrist Porter, 1850–52; Alfred W. Lamb, 1852–54; Gilchrist Porter, 1854–56; Thomas L. Anderson, 1856–60; James S. Rollins, 1860–64; George W. Anderson,

---

*The latter died during the session of the Legislature and January 27, 1851, Tully R. Cornick was elected to fill the vacancy.

1864; David P. Dyer, 1868–70; Andrew King, 1870–72; Aylett H. Buckner, 1872–84; J. E. Hutton, present incumbent, 1884–88.

CIRCUIT COURT CLERKS.

John Ruland, 1819–20; Bennett Palmer, first half of 1821, to his death in August; Francis Parker, 1821–48; Thomas G. Hutt, 1848–54; Alexander H. Martin, 1854, to his resignation in 1869; William Colbert, 1869–87; Benjamin F. Reed, present incumbent, elected in 1886.

COUNTY COURT CLERKS.

Bennett Palmer, from organization of the court, January 15, 1821, to his death, in August following; Francis Parker, 1821–54; N. H. Meriwether, 1854, to his death in March, 1857; James A. Ward, 1857–58; Francis C. Cake, 1858–75; William A. Woodson, 1875–87; Jesse J. Shaw, the present incumbent, elected in 1886.

SHERIFFS.

David Bailey, 1819–23; Jonathan Riggs, 1823–27; Robert Stewart, 1827–31; Henry Watts, 1831–35; Valentine J. Peers, 1835–39; William Sitton, 1839–43; Richard Wommack, 1843–47; Henry T. Mudd, 1847–49; Joel Blanks, 1849–53; Richard Wommack, 1853–57; Joel Blanks, 1857–59; Peachy G. Shelton, 1859–61; Elias Norton, 1861–63; John R. Knox, 1863–67; Shapleigh R. Woolfolk, 1867–71; Frederick Wing, 1871–73; Thomas M. Carter, 1873–77; James C. Elmore, 1877–81; A. C. Snethen, 1881–85; Beverly Duey, present incumbent, elected in 1884, and re-elected in 1886.

COLLECTORS.

David Bailey, 1819–23; Daniel Draper, 1823–25; William Hammock, 1825–26; Austin C. Woolfolk, 1826–27; Daniel Draper, 1827–29; Walter Wright, 1829–32; H. Watts, 1832–34; Freland W. Rose, 1834–35; Benjamin Ford, 1835–39; William Sitton, 1839–42; John A. Woolfolk, 1842–43. From the latter date until 1873 the sheriffs of the county were *ex-officio* collectors of the revenues thereof. In 1872 the separate office of collector was established, and the following is a list of the collectors from that date: William W. Shaw, 1873–75; Peachy G.

Shelton, 1875-79; William B. Thornhill, 1879-83; Peachy G. Shelton, 1883-87; William Moore, present incumbent, elected in 1886. During the first three years of the existence of the county Sheriff Bailey collected the revenues, and from that time up to 1843 the taxes were collected part of the time by the sheriffs, and part of the time by collectors other than sheriffs.

TREASURERS.

Daniel Draper, 1825-26; Henry Watts, 1826-27; Francis Parker, 1827-33; R. H. Woolfolk, 1833-35; Charles Wheeler, 1835-42; William Young, 1842-46; James H. Britton, 1846-52; Charles Wheeler, 1852-58; S. R. Woolfolk, 1858-66; Frederick Wing, 1866-68; James D. Shelton, 1868-70; James K. Cannon, 1870-72; John McDonald, 1872-78; Thomas J. Nalley, 1878-84; William S. Bragg, 1884 till March, 1888, when he resigned, and was succeeded by H. W. Perkins, the present incumbent, who was appointed to fill the vacancy.

ASSESSORS OF REVENUE.

Philip Sitton, 1831-32; Austin C. Woolfolk, 1832-33; Robert Shelton, 1833-34; John M. Hopkins, 1834-35; James Reid, 1835-39; Richard Wommack, 1839-41; William Jameson, 1841-42; Henry T. Mudd, 1842-46; Edward J. Peers, 1846-48; Morgan Wright, 1850-52; Alex. H. Martin, 1852-53; Richard Wells, 1853-54; John M. Reed, 1854-58. In 1858 the county was divided into four assessors' districts, and William Miller, William T. Wilson, William H. Martin and Richard Wommack were appointed by the county court as assessors. Joseph S. Gear, 1860-62; David B. Smiley, 1862-66; James K. Cannon, 1866-68; Norman Porter, 1868-70; Elijah Myers, 1870-74; John Wilson, 1874-77; David C. Downing, 1877-80; Thomas H. Hammond, 1880-84; R. S. Gililland, 1884-86; William R. Clark, present incumbent, elected in 1886.

CORONERS.

Barnabas Thornhill, 1820-22; Jehu L. Sitton, 1822-24; John Parkinson, 1824-26; John Chandler, 1826-28; Thomas Armstrong, 1828-30; Bluford Stone, 1830-32; John B. Stone, 1832-

36; Joseph B. Kelsick, 1836-38; Barnabas Thornhill, 1838-40; Alexander Wilson, 1840-42; Baldwin D. Talliafero, 1842-46; William Murphy, 1846-48; William A. Sallee, 1848-50; Samuel Barker, 1850-52; Jordan S. Sallee, 1852-54; Joseph Chandler, 1854-56; J. B. Campbell, 1856-60; J. W. Thurman, 1860-66; J. B. Campbell, 1866-70; R. A. Nurnelly, 1870-74; George W. Elder, 1874-76; Robert L. Robinson, 1876-82; Talbot N. Bragg, 1882-86; Charles D. Avery, 1886-88.

PUBLIC ADMINISTRATORS.

Elective since 1858: Eugene N. Bonfils, 1858-62; Samuel Howell, 1862-64; Robert H. Hudson, 1864-66; J. B. Allen, 1866-68; Elbridge G. Sitton, 1868-72; Josiah Creech, 1872-76; Jeptha Wells, 1876-80, H. Avery, 1880-84; Josiah Creech, 1884-88.

SCHOOL COMMISSIONERS.

William Young, 1853; A. V. McKee, 1854; Francis C. Cake, 1857; John R. Knox, 1860; Francis C. Cake, 1861; James M. McLellan, 1866; William S. Pennington, 1871; John Wilson, 1873; James M. McLellan, 1875; Thomas P. Dyer, 1879; Horace Rose, 1881 to his death in 1885; W. T. Baker, 1885, present incumbent.

SURVEYORS.

Joseph Cottle, 1819; William Herbert, 1828-30; James Finley, 1830-38; James Reid, 1838-40; Nixon Palmer, 1840-46; J. J. Pritchett, 1846-51; James Reid, 1851-55; A. R. Finley, 1855-57; G. G. Wilson —; John C. Downing, 1867-72; John F. Wilson, 1872-88.

RECORDERS.

The office of recorder, in Lincoln County, was never separated from that of the circuit court clerk until 1886, when J. H. Alexander, the present incumbent, was elected recorder. He assumed the duties of his office January 1, 1887.

The following is a list of the judges of the circuit court and also of the justices and judges of the county court. Of the latter the time that each individual officer actually served, as shown by the records, is given, and may not in all cases cover the whole time during which they held office. The county court was sometimes composed of several officers, only two or three of whom met to hold the sessions. The list has been obtained by an actual and careful search of the records of the proceedings of the court.

CIRCUIT COURT JUDGES.

David Todd, 1819–21; Rufus Pettibone, 1821–23; Nathaniel Beverly Tucker, 1823–30; Priestly H. McBride, 1830–36; Ezra Hunt, 1836–49; Carty Wells, 1849–57; Aylett H. Buckner, 1857–62; Thomas J. C. Fagg, 1862–67; Gilchrist Porter, 1867–72; W. W. Edwards, 1872–81; Elijah Robinson, 1881–87; Elliott M. Hughes, present incumbent, elected in 1886, and assumed the duties of his office in 1887.

COUNTY COURT JUSTICES.

Ira Cottle, 1821–24; Jonathan Riggs, 1821–22; John Geiger, 1821–23; Benjamin Cottle, 1822–25; James Duncan, 1823–25; John Lindsey, 1825–28; Thompson Blanton, Philip Sitton, Daniel Draper, Benajah English, William Hammock, Barnabas Thornhill and Jonathan Cottle, 1825–26; Samuel Smiley, 1825–27; Gabriel P. Nash, 1826–28; William W. Woodbridge, John Love and Ira Cottle, 1826–27; Caleb McFarland, 1827–46; James Duncan, 1827–31; Joseph H. Allen and Henry Watts, 1828–30; Charles Wheeler, 1830–31; John S. Besser, 1831–34; George W. Zimmerman, 1831–35; William Young, 1834–39; Price W. Hammock, 1835–54; Lewis Castleman, 1839–42; Solomon R. Moxley, 1842–44; Thomas W. Hutt, 1844–46; Charles Ferry and Solomon R. Moxley, 1846–50; M. A. Shelton, 1850–54; James Wilson, 1850–58; Horatio N. Baskett and Charles W. Martin, 1854–58; Solomon R. Moxley, 1858–64; John South, 1858–60; Milton L. Lovell, 1858–70; William W. Shaw, 1860–61; Samuel T. Ingram, 1862–73; James Wilson, 1864–67; Solomon R. Moxley and James K. Cannon, 1867–69; Norman Porter, 1867–70; Alexander K. Wilson, 1869–75; John C. Downing, 1869–70; Levi Bickel, 1870–71; Charles W. Martin, 1870–77; Henry T. Mudd and N. H. Baskett, 1875–79; Nathan D. Prescott, 1877–79. District No. 1.—Gion G. Wilson, 1879–83; Jerome B. Sitton, 1883–84; John T. Gilmore, 1884–86; Wilson

W. Reid, 1886–88. District No. 2.—B. B. Harvey, 1879–80; Lawrence B. Sitton, 1880–83; A. Y. Brown, 1883–88. Presiding justices—Charles U. Porter, 1879–83; G. G. Wilson, 1883–88.

PROBATE JUDGES.

In 1825 Gabriel P. Nash was appointed for four years by the Governor. Before the organization of the county court in 1821, the circuit court exercised probate jurisdiction, and from that time forward, excepting the administration of Judge Nash, the county court exercised probate jurisdiction until 1870, when the probate court, as it now exists, was created by law. Since then the judges have been Solomon R. Moxley, 1870–74; E. N. Bonfils, 1874–78; Benjamin W. Wheeler, 1878; re-elected in 1882, and again in 1886—present incumbent.

PROSECUTING ATTORNEYS.

Benjamin W. Wheeler, 1872–74; Josiah Creech, 1874–76; George T. Dunn, 1876–78; Robert Walton, 1878–82; Jeptha Wells, 1882–84; Howard S. Parker, 1884, to his death January 3, 1886; Nat. C. Dryden, 1886—present incumbent.

BRIEF SKETCHES OF COUNTY OFFICERS.

Following are brief biographical sketches of many of the county officers, as given by Dr. Mudd in the county atlas, together with necessary changes and additions to make them complete at this time:

Increase Adams came from Maine. He conducted a mercantile business several years in Louisville, and left this county in 1860, to reside in Mexico, Audrian County, where he died June 5, 1874, aged about sixty-five years.

Joseph Benson Allen was born in Truxton, this county, December 12, 1841; commenced the practice of law in 1860; served in the Eighth Illinois Volunteers during the war. Now resides in Troy and is president of the Temperance Benevolent Association.

Thomas Armstrong was a pioneer settler and preacher. He went to Texas many years ago.

Joel Blanks was born in Pittsylvania County, Va., February

27, 1800. Married Miss Nancy Compton, January 4, 1827, came to this county in 1831, and settled on Big Creek. He died in Monroe Township at the residence of his daughter, Mrs. Witcher, February 25, 1875.

Eugene N. Bonfils was born in Tuscaloosa, Ala., October 13, 1820; moved to St. Louis, July, 1842; to Lexington, Ky., in 1846; graduated at Transylvania University, July, 1849; came the following month to St. Louis County, where he taught school; came to Troy in May, 1852, and commenced the practice of law. Besides offices named above, was probate clerk for four years preceding his election as judge, and held other positions of trust.

James H. Britton was born in Page County, Va., July 11, 1817. His early training was in the mercantile business. He married in 1838, came to Troy in 1840, and commenced business. Besides the offices named he was for a time postmaster of Troy; in 1848 he was secretary of the State Senate, and during the session of 1856–57 was chief clerk of the House of Representatives. In 1857 he was appointed cashier of the Southern Bank of St. Louis, and moved to that city; in 1864 he was elected its president. He held several other positions of trust, among them the office of president of the Life Association of America, and that of treasurer of the Illinois & St. Louis Bridge Company.

Warner Edward Brown was born in Union County, Ark., February 6, 1847; came to Wentzville in 1856; served in the Confederate army the latter part of the war. He graduated in medicine at Washington University, Baltimore, February 22, 1870, and located at Chain of Rocks. He abandoned the practice of medicine years ago and engaged in farming. He was commissioner of the Chain of Rocks bridge, and the principal originator of the project.

Francis C. Cake was born in Deerfield, Cumberland County, N. J., November 9, 1820, came to Troy October 16, 1840, and engaged in mercantile business until 1849. April 12 of that year he started to California by way of the plains, prospected from Nelson Creek in the northern mines to Sonora in the southern: was in Sacramento before there was a frame house erected in the city. He returned to Troy by way of Panama and New York. In 1857 he was appointed on the staff of Gov. Robert M. Stewart, with the rank of colonel. He is now deceased.

Thomas Miller Carter. [See biography elsewhere in this work.]

Elijah Collard, one of the early pioneers, came from Kentucky. He was a ranger in the War of 1812. He went to Texas many years ago.

Enoch Emerson was a native of Maryland. He was a merchant, and went to California in 1849 or 1850.

Andrew R. Finley came from Kentucky, and from here he went to California about the year 1870.

James Finley also came from Kentucky, and died years ago in this county.

Richard Gladney was a native of South Carolina, and came to this county with his parents when quite young. He went to California in 1870, and shortly afterward died.

George Webb Huston was born April 18, 1810, in New Market, Shenandoah County, Va. He came to Troy in 1834, was elected State registrar of lands in 1856, and held the office for four years. He died in April, 1862.

Thomas G. Hutt was born in Westmoreland County, Va., May 21, 1817, came to this county in 1837, and has ever since resided here.

Thomas W. Hutt was born in Westmoreland County, Va., September, 1798, and came to this county in the fall of 1832.

John R. Knox was born in this county September 16, 1836, was admitted to the practice of law in 1859. He traveled for his health about three years prior to his death, which occurred in Austin, Tex., May 3, 1876.

Charles William Martin was born in Campbell County, Va., September 29, 1810. He came to this county in 1838. He died at his home, near Troy, July 14, 1888, in his seventy-eighth year.

Nixon Palmer came from Garrard County, Ky. He died in 1845.

Francis Parker was born in Windsor, Vt., April 27, 1797. His grandfather, William Parker, came from the county of Londonderry, Ireland, about the year 1750, settled at Londonderry, N. H., and served throughout the entire war of the Revolution.

His maternal grandfather, Tyler Spafford, of English descent, also served throughout the war. His father, Henry Parker, died in 1814; and in 1817 he came to Jonesboro, Union County, Ill., where he held several important county offices, and where he married, in 1819, Miss Catharine Clapp, by whom he had eight children. He came to this county in 1821, and married his second wife, Miss Sarah Cochran, of this county, in 1833. By reference to the list of county officers it will be seen that he was county clerk for thirty-two years, and circuit clerk for twenty-six years. He died September 4, 1868. He was greatly esteemed as an honest, industrious and capable officer, and a sincere and earnest Christian.

John Parkinson was a native of England. He left this county many years ago, and died at Galena, Ill.

Edward J. Peers came from Kentucky; he was a graduate of West Point and a major of militia. He died in Troy, September 9, 1862.

Valentine J. Peers was a brother of the preceding; he married a daughter of Maj. Christopher Clark, and died some years ago in St. Louis.

J. J. Pritchett was a native of Pennsylvania; he left this county about 1856 or 1857.

Alexander Reid came from Kentucky; he died at Jefferson City while in office, as stated elsewhere.

James Reid was a native of Kentucky, and long a resident of this county, where he was widely known and greatly respected; he died in 1870.

Jonathan Riggs was a native of Campbell County, Ky., and the son of Rev. Bethuel Riggs, the first Baptist preacher of this county. He came to this county in 1812, and made an honorable record during the war. He married Miss Jane Shaw, by whom he had eleven children. After the war he settled north of the Cuivre, on the Troy and Auburn road, where he died in 1834. He was a brigadier-general of militia.

James David Shelton was born in Pittsylvania County, Va., June 11, 1816; came to this county in November, 1829.

Philip Sitton was born in North Carolina about the year 1772, and came with his father, Joseph Sitton, and several of his brothers, to this county in 1818. He was very prominent in public affairs, and died in this county in 1862 or 1863.

Jehu L. Sitton, a brother of the preceding, came to this county at the same time. He died about 1868, in Pike County, Ill.

William Sitton, a brother of the preceding, was born April 26, 1778. He was a captain in the army during the War of 1812, and was at the battle of New Orleans. He died in 1865. The last vote he cast was for John C. Breckinridge, for president.

Joseph Winston Sitton, son of the preceding, was born in 1806, in Tennessee.

Hans Smith was a native of Pennsylvania, and came to this county in the summer of 1828, just two years before he was elected to the Legislature. He was a brilliant orator and a very popular man. He went to Arkansas in 1846 or 1847, and was shortly afterward elected to the State Senate. He finally went to Texas, engaged in mercantile business in Austin, and was drugged, robbed and murdered.

John Snethen was born in Estill County, Ky., and came with his father to Montgomery County in 1808. During the War of 1812 he was in the forts in Howard County, and went to school with Kit Carson. He married Miss Euphemia Wells, sister of Judge Carty Wells, by whom he had six children. He was a merchant of Troy for thirty-seven years.

David Stewart was born in Montgomery County, Ky., January 24, 1798; came to this State and settled near Palmyra in 1829, and came to this county the following year. He was a brigadier-general of the militia. He and his wife were both killed by a runaway horse attached to a buggy, while on their way to church at Louisville, on Sunday, June 11, 1871. He was a prosperous farmer, and enjoyed, to the day of his death, the confidence and esteem of all who knew him; he was a sincere Christian gentleman.

Robert Stewart came from North Carolina, and was an early settler; he accumulated considerable property and died in this county. Henry Watts was born in Kentucky, and at an early age came to this county. He was colonel of militia, and was under marching orders with his regiment in Gen. Jonathan Riggs' brigade for the Black Hawk War, in 1832. He died in 1840.

Charles Wheeler was born in Hanover County, N. H., April 1, 1794; moved to New Castle, Henry Co., Ky., in 1820; had charge of New Castle Academy nine months; went next year to Bedford County, and taught school. He came to Alexandria, in this county, in 1825; went to Jefferson County, Ky., in 1828, taught school one year, and returned in 1829 to Troy, where he lived until his death, January 21, 1873. He was brother of Capt. Otis Wheeler. He held the office of justice of the peace from July 31, 1829, to within a week of his death, when he resigned it—a period of forty-four years. He was a graduate of Dartmouth College, both in law and literature, in the class of 1818. John Wilson was born in Muirkirk, Prince George's Co., Md., and came with his parents to this county about 1856. He served in the Confederate army during the late war, and lost an arm in battle. He was a brother of Maj. James Wilson, of the Federal army, who was killed at Pilot Knob. He died in June, 1877, of consumption.

Richard Wommack was born in Halifax County, Va., January 10, 1804, and departed this life at his residence in Lincoln County, March 25, 1880. He moved with his parents to Tennessee, where his father died, and from there moved with his mother to this county in October, 1823. He was married three times; first to Miss Cynthia Smiley; in 1831 to Mrs. Harriet Gilmore, and in 1873 to Mrs. Mary Morris; had ten children. He held prominent positions in public affairs; was a liberal and public-spirited citizen, and lived an exemplary life. He held the office of assessor two terms, that of sheriff four terms, and that of representative in the Legislature four terms. Of him it can truthfully be said to all the world, with all that the language can imply, "This was a man."

William Anderson Woodson was born in Monroe Township, in this county. For years he followed merchandising in Troy, where he now resides.

Richard Henry Woolfolk was born in Jefferson County, Ky., in October, 1803; studied medicine in his native State, and came to Troy in 1825; established and maintained a good practice in this and St. Charles Counties for about twenty-five years. In May, 1828, he married Miss Helen B. Wells, sister to Judge Carty Wells. He died in this county.

Morgan Wright was born in Bourbon County, Ky., and came at an early day to this county; he was a brother to the late Edward Thomas J. Wright; he married a daughter of Judge James Duncan, of this county, and died at his home in Clark Township about the year 1852.

For information concerning other prominent county officials the reader is referred to "bench and bar," and the biographical department of this work.

CHAPTER IX

ELECTIONS, JUDICIARY, ETC.

The first election held in Lincoln County was in 1819. The places for holding the elections, and the judges to conduct them, have been mentioned in connection with the county organization.

For the election in 1820, Prospect K. Robbins, Ira Cottle and Joseph Oldham were appointed judges in Monroe Township, and the election was ordered to be held "at the place for holding courts" in Old Monroe. Elijah Collard, James Duncan and Benjamin Blanton were appointed judges in Bedford Township, and the election was ordered to be held at the house of Benjamin Cottle. Robert Jameson, Philip Sitton and Samuel Gibson were appointed judges for Union Township, and the election was ordered to be held at the house of the latter. Benjamin Allen, Jesse Sitton and David Diggs were appointed judges for Hurricane Township, and the election was ordered to be held at the house of James Barnes. Afterward, from time to time, with the change of the municipal townships, new election precincts were established, and new places appointed for the holding of the elections.

In August, 1875, the county court appointed the following named places and judges for the holding of the special election to be held on Saturday, October 30, following, on the adoption or rejection of the new constitution of the State: Chain of Rocks, John K. Lindsey, William Eggering and Lawrence B.

Sitton; Chantilla, Alfred Y. Brown, William Lindsey and Robert Ricks; Drydensville, in Snow Hill, Andrew Cunningham, John J. Alexander and Christopher W. Ricks; Burr Oak Valley, Charles L. Alloway, Thomas R. Reid and Frank D. Hardesty; New Hope, William W. Reid, William F. Wilson and J. Winston Sitton; Hickory Grove schoolhouse in Clark Township, James A. Miller, Casper Extine and Royal J. Williams; Troy, James Wells, Jordon R. Witt and Charles U. Porter; Auburn, Alex. K. Wilson, Andrew F. Downing and John M. Reeds; Millwood, William W. Haynes, Francis B. Clare and Thomas Jackman; Truxton, Robert B. Allen, Williamson C. Giles and Henry Dewell; Nineveh, James C. Elmore, William W. Shaw and James Porter; Louisville, John T. Kimler, J. S. R. Gregory and Samuel C. Motley, Sr. The elections were held accordingly, and on the 12th day of November the returns were canvassed, and out of 1,239 votes cast, it was found that 1,209 were for the adoption of the new constitution, and 30 against it.

PRESIDENTIAL VOTE OF 1884.

The vote for President in 1884, at the several voting places in Lincoln County, was as follows:

PLACE.	Cleveland.	Blaine, Butler and Fusion.
Troy	281	227
Richardson's Mill	24	32
Hubbard's Schoolhouse	152	72
Linn's Mill	63	87
Truxton	57	98
Olney	109	68
Louisville	148	89
Millwood	149	60
Whiteside	126	35
Auburn	96	69
New Hope	173	86
Elsberry	215	125
Smith's Schoolhouse	48	9
Snow Hill	112	32
Burr Oak	119	95
Winfield	114	75
Chain of Rocks	136	54
Chantilla	91	58
Total	2243	1321

St. John received one vote at each of the following places: Whiteside, Elsberry and Smith's schoolhouse.

For the political phase of Lincoln County from 1836 to 1884, the reader is referred to the table showing the votes by counties at the presidental elections, found in the State history in this volume. In 1860, Abraham Lincoln, Republican, received only three votes.

AN ANECDOTE.

For the amusement of the reader the following joke on candidates, as reported in the Troy *Free Press*, in May, 1882, is here inserted:

"One day last week a lady from below Troy was engaged in shopping here, and having occasion to make some purchases at C. M. Hamilton's, was waited upon in the most polite and accomplished manner by our venerable friend Mr. P. G. Shelton, who, we may observe parenthetically, is a candidate for collector. Mr. Shelton, with the grace of a Parisian, assisted the lady upon her horse, and by his actions and delightful conversation so captivated her that on her way home she stated to a friend that she would certainly see that her husband cast a solid vote of the whole family for Mr. Shelton. This news immediately reached Troy, and now observe the effects. On Thursday last, another very sprightly and charming lady, who lives about four miles south of Troy, and who we will call Mrs. J., for short—came to Troy on a shopping expedition, and the first persons she met were Prince Birkhead and Capt. Colbert. The former, in behalf of the livery stable, tried to outdo Mr. Shelton in politeness, in the way of assisting the lady to alight and in taking charge of her horse, the Captain, in the meantime, standing still and scratching his head in a bewildered manner, looking for an opportunity to show off in the same way.

"Mrs. J. intimated to him that he ought not to be outdone by Messrs. Shelton and Birkhead—that Mr. Shelton had made one vote by assisting a lady last week, and that he (the Captain) might do as well this week by following the same plan. The Captain acknowledged it, excused himself for not being as quick as his young friend, mentioned the infirmities of age, etc., and promised that he would get her horse and assist her when she got ready to start home. After the lady had finished shopping, she looked around, but could not see the Captain, and concluded to send him a note by a convenient colored boy, who happened to be on hand, notifying him that she was ready to start. The boy carried the note to the courthouse, and in a minute the Captain was seen coming down the street, bareheaded and on a full run—but, alas! he was too late, as seventeen candidates had already gotten the horse, assisted the lady in the saddle, and she was going down the street toward home in a canter. It is hardly necessary to observe that the Captain was greeted with the cheers of the lucky seventeen."

SUPREME AND CIRCUIT COURTS.

When the county of Lincoln was organized, in 1819, under the Territorial laws, it belonged to what was then designated as the Northwestern Circuit, including, probably, all the settlements in Missouri Territory north of the Missouri River. Under the State organization the county was made a part of the Second Judicial Circuit, and under this head the first term of the court was held in February, 1821. In 1825 the Legislature passed an act establishing judicial districts and circuits, and prescribing the times and places for holding courts. The act was approved February 5, and by its provisions the State was divided into four judicial districts—the counties of Callaway, Montgomery, St. Charles, Lincoln, Pike and Ralls composing the Second. In each of the four districts the Supreme Court of the State was to be held alternately—the sessions to be held in the Second District, at St. Charles, beginning on the fourth Mondays of April and October in each year.

Judicial Circuits.—The act also provided that the counties composing each judicial district should constitute a judicial circuit, and the time for holding the circuit court in Lincoln County was fixed on the first Mondays of February, June and October. Thus the districts and circuits remained, with additions of new counties, until 1835, when, by an act of the Legislature, approved March 17, the judicial districts and circuits were reorganized. The Second District was composed of the counties of Montgomery, Warren, Lincoln, Pike, Ralls, Marion, Lewis and Shelby.

The sessions of the supreme court for this district were to be held at Bowling Green, in Pike County, commencing on the third Mondays of April and August in each year. The Second Judicial Circuit was composed of the counties of Montgomery, Warren, Lincoln, Ralls, Marion, Lewis and Shelby. The time for holding the circuit court in Lincoln County was fixed to commence on the first Mondays of March, July and November. Another reorganization of the judicial districts and circuits took place in accordance with an act of the General Assembly, passed in February, 1837, and in February, 1843, an act was passed to concentrate the supreme court. It provided that after that date the sessions of the supreme court should be held at Jefferson City only—to be held twice a year, commencing on the second Monday of January, and the first Monday of July in each year. The judicial districts for supreme court purposes were then abolished.

An act of the Legislature, approved March 27, 1845, provided that two sessions of the supreme court should be held annually, at the capitol of the State, commencing on the second Monday of January and the first Monday of July; and that two sessions should be held annually, commencing on the third Mondays of March and October, to hear causes from the Eighth Judicial Circuit, it being composed of the county of St. Louis only. This virtually divided the State into two supreme court districts—the one being composed of the county of St. Louis, and the other of all the other counties. The same act divided the State into fourteen judicial circuits, and made the third one consist of the counties of Marion, Ralls, Pike, Lincoln, St. Charles, Warren and Montgomery, and fixed the time for the holding of the sessions in Lincoln County on the fourth Mondays of April and September, of each year.

An act approved November 17, 1855, provided for the holding of two annual sessions of the supreme court "in the capitol, at the seat of government, on the second Monday in January and the first Monday in July," and also two sessions annually at the city of St. Louis, commencing on the third Mondays in March and October. Another act approved December 12, 1855, divided the State into sixteen judicial circuits, and made the third consist of the counties of Pike, Lincoln, St. Charles, Warren and Montgomery, and fixed the time for holding the sessions in Lincoln County, commencing on the second Mondays after the fourth Mondays of April and September of each year. In 1864 the law was amended so as to require two annual sessions of the supreme court to be held in the city of St. Joseph, commencing on the third Mondays of February and August. According to the revised statutes of 1866, the State was divided into six districts, in each of which a district court was established, the particulars of which are beyond the scope of this work. At the same time the State was divided into twenty judicial circuits, and the third was made to contain the counties of Pike, Lincoln, Montgomery, Warren and the Louisiana Court of Common Pleas. The time for holding the sessions in Lincoln County was fixed to commence on the second Monday of April and the fourth Monday in September in each year.

According to the revised statutes in 1872 (Wagner's Statutes) the State was divided into twenty-nine judicial circuits, and the nineteenth was made to consist of the counties of Lincoln, St. Charles and Warren, and the time for commencing the sessions in Lincoln County was fixed on the first Mondays after the fourth Mondays in March and September in each year. Afterward, by the revised statutes of 1879, the law was so amended as to make the nineteenth district consist of the counties of St. Louis, St. Charles, Lincoln and Warren, and the time for commencing the terms of the court in Lincoln County was fixed on the first Monday after the fourth Monday in March, and on the second Monday in October. Subsequently, by an act of the Legislature approved March 18, 1881, the law was again amended so as to take Lincoln County out of the nineteenth judicial circuit, and make it constitute a part of the third again. By this act the third circuit was composed, as it now exists, of the counties of Audrain, Montgomery, Lincoln, Pike, and the Louisiana Court of Common Pleas. The time for commencing the terms of the Lincoln Circuit Court is now fixed on the first Monday after the fourth Monday in March, and on the third Monday in September of each year. A list of the judges of the circuit court can be seen elsewhere in this work.

THE COUNTY COURT.

The first term of the county court, as has already been stated, was held on the 15th day of January, 1821, the law providing for its formation having been passed in 1820. It was composed of three justices of the county court, first appointed by the Governor and afterward elected by the people, and continued to be thus composed until 1825, when by an act of the Legislature, approved January 7, it was made to consist of all of the justices of the peace within the county. This act provided that the justices of the peace, or a majority of them, should meet on the first Monday of March, 1825, and designate not less than three nor more than seven of their number to serve as justices of the county court for the ensuing year, and that this designation should continue to be made at the first meeting of the justices of the peace in each year. The law also provided that there should be four terms of the county court held in each year, commencing on the first Mondays of February, May, August and November, and that each county should procure and keep a seal with such emblems and devices as it might desire. This method of composing the county court did not prove satisfactory, and the law being repealed, it did not continue later than 1830, after which the county court was composed of three justices of the county court as it was originally organized. An act approved March 7, 1835, provided that these justices should be elected for a term of four years, and that they should choose one of their number to act as president of the court.

The county court continued to be thus composed until it was reorganized under the new law of 1877. This law, entitled "An act to provide for a uniform system of county courts," approved April 27, 1877, provided that each county should be divided into two districts as nearly equal in population as possible, without dividing municipal townships; and at the general election in 1880, and every two years thereafter, there should be elected in each district an associate justice of the county court, and that at the general election in 1882, and every four years thereafter, a presiding justice of the court should be elected at large. In accordance with this law the county court at its November term (1877) divided the county into districts, by an order, of which the following is a copy: "It is ordered by the court that the municipal townships of Hurricane, Burr Oak, Snow Hill, Union, Waverly and Millwood constitute election district No. 1 of the county of Lincoln, and that the municipal townships of Monroe, Clark, Bedford, Prairie and Nineveh constitute election district No. 2, of said county, for the election of judges of the county court." The law of 1877 continues in force, and under its provisions the county court has been, and continues to be, composed. A complete list of the officers of the county court, from its organization to the present writing (1888), appears elsewhere in this work.

TOWNSHIP ORGANIZATION.

An act of the General Assembly approved in March, 1872, provided that counties might, by a popular vote, adopt "township organization," under which the county court would consist of all the justices of the peace, similarly as it did under the law of 1825. In accordance with the provisions of this act, Alfred H. Cheneworth, and 114 other citizens of the county, presented a petition to the county court at its August term, 1872, praying the court to submit the question of township organization to the qualified electors of the county. The prayer of the petition was granted, and the question ordered to be submitted at the general election in November of that year. The question was submitted accordingly, and when the election returns were canvassed by the court, it was found that a majority of the qualified voters were opposed to township organization.

PROBATE BUSINESS AND PROBATE COURT.

The circuit court exercised jurisdiction over all probate business until the county court was organized in 1821. The latter court then assumed probate jurisdiction, and held it until 1825, when, by act of January 7, the Legislature created a separate probate court, and authorized the Governor, "by and with the advice and consent of the Senate, to appoint and commission a competent person as judge of the probate court in each county of the State, to serve four years." Under this act Hon. Gabriel P. Nash was appointed and commissioned, and held his first term of the probate court in June of that year. The court being abolished, he held his last term in September of the following year. The county court then resumed jurisdiction of probate business, and exercised it until the close of the year 1870, when the probate court, as it now exists, was first established. The first term of the present probate court began January 9, 1871. [See elsewhere in this work for list of probate judges.]

The first probate business transacted in Lincoln County was the granting of letters of administration to Dr. Benajah English, on the estate of Daniel Epps, May 10, 1819. The first petition for partition was presented in August, 1819, by Benjamin O'Fallon, B. G. Farrar, Samuel D. Holmes and Thomas Hempstead; and at its second term, August, 1819, when, upon petition of Benjamin O'Fallon, B. G. Farrar, Samuel D. Holmes, Thomas Hempstead and Charles S. Hempstead (all non-residents), for the partition of 3,056 arpents of land, being an undivided part of a tract of land, containing 7,056 arpents, granted to Augustus A. Chouteau, by Don Carlos Dehault De Lassus, late Governor of the Province of Upper Louisiana, and confirmed to said Chouteau, the Court appointed as commissioners to make such partition Prospect K. Robbins, Joseph McCoy, Joseph Cottle, E. Collard and David Bailey.

The first guardian appointed in Lincoln County was James Murdock, who was appointed, in April, 1820, as guardian of Daniel, Joseph, Hynes, Clever and William Lynn, heirs under fourteen years of age, of William Lynn, deceased. Murdock gave bond for the faithful performance of his duties in the premises, in the sum of $1,000, with Samuel H. Lewis, Zadock Woods and Jacob Groshong as sureties.

FIRST WILLS PROBATED.

The first record of wills found among the public records begins with 1825. The following is a list of the names of the first persons in the county dying testate, with the date of the probate of their wills annexed: Robert Robertson, June 8, 1825; James Paxton, November 5, 1827; Thomas McCoy, July 12, 1828; William Hammack, November 4, 1828; Daniel Moss, January 21, 1829; Abraham Hoff, April 5, 1830; Cary A. Oakley,

February 21, 1831; Littleton Davis, November 7, 1831; Joseph Sitton, February 10, 1832. According to this it is observed that the deaths of testators during the early existence of the county were not numerous.

CIVIL ACTIONS.

The first civil action ever brought in Lincoln County was filed in the circuit court at its second term, being in August, 1819. It was entitled "William Howdeshell vs. James White," pleas of debt for $200. The defendant filed his plea of payment, and the cause was continued to the next term, when it was submitted to court, neither party requiring a jury, and judgment was rendered in favor of the plaintiff for $100.50 debt, and $6.43¾ damages.

FIRST CRIMINAL PROCEEDINGS.

At the term of court referred to the grand jury found and returned indictments against William Petty, Isham Petty, James Petty, John Petty, Alexander McNair, Robert McNair and Moses Oldham, for "hog-stealing;" Washington Jameson for stealing a bridle, and two against Zadock Woods, for assault and battery. At the next term of court the defendants charged with hog-stealing were arraigned and granted separate trials.

THE FIRST PETIT JURY.

The first petit jury in the Lincoln Circuit Court was thus empaneled: Ira Cottle, foreman; John Lindsey, Guyan Gibson, Jacob Williamson, George Jameson, Samuel Gibson, Robert Jameson, Sr., Thacker Vivion, Isaac Cannon, Ahijah Smith, Hugh Barnett and Andrew Cottle. Before this jury defendant Robert McNair was tried, and the following is a copy of the verdict: "We, the jurors, find the defendant not guilty of any of the charges against him in the indictment, and furthermore that the prosecutors pay the costs of suit." Accordingly, the prisoner was dismissed, and judgment for the costs was rendered to Christopher Clark and Jeremiah Groshong, the prosecutors. When the cases against the other defendants were called the prosecuting attorney dismissed them, there not being sufficient evidence to convict either one. In each case the costs were adjudged against the prosecutors, Clark and Groshong. Zadock Woods was then tried on one of the cases against him for assault and battery, and was acquitted. To the other case he plead guilty, and was fined $1 and costs. This was the first criminal conviction in the Lincoln Circuit Court.

At the next term of court, December, 1819, the grand jury returned presentments against the following parties for the following violations of law, viz.: Joshua N. Robbins, for Sabbath-breaking; James McCoy, assault and battery (three cases); James McCain, immorality; Zadock Woods and Alex. B. Faith, assault and battery; Seth Allen and Lee F. T. Cottle, selling liquor without license. It is not deemed necessary to follow the result of these cases. The early criminal cases were mostly, as they are now, for assault and battery, larceny, and selling liquor without license, the greater number being for the latter cause.

MISCELLANEOUS ITEMS.

In January, 1822, the county court, under an act of the Legislature, pointing out the manner in which executions might be stayed, and how the sale of property under execution should be made, appointed the following persons to appraise all and every manner of property taken under execution in their respective townships: For Bedford — Christopher Clark, John Hunter and Andrew Cottle; Union—Samuel Gibson, Philip Sitton and Thomas Hammond; Hurricane—Francis Riffle, Jonathan Cottle and Elijah Myers; Monroe—Thomas Slayton, Samuel Bailey and William Talbert.

The first foreigner naturalized in Lincoln County was Eleazer Block, a late citizen of Germany, who, on the 6th day of February, 1827, appeared before the county court and declared his intention to become a citizen of the United States, and took the oath of allegiance thereto.

Dram Shops.—At the November term, 1841, of the county court, licenses were granted to Bradford and Robert Thornhill, and Joseph Youngblut, to keep dram shops for a period of six months. The Thornhills were charged $15.50 for State purposes, and the same amount for county purposes; and Youngblut was charged 15.02\frac{1}{2}$ for State, and the same for county purposes.

In searching the records, these appeared to be the first licenses granted for keeping dram shops; but licenses had, from the organization of the county, been granted to individuals to keep "tavern," which answered all the purposes for the accommodation of "tipplers."

Criminals to Break Rocks.—At the May term, 1882, of the county court, the following order was made and entered of record: "Ordered that the sheriff of this county cause any person or persons, who have been convicted and sentenced by a court of competent jurisdiction, for crime, the punishment of which is defined by law to be a fine, to break rocks for macadamizing purposes, and work out the full number of days for which they may be sentenced; and if the punishment is by fine, and the fine be not paid, then for every dollar so fined said prisoner or prisoners shall work one day." The sheriff was also ordered to furnish a supply of rocks in the jail yard for the purpose of keeping such prisoners employed.

CHAPTER X.

BENCH AND BAR.

Men of State and national reputation, and of the ablest legal talent in the country, have practiced at the Lincoln County Bar. The first attorney admitted to this bar, as shown by the record, was Peyton Hayden, who, at the August term of the court, in 1819, presented a deputation from John S. Brickey, the then circuit attorney of the Northwestern Circuit, authorizing him (Hayden) to officiate in his stead. At the same term, John Payne, William Smith and Robert McGavock were admitted to practice, and at the next term LaFayette Collins and Ezra Hunt were admitted. In April, 1820, James McCampbell and John S. Brickey were admitted. The latter lived at Potosi, in Washington County. The lawyers in those days, like Methodist preachers, were "circuit riders," it being the custom then to follow the Judge around through his judicial circuit so as to be present and ready to accept whatever business might be presented to them. In this way the bar of each county was composed of all the able lawyers in the whole circuit; hence each bar had a concentration of legal talent. That custom, however, was discontinued long ago, and now the lawyers do not go abroad to seek clients and business, but go only when employed by their clients.

ATTORNEYS IN LINCOLN COUNTY.

The following is a list of the names of the attorneys, in addition to those already given, who served with the Lincoln County Bar prior to 1848, together with dates of admission so far as given on the roll of attorneys: Charles S. Hempstead, John C. Naylor, William Young, June, 1827; Charles Wheeler, George Shannon, Alfred W. Carr, John B. Gordon, Thomas A. Young, Francis K. Buford, L. Rogers, A. B. Chambers, Carty Wells, Samuel Moore, October, 1829; Thomas L. Anderson, February 15, 1831; John Anderson, William M. Campbell, February 15, 1831; Albert G. Harrison, September 20, 1831; Foster P. Wright, January 16, 1832; Thomas W. Cunningham, James F. Moore, May 20, 1833; William Porter, May 20, 1833, John Jameson, May 20, 1833; Henry L. Geyer, Bryan McMurphy, January 21, 1834; David Barton, September 15, 1834; George W. Huston and Joseph E. Wells, July 5, 1836; Beverly Allen, Urial Wright, Wilson Primm, Alonzo W. Manning and Alexander Hamilton, November 8, 1836; Gilchrist Porter, April 10, 1837; Henry Cave, August 8, 1837; Aylett H. Buckner and A. Backus Bacon, April 29, 1839; Victor Monroe, September 3, 1839; Garland C. Carr, November 30, 1840; W. V. Bouie and A. O. Forshey, October 20, 1841; James O. Broadhead, July, 1842; J. S. Samuels, August 18, 1842; Gustavus A. Bird, November 6, 1843; G. W. Buchner, Smith S. Allen, Abraham H. John, Rufus Sanders, Abner Green, A. P. Minor, October 7, 1840; Charles E. Perkins, John Scott, William Murphy, October 9, 1844; T. G. C. Fagg and S. F. Murray, May 6, 1845; L. A. Welch, September 22, 1845; David W. Nowlin, A. W. Lamb, September 28, 1846; S. M. Bowman, R. H. Parks, James K. Shelby and Thomas L. Wells, May 4, 1847. Edward Bates was also an early practitioner of the bar, but neglected to sign the roll. Many of the foregoing were very able and prominent, and some of them, at some time during life, filled very important official positions, from a cabinet officer down to that of justice of the peace. Some became judges and others congressmen. [See list of officers elsewhere in this work.] The homes of these attorneys were scattered from the Iowa line down to and including Washington County. Among the late prominent attorneys of the local bar of Lincoln County were Archibald V. McKee, Jeptha Wells and Howard S. Parker, all of whom, after becoming prominent in the history of the county, have passed on to "that undiscovered country, from whose bourne no traveler e'er returns."

The following is a list of the names of the resident members of the Lincoln County Bar at present: Richard H. Norton, Nat. C. Dryden, Charles Martin, Benjamin W. Wheeler, O. H. Avery, George T. Dunn, George W. Colbert, Joseph B. Allen, James M. McLellan, J. W. Powell, E. B. Woolfolk, W. A. Dudley and John H. Murphy [see biographical department]. Benjamin W. Wheeler, being judge of the court, is not now in active practice, and Joseph B. Allen and James M. McLellan have retired from active practice. The bar, as a whole, compares favorably in point of ability with local bars of the State. Some of the older attorneys practice in all the higher courts of the States and in other counties. The professional lives of some of the most prominent of the former members of the Lincoln County Bar, and of the judges of the judicial circuit of which the county has formed a part, are worthy of record, as given below:

Judge Carty Wells, formerly a prominent member of the Lincoln County Bar, was born in February, 1805, in Prince William County, Va. At the age of five he was taken to Shelby County, Ky., where he afterward received a good English education, and commenced the study of law. In 1827 he came to Missouri, finished his studies at St. Charles, where he was admitted to practice, and opened his office there in the autumn of 1828. Five or six years later, when Warren County was organized, he was appointed clerk of the circuit and county courts. After holding this office a few years, he resigned, and moved on a farm near Troy, Lincoln County, but continued to practice law. In 1840 he represented this county in the Legislature. From about 1843 to 1847 he resided at Palmyra, and while there served one term in the State Senate. He served as judge of the Lincoln Circuit Court from 1849 to 1857, and then returned to his farm. He was an able lawyer, genial in nature and had a host of friends. As an advocate he aimed not at oratory, but, with candor and logic, appealed to the understanding of a jury and seldom failed of success. He died in Troy in 1860.

Judge Thomas J. C. Fagg was born July 15, 1822, in Albemarle County, Va. His father, John Fagg, was a farmer in that State, and when Burgoyne's army was sent as prisoners to Virginia, it occupied part of his farm. John Fagg married Elizabeth W. Oglesby, a relative of ex-Governor Richard J. Oglesby, of Illinois, and in 1836 moved with his family to this State, and settled in Pike County. Thomas was educated at Illinois College, at Jacksonville, and there commenced reading law with Murray McConnell and James A. McDougal, and finished with Hon. Gilchrist Porter, then of Bowling Green, and was admitted to practice at Troy, this county, in April, 1845. Mr. Fagg opened an office at Bowling Green, and for some years was in company with the Hon. J. O. Broadhead, and afterward alone. In 1856 he moved to Louisiana in the same county, where he lived for more than a quarter of a century, and was in some public office much the larger part of the time. Before leaving Bowling Green he had become greatly interested in politics, being a Benton Democrat. As such, in August, 1850, he was a candidate for the Legislature, and was defeated. In November of the same year he was elected judge of probate, and established that court in Pike County. He was re-elected in 1854. At a special election in 1855 he was elected on the American ticket, in Pike County, to fill a vacancy in the Legislature. In 1856 Mr. Fagg was defeated on the State ticket as a candidate for commissioner of the board of public works. About this time he was appointed to the vacant office of judge of the court of common pleas, Louisiana being the seat where the court was held. In 1858 Judge Fagg was again sent to the Legislature, and in 1860 was the candidate for lieutenant-governor on the ticket headed by Hon. Sample Orr.

Though born and partly reared in a slave State, he was

opposed to the spread of slavery, and when the civil war began he was an outspoken Union man. In July, 1861, he was appointed brigade inspector, and in that and the following months mustered many State troops into service. He was elected colonel of the Fifth Regiment of Missouri Home Guards, and served in the field in Northeast Missouri until February, 1862. In that month he was appointed judge of the Third Judicial Circuit, of which Lincoln County composed a part, and in 1864 was elected to the same office for the full term of six years; but in September, 1866, he was appointed by Gov. Fletcher to a seat on the bench of the Supreme Court, to fill a vacancy caused by the death of Judge Lovelace, which position he held until the close of 1868. An old associate of his says, "Judge Fagg was always considered a good lawyer and an able advocate. On the bench he was cool, impartial and just, and left his judicial seat with an irreproachable character." On leaving the bench, Judge Fagg returned to the practice of his profession at Louisiana, and was in company with Col. Dyer, and later with others, until he removed to St. Louis, in 1882, where he resides at this time. In 1872 he was the Republican candidate for Congress in the Ninth District, and in 1878 in the Thirteenth, both strongly Democratic districts, and was defeated.

Judge William W. Edwards, a son of Henry and Sarah Ann (Waller) Edwards, was born in Henry County, Va., June 3, 1830. The Edwardses are of Welsh descent, and settled in Virginia long before the American Revolution. When William was six years old the family came to Missouri and settled in St. Charles County. The subject of this sketch was reared at farm work, attending winter school, meantime, until eighteen years old, when he commenced teaching in Lincoln County. He read law in the office of Robert H. Parks, of St. Louis, and at the end of one year entered the law department of the University of Virginia, at Charlottesville, and took a full course of lectures. Returning to Missouri, Mr. Edwards was admitted to the bar, and opened an office in St. Charles, where he soon proved his adaptability to his chosen profession. He was elected to the office of public administrator, and in 1858 to that of prosecuting attorney for the Nineteenth Judicial Circuit. This he resigned in 1862 to accept the appointment of United States district attorney for the Eastern District of Missouri, from which office he was removed the next year for political purposes. In November, 1863, Mr. Edwards was elected judge of the Nineteenth Judicial Circuit, and held that office for a series of years. Afterward, from 1872 to 1881, he served as judge of the Lincoln Circuit Court, and aimed to have exact justice done in all cases. He was cool and impartial, and his kindness to the members of the bar bound them to him by ties of lasting friendship.

Judge Elijah Robinson, son of Owen C. and Elizabeth (Salmons) Robinson, of Troy, was born in Lincoln County, Mo., February 9, 1849. He finished his education in the Watson Seminary, Pike County; read law at Troy in his native county, with Archibald V. McKee; was admitted to the bar in 1869, and at twenty years of age commenced practice at Bowling Green, Pike County. In February, 1870, he was appointed county attorney; was elected prosecuting attorney in the autumn of 1872, and re-elected in 1874, holding the office four years, and leaving a brilliant record as a prosecutor. In the autumn of 1880 Judge Robinson was elected judge of the judicial circuit including Lincoln County, served a full term of six years, and then resumed the practice of his profession at Bowling Green, where he resides at this writing. As a judge he gave good satisfaction, administering his duties with ability. His political affiliations have always been with the Democratic party.

Judge Elliott McKay Hughes was born in Lincoln County, Mo., November 7, 1844. His father, Elliott Hughes, was a native of Kentucky, a teacher in early life, and later a merchant, and his grandfather was a native of the Old Dominion. The mother of Elliott M. was Jane S. McConnell, a native of Kentucky. In 1845, before he was a year old, the family moved to Danville, Montgomery County, this State, where the father died in 1862, and the mother in 1866. Having obtained a common-school education, Mr. Hughes, with careful studying outside of the schoolroom, fitted himself for teaching. He taught three years in Adams and Pike Counties, Ill.; read law at Jacksonville, Morgan County, that State, and was admitted to the bar at Danville, Mo., in 1867. He was county superintendent of schools in

1870-71; was elected prosecuting attorney in 1872; re-elected in 1874 and 1876, and served six years, making a popular and efficient official. In 1886 he was elected judge of the judicial circuit of which Lincoln County composes a part, and is now filling his office, and performing the duties thereof, to the general satisfaction of the people.

Hon. Archibald V. McKee was born November 6, 1831, in Harrison County, Ky. His father, Archibald McKee, belonged to an old Virginian family, and was engaged in mercantile and agricultural pursuits, dying in Indiana in 1856; and his mother, whose maiden name was Lilly McClure, was a native of Boone County, Ky. She died in Iowa in 1871. In 1840 the subject of this sketch went to Hanover College, Indiana, where he graduated in 1851. He read law at Greensburg, same State, attended law lectures at the Indiana State University, and was licensed to practice at Indianapolis, in 1853. The next year he came to Troy, where he soon became well established in the practice. In 1862 he married Miss Clara S. Wheeler, daughter of Capt. Otis Wheeler. He occupied a high position at the bar, and died in Troy, July 13, 1884.

Hon. Jeptha Wells, was born in Troy, Lincoln Co., Mo., September 18, 1852. His father, Dr. John C. Wells, who was a native of Kentucky, and a graduate of the medical department of the Louisville University, came to this State when a young man, married Kitty Custer, a cousin of the late Gen. Custer, of the United States army, and was in practice at Troy at the time of his death, in 1857. Jeptha was educated at the Christian Institute, Troy, and graduated at the St. Louis Law School, in the class of 1874. He then began to practice in his native town, and in 1876 was elected to the office of public administrator, which he held four years. In 1882 he was elected to the office of prosecuting attorney and held it one term. He was a nephew of Judge Carty Wells.

Hon. William Young, son of James and Ann Frances (Booker) Young, natives of Virginia, was born in Shelby County, Ky., March 26, 1803. He was educated at Shelbyville Academy, and Transylvania University, Lexington, Ky., being a graduate of the class of 1824, studied his profession at Shelbyville, came to Missouri in 1827, and, after being one year in St. Charles, settled in Troy. He held several offices, was made one of the justices of the county court in 1834, and held the office four years; was county treasurer the same length of time, 1842-46; was public administrator one or two terms; county school superintendent for a time, commencing in 1853, and taught the Troy Academy one year, 1839. He was a member of the Presbyterian Church from 1833, and served in the office of elder for a long period. Part of the time he lived in the city, and part of the time on his farm, near Troy. He left the farm in 1876, and sold it in 1881. He died in Troy, March 23, 1886.

Hon. Howard S. Parker was born in Fayette County, Ky., September 5, 1853. His parents, Warren O. and Rebecca E. (McConnell) Parker, were also natives of that State. Howard was educated in the Kentucky University, Lexington, graduating in the law department thereof in the class of 1874. After practicing a few months in his native State he came to St. Louis, where he practiced two years, and then, in July, 1876, settled in Troy, Lincoln County. He represented this county in the Thirty-first and Thirty-second General Assemblies, and was chairman of the committee on constitutional amendments in the Thirty-first, of the judiciary committee and also temporary speaker of the Thirty-second. He held, as it is seen, in the latter General Assembly, one of the highest positions in a legislative body, and as chairman of the judiciary committee his legal talents and attainments were shown to good advantage. He was the youngest member ever chairman of that committee in Missouri, and the youngest speaker. In 1884 he was elected prosecuting attorney of Lincoln County, and held the office until his death, January 3, 1886. His business took him into the several courts of the State, and also into the Federal courts. He was considered an able attorney, and especially adapted to the criminal practice.

Hon. James R. Abernathy was one of the earliest practitioners in Northeastern Missouri, and served many years as circuit attorney. He was born in Lunenburg County, Va., February 25, 1795, but was raised principally in Fayette County, Ky., where he lived until 1817, when he came to Missouri. He was admitted to the bar at an early age, and was elected circuit attorney of a circuit embracing twelve counties, and filled the place with ability. He was first treasurer of Monroe County, and was justice of the peace sixteen years. He was the father of Mrs. Hugh Glenn (the California millionairess), a soldier in the War of 1812, and was well known all over Northeast Missouri. He was a resident of Monroe County when he died, January 23, 1883.

CHAPTER XI.

CRIMINAL RECORD.

Lincoln County, like most of the Missouri counties, has had to contend with a considerable amount of crime. While its record of crimes committed is greater than that of some counties, it is much less than that of others. Among the homicides that have taken place, the history of the following cases are given:

MURDER OF THE FLORENCE CHILDREN.

In 1834 William Florence settled on a tract of land about two miles north of west of Auburn, and there erected a rude horse-power grist mill. Four years later his family consisted of himself and wife and two bright, intelligent boys, William and Thomas, the elder being nine years old. About 2 o'clock P. M. on the 1st day of September, 1838, Florence rode over to Auburn, leaving his mill and place in charge of his slave, Aaron. On returning home his wife informed him that she had given the boys permission to go to the orchard of William C. Prewitt, who lived near by, to get peaches. Florence had repeatedly refused the boys this permission, fearing that Fanny, one of Prewitt's slaves, who had made threats, might do personal violence to them. He then walked over to the orchard, but seeing nothing of his boys, went to the house, and interrogated Fanny, who denied having seen them. He then went home and told his wife of his apprehensions. Search was at once instituted, and the next day more than a hundred men had collected, among whom were many of the most prominent citizens, such as Sheriff William Sitton,

Hans Smith (a member of the Legislature, and one of the most brilliant orators of the day), Burton Palmer (one of the early surveyors) and others. The search continued until Tuesday, when Mr. Palmer found the bodies of the children in Mill Creek, weighed down with stones. The water, which was high when the bodies were deposited there, had fallen and partially exposed them, so that the buzzards had begun to prey upon them. The flesh of the face and arms of Thomas had been partially devoured. It was the presence of these birds of prey that led Palmer and others to the place.

That evening Sheriff Sitton arrested Fanny, Ben, her husband, and Elick, her son. The latter, on being taken out and examined alone, confessed that his mother told him that she had killed the boys and thrown them into a sink hole in the creek, and showed them the stick with which the killing was done—the end of a horse-yoke. They then took the boy to the woods, put a rope around his neck, and tried to get further information, but failed in obtaining it. The prisoners were then taken before Squire Lawrence B. Sitton for preliminary trial. Elick, the boy, was released, and Fannie and Ben were committed to jail to await the action of the grand jury. Mr. Prewitt, who had been to Philadelphia, returned and prepared to defend his slaves. For this purpose he employed Judge Carthy Wells and the Hon. Edward Bates. The latter enjoyed a national reputation and was afterward a member of President Lincoln's Cabinet. Ezra Hunt was then judge of the circuit court, and Gilchrist Porter circuit attorney. Court convened on the first Monday in November, 1838. The grand jury was composed of nineteen men, of which Lewis Castleman was foreman. Upon the evidence given before this jury by Elick, he and Fanny, his mother, were indicted and Ben discharged On application of Prewitt, the owner of the defendants, a change of venue was granted to Warren County. The prisoners were then sent to the Pike County jail for safe keeping. In April, following, Fanny was tried at Warrenton, found guilty of murder in the first degree, and sentenced to be hung. On the trial Elick swore that he knew nothing about the murder, and that what he had confessed had been extorted from him.

The case was appealed to the supreme court, where a decision was rendered at the October term, 1839, reversing the decision of the lower court on the ground that the Warren Circuit Court had no jurisdiction, for the reason that a slave holder was not entitled to a change of venue for a slave. The case was remanded to Lincoln County, with directions that the testimony of Elick, the son, should not be admitted in evidence. At the succeeding trial there being no sufficient evidence she was acquitted. The people were indignant that the technicalities of law should defeat justice.

MURDER OF JOSEPH PLUMMER.

The Plummers lived on the bluff about a mile west of King's Lake. Some difficulty arose between the children of Philemon Plummer and those of his sister, Mrs. Anna Barker. On one occasion his children returned from his father's house and reported that they had been insulted by a negro woman and her children, belonging to the old man, and that their aunt, Mrs. Barker, supported them in their abuse. Afterward, on or about April 22, 1839, Philemon went over to his father's house with two of his children as witnesses, and wanted his father to whip the black woman. This the old gentleman refused to do. Philemon was about to whip the black woman himself when Mrs. Barker came up and interfered in behalf of the slave, and struck him two or three times on the mouth. He then gathered her hands into one of his, and raised a switch in the other. Joseph Plummer then came running up with a stone in his hand to defend his sister, and threatened to knock Philemon down if he struck her. Mrs. Barker, getting her hands loose, picked up a pitch-fork lying on the treading yard or floor, where they happened to be, but Philemon wrenched it from her hands, and with it struck Joseph a blow on the right side of the head, causing his death.

Philemon was indicted the same month for the murder of his brother, the indictment charging in substance that on or about April 22, 1839, he struck his brother Joseph on the right side of the head, with a stick seven feet long and three inches in diameter. On evidence the "stick" proved to be a pioneer pitch fork, made out of a sapling "about seven feet long, and about as thick as one's wrist," with one end split to form the prongs. Mrs. Barker testified that the bars to the entrance of the treading yard were all down except the top one, and that Philemon struck the fatal blow as Joseph was rising up after having passed in a stooping position under the top bar on his way to her assistance. Philemon was tried the same month and found guilty of manslaughter in the third degree, and was sentenced to serve three years in the penitentiary. The case was appealed to the supreme court, where the finding and sentence of the lower court were sustained. The prisoner was prosecuted by Gilchrist Porter, the circuit attorney, and was defended by the great lawyer, Edward Bates. It is said that his appeal in behalf of his client was the finest ever heard in the Lincoln Circuit Court.

BURNING OF GILES, A SLAVE.

In 1858 Simeon Thornhill and his family lived near the center of Section 20, in Township 49 north, Range 1 east, being north of east of Troy, and about three and one-half miles distant therefrom on a straight line. Thornhill was the owner of a slave named Giles, and when he and his slave were both sober they were on as good terms as generally existed between a slaveholder and his servant. In those days the greater part of goods sold at Troy were hauled on wagons from the landing at Cap-au-Gris, on the Mississippi. One of the leading articles thus conveyed was whisky, and it was customary with the drivers of the teams hauling it out from the river to carry gimlets with them with which they tapped the barrels, and by the use of a straw, sucked therefrom, to their full satisfaction, the death-producing liquid. Thornhill and his slave frequently hauled goods from Cap-au-Gris to Troy, and indulged according to the custom, and also usually carried home a jug of the "ardent." Giles was allowed to have whisky whenever he could procure it, and as it was both cheap and free in those times he had no difficulty in obtaining it. It is said by a prominent citizen, who lived in the Thornhill neighborhood, and who was well acquainted with the parties, that when Thornhill had a jug of whisky Giles always had a share of the contents, and *vice versa*, when the slave had whisky he always divided with his master, and thus they mutually imbibed.

On the night of December 24, 1858, they were together in the negro's cabin, which was inclosed in a little yard near the residence of Thornhill. Here they were drinking. The hours "wore away," and all retired for their usual rest save the master and his slave, who continued to indulge in the dangerous amusement. Presently they disagreed, then grew angry, became desperate, and the negro, being the larger and stronger man, made a pass at his master, who fled for safety toward his house. The negro caught him while crossing the yard fence, and with his knife stabbed him in several places, mostly on the back of his body, but did not kill him instantly. This aroused the sleepers, and Thornhill was carried into his house and cared for. The next day (Christmas) the negro was arrested without process of law and placed in jail at Troy. Capt. Jordan S. Salle, who still resides in Troy (and to whom the writer is indebted for some of these facts), was then the jailer. Some of the neighbors of Thornhill, and others residing east of the Cuivre, became terribly incensed at the negro, and in a few days after he was incarcerated in jail they assembled and started toward Troy, for the purpose of lynching him and putting an end to his existence; but upon reaching the river they found that it had so swollen that they could not cross, and thereupon disbanded and returned to their homes. Thornhill lingered until the 30th of the month, and then died from the effects of the wounds inflicted by his slave. On the following day Capt. Salle, the jailer, anticipating the action of the mob, and being anxious to have a legal right to hold his prisoner, in case of a demand for his release or an attack upon the jail, filed his affidavit with Charles Wheeler, a justice of the peace, charging Giles with the murder of Thornhill. In the affidavit he stated that on the day that the negro was delivered into his custody he "acknowledged that he had stabbed his master, Simeon Thornhill, several times on the night before, and that he tried his best to kill him, and would have cut his head off and cut him in two if he had had anything to have done it with at the time."

A warrant for the formal arrest of Giles was then issued by Squire Wheeler. The prisoner was taken before this officer and given a preliminary trial, during which he (Giles) stated that he and Thornhill were both drinking when the difficulty took place, and that Thornhill threatened several times to kill him, and did actually stab him first. Upon the evidence adduced at this trial he was legally committed to jail, and thus the jailer obtained a legal right to hold him.

On the second day after Thornhill died, it being January 1, 1859, the mob re-assembled and went in a body to Troy. A little after noon James Callaway stepped upon a "horse block" near where Mr. Hart's store now stands, and made a short speech to the crowd there assembled. They then started, yelling, on the way toward the jail. Arriving there they demanded of Capt. Salle the keys, but he, very properly, refused to give them up. Runners then started down town for tools with which to break down the doors. The tools being brought the doors were finally broken down, the negro was taken out, and his feet were chained to a stake driven into the ground in the jail yard, and his hands were tied behind him. Then the irate members of the mob, in haste and with a seeming relish and delight, piled wood around the wretched and defenseless victim, and prepared to burn him alive. Here he stood in this awful condition, facing death with a brave and unnatural courage—confessed his crime and repented not, but told his executioners that when he committed the crime he was drunk, otherwise he would not have done it, and that they, being sober, ought not thus to take his life in retaliation.

When the funeral pile was completed, it was set on fire. The fuel being dry, the lurid flames enwrapped the victim, yet minutes passed ere death ensued. But death did not satisfy the wreakers of vengeance. They added fuel to the flame, and stirred up the fire, and persevered in the fiendish work until the body was all reduced to ashes. It is said that the scene was horrible to behold.

On this lamented occasion, many spectators, who neither approved of the act, nor rendered any assistance to the perpetrators thereof, assembled to witness the burning; while others, who came into town for the purpose of witnessing the scene, considered the cruelty and the enormity of the crime, and went away without seeing it. Perhaps the most remarkable thing in connection with the matter was the indifference manifested in the conduct of the negro—the stolid demeanor in which he met his death—the fact that he confessed his crime, yet expressed no sorrow for it, but entered into eternity defiant and unrepentant. By what method of reasoning can any one account for such unnatural conduct! And it may be asked with propriety, by what method of reasoning can any one account for the cruel and illegal conduct of the men who burned the negro at the stake!

On the 25th day of March, 1859, three of the leaders of the mob, James Callaway, James Segrass and Samuel Carter, were indicted for the murder of Giles, the slave. At the following fall term of the Lincoln Circuit Court they were arraigned for trial, and Thomas P. Hoy was appointed circuit attorney *pro tem.* to prosecute them. On being arraigned they plead "not guilty." The following jurors were then empaneled, and sworn to try the defendants: James H. Reeds, Smith McGinnis, D. H. Chambers, G. W. Stonebraker, John W. Rice, Gabriel Thompson, Charles Kimler, William Hopkins, Zach. Lovelace, William Birch, Gion G. Wilson and James Horton. At this stage of the proceedings the circuit attorney dismissed the case, and thus ended the prosecution. The burning of the negro has always been and is still regretted by the best people of Lincoln County. All countries have suffered from the practice of lynch law. While there are many citizens now in Lincoln County who resided here when this affair took place, it is said that not one of the members of the organized mob that perpetrated the act remains in the county; that nearly all of them died early in life, and that only one of them was known to be living at a recent date, and he was then residing in Taylor County, and is probably still living. He was one of the leaders.

KILLING OF JAMES M. TEAGUE.

Some time in the year 1874 a horse was stolen from Mr. Isaac Ellis, of Lincoln County, and James M. Teague, formerly of this county, but then of Cole County, where he had recently been released from the fulfillment of a second term in the penitentiary for former crimes, was arrested for the theft and brought back to Auburn, and was there in custody of Constable Robert F. Waters. Benjamin W. Wheeler, the prosecuting attorney, went over to prosecute the prisoner. Waiving trial before the justice of the peace, he started in custody of the constable and in company with the prosecutor for lodgement in the jail at Troy. When the party was about two and one-half miles south of Auburn they were met by a mob of men with blackened faces, one of whom shot the prisoner, causing him to fall from his horse. The rope with which his feet were tied remained fast to the saddle, and as he fell the horse frightened and ran down the road a distance, dragging the man over the rough rocks, then turned and ran back a distance, still dragging him along, until the rope was cut, and he was left lying in the road. The attacking party then rode by him, each firing at him as he passed, and all missed him. Supposing they had accomplished their work well, they rode on out of sight. The prisoner was picked up and carried to a cabin near by, cared for, and then conveyed to Troy and placed in jail, where he remained from November 14 to 19, at which latter date he died from his injuries. An effort was made to capture the members of the mob, but they could not be found.

THE KILLING OF EDWARD W. RECTOR.

On the 16th of July, 1878, a "picnic" was held near Auburn, on the road leading to New Hope. The farmers, with their sons and daughters and little children, had assembled for a day of pleasure, rest and recreation, and to hear the speeches of the aspiring county candidates. Enjoyment and plenty were there in store for all. Nothing marred the festivities of the occasion until a gentleman was accosted by some one with the remark, "If you want to see Ed. Rector killed wait here about five minutes." Not wishing to see the tragedy the gentleman walked away. Soon the report of a pistol was heard, a crowd rushed to the spot where the shot was heard, and there found Rector in a dying condition, a bullet hole through his bowels, the back of his head crushed in, and the brains oozing out. Coroner Robinson was present and immediately summoned a jury and held an inquest. The jurors were J. L. Sanders, J. J. Bradley, T. Moseley, B. M.

Vance, John Cochran and D. J. Moxley. This jury, after hearing the evidence, rendered the following verdict: "Edward Rector came to his death by a pistol shot in the bowels, and a lick over the head with a pistol by John and George Calhoun."

A feud had long existed between the parties, and upon making the assault (as shown by the evidence) one of the Calhouns used insulting language to Rector. The evidence showed that the pistol was held and used by George Calhoun, after John Calhoun and Rector became engaged in a scuffle. Warrants were issued for the arrest of the Calhouns (who fled immediately after the perpetration of the act) and placed into the hands of Deputy Sheriff Snethen, who started in pursuit. The next morning John Calhoun gave himself up, and was taken to Troy and put in jail. It seems that Rector was regarded as a dangerous man, having, at the close of the war, been tried and acquitted for the murder of one Joseph Hamilton, and that not much regret was felt at his death. He left a wife and four children.

At the following term of the circuit court John Calhoun was indicted for the murder or for being a principal in the murder. He was prosecuted by the prosecuting attorney, George T. Dunn, assisted by A. V. McKee, and defended by Nat. C. Dryden and R. H. Norton. He was defended on the ground of "self defense." The State gave evidence to the effect that Calhoun was the aggressive party, and that Rector retreated; that he (Calhoun) took hold of Rector and that George Calhoun did the shooting; that Rector had a cane which he held in the middle and not in a striking posture. The evidence of the defense was that three or four hours before the difficulty took place Rector showed the head of his pewter-top cane to a witness and said he would "stick it into the heads of the Calhouns before night;" that he raised his cane to strike John Calhoun when they met, etc., and that about a year previously Rector had threatened to kill the Calhouns. The State, on rebuttal, proved by good witnesses that for the last six months Rector had sustained a good reputation as a peaceable citizen, and had resolved to lead a better life. The jurors were J. A. Street, W. J. Wade, J. H. Pollard, G. A. Jennings, D. A. Dyer, J. B. Dyke, Jacob Geiger, Montgomery

Geiger, Hannon Sneed, M. C. Blanks, H. C. Bahar and George Lovell. The theory of the prosecution was that Calhoun sought and brought on the difficulty, and therefore neither threats nor the bad character of Rector could justify the killing. The theory of the defense was, that Rector, being a dangerous man and having repeatedly made threats against Calhoun's life, and, according to some of the evidence, attempted to strike Calhoun at the time, he was in fear of a deadly assault, and justified in the killing. The verdict of the jury was "not guilty," and the prisoner was released.

KILLING OF ALEXANDER CARTER, COLORED.

In February, 1875, John Crouch killed Alexander Carter, colored. There had been a dispute at the courthouse, which arose from Carter assisting a decrepit old colored man to the polls, at the same time crying out, "Hurrah for the railroad!" It is said that Crouch insisted that the negro had no right to vote taxes on him, and Carter maintained that he paid taxes and had a right to vote. Crouch seized an ax and struck Carter on the left breast, making a slight wound. Carter then knocked Crouch down, and struck him in the face two or three times before they were separated. Crouch went down street and procured a pistol, soon met Carter on the street, and shot and killed him.* Crouch was arrested and given a preliminary trial (which lasted about a week) before J. B. Allen, a justice of the peace, who associated with him Squire John M. Reid. This tribunal, after hearing the evidence, which amounted to 27,000 words as counted on the manuscript, committed the prisoner to jail to await the action of the grand jury at the next term of court. Crouch was then conveyed to St. Charles by Sheriff Thomas M. Carter, and there placed in jail. In the trial the State was represented by Prosecutor Josiah Creech and R. H. Norton, and the defendant by McKee and McFarland. On the 31st day of March, following, the grand jury being in session considered the matter and refused to find a bill of indictment against Crouch for the killing of the negro. Upon presentation of their finding, the judge of the court "ordered, adjudged and decreed that the prisoner be dis-

---
* *Herald* account verified by living witnesses.

charged, and that he go hence without day." This ended the matter in temporal tribunals of justice.

It was on the occasion of the election held at the courthouse in Troy February 20, 1875, for the purpose of taking the expression of the taxpayers and voters of Bedford Township upon the proposition of subscribing $55,000 to the capital stock of the St. Louis & Keokuk Railroad Company, to secure the building of the machine shops at Troy, that Crouch killed Carter. The people in the town were anxious to make the subscription, and consequently the leaders in the movement did all they could to secure the colored vote in its favor, while the people in the country, in view of the fact that the county had already subscribed $300,000 to the railroad, were generally opposed to making the further subscription of $55,000 by Bedford Township. Crouch lived in the country, and was opposed to voting the tax, while Carter, the negro, lived in town, and voted for the tax. Intense excitement prevailed in regard to the subject matter of the election, between the parties in favor of and opposed to voting the additional tax. The excitement grew into bitterness, and much bad blood was engendered. Those opposed to the proposed subscription of stock combined to furnish means for the defense of Crouch, and an overwhelming pressure was brought to bear in his favor.

THE KILLING OF THOMAS B. WALKER.

Thomas B. Walker lived about two miles east of Troy, and the parties charged with his murder, Monroe Thomason and Franklin Hartman, lived in the same neighborhood. A feud had existed for some time between Walker and Thomason. The former cut a saw-log on land he was clearing and it was washed in a high water freshet onto the land where Thomason and Hartman were cutting timber. These men claimed the log and attempted to haul it away. Walker, seeing them, went to them and placed his hand on Hartman's arm, and warned him against moving the log. Hartman then struck Walker with his hand-spike, and in turn Walker felled Hartman with his fist, whereupon Thomason approached with a bludgeon and delivered a blow on Walker's head, crushing the skull and killing him. They then carried Walker to his clearing, where he was found the next day, partially consumed by hogs.

The killing of Walker occurred August 26, 1875. He was said to have been a peaceable and industrious citizen. He left a wife and four children. A coroner's inquest was held by Squire Allen acting as coroner, and the verdict of the jury implicated Thomason and Hartman in the murder. They were arrested, and at the following October term of the court were indicted for the murder. Thomason was tried October 13, the jury disagreed, and he was remanded to jail. His second trial began November 5, following, and the jury again disagreed. On the 7th day of December, following, he was arraigned the third time for trial. He then withdrew his plea of "not guilty," and entered a plea of "guilty as charged in the indictment," whereupon the judge sentenced him to serve a term of ten years in the penitentiary. At the same time, Hartman, whose case had been continued up to this time, withdrew his plea of "not guilty," and entered a plea of "guilty as charged in the indictment," and likewise received a sentence of ten years in the penitentiary.

MURDER OF MISS MARY ELLEN CALLAWAY.

On the 5th day of September, 1875, Meredith Waters, aged eighteen years, shot and killed Miss Mary Ellen Callaway, aged sixteen years, at or near the residence of her parents, in the vicinity of Old Monroe. Waters was arrested, and on being arraigned for examination before Squire Admire, he waived trial and was committed to jail. He claimed from the first that the shooting which caused the death of the young lady, was, on his part, accidental. In October, following, he was indicted by the grand jury for the murder. The indictment charged in substance that the wound which caused the death of Miss Callaway was received in her left breast from a double-barreled shot-gun, held in the hands of Waters. The State was represented by Attorneys Josiah Creech, prosecutor, assisted by McKee and McFarland, and the defendant by Stewart, Magruder, Avery and Wells. The jurors empaneled were Henry F. Wells, foreman; W. A. K. Elsberry, John Ward; E. Hines, Barton Hubbard, H. C. Pennington, Thomas H. Harris, S. H. Uptegrove, Henry Wehrman, I. B. Thomas, William Sitton and Joseph Cantril.

After hearing the evidence, argument of counsel and charge

of the court, the jury retired, and after deliberation returned into court a verdict of guilty of murder in the first degree. This was the first verdict for murder in the first degree ever found against a criminal in Lincoln County, it being then fifty-six years after its organization. It should be observed here that the defense was made on the ground of accidental shooting, but evidence was given to show that the defendant was a rejected suitor of the young lady, and from this and other evidence the jury became satisfied that the shooting was intentional and not accidental.

Motions for arrest of judgment and for new trial were made by defendant's attorneys, and overruled by the Court. Sentence was not pronounced until after Henry Reakey was tried for the murder of his wife and also found guilty in the first degree.

MURDER OF MRS. ELIZA REAKEY.

Mrs. Eliza Reakey, who lived with her husband near Grant's Ford on the Cuivre, disappeared from home on Thursday, September 9, 1875. Reakey followed her, and after being gone about four hours returned with some clothes which it was alleged she had taken away, and said he could not find her. On Sunday following (September 12), her body was found in the Cuivre at the ford, by Dr. Lindsey. At the following November term of the Lincoln Circuit Court, Reakey was indicted for the murder. Out of eighty men summoned, the following jurors were selected and empaneled to try the accused, viz.: Thomas J. Nally, Robert Black, E. A. Holmes, Douglas Wyatt, A. B. Ellis, Montgomery Geiger, W. J. Hardesty, John Sleet, C. W. Janes, J. W. Sitton, T. W. Wright and W. J. Holmes. The State was represented by Josiah Creech and G. T. Dunn, and the defendant by W. A. Alexander, of St. Charles, and McKee and McFarland. The testimony was voluminous. The marks of violence on her body showed that a murder had been committed, and the connection of Reakey with the tragedy was shown by evidence of his beating her on the evening of her disappearance, throwing her out in the yard, and leaving bloodstains on the floor. On this occasion Larkin Creech passed by and Reakey then desisted. After Creech had ridden out of sight he again heard the shrieks of the woman. Other evidence tending to the guilt of the accused was given. His plea of defense was that at times the woman was considered crazy, and that on this occasion she had committed suicide. The jury, after hearing the evidence, argument of counsel, and charge of the judge retired for deliberation and returned the following verdict:

"Troy, Missouri, November 4, 1875. We, the jury, find the defendant guilty of murder in the first degree.
(Signed) DOUGLAS WYATT, *Foreman.*"

Afterward, at the same term of court, the Judge ordered the sheriff to bring the convicted prisoners, Meredith Waters and Henry Reakey before him, and upon their arrival, he addressed them as follows:

"I have sent for you, Mr. Waters and Mr. Reakey, to pass sentence upon you in accordance with the law and the finding of the jury in your respective cases. In this trying ordeal I shall perform the unpleasant duty that devolves upon me—the first of the kind I have ever been called upon to do in all my official life—with but few words. I consider it out of place to use many words on an occasion of this kind. You have been tried according to the requirements of the law, and the juries, composed of good, intelligent, conscientious men, have found you guilty of murder in the first degree. I must say that my deliberate judgment endorses their verdict. Your trials have been fair. No testimony that could have benefited you was excluded. You have had every advantage shown you that the law allowed. You have been ably and faithfully defended. Your counsel have seen fit, and very properly, too, in the exercise of their legal opinion, to ask for an arrest of judgment and a new trial. In the most searching review of the matter in all the points presented, I found no cause to grant either, and your counsel have given notice of an appeal to the supreme court. I deem it proper to say in your case, Mr. Waters, that the reason assigned for a new trial by your counsel—that the panel of jurors and a copy of the indictment were not placed in their hands forty-eight hours before trial—is one that might possibly have some weight in determining the action of the higher court. I do not mention this to give
i

you any hope of a result different from that already arrived at. It would be wrong to excite within your breast a hope that my honest conviction tells me will prove fallacious." He then asked the prisoners if they had anything to say, either by themselves or by their counsel, why sentence should not be passed. A. V. McKee, speaking for Reakey, and Jeptha Wells for Waters, replied they had not. The Judge then resumed:

"It now remains for me to perform the awful duty imposed upon me by law. It is with the greatest feelings of regret that I do so. I wish you to understand that this is not my judgment but that of impartial jurors, and the sentence is that of the law. I beg of you to remember that. The sentence is this: That you be taken hence by the sheriff, in whose custody you are, to the usual place of confinement, and there to be confined until the 31st day of December, 1875, and on that day that you be brought to the place previously prepared for your execution, and that between the hours of 1 and 3 o'clock in the afternoon, you be hanged by the neck until dead. And may God grant you His patience in this the hour of your greatest trial; and may He mercifully grant you a true and sincere repentance for all the sins of your past lives."

In accordance with the foregoing sentence, a gallows was erected in the courtyard, and preparations for the execution of the condemned men were fully made. Meanwhile both cases had been appealed to the court of appeals at St. Louis, and a stay of the execution was granted by that court. The notice of the stay of executions was not received until the evening before the day that the unfortunate men were sentenced to be executed. The people of the country, not knowing the turn that affairs had taken, assembled in Troy early on the day appointed for the execution, but all were disappointed in witnessing the tragic scene. During the night, after the notice of the stay of execution was received, some parties in Troy, fond of amusement, made an effigy and hung it upon the gallows. This device had the effect to make it appear to some persons coming from the country, before they learned the true state of affairs, that one of the criminals had been executed before their arrival. In this way the anticipated serious matter was turned into that of amusement.

In the case of State *vs.* Waters, the judgment was reversed on an error of the lower court, and the cause remanded for a new trial. In the case of State *vs.* Reakey, the judgment was reversed on account of the insufficiency of the indictment, and the cause remanded for a new trial.

SECOND TRIAL OF MEREDITH WATERS.

In April, 1876, Meredith Waters was again arraigned for trial, and the following jury was empaneled: Richard L. Janes, Thomas Buford, William D. Shaw, E. G. Dehart, James M. Hall, W. H. Grimmett, D. R. Porter, W. A. Taylor, Andrew Wilson, Tobias E. Henry, Edmund Lahart and John G. Koster. The State was represented by Josiah Creech and Nat. C. Dryden, and the defendant by O. H. Avery, P. P. Stewart, A. H. Edwards and Jeptha Wells. The following is the verdict of the jury:

"We, the jury, find the prisoner guilty of murder in the second degree, and assess his punishment at sixty years' imprisonment.
"R. L. JANES, *Foreman.*"

The Judge, in mercy, threw off fifteen years, and sentenced the defendant to a term of forty-five years in the penitentiary. In accordance with the sentence, Waters was conveyed to the penitentiary and incarcerated therein until Christmas Day, 1887, when he was released by executive clemency.

SECOND TRIAL OF HENRY REAKEY.

On the 4th of April, 1876, a new indictment was found against Henry Reakey, and he was again put on trial for the murder of his wife. The jurors empaneled were Lewis Meyer, T. B. Green, J. P. Ellis, Thomas G. Branch, J. W. Palmer, Weston Ives, William Subert, T. G. Mitchell, John S. Cunningham, H. K. Elmore, T. B. Dyer and T. L. Elmore. After trial the jury returned the following verdict: "We, the jury, find the defendant guilty of murder in the second degree, and assess his punishment at twenty-four years in the State penitentiary."

[Signed.] TAYLOR B. GREEN, *Foreman.*"

Sentence was rendered in accordance with the verdict, and the prisoner was conveyed to the penitentiary, and remained therein about ten years, and was then pardoned out by the Governor.

It should have been said in a more appropriate place, that in both the Waters and Reakey cases, an appeal was taken from the court of appeals to the supreme court, where the decision of the court of appeals was affirmed.

KILLING OF CHARLES C. RANSDELL.

A difficulty arose between the sons of Francis C. Cake, Sr., and the step-sons of Charles C. Ransdell, the latter being the Bragg boys. These parties all lived in Troy. On the night of the 2d of August, 1879, they happened to meet in front or a little south of the front of King's drug store. As shown by the evidence in the case Francis C. Cake, Sr., and his son, Francis C. Cake, Jr., came out of the drug store and started southward and after going only a few steps they came even with Charles C. Ransdell and one or more of his step-sons. Some of the parties clinched and became engaged in a struggle. Francis C. Cake, Jr., was seen to step out of the struggling crowd and with his pistol fire two shots into it. After the firing of the first shot, or perhaps after the second was fired, Charles C. Ransdell was seen to reel from the struggling crowd and fall. Other shots were fired by one or two other parties. Ransdell was carried into the drug store, where he died immediately from the effects of a pistol-shot wound. In the fracas Francis C. Cake, Sr., received a slight wound on his head, and Francis C. Cake, Jr., was wounded in one arm.

Joseph B. Allen, justice of the peace, and acting as coroner, summoned a jury and held an inquest over the dead body of Ransdell. The following is a verdict of the jury: "That said Charles C. Ransdell came to his death by a bullet being fired from a pistol and passing through the upper and left portion of his heart, and that said pistol was fired by and in the hands of Francis C. Cake, Jr., and which the jury do find was the immediate cause of said Charles C. Ransdell's death." Mr. Cake was arrested and given a preliminary trial before Squires Robert F. Waters and M. H. Brown, who held him under bond for his appearance at the next term of court. The State was represented by Prosecutor Josiah Creech and Norton & Dryden, and the defendant by Walton & Avery and Elijah Robinson. At the following October term of the circuit court Cake was indicted for the murder of Ransdell, and upon giving bond for his appearance at court his case was continued until April 2, 1880. He was then arraigned and plead "not guilty." The following jury was then impaneled to try the cause: Q. M. Wilson, John Fleener, W. T. Hall, J. W. Rush, N. M. Robinson, T. P. Moxley, J. A. Enusmaer, H. B. White, Berry Porter, Thomas D. Wilkinson, Robert Stewart and T. J. Henry. After hearing the evidence, argument of counsel and the instructions of the Court, the jury retired, and after deliberation returned their verdict, finding the defendant guilty of manslaughter in the third degree, and assessed his punishment at a fine of $500. Sentence was rendered accordingly, the prisoner to stand committed until the fine and costs were paid. The next day defendant's counsel made a motion for a new trial, which was overruled. Afterward, on petition of the defendant, accompanied with his affidavit of insolvency, Judge W. W. Edwards ordered that he should be discharged at the end of fifty days from date of his conviction.

MURDER OF OLIVER BARNES.

In the summer of 1880 Oliver Barnes and his step-son, John Howdeshell, aged eleven years, went into a field near the residence of James Cox, not far from old Alexandria, to catch some horses for the purpose of attending a picnic in that vicinity. They separated, and, after going to the house, the boy went back and found Barnes lying dead, about sixty or seventy yards from the house of Cox. His skull had been crushed, and circumstances pointed to Jesse Cox as the perpetrator of the foul deed, there having been some dispute about Barnes' right to pasture his horses in the field. Squire R. F. Waters summoned a jury and held an inquest over the body. The jurors were L. Hull, W. R. White, Felix Raney, James Raney, William Broyles and Jacob Raney. Their verdict was "that Oliver Barnes met his death at the hands of Jesse Cox." A warrant for the arrest of Cox was issued and placed into the hands of Deputy Sheriff Snethen, who executed it by placing Cox in jail. A preliminary trial was had before Squires Shelton and Waters. Attorneys Creech, Wells and Parker appeared for the State, and Walton & Avery for the defendant. According to the evidence Cox, who was a half-brother to Mrs. Barnes, lived on her farm. She testified that Cox had told her that he laid out by the brush fence all day, waiting for Barnes to come after the horses, but did not say what he was going to do. The Deputy Sheriff found a coat in the house of Cox with blood on it, and Mrs. Cox said the coat belonged to her husband. The attorneys for the defense submitted the case without offering testimony. The prisoner was remanded to jail to await the action of the grand jury.

He was indicted and tried at the following October term, and the jury disagreed. He was tried again at the following spring term of court, found guilty of murder in the second degree, and was sentenced to serve a term of fifteen years in the penitentiary, from which place he was released in 1886 by executive clemency.

KILLING OF MORGAN SHOW.

The Show family, consisting of several brothers and one or more sisters, and their widowed mother, lived on their deceased father's old homestead, in Pike County, about eight miles north of Louisville. In farming the place the brothers quarreled about the crops, etc., and it is said that during one season they were so angry and hostile each to the other that they carried their shot-guns strapped across their backs while at work in the fields. It seems that Morgan was the one most feared, and stood somewhat alone in his hostility toward the other members of the family. Early one morning, while Parrin Show, aged about twenty-one years, was at the barn feeding the stock, Morgan, his brother, went out and shot and killed him. Morgan was arrested and afterward indicted for the murder in Pike County. His trial was continued and finally moved to another county on change of venue. Mrs. Weatherfield, a sister of the Show brothers, lived with her family in the northwestern part of Lincoln County. After the killing of Parrin, it seems that Morgan was rejected in general by all the other members of the family; but as time passed on he began to repent of his conduct, or at least professed to repent, and said that he intended to lead a better life. In so doing he became, in a measure, reconciled to all the surviving members of the family, except his brother Marshall, who was not disposed to forgive him.

In the latter part of December, 1881, and the beginning of January, 1882, Morgan Show was out subpœnaing witnesses to attend his trial for the killing of his brother, Parrin; and on the evening of January 1, 1882, stopped at the house of his sister, Mrs. Merriweather, to stay over night. Presently, Mrs. Merriweather discovered her brother Marshall approaching, and knowing the bitter feeling that existed between the brothers, she met Marshall, told him that Morgan was in the house, and entreated him not to stop on the occasion. Morgan then came out and invited his brother to dismount and come in, at the same time proposing that they should make up and become friends. The two brothers and their sister then went into the house together. Mrs. Merriweather retired immediately to get some fuel to replenish the fire. Her daughter, aged thirteen, was in an adjoining room (the kitchen). While the brothers were left thus alone pistol shots were heard. Morgan Show retreated from the room and fell dead near the outer door.

On January 5 Robert D. Walton, the prosecuting attorney, filed an affidavit before B. A. Gililland, a justice of the peace at Olney, charging Marshall Show with the murder of his brother Morgan. A warrant for the arrest of the accused was issued, and in due time he was brought before Squire Gililland for trial. He was prosecuted by Prosecutor Walton, and defended by Champ Clark and D. A. Ball. The witnesses testified to the facts pertaining to the killing as here given. Mrs. Merriweather testified positively that she heard three shots, and thought she heard two more. The little girl testified also to the hearing of the firing. Dr. T. M. Luce testified that he was called, and that upon examination of the body of Morgan Show he found three distinct wounds, two in the body and one in the head, that either of the wounds in the body was probably fatal, and that the one in the head was such a wound as would cause instant death; that the murdered man might have walked to the place where he fell with one or possibly both of the wounds in his body, but could not have done so after receiving the wound in the head. Several other witnesses were examined, nearly all of whom testified that Morgan Show was generally regarded as a bad and dangerous man, and that Marshall Show was regarded as a quiet and peaceable citizen. The defendant claimed that when left alone in the room with his brother Morgan, he (Morgan) first attempted to shoot, and that he (Marshall) acted in self-defense. Be that as it may, the latter was acquitted, and there the whole affair ended.

KILLING OF J. F. M. BROWN.

On the night of the 17th day of February, 1882, J. F. M. Brown, while in a state of intoxication, was knocked down on the sidewalk near the southwest corner of the Laclede Hotel, in Troy. The following day he died. A coroner's inquest was held, and the following verdict rendered by the jury: "That J. F. M. Brown came to his death by wounds received in a difficulty with John E. Worsham, on the 17th of February, 1882, in the town of Troy, Lincoln County, Mo. The precise manner in which said wounds were inflicted is unknown to the jury." At the following term of the Lincoln Circuit Court Worsham was indicted for the killing of Brown, charging that in the heat of passion and without design he struck Brown on the head and knocked him down, thus causing his death, which resulted the next day. Worsham was finally tried for the offense on the 6th day of April, 1883, and the verdict of the jury was "not guilty." At the time of this unfortunate affair Worsham was clerking at the Laclede Hotel, and was aggravated by the ill-conduct of the unfortunate man.

MURDER OF MORDECAI W. WILKINSON.

On the morning of July 17, 1883, at about 1 o'clock, Mordecai W. Wilkinson, living about half a mile north of Elsberry, was shot and killed while lying in his bed. The only persons known to have been in the house at the time were Mr. Wilkinson and his wife, Maggie, and William Wesley Gibson. Two or three colored persons slept in a house in the same yard. After the murder was committed, Mr. Gibson gave the alarm to James Evans and others who lived near by. A coroner's inquest was held by J. W. Ellis, a justice of the peace. Dr. W. A. Hemphill, of Elsberry, and Dr. Kerr were called to examine the wounds of the murdered man, and Dr. Hemphill took down the evidence at the inquest. The verdict of the coroner's jury was that "the deceased came to his death by a shot from a shotgun loaded with buckshot, in the hands of an unknown person."

Circumstances soon caused suspicion to rest upon the parties heretofore named, who were in the house with Mr. Wilkinson. The body of the murdered man was disinterred, and a *post-mortem* examination was made by Dr. W. A. Hemphill and Dr. Kerr, and several shots were found within it besides the one found on examination at the coroner's inquest. On the 21st of the same month, Prosecutor Jeptha Wells filed his affidavit before George W. Colbert, a justice of the peace, implicating William Wesley Gibson with the murder. Upon this, a warrant was issued and placed into the hands of Sheriff Snethen, who executed it by arresting Gibson and lodging him in jail at Troy. On Saturday following he was arraigned before Squire Colbert on charge of murder. Jeptha Wells appeared for the State, and Messrs. R. H. Norton and Nat. C. Dryden for the defendant. Upon agreement, July 30 was appointed as the day for preliminary examination.

On the day appointed the prisoner was arraigned for trial. Prosecutor Jeptha Wells was assisted in behalf of the State by Hon. Marshall F. McDonald, of St. Louis, and Howard S. Parker, of Troy. The defendant was represented as before by Norton & Dryden. The State made a formidable array of circumstantial evidence to establish the guilt of the prisoner. Some of the strong points in the evidence were, that when the neighbors assembled at the house of Wilkinson, on the call of Gibson, immediately after the murder was committed, the bed in which Gibson claimed to have been sleeping when he heard the report of the murderer's gun was made up and did not have the appearance of having been used that night; and the side of the murdered man's bed, where his wife was presumed to sleep, did not have the appearance of having been used that night. Mrs. Wilkinson swore, at the coroner's inquest, that she was in bed when her husband was shot—that the first she knew of the affair she heard the dog bark, and after that she went to sleep. Prior to this, though, Gibson had stated to one of the persons present that the dog did not bark. The State proved that when Mrs. W. said "the first she knew of the affair she heard the dog bark," Gibson, in a low whisper, said to her, "Hold on there; you are too fast."

Other witnesses testified to certain conversations, some of them with Gibson about a criminal intimacy which was alleged to have existed for the last two years between Mrs. W. and himself. The State also produced in evidence the will of Wilkinson, made a short time before his death, whereby he bequeathed to William Wesley Gibson, the defendant (who was his nephew), a note on a certain party for $800, and a lot of farming implements, and that after certain other legacies specified in the will were paid, all the residue of his estate, both personal and real, of whatsoever nature, should go to his wife. This latter would amount to several thousand dollars. The State also proved that both the wife of the murdered man and the defendant knew of the contents of the will.

On the part of the defendant, evidence was given that just after the murder was committed, an unknown man was seen going from the house, and that the bed in which Gibson slept was made up after the murder was committed and before the neighbors arrived. The evidence was voluminous, and space will not admit of further recital of it here.

Wilkinson had raised the defendant Gibson, the latter being a nephew, or half-nephew of the former. He (Wilkinson) was a middle-aged man when he married his wife. Her maiden name was Maggie Elsberry, and her age at date of marriage was twenty-one years. He had been ailing during the spring of 1883, and was sick at the time he was murdered. At the conclusion of the trial before Squire Colbert, Gibson was remanded to jail to await the action of the grand jury. At the following fall term of the circuit court he was indicted for the murder, but was not tried until in January following. In this trial the State was represented by Prosecutor Jeptha Wells, M. F. McDonald, D. P. Dyer, Howard S. Parker and David A. Ball, and the defendant by his former counsel, Norton & Dryden, assisted by

Josiah Creech. The jurors before whom the defendant was tried were J. W. Owen, W. N. Wright, A. J. Powell, F. M. Gear, William Dixon, T. J. Pollard, William Smith, P. Layne, M. W. Lindsay, G. W. Cohea, W. B. Morris and George Bridges.

The evidence adduced was substantially the same as that given on the preliminary trial. The argument of counsel commenced on Wednesday morning and continued until Friday at noon. The evidence against the prisoner was wholly circumstantial. After the case was submitted the jury retired and remained out about one hour, and then returned a verdict of "not guilty." This was a great surprise to many people, and much indignation was manifested.

Indignation Meetings.—On the 23d of January, a few days after Gibson was acquitted, a large number of citizens assembled in the schoolhouse at Elsberry, organized a meeting, and "*Resolved*, That the guilt of no party was ever more clearly proven by circumstantial evidence than that of Wesley Gibson for the murder of M. W. Wilkinson." Another resolution of this meeting censured Sheriff Snethen in severe terms, charging him with acting under undue influence in selecting the men from whom the jury was drawn and empaneled. Another resolution was as follows: "*Resolved*, That we believe it would be policy for the Legislature to authorize the county courts to select all special as well as regular juries, and thus put it out of the power of unscrupulous attorneys, by means of flexible and unworthy sheriffs, to convert a trial by jury into a contemptible farce." Other resolutions expressive of the indignation of the members of this meeting were passed. The next week Sheriff Snethen replied to the published resolutions of this meeting through the medium of the press, vindicating his conduct, and claiming that the jury was drawn from the best citizens of the county. He also denounced the resolutions relating to his conduct as "wicked, poisonous, libelous, and as a mass of falsehoods as black as hell." This led to further controversy in the papers. Another indignation meeting was held in the schoolhouse at Auburn, on February 2 following the trial, attended by about 150 persons. Resolutions in regard to the Gibson trial, similar in their nature to those passed by the Elsberry meeting, were adopted and passed.

In the indictment found against Gibson, Maggie Wilkinson, wife of the murdered man, was also indicted and charged with aiding, abetting and assisting Gibson in the commission of the felony. Her case was continued until the April term of court following the acquittal of Gibson, and then *nolle prosequied* by the State. The trial of Gibson was undoubtedly the most exciting one ever held in Lincoln County, and his acquittal probably caused the greatest indignation. A theory is entertained by some persons that the negro male-servant, who usually slept in the out-house, at the residence of Wilkinson, assisted in the murder, and actually did the shooting at the instigation of the other parties implicated.

MURDER OF CAROLINE THORNHILL, COLORED.

In November, 1884, Caroline Thornhill was found dead in her bed, at her residence in Troy. A coroner's inquest was held over her dead body, and the verdict of the jury was that she came to her death, on the night of November 6, by being struck on the top and back of her head with an ax, in the hands of her husband, Green Thornhill. On the 12th day of the same month, court being then in session, Thornhill was indicted for the murder, arraigned for trial, and plead guilty as charged, and thereupon was sentenced, by Judge Robinson, to the penitentiary for the term of " during his natural life."

KILLING OF HENRY TURNER.

Early in December, 1884, Henry Turner and George W. Sitton met in a saloon in Elsberry, Lincoln Co., Mo., and quarreled about a settlement. Turner called Sitton a liar, and in turn Sitton knocked Turner down, and stamped him on the breast and stomach. Turner was assisted from the floor by parties who were present, and he and Sitton, both being intoxicated, made friends, and the latter treated the crowd. That evening the town marshal assisted Turner into the caboose attached to the north-bound freight train, bound for Dameron, his home. The train moved while he was getting on, and he slipped and fell so that the wheels tore off a portion of the calf of his left leg. Turner died on Friday, was buried on Saturday, and was disinterred on Sunday. A coroner's inquest was held, and Drs. Lee, Kerr and Hemphill made a *post-mortem* examination, and declared that in their opinion the wound of the leg did not cause his death. The inquest was held by J. W. Ellis, a justice of the peace, acting as coroner. The jury, on this occasion, found that "the deceased, Henry Turner, came to his death by being stamped on the chest and bowels by George W. Sitton." A warrant was issued for the arrest of Sitton, and placed in the hands of Constable A. W. Farmer, who executed it by arresting the accused, and taking him before Squire J. W. Ellis on the 8th day of the month. Sitton was released on bond of $500 for his reappearance on the 10th of the month. He then appeared with his attorney, Nat. C. Dryden, and upon application was granted a change of venue to Squire G. W. Colbert, at Troy, and was held to appear before that officer on the 13th of the month, for trial. The preliminary examination was closed before Justice Colbert on the 19th, and, the Court finding the evidence insufficient for conviction, acquitted and discharged the defendant. So it was not decided whether the whisky, or the injury received from Sitton, or the wound received at the train caused Turner's death. Probably all combined contributed to that sad result. This is another argument against saloons and intemperance.

HOMICIDE AND SUICIDE.

About 4 o'clock on the morning of March 4, 1885, Stephen Coose, after having set up with Louis Coster, returned home to his father's house, near Silex, and kindled and started a fire. His brother, Horatio, got up, observed the time, and went back to bed. They quarreled, and Stephen shot Horatio and then shot himself, both shots being fatal. Stephen died about 7 o'clock A. M., and Horatio about 3 P. M.

CHAPTER XII.

MILITARY ITEMS.

At the time of the first settlement of the territory composing Lincoln County, the country here was commonly called New Spain. [See State History.]

After being ceded to the United States it was temporarily assigned to the government of the Territory of Indiana, of which Gen. William Henry Harrison was governor, with seat of government at Vincennes. On the 21st day of December, 1804, Gov. Harrison commissioned Christopher Clark a captain of volunteers, and he was sworn into office February 9, 1805. Clark's company used to muster at Zumwalt's Spring, since known as Big Spring Mills, near Flint Hill. This was perhaps a central point, but the chief attraction was the whisky that was made from Adam Zumwalt's two distilleries.

In 1824 Peter Yates gave bond to the county court in the sum of $1,000 as paymaster of the Eleventh Regiment, First Division, Missouri Militia.

MUSTERS.

One of the first musters of the militia in Lincoln County, for the purpose of drilling, took place in a little patch of cleared ground around Philip Sitton's spring, which is just below the one known as the old Perry Parks Spring. This was some time before the Black Hawk War. Henry Watts, who lived about two miles from Louisville, was captain. It took the whole northwest part of the county, including the Forks of Cuivre, to make up his company. The general musters of the militia in those days were held ostensibly for the purpose of teaching the settlers the tactics of military drill, but for this purpose they were an entire failure. As a rule the officers, with only a few exceptions, knew very little about military tactics, consequently they could not make it interesting for the men, and the men having no relish for the exercise, the result was that the musters on "general training day" were usually turned into fun and frolic, and no inconsiderable amount of twenty-five cents per-gallon whisky would be consumed, and frequently there would be a few rounds of "fisticuffs." Wrestling, racing, shooting at a mark and other amusements usually accompanied, and thus "training day" was a day of sport. Samuel Howell, a prominent old settler, mustered in the militia company of Capt. William Brunk, which was afterward commanded by Capt. William Barnes. He and his neighbors, Armstrong Kennedy and Thomas East, were drafted during the Black Hawk War, and were equipped and ready to join Gen. Scott's army when orders for disbandment came. Mr. Howell was also enrolled at the call of the Governor for the war known as the Iowa War, which grew out of a dispute between the State of Missouri and the Territory of Iowa about the location of the boundary dividing these commonwealths. The battalion raised and organized here for that anticipated war was never called into active service. Though troops were assembled on both sides of the line, the Iowa War never resulted in a clash of arms, the question being settled by the action of Congress and the supreme court of the United States. This battalion was commanded by Henry Watts, who now enjoyed the title of colonel. John S. Besser and Jonathan Riggs were captains under him. Ezekiel Downing was a candidate for captain, but was defeated by one of the individuals mentioned.

The Sioux Indians were allowed to remain here until about five years after the termination of the Black Hawk War. About 1831 or 1832 Col. David Bailey, who was the agent of the General Government for the removal of the Seneca Indians from Ohio to the Indian Territory, was encamped for several months in Monroe Township, in this county, with the whole tribe.

THE "SLICKER" WAR.

The following is the full history of this war, as related by Dr. Joseph A. Mudd:

"During the years 1843, 1844 and 1845 there raged in this county what was known as the 'Slicker' War. The term originated elsewhere, probably in Benton County, about the year 1841, and came from the peculiar mode of punishment inflicted by the regulators—whipping with hickory withes, or 'slicking,' as the backwood parlance of that day termed it. An organized band of counterfeiters and horse and cattle thieves existed in many counties of this and other western States, and about the period mentioned above the people of the eastern part of the county found it necessary to organize for the protection of their property, so extensive were their depredations. It has been said that the parties who operated in this county sold 1,200 horses, during a single season, at one sale stable in St. Louis. Of course not all these were taken from this county. Their operations in beef cattle were on as large a scale. Sometimes the thieves would be taken with the stolen property in their possession, but would always manage to have enough convenient witnesses on hand to secure acquittal, and would march off with the stock before its owner's eyes. This aroused the greatest indignation, which was heightened by the fact that the prevalence of counterfeit money, both metal and paper, seriously affected the transaction of business. A company of regulators was organized, with James Stallard, of Hurricane Township, as captain. Some of the very best men of the eastern half of the county went into it. Brice Hammock drew up its constitution and by-laws. Had the spirit of these been strictly followed some bloodshed and much ill-feeling might have been avoided. Some inexcusable excesses were committed, partly the result of the excitement of the times, but more from the fact that a few unprincipled men took the opportunity, either as active members of the organization or as pretended friends, to settle personal grudges.

"When the evidence against a suspected person became satisfactory to the regulators, such person was either 'slicked' or ordered to leave the county by a given date, or both, and the penalty for a refusal or a failure to leave was either 'slicking' or death, according to the merits of the case. The principals all fled the county. John Plummer, who was notified to leave, and was preparing to do so, went to Troy on the very day on which his period expired, and on the way home was shot and killed, it probably not having been known that he intended to leave. Several against whom suspicion was not very strong had their time extended by reason of sickness in family, or other sufficient cause. James Turnbull refused point blank to leave. Turnbull was a very peculiar man, but at this day nobody doubts that he was honest. The cause of suspicion against him was that a notorious thief and counterfeiter, Hal. Grammar, was intimate with his son Ezekiel, and used sometimes to stop at his house. It is not thought that Turnbull was aware of Grammar's real character. Turnbull lived on Bob's Creek, in Section 32, Township 49, Range 2 east, on land that he bought, in 1840, from Dominique Francois Burthe, of New Orleans, and Marguerette Susanne Delor Sarpy Burthe, widow of the Baron Andre Burthe d'Anelet, of Paris, France. The house was a solid log structure, and was generally called Turnbull's fort. When the 'Slickers' came to enforce their demands, Turnbull and one of his daughters went out to dissuade them from their purpose, declaring the innocence of the family. The conference was unavailing, and the one side prepared for attack and the other for defense. It is not known who commanded the attacking party, nor how many were present. Some random firing was done on both sides, and the 'Slickers' attempted, but unsuccessfully, to fire the house. It was then determined to make an assault, batter down the door, and make short work of the matter. Malachi Davis was the first man to enter; he received a bullet in the bowels, from the effect of which he died the next day. John Davis, his brother, rushed forward, thrust his pistol under the chin of James Turnbull, Jr., and fired. The latter fell, apparently dead, but finally recovered, except a partial paralysis which rendered him an invalid for life. Davis then raised his rifle and put a ball into the hip of Squire Turnbull, which caused his death some weeks afterward. Washington Norwell came in by the side of John Davis. As he crossed the threshold, one of Turnbull's girls cleft his skull with a corn-knife. The wound was about six inches long, and extended an inch down the forehead, penetrating the brain and involving a considerable loss of its substance. Norwell fully recovered. He died a few years ago. The 'Slickers' retired without accomplishing anything further.

"This affair caused great excitement, and a company of 'anti-Slickers' was organized the next day in the vicinity of Flint Hill, St. Charles County, for the avowed purpose of protecting the Turnbull family, and checking the excesses of the regulators. This company made several incursions into this county, removed the Turnbulls to Flint Hill, and maintained guards and pickets on the fords of Cuivre. On one occasion the 'Slickers' gathered in a force to drive them from this county, and made a rapid march to where the 'antis' were supposed to be, but arrived an hour too late. One evening Joseph L. Woodson and James Burdyne were coming from Troy, and just opposite Mont. Cottles', Burdyne a few feet behind, sitting sideways, was telling about a game of poker that he had gotten into that day: 'I had,' said he, 'three jacks and a pair of aces, and'—when the report of firearms rang out, and the blaze from the gun was seen in the bushes on the side of the road. Neither was hurt, but they quickened their pace considerably, and the luck of the three jacks and pair of aces was never told. After riding a hundred yards, Burdyne remembered that he had a horseman's pistol, and proposed to go back and 'give 'em a shot,' but he was overruled. That same evening William Holmes and his brother were riding into the gate of their uncle, Levi Bailey, when they were fired upon by two men, one ball wounding a horse and one penetrating the clothes of the other rider. Some time after this James Shelton, who had been the captain of the 'anti-Slickers,' was in Chain of Rocks, and, as he was crossing the river in a skiff, had his arm fractured by a shot from the bank. When the legitimate purpose for which the regulators had been formed was accomplished, the organization was disbanded, but it was a long time before the animosities engendered by the civil strife died out."

THE CIVIL WAR.

Upon the approach of the war of 1861–65 the sentiment of a large majority of the people of Lincoln County was undoubtedly in favor of the Southern cause, though, perhaps, the majority was not in favor of a disruption of the Union, as it is true that the county elected delegates to the State Convention, held in Jefferson City, February 28, 1861, who were in favor of the Union. After the inauguration of President Lincoln, and especially after the first gun was fired, and the President made his first call for troops for the preservation of the Federal Government, the sentiment in favor of the Southern cause became more positive and outspoken, and for a time it was somewhat unsafe for a Union man to express his sentiments. Two companies of soldiers, commanded, respectively, by Capts. Thomas M. Carter and George Carter, were raised for the Confederate army, in the summer of 1861. In the fall of 1861 Col. John B. Henderson brought his regiment, or a portion of it, to Troy, and took possession of the county. These were the first Federal troops brought to Troy. This put a stop to open recruiting for the Southern army; however, recruiting for the Southern forces continued in a quiet way for some time thereafter. Individuals or small squads continued to go out of the county and join organizations of that army at other points. Col. Hendersen continued to occupy Troy but a short time, and was then followed by other Federal forces. In 1862 Col. Krekle, of St. Charles, occupied Troy for a time, with a portion of his regiment. Later Capt. McVaden, of Warren County, had a battalion of Federal troops in Troy, and in the winter of 1864-65 the town was occupied, for a time, by Capt. Kimpinski's company of the Forty-ninth Regiment, Missouri Volunteers. Afterward Col. Charles W. Parker, of the Thirty-seventh Enrolled Missouri Militia, commanded the post of Troy until the close of the war. He had it garrisoned alternately by the different militia companies of the county composing his regiment.

Portions of the following commands, for the preservation of the Government, were recruited in Lincoln County, and scattering individuals probably joined other commands organized outside of the county.

THIRD REGIMENT CAVALRY, MISSOURI STATE MILITIA.

Company G, of this regiment, commanded by Capt. Richard Wommack, was raised in Lincoln County, and a portion of Companies C and D, from Pike County, commanded respectively by Capts. S. A. C. Bartlett and Robert McElroy, were recruited in this county. The following is the official roster of the staff officers of the regiment, and the officers of Company G:

Col. Edwin Smart, enl. May 8, 1862, com. May 5, 1862, res. May 20, 1863.
Col. Richard G. Woodson, enl. May 25, 1863, com. May 21, 1863, dis. by S. O. No. 35, Headquarters of Mo., Feb. 27, 1864.
Col. O. D. Greene, enl. April 4, 1864, com. April 4, 1864, not mustered.

Lieut.-Col Frederick Morsey, enl. May 8, 1862, com. May 5, 1862, res. May 23, 1863.
Lieut.-Col. J. O. Broadhead, enl. June 8, 1863, com. June 8, 1863, res. Feb. 6, 1864.
Lieut.-Col. H. M. Matthews, enl. Feb. 18, 1864, com. Feb. 18, 1864, m. o. expir. of term, April 20, 1865.
Maj. Richard G. Woodson, enl. May 8, 1862, com. May 25, 1862, pro. to Col. May 21, 1863.
Maj. Robert McElroy, enl. June 20, 1863, com. June 20, 1863, dec'd by Maj. McElroy.
Maj. James Wilson, enl. July 11, 1863, com. June 20, 1863, capt. at battle of Pilot Knob, Sept. 27, 1864, and murdered by the enemy in Washington Co., Mo., Oct. 3, 1864.
Maj. Henry C. Campbell, enl. Dec. 2, 1864, com. Dec. 21, 1864, m. o. as Adj't at expir. of term, May 8, 1865.
Maj. H. S. McConnell, enl. June 14, 1862, com. May 16, 1862, res. July 3, 1863.
Maj. S. A. C. Bartlett, enl. May 12, 1864, com. May 12, 1864, m. o. expir. of term, May, 1865.
Maj. H. M. Matthews, enl. Mar. 25, 1863, com. Mar. 18, 1863, promoted to Lieut.-Col. Feb. 18, 1864.
Lieut.-Adjt. H. C. Campbell, enl. Oct. 21, 1862, com. Oct. 21, 1862, prom. to Maj.
Lieut.-Q. M. J. F. L. Jacoby, enl. May 18, 1863, com. May 18, 1863, m. o. at expir. of term, May 8, 1865.
Lieut.-Com. H. R. Woodruff, enl. Feb. 6, 1863, com. Feb. 6, 1863, m. o. expir. of term, Feb. 22, 1865.
Surg. William L. Short, enl. May 17, 1862, com. April 22, 1862, m. o. expir. of term, May 8, 1865.
Asst. Surg. William L. Short, enl. Mar. 6, 1862, com. Mar. 6, 1862, pro. to Surg.
Asst. Surg. H. E. Jones, enl. May 17, 1862, com. Apr. 22, 1862, res. Feb. 27, 1863.
Asst. Surg. James Hollister, enl. Apr. 11, 1863, com. Apr. 11, 1863, res. June 10, 1864.
Asst. Surg. William C. P. Buttman, enl. July 11, 1864, com. July 11, 1864.

COMPANY G.

Capt. Rich. Wommack, enl. Feb. 17, 1862, com. Feb. 15, 1862, res. Apr. 24, 1862.
Capt. James Wilson, enl. May 5, 1862, com. May 3, 1862, promoted to Major June 20, 1863.
Capt. Charles W. Rush, enl. July 30, 1863, com. July 27, 1863, m. o. expir. of term, July, 1865.
1st Lieut. John M. Reeds, enl. Feb. 17, 1861, com. Dec. 13, 1861, m. o. expir. of term, July, 1865.
2d. Lieut. Isaac W. Cannon, enl. Feb. 17, 1862, com. Feb. 15, 1862, res. May 6, 1862.
2d. Lieut. Chas. W. Rush, enl. May 10, 1862, com. May 10, 1862, promoted Capt. July 30, 1863.
2d. Lieut. Elbert May, enl. July 30, 1863, com. July 28, 1863, m. o. expir. of term, 1865.

The following communications from commanding officers constitute the history of this regiment:

HEADQUARTERS THIRD REGIMENT, MISSOURI STATE MILI-
TIA CAVALRY, PILOT KNOB, MO., December 19, 1863.

"COL. JOHN B. GRAY, ADJUTANT-GENERAL OF MISSOURI,

"*Sir:*—In compliance with your request, I submit the following report of the history of battles, marches, etc., of the Third Regiment Cavalry, Missouri State Militia: The Third Cavalry, Missouri State Militia, was organized on the 5th day of May, 1862, at Louisiana, Pike Co., Mo., composed of five companies recruited at Louisiana, and three from Warrenton, recruited principally under the superintendence of Lieut.-Col. Morsey, with 740 aggregate, and commanded by Col. Edwin Smart. For two months it was engaged principally in guarding the line of the North Missouri Railroad, with its headquarters at Louisiana, Mo. As soon as the rebel Porter commenced organizing his forces in Northeast Missouri, the regiment was placed in the field, and continued there continually until the following November. A part of the command was in the first engagement with Porter the latter part of July, on Salt River, Monroe Co., Mo., in connection with the Third Iowa Cavalry, Maj. Caldwell in command. It was next engaged with Porter's forces a few days after at Moore's Mill, in Callaway County, Mo., Col. O. Guitar commanding. It then went in pursuit of these forces through Northeast Missouri, to the Iowa line, and one company was in the engagement at Kirksville, Mo., Col. John McNeil, commanding. After this, the rebel forces being dispersed, it was engaged in pursuing and capturing them, having frequent skirmishes with Porter's, Poindexter's, Cobb's and other guerrilla parties which so infested that region during the fall of 1862.

"On the 18th of October it engaged and successfully dispersed a large force of these guerrillas near the Avonix Church, in Callaway County, Mo., who were attempting to cross the river and get south. This was the breaking up of the campaign of that fall. During the time many rebels, horses, etc., were captured, and many were surrendered to the command. On the 10th day of December the regiment took up its march to Jefferson City, thence to Rolla, where it remained but a short time, when it was ordered to Pilot Knob, Mo., at which place it arrived on the 28th day of December, 1862. It remained there until the middle of

March, 1863, during which time it was engaged in guarding the post, and escorting trains to Gen. Davidson's command, then in Southeast Missouri. In March it marched to Patterson, Mo. There, on the 20th day of April, 1863, it was attacked by Marmaduke's command of eight thousand men, and being so outnumbered, and no artillery, it was forced to fall back on Pilot Knob, which it did in order, losing in killed and wounded only about thirty men. This engagement lasted from twelve o'clock, M., until sundown. It then joined the forces of Gen. Vandever, and pursued Marmaduke out of the State, being in all the engagements from Jackson to Chalk Bluff. Since this time it has been continually in the field, having many skirmishes with guerrillas in Southeast Missouri and Arkansas.

"In August last it made a raid into Arkansas, which succeeded in the capture of Gen. Jeff. Thompson and staff.

"In October it was again (under command of Maj. Wilson) in that State, and captured a company of sixty men, with their officers, at Evening Shade. At the same time another portion of it, under Capt. Leeper, entered the State at a different point and had a skirmish with rebel force under Reeves, a notorious guerrilla leader. The regiment has just taken winter quarters, with headquarters at Pilot Knob, and its companies occupy several other posts in Southeast Missouri.

"I am, colonel, very respectfully, your obedient servant,
"R. G. WOODSON,
"*Colonel Third Missouri Militia Cavalry.*"

"HEADQUARTERS THIRD MISSOURI CAVALRY,
"WESTON, MO., December 22, 1864.

"*General:*—At the beginning of the year 1864, the headquarters of the regiment were at Pilot Knob, Mo., with companies occupying the outposts of Patterson, Centerville, Fredericktown, Potosi and Farmington, Maj. James Wilson commanding. The stations of the companies and command of the regiment remained unchanged during the severe winter months of January and February, very little being done by the command except the usual routine of camp, post and escort duty.

"About the 1st of March Maj. H. M. Matthews was promoted

to lieutenant-colonel and assumed command of the regiment. During this month Maj. Wilson, in pursuance to orders from Brig.-Gen. Fisk, made a successful raid into Arkansas from Pilot Knob, with 100 picked and well mounted men, killing twenty-one guerrillas and scattering the bands that then infested that country. Shortly after this a battalion was sent to Patterson, under the command of Maj. Wilson, and the work of exterminating bushwhackers and guerrillas commenced in earnest. Scouts from the regiment were continually sent to the border and into Arkansas, and if an enemy were anywhere in that country he was sure to be hunted out and justice meted out to him. The regiment had, by scouting the country so frequently, learned every path and by-road, and this was the cause of their great success in hunting down the marauding parties. No district of country in Missouri, so much exposed, has, within the last year, been kept more quiet from the bands that have infested our State than this.

"In June the Second Battalion was detached from the regiment, placed under command of Maj. Bartlett, and ordered to the District of North Missouri, where it did good service during the summer and fall in hunting down the numerous guerrilla parties in that district. The battalion also lost quite a number of men wounded, captured, and afterward murdered by the rebels.

"Lieut.-Col. Matthews being detached from the regiment early in June, Maj. Wilson assumed command, with headquarters at Patterson, Mo. On the 18th of July, Maj. Wilson, with 125 men, started on a raid into Arkansas, marched to Bloomfield, Mo., and reported to Lieut.-Col. Burris, Tenth Kansas Volunteers, who commanded the expedition, which lasted for twenty-six days, during intensely hot weather, and for the part performed by the Third Missouri State Militia Cavalry we refer to Col. Burris' report.

"On the 2d day of August, and on our return from Osceola, which place we had taken, with a large number of prisoners, engaged the Second Missouri rebel regiment, commanded by Lieut.-Col. Erwin, Pemiscot County, Mo.; charged, in connection with the First and Sixth Missouri Volunteer Cavalry, killing and capturing the greater portion of the command and dispersing the remainder. In this engagement the regiment lost Capt. Evans Francis, Company L, killed. Capt. Francis was a young man, just promoted, a fine officer and a gentleman in every respect, and bid fair to make a name worthy of the cause in which he was engaged.

"Upon the return of the regiment from this expedition, Lieut.-Col. Matthews again assumed command, with headquarters at Sturgeon, Mo., District of North Missouri, and Maj. Wilson was placed in command of the sub-district of Pilot Knob, Mo.

"During September, and when Price was expected into Missouri, the District of Southeast Missouri again began to swarm with guerrillas and recruiting parties from the rebel army, and the regiment was kept on the march night and day clearing out the parties and obtaining information in regard to Price's movements.

"On the 17th of September Lieut. Pape, Company K, with a small detachment of the regiment, moved to Doniphan, found the advance of Shelby's division, charged them, drove them from the town and across Current River, and for several miles back toward the Arkansas line. He then fell back and encamped on Black River. During the night the enemy advanced in heavy force; succeeded, under the cover of the night, in surrounding the little camp, and next morning made the attack with mounted and dismounted men. Lieut. Pape mounted his men, and finding himself surrounded by a vastly superior force, ordered them to charge, which they did four times before they succeeded in breaking the enemy, who were formed three lines deep. They succeeded in cutting their way out, with the loss of Lieut. Brawner, Company K, killed, and several men killed and wounded.

"This is but one instance of the many severe skirmishes in which the regiment was engaged during and before the raid of Price into Southeast Missouri.

"Two battalions of the regiment were engaged in the battle of Pilot Knob, Mo., on the 26th and 27th of September, 1864. There and on the retreat to Rolla the regiment lost heavily; among the number, Maj. James Wilson, who, with six men, was captured at Pilot Knob, and afterward shot by order of the rebel Gen. Price. For the honorable and heroic part the regiment acted at that battle and on the retreat, we refer to the official report of the commanding general.

"When the forces in Missouri were ordered to concentrate at Jefferson City, Lieut.-Col. Matthews, who was then at Rocheport, moved to that place; arrived there with the Second Battalion, on the 3d day of October, and was there joined by a detachment under command of Lieut. Blain, who had come through ahead of the enemy from Gen. Ewing's command. On the 4th the battalion moved out and met the enemy on the Osage; was there engaged until forced back, with the balance of the command, slowly to the city. It then followed in pursuit of the enemy to Boonville, under the command of Gen. Sanborn, until Gen. Pleasanton assumed command, when it was placed in McNeil's brigade and continued the pursuit to Independence and was engaged in that battle. It was then detached from the command and left to garrison the post.

"After the Price raid the regiment concentrated at St. Louis. From there moved by rail to St. Joseph, where five companies are now stationed, headquarters at Weston, Mo.; two companies at Liberty, one at Parkville, one at Chillicothe, two at Carrollton and one at Weston, Mo.

"This is but a brief summary of the operations of the regiment, it being impossible to give a detailed account of the movements, marches, scouts, skirmishes, etc., in which it has been engaged during the last year.

"The total enlisted strength of the regiment is 803; aggregate, 840.

"Very respectfully, your obedient servant,
"H. M. MATTHEWS,
"*Lieutenant-Colonel Commanding.*"

Immediately after the Price raid into Missouri, which continued until the latter part of 1864, this regiment was concentrated at St. Joseph, Mo.

On the 1st of January, 1865, the headquarters were at Weston, Platte County, Mo., where they remained until most of the regiment was mustered out.

The companies garrisoned the posts of St. Joseph, Liberty,

Weston and Parkville, on the north side of the Missouri River, and Pleasant Hill and Lone Jack, on the south side.

During this time they were energetically engaged in hunting down the guerrillas that then infested that portion of the State, and did good service in restoring peace and quiet within the limits of their district.

With the exception of recruits, this regiment was mustered out at expiration of term, during the months of January, February and March, 1865. The recruits were consolidated into one company (A), which, under instructions of the War Department, dated June 23, 1865, was mustered out July 13, 1865.

FORTY-NINTH INFANTRY, MISSOURI VOLUNTEERS.

Company A of this regiment, commanded by Capt. William Colbert, was raised in Lincoln County; and Company E, of the same regiment, was also mostly raised there. The following is the roster of the regimental staff and of the officers of the companies serving in the regiment from this county:

Col. David P. Dyer, enl. Jan. 3, 1865, com. Jan. 3, 1865, m. o. Aug. 5, 1865.
Lt.-Col. David P. Dyer, enl. Oct. 17, 1864, com. Sept. 20, 1864, promoted to Col.
Lt.-Col. Edwin Smart, enl. Jan. 3, 1865, com. Jan. 3, 1865, m. o. Aug. 2, 1865.
Maj. Edwin Smart, enl. Oct. 20, 1864, com. Sept. 15, 1864, promoted to Lt.-Col.
Maj. Israel W. Stewart, enl. Jan. 3, 1865, com. Jan. 3, 1865, m. o. Aug. 2, 1865.
Adjt. Wm. R. Hardin, enl. Aug. 11, 1864, com. Aug. 11, 1864, m. o. May 15, 1865, S. O. No. 272, W. D.
Adjt. Wm. Lansdown, enl. July 19, 1865, com. July 19, 1865, m. o. as 1st Lieut. Co. F, Aug. 2, 1865.
Q. M. T. M. Guerin, enl. Aug. 7, 1864, com. Aug. 7, 1864, res. Nov. 3, 1864.
Q. M. Wm. D. Bush, enl. Nov. 3, 1864, com. Nov. 3, 1864, m. o. Aug. 2, 1865.
Surg. Oscar Monig, enl. Sept. 9, 1864, com. Sept. 9, 1864, m. o. Aug. 2, 1865.
Asst. Surg. Thos. S. Ruby, enl. Aug. 26, 1864, com. Aug. 26, 1864. m. o. Aug. 2, 1865.

COMPANY A.

Capt. Wm. Colbert, enl. Sept. 14, 1864, com. Aug. 31, 1864, m. o. Aug. 2, 1865.
1st Lieut. Jos. H. Mitchell, enl. Sept. 14, 1864, com. Sept. 14, 1864, m. o. Aug. 2, 1865.
2d Lieut. Reuben W. Colbert, enl. Sept. 14, 1864, com. Aug. 31, 1864, m. o. Aug. 2, 1865.

COMPANY E.

Capt. Jno. E. Ball, enl. Sept. 22, 1864, com. Sept. 22, 1864, m. o. Aug. 2, 1865.
1st Lieut. Fritz Eversmeyer, enl. Sept. 22, 1864, com. Sept. 22, 1864, m. o. Aug. 2, 1865.
2d Lieut. Herman H. Schafer, enl. Sept. 22, 1864, com. Sept. 22, 1864, m. o. Aug. 2, 1865.

This regiment was organized at Warrenton, in Warren County, in August and September, 1864, and on becoming full it moved to Mexico, and from there, on the occasion of the Price raid into Missouri, it moved to Jefferson City, and during Price's stay in the State it did service up and down the Missouri River for the purpose of preventing the Confederate army, or portions thereof, from crossing to the northern side. After Price retreated from the State the Forty-ninth Missouri regiment returned to Mexico. The companies were then distributed to different points, mostly in Callaway, Boone, Audrain and other counties. Capt. Colbert's company was sent to Columbia, Boone County, and Company F, commanded by Capt. A. Kimpinski, was stationed for a short time at Troy, in Lincoln County. The following letter, addressed to the adjutant-general of Missouri, completes the history of this regiment:

"LOUISIANA, PIKE COUNTY, MISSOURI,
October 20, 1865.

"COLONEL SAMUEL P. SIMPSON, ADJUTANT-GENERAL OF MISSOURI,

"*Sir:*—In obedience to your request of the 17th inst., I have the honor to submit the following as a history of the operations of my command from the commencement of the present year to the date of the muster out:

"On the 1st day of January, 1865, the regiment was scattered throughout several counties in North Missouri, principally along the line of the North Missouri Railroad. The regiment was at that time under the command of Lieut.-Col. Smart (leave of absence having been granted to me to attend a session of the State Legislature). On the 30th of January orders were received by Lieut.-Col. Smart to report with his command at St. Louis, Mo. On the 1st day of February I reported at St. Louis and assumed command of the regiment, and thereupon received orders from Gen. Dodge to proceed to New Orleans and report to Maj.-Gen. E. R. S. Canby, commanding military division of West Mississippi. On the 10th day of February we embarked at St. Louis, and on the 21st of same month reported to Gen. Canby at New Orleans, and by him were assigned to the Sixteenth Army Corps, Maj.-Gen. A. J. Smith commanding. My regiment was, by order of Gen. Smith, assigned to the Third Division, Sixteenth Army Corps, Brevet Maj.-Gen. E. A. Carr commanding. The regiment remained at New Orleans until the 10th day of March, at which time it embarked on steamer, under orders to report at Dauphin Island, the entrance to Mobile Bay. On the 20th of the same month left Dauphin Island and proceeded by way of Gulf of Mexico to Fish River, which we ascended for a distance of some twenty miles, and then disembarked, proceeding across the country in the direction of the city of Mobile, and on the morning of the 27th of March commenced operations against Spanish Fort, situated on the eastern side of Mobile Bay, and opposite the city; that fort and Fort Blakely, situated four miles above, comprising the main defenses of the city in this siege, which lasted for thirteen days. My command held a portion of the main line investing the fort, being near the center of the division, and the division occupying the right of the line. My loss during the siege was twenty-one killed and wounded. On the 9th of April the garrison surrendered, and on the next day we started in the direction of Fort Blakely, which, before our arrival, had also surrendered. From there we marched to Montgomery, Ala., a distance of 200 miles, reaching there on the 26th of April. At this latter place the regiment remained until the 14th of July, at which time eight companies of the regiment were ordered to report for muster out and discharge. Left Montgomery on the night of the 14th, and proceeded by the way of Selma, Meridian, Jackson and Vicksburg to St. Louis, reporting at the latter place to Col. B. L. E. Bonneville for muster out, and were, on the 2d of August, finally mustered out and discharged. The two remaining companies, H and K, commanded respectively by Capt. Gentry and Grabenharst, are at this time at Eufaula, Ala., awaiting the expiration of their term of service.

"The men composing the several companies of the regiment were not acclimated, and hence, during the summer season, a great deal of sickness prevailed, with fearful fatality. During the encampment at Montgomery, Ala., a little more than two months, we buried of our number fifty-two, thirty-eight of whom sleep side by side in one graveyard.

SCENE ON THE MISSOURI PACIFIC R. R.

"I have the honor to be, very respectfully, your obedient servant, "D. P. DYER,
"*Late Colonel Forty-ninth Missouri Infantry Volunteers.*"

The two companies mentioned as remaining in the service were in due time thereafter mustered out.

On the 1st day of August, 1864, when a draft was pending in Missouri to raise her quota of soldiers for the United States army, the county court of Lincoln County, in order to avoid the enforcement of the draft therein, by virtue of an act of the General Assembly of the State of Missouri, entitled: "An act to encourage volunteer enlistments in the United States military service," approved February, 1864, ordered that $100 should be paid to each citizen of the county who would volunteer to enter the service to fill her share of the quota, the aggregate number of men to receive such bounty not to exceed 205. The court further ordered that an amount of money not exceeding $15,000 should be borrowed for the payment of such bounties, at the rate of 10 per cent interest, the interest to be paid annually, and that bonds or orders on the county treasurer, signed by the president of the court, and countersigned by the clerk thereof, should be issued for the payment of the money borrowed.

At a special term of the court held in March following, when another draft was pending, it was ordered, by virtue of the aforesaid legislative act, that $200 should be paid to each citizen of the county "who would volunteer for the term of twelve months in the Missouri Volunteers for the United States service," $100 to be paid upon enlistment and $100 at the expiration of term of service, the aggregate number of men to receive such bounties not to exceed 103 men.

On the 22d day of the same month (March, 1865) the Court ordered "that $200 bounty be paid to each soldier who should volunteer for the term of three years in the Missouri Volunteers for the United States service, to be credited to the quota of Lincoln County, $100 to be paid when accepted, and $100 to be paid at the expiration of twelve months, with 10 per cent interest from date. Bonds or orders to be issued for the deferred payments. The aggregate number of men not to exceed the number required to fill the quota. The Court appoints Maj. Alex. H. Martin commissioner to contract for and superintend the filling of the quota for the county for the impending draft." On April 7, following, the Court made an order to borrow from the school fund such amount as proper to pay the bounties, and to execute bonds to the State for the same.

On the 10th day of April, following, the Court rescinded the orders made on the 22d of March and 7th of April preceding, and made the following order instead:

"By virtue of an act of the General Assembly of the State of Missouri, entitled 'An act to encourage volunteer enlistments in the United States military service,' approved February 26, 1864, it is ordered by the Court that the sum of $15,000 be appropriated for the payment of substitutes to fill our quota for the present draft. The Court also appoints Maj. A. H. Martin a commissioner to contract for and superintend the filling of said quota, limiting him to an amount not to exceed $200 for each substitute furnished for one, two or three years. It is further ordered by the Court that Shapley R. Woolfolk, treasurer of this county, pay over to said commissioner any proportion of the aforesaid amount of $15,000 which he may require from time to time for the payment of said substitutes, and charge to any fund to which it properly belongs."

In accordance with these several orders of the Court, bounties were paid to a sufficient number of volunteer soldiers to exempt the county from the enforcement of any draft.

CASUALTIES.

During the continuance of the war a number of cruel actions were committed, which might have been avoided. Several individuals were killed, undoubtedly without sufficient cause. Among those killed were the following: A German living a few miles north of Troy, and whose name was Chitty, was arrested by some Federal soldiers, and, while being brought to town, he attempted to escape from his guard, who shot and killed him. He was the first man killed in the county during the war period.

Dr. Benjamin Todd, living at his home on Highland Prairie, about ten miles east from Troy, who was a Southern sympathizer, though a quiet citizen, was killed at or near his home by a Federal scout.

Dr. Bourland, who lived near Hawk Point, was killed, it is supposed by some one or more persons belonging to the army, for his money.

Harrison Hubbard, who lived about four miles south of Troy, being accused of harboring rebel bushwhackers, was killed by a party of Federal scouts from Troy.

William M. Allen, while passing on the road south of Olney, in company with William Adams, was shot and killed by a bushwhacker. This was in the fall of 1864. No clue to the murderer was found.

Pleasant J. Davis and William Hazlett were killed near Louisville.

Tid Sharp and a Mr. Hill were killed by some Federal scouts near Big Creek.

Sanders Warren, who resided between Troy and Truxton, was killed by one of a squad of soldiers that went out from Troy. On this occasion he and the soldiers suddenly discovered each other, when he started off on a run, was commanded to halt, and, upon refusing to obey, was shot and killed. His running created a suspicion in the minds of the soldiers that something was wrong. Had he not started to run, or even obeyed the command to halt, he probably would not have been disturbed.

Sylvester Millsap, one of the three men in this county who voted for Lincoln in 1860, was killed in the fall of 1863 by a bushwhacker who was concealed in the bushes.

CHAPTER XIII.

CITIES, TOWNS AND VILLAGES.

ALEXANDRIA,

Located on the Auburn road, five miles north of Troy, was surveyed and laid out in 1822, and was the second place where the county seat was established. The plat is not recorded. It was the best planned town ever laid out in the county. The streets were broad, crossing at right angles. There were spacious public squares, parks and reservations for public buildings. As the county seat remained there only a short time, it did not become a place of importance, and it now exists only on paper.

AUBURN,

A small village ten miles north of Troy, was laid out in April, 1838, on lands of Daniel Draper, Sr., and Philander Draper, on the east half of the southeast quarter of Section 2, Township 50 north, Range 1 west. The plat was acknowledged before James Wilson, a justice of the peace. The latter is now residing at Auburn, at the advanced age of ninety-four years. The vicinity of Auburn was noted, in the early history of the county, on account of the prominent men who settled there, and on account of Stout's Fort, which was erected at the spring, a short distance south of where Auburn stands. In the early days Thacker Vivion had a cotton-gin near Auburn, and it was a common sight, so says a noted old settler, Walter Perkins, now departed, "to see cotton-seed in heaps larger than the gin-house." For many years Auburn was a place of considerable business, but since the railroads were completed through the county, it has declined, so that at the present writing it contains one general store and the postoffice, kept by J. M. Terrell; a blacksmith shop, by C. Teauge; a Cumberland Presbyterian Church, and a few residences. Dr. William McClure is believed to have been the first physician who practiced at Auburn. The present resident physician is Dr. Joseph A. Knox. James Wilson was a justice of the peace in the Auburn vicinity for a great many years. The first marriage ceremony he performed was in 1833. The contracting parties were Hiram McDonald and Eliza Ann Tilford. Auburn has about seventy-five inhabitants.

BRISCOE,

On the St. Louis & Hannibal (Short Line) Railway, was laid out in 1883, on lands owned by Samuel Briscoe and others, in Sections 21 and 22, Township 50 north, Range 1 west.

BREVATOR

Is a station on the St. Louis, Keokuk and Northwestern Railroad, forty-five miles from the city of St. Louis. A town was surveyed and laid out here in 1880, but it contains nothing but a small railroad depot. It is situated in Township 48 north, Range 2 east.

CAP-AU-GRIS

Is situated on the west bank of the Mississippi River, in Township 49 north, Range 3 east, about sixteen miles east of Troy. It was laid out in November, 1845, on land of David Bailey, in Survey 1653. The plat was acknowledged before Charles Wheeler, a justice of the peace. At the August term of the county court, in 1875, it was incorporated under the name and style of "The Inhabitants of the Town of Wiota," the old name being discarded; however, the people never became accustomed to the new name, but continued to use the old name. The board of trustees appointed, when the place was incorporated, consisted of William Jewell, Antoine Guion, Patrick Wyland, Lem A. Springerstun and F. G. Hoyt. In an early day it was a shipping point for Troy and some other places, and before the railroads took away its trade it was a place of considerable business and importance. In 1875 when it was incorporated, being some years before the railroads in this county were completed, it contained inhabitants enough to compose at least a board of trustees, but at present the town exists only in name.

CHAIN OF ROCKS

Is situated on the north side of the Cuivre River, about four miles above Old Monroe. In 1885 the *Free Press* published the following sketch of this village: "It is one of the places that might have been, for two railroad surveys were run through the place— one for the long and one for the short line.* When these surveys were made much business was transacted at Chain of Rocks. There were three general stores, a mill, a box factory, a blacksmith shop, two boot and shoe shops, three doctors and a saloon. During most of the year a line of steamboats made regular trips and bore away the produce, and when boating was impracticable, the produce was hauled to St. Louis direct, or to O'Fallon, on the North Missouri (now the Wabash). After the

---

*The St. Louis, Keokuk & Northwestern Railroad is commonly called the "long line" and the railroad via Troy, the "short line."

completion of the two railroads the business of the town gradually decreased down to one store, a blacksmith shop and one physician. It afterward revived, and now (1885) there are three general stores, a blacksmith shop and wagon shop, a shoe shop, two doctors, and a telegraph line to Old Monroe. Reller & Pollard conduct the largest business in the town, consisting of dry-goods, groceries, clothing and tinware. J. T. Schacher, general merchandise; J. T. Haislip, groceries; Conrad F. Schacher, blacksmith; Geo. J. Pohlmeyer, wagon-maker; George Schacher, boot and shoe maker; J. J. & L. C. McElwee (father and son) physicians; Stephen Reller, postmaster. The telegraph line to Old Monroe was completed in March, 1885, the money being raised by subscription from the business men of the Chain and Monroe, and the farmers of the Chain vicinage. It was erected by C. K. Sitton and Dr. L. C. McElwee. A handsome wagon bridge across Cuivre to St. Charles County, 192 feet span, fourteen feet wide, with a tested capacity of three threshing engines, was erected by the two counties, and by subscription of the residents of the contiguous neighborhoods in each. The bridge is partly iron and partly wood, and cost originally over $6,000. Dr. W. E. Brown was commissioner for Lincoln and A. P. Gill for St. Charles."

Since the above was published the town has again slightly retrograded, the business at present (1888) consisting of two general stores, kept respectively by Reller & Pollard and J. F. Schacher, and a blacksmith shop by C. F. Schacher. The telegraph line remains, and a daily mail is had from Monroe. The town was laid out on a Spanish grant about the year 1835. The name was given it by Gen. Amos Burdyne, on account of a section of archimides limestone exposed in the bank of the Cuivre River in front of the town.

CHANTILLA

Was laid out July 2, 1852, on land of Robert McIntosh, on the southwest quarter of the northwest quarter of Section 19, Township 49 north, Range 2 east. The plat was acknowledged before Francis Parker, clerk of the circuit court. It is a small post village.

ELSBERRY

Is situated on the St. Louis, Keokuk & Northwestern Railroad, fifty-eight miles north of the city of St. Louis. It is located at the western margin of the Mississippi bottom, and on the north side of Lost Creek, which cuts through the bluffs and flows to the Mississippi River. It was surveyed and platted in August, 1879, by Z. E. Freer, civil engineer, for Robert T. Elsberry, John C. Roberts, William McIntosh and Henry S. Carroll, the original proprietors, and named in honor of the former. The plat was acknowledged by these parties May 21, 1881. As shown by this plat the town originally contained twelve blocks of ten lots each, the lots being 50x115 feet in size. In June, 1885, the same proprietors laid out an addition to the town, and in the same month Robert T. Elsberry laid out a second addition. The first house built in Elsberry was a railroad warehouse, which is still standing. The first merchants were Smither, Carroll & Co., who came from Clarksville with a stock of groceries and hardware, and occupied the warehouse first built, one end of it being cut off for a store room. Soon after this Messrs. Elsberry & Wilkinson put up a two-story frame building, in which they opened a general store. This house was located on the hill some 300 yards from the depot, the town being now divided into two parts, "on the hill" and "under the hill." This firm did not remain long, but sold out, and after several changes the house came under the control of the Cannon Bros., who still continue the business. After this house was built the "boom" had a slight cessation, but early in 1880 a number of business houses were erected, among which was the Etter building, on Main Street, "under the hill." Three other buildings, on the north side of the Etter building, all under the same roof, were constructed at the same time, one being occupied by R. T. Wigginston & Co., another by Smither, Carroll & Co., and the other by J. M. Gibson, druggist. Later in the spring of 1880 Sour & Reuter erected a business building near the depot, and commenced merchandising, but soon went into bankruptcy.

The following is a statement of the business of Elsberry in 1883, when the town was only three years old: Dry-goods, Cannon & Sons, Etter's O. P. C. H. (one price cash house); groceries, Gibson & Shipp and Brother & Singleton; drugs, J. W. Bibb, Nicklin & Hawkins and Lee & Howard; hardware, "Yank" Elliott; farm implements, Watts & Elsberry and Gibson & Shipp; jewelry, J. W. Steadman; millinery, the Misses Knox; boots and shoes, H. H. Reuter; lumber and undertaker's goods, Robert E. Black; grain dealers, Watts & Elsberry, also the Elsberry Milling Company; cooper shop, James Cooper; boot and shoe shops, Tim. Mulcar and T. J. Potts; livery, Gentry & Cannon; hotel, "Richards' Hotel," by Samuel Richards; restaurants, W. N. Gibson and Mrs. H. Hitt; blacksmith shops, H. W. Leo, Gordon T. Felty and J. K. Gililland; wagon shops, John Carter and John Dawkins; butcher shops, Elsberry & Gatewood and C. L. Gennie; ice dealers, Robert T. Elsberry and C. L. Gennie; merchant tailor, James Saulsberry; saloons, Watts & Elsberry and R. T. Booth & Co.; physicians, R. T. Hawkins, S. H. Kerr, B. J. Lee and W. A. Hemphill. The Elsberry Flouring Mills, erected by the Elsberry Joint Stock Milling Company, was doing an extensive business in 1883, manufacturing flour and meal and shipping the same to other points. The foregoing shows a large number of business houses and business enterprises for a town only three years old. In fact, the business was overdone, several parties having commenced business with a small capital, expecting the place to grow so rapidly and the demand of "home consumption" to become so great that their success was assured. This, however, was not to be; a railroad in a country lying close to large towns and cities could not cause a city to come into existence, as if by magic, at the site of Elsberry. But being located as it is in an excellent agricultural country, there was, and is, a good prospect for a substantial and prosperous town at Elsberry, notwithstanding the fact that at first too many individuals embarked in business enterprises.

The following is a directory of the business of the town in 1885: General stores, Gibson & Eastin, and Cannon Bros.; groceries, A. D. Shipp and B. S. Cannon & Bro.; drugs, Nicklin & Hawkins and C. M. Howard; boots and shoes, H. H. Reuter; millinery, the Misses Knox and Mrs. T. R. Goodman; lumber, undertaking goods, plaster, lime, etc., R. E. Black; builder and contractor, A. A. Brother; hardware, G. C. Elliott;

blacksmiths, G. T. Felty and J. M. McDonald; wheelwright, J. C. Carter; livery, J. S. Cannon; hotel, C. B. Lindsey; restaurant, Mrs. Hitt; saloon, W. W. Watts; butcher shop, J. A. Sour; barber, L. D. Gatewood; apiary, Hemphill & Goodman; physicians, S. H. Kerr, Lee & Bailey, and W. A. Hemphill. Up to this time one church, the Methodist Episcopal South, had been erected, and was then used by several denominations. The large high-school building was erected prior to 1883. It is one of the largest and best school buildings in the county, and is constructed of brick. In 1883 Prof. Seaman, principal, and Miss Callie Towles and Miss Nonie Elgin taught the schools. In 1885 the schools were taught by Prof. Nichols and his assistant, Miss Sophia Seaton, of Troy.

The business of Elsberry at this time, July, 1888, is as follows: Dry goods, Rose & Eastin, Cannon & Alloway; groceries and farm implements, A. D. Shipp, B. S. Cannon & Bro.; drugs, D. F. Foley; furniture and harness, Bailey & Morris; millinery, Mrs. T. R. Goodman; millinery and dressmaking, the Misses Knox; farm implements, W. W. Watts; restaurants, Mrs. Pfordt and Mrs. Hitt; blacksmiths, James McDonald and W. P. Morton; livery, Cannon & Bro.; boot and shoe shop, John Stahl; hardware and lumber, Black & Luckett; barber, L. D. Gatewood; "Hotel Palmer," William Palmer, Jr.; bank, Blank, Block & Harvey. The large flouring mill is now idle. It is claimed that all the mills on the line of the St. Louis, Keokuk & Northwestern Railroad in Lincoln County cannot compete with other mills until they are provided with the roller apparatus and machinery, there being no demand for flour manufactured by the old buhr method. Attached to the mill of the Elsberry Milling Company is a large warehouse, and there is another warehouse near the railroad depot owned by Elsberry & Watt. The physicians of Elsberry are Samuel M. Bailey and B. J. Lee. The town now contains four frame churches, one owned by the Southern Methodists, one by the Baptists and Presbyterians combined, one by the colored Baptists, and one by the colored Methodists.

There is a lodge each of the I. O. O. F. and A. O. U. W., and both use the same building. There is also a lodge of colored Odd Fellows.

The Elsberry *Advance*, a weekly newspaper, was established by H. F. Childers, who published the first number October 8, 1880, and continued to publish the paper alone until March, 1881, when J. P. Powell, bought a half-interest. Childers & Powell then continued its publication until December, 1861, when Powell bought his partner's interest. Mr. Powell then continued the paper alone until February, 1884, when he sold it to W. T. Reeds, who published it until May, 1885, and then sold it to J. W. Powell and R. T. Robinson. These gentlemen published it together until July, 1887, when Robinson sold his interest to R. H. Womack. Messrs. Powell & Womack, the present publishers, have since continued its publication.

Elsberry has two local attorneys, J. W. Powell and W. A. Dudley.

In 1883, H. W. Lee, J. C. Carter and fifty-two other citizens of Elsberry, petitioned the county court, praying for the incorporation of the town. In November of that year the court granted the prayer of the petition, and duly incorporated the town according to Article 6, Chapter 89, Revised Statutes of Missouri. The boundary line of the district incorporated was described as follows: "Beginning at a stone on the north bank of Lost Creek, where a continuation of the Bluff Road south would intersect said creek; thence north with said Bluff road to the northern line of Lincoln Street, as shown by the recorded plat of said town; thence east on Lincoln Street to Sixth Street; thence north on Sixth Street to the north line of Hill Street; thence east on the north line of Hill Street to the St. Louis, Keokuk & Northwestern Railroad; thence southwest with said railway to Lost Creek; thence west along the north bank of Lost Creek to the place of beginning." The town was incorporated under the name and style of "The inhabitants of the Village of Elsberry." The board of trustees appointed by the court were James W. Powell, J. M. Gibson, Charles A. Mayes, J. R. Cannon and George C. Elliott.

Elsberry is very pleasantly located at the western margin of the valley, that portion of the town known as "under the hill" being on an even plateau gently sloping eastward toward the Mississippi, and that part known as "on the hill" being located on an elevated plateau, that might with propriety be called a bench of the bluffs. From this bench, where a part of the business houses and most of the residences are located, a delightful view of the Mississippi Valley and of the hills beyond the river on the Illinois side is obtained, and by looking southward and southwestward, a pleasant view of the hills of the western bluffs is obtained. On the whole Elsberry has a picturesque location.

FALMOUTH.

Falmouth (Westport) is a landing on a side channel of the Mississippi, about two and a half miles east of Elsberry. It was surveyed and laid out as a town October 12, 1836, on lands of James Finley, Charles Cox and John Galloway, on the fractional Section 24, Township 51 north, Range 2 east; acknowledged before E. H. Powers, justice of the peace. Formerly this was a place of considerable business, being the place where Uncle Hiram Wommack, well known throughout Lincoln County, made his start in life. At that time all stock and grain of the northeastern part of the county were shipped by river from Falmouth, while all the necessary merchandise for the people of that vicinity was shipped by the river to this point. The building of the railroad and the establishment of Elsberry was the death knell to Falmouth. Elsberry has absorbed the business, and left Falmouth only its name and the place of its former greatness.

FOLEY.

Foley is situated on the St. Louis, Keokuk & Northwestern Railroad, fifty-one miles from St. Louis, and on part of Section 1, Township 49 north, Range 2 east, and on parts of Surveys 425 and 741. A short time before the railroad was completed to this point B. F. Robertson bought six acres of land and gave the company $500 in consideration of their locating the depot on his land, where it now stands. About this time Mr. Robertson bought 144 acres more adjoining the town, and associated himself in partnership with John C. Downing, with whom he laid out the town in October, 1879. Then William McQuire, administrator of the Foley estate, laid out an addition to the town, and gave other lots to the railroad company on condition that they would locate the depot where it is, and name the town Foley, in honor of Miss Addie Foley (since Mrs. Dr. D. H. Young, of Fulton, Mo.). The donations were accepted and the town named accordingly. D. N. Trescott erected the first storehouse in Foley, the same year that the depot was built. Afterward B. F. Robertson put up his fine two-story house, and then came the building boom. The large flouring mill in the south end of the town was the original Burr Oak Valley Mills, brought to Foley in 1880, by Messrs. Mildenstein & Anderson, who operated it until 1884, when the former sold his interest to Broyles and the latter to Trescott. It is now owned by Columbus Broyles, who uses it as a grain elevator, but not for grinding.

The following is a directory of the business of Foley in 1885: Flouring mill, Broyles & Trescott; general stores, Robertson & Marks, and Lee Frank; Foley House, Matthew Crouch; grocery and boarding house, Mrs. Lucinda J. Pfordt; boot and shoe shop, Bernard Wagner; blacksmith shop, John Bricker; drugs, J. M. Tipton.

The following is a directory of the business of Foley at the present writing, July, 1888: General merchandise, Robertson & Marks, Lee Frank and Wagner Bros.; drugs, Thirstin & Tipton; grain dealer, Columbus Broyles; Foley House, Mrs. Dodge; blacksmith shop, John Bricker; wagonmaker, O. McNutt; shoemaker and harness-maker, B. Wagner, Sr.

Foley is a great depot for the shipment of railroad ties. In March, 1888, there were 26,000 ties in the yard at this place. The school building and Odd Fellows' Hall is a large, two-story frame structure, and was erected and is owned in partnership by the Odd Fellows and the school district. The school occupies the first story.

Burr Oak Lodge No. 378, I. O. O. F., was chartered and located at Burr Oak in 1877. It was moved to Foley in the fall of 1882. Its present membership is about thirty-five. It owns the hall in which it meets, is out of debt, and has money in its treasury. There is no church building in Foley, but the Baptists, Methodists and Christians hold services occasionally at the school house. The people of Foley and vicinity erected the iron bridge, fifty feet in length, over Sandy Creek, just west of the town.

HURRICANE.

Hurricane is a station on the St. Louis, Keokuk & Northwestern Railroad, between Elsberry and Foley. It contains one general store.

JONESVILLE.

Jonesville was laid out in 1883 by Martin T. Jones and wife, on the east half of the northwest quarter of the northwest quarter of Section 26, Township 49 north, range 1 west, being about a mile from Troy. It remains only a paper town. It may have been intended as a suburb for Troy.

LOUISVILLE.

Louisville is situated in the northwest corner of the county on Section 7, Township 51 north, Range 2 west; being about twenty-two miles northwest from Troy. It was laid out and platted in 1832 by Hannibal Marshall, Enoch Emerson and Dayton Crider, the original proprietors. It was surveyed into nine blocks each containing eight lots. Col. Meredith Cox was, perhaps, the most prominent early settler in that vicinity, and there he established and maintained a whisky distillery for a number of years in pioneer times. Following the use of the horse-power mills a Mr. Brown erected a steam mill at or near Louisville. In 1829 a man by the name of Scroggins kept a store at the site of Louisville. This village is situated in a good agricultural country, and has been a place, especially before the railroads came near it, of considerable importance. Latterly its business has been drawn away to some extent to the railroad towns. The town contains, at present writing, one general store, kept by H. H. & T. J. Higginbotham. These gentlemen keep one of the most complete stores in the country, having all classes of goods, including dry goods, clothing, groceries drugs, hardware, agricultural implements, saddles, harness, queensware, coffins, etc., in short, every thing the community needs. A good hotel is kept by Mrs. Erlinda Bartlett. There are two blacksmith shops, run, respectively, by S. Y. Dixon and S. E. Estes, and a carpenter shop by Samuel Myers. The physicians are Drs. R. C. Prewitt, and G. N. Tinsley; postmaster, T. J. Higginbotham. In addition to the above there is a public schoolhouse, a select schoolhouse and Masonic hall combined, and the Christian Church. The latter is a brick structure which was erected in 1874.

Louisville Lodge No. 428, A. F. & A. M., was granted a dispensation July 5, 1870. The original members were J. R. Tinsley, J. S. R. Gregory, C. T. Nash, H. F. Reeds, E. J. Fisher, Levi Thomas, James Merritt, H. Hopke, John Stone, H. H. Higginbotham and P. H. Tucker. The lodge received its charter October 16, 1872, with J. R. Tinsley, W. M., J. S. R. Gregory, S. W. and C. T. Nash, J. W.

The present membership is twenty-seven, and the officers are J. L. Butler, W. M.; J. F. Young, S. W.; D. Y. Morris, J. W.; D. C. Reeds, Secretary; H. M. Reid, Treasurer; S. E. Estes, S. D.; H. H. Higginbotham, J. D., and Josiah Young, Tyler.

In 1882 this lodge and the high school board jointly erected a two-story frame building, 24x46 feet in size, at a cost of about $2,100, the former paying three-sevenths and the latter four-sevenths of the amount. The first story is occupied by the high school and the second by the lodge. The building is paid for, and no debt is pending with either lodge or school board.

On petition of two-thirds of the taxable inhabitants of Louisville, it was incorporated by the county court at its May term, 1874, under the name and style of "The Inhabitants of the Town of Louisville," and Edward Huntsman, A. J. Dixon, William H. Bartlett, F. M. Dixon and W. J. Wales were constituted the first board of trustees.

MONROE.

Monroe, or "Old Monroe," as it is commonly called, is situated on the St. Louis, Keokuk & Northwestern Railroad, at the crossing of the Cuivre, the town being wholly on the north side of the river. It is located in the southeastern part of Lincoln County, and, having been the first county seat thereof, it is one of the most historic places in the county. It is also noted for the beautiful mounds that have been constructed there in former ages. The site is beautiful, but the town is small. The original town was laid out some time prior to 1819, by Ira and Almond Cottle and Nathaniel Simonds, the original proprietors. A large portion of it was donated in 1819 to the county for the seat of justice. The large brick house now owned and occupied by Herman Niemeyer was built some seventy-eight years ago, about the year 1810. The county was organized in this house, and the courts held therein while the county seat remained at Monroe. In August, 1820, Almond Cottle was licensed to keep a "tavern," the fee being $10 for a year. It is presumed that this is the house in which the "tavern" was kept. With the exception of the Niemeyer residence there had been nothing at Monroe, in the way of buildings, for many years, until the railroad drew near its completion, when it began to revive. It was re-surveyed in 1880 by Charles Du Bois, a civil engineer, and since that time the town as it now exists has principally been built. It contains two general stores kept, respectively, by Albert Isenstein and Herman Niemeyer; a hotel, grocery and livery stable by W. H. Pollard; a hotel by Henry H. Pieper, and a blacksmith shop by Herman Brunes. Isenstein also deals in furniture and farm implements. There is a daily mail between Monroe and Chain of Rocks. The railroad bridge, across the Cuivre at Monroe, has twice been swept away by the pressure of drift collected when the water was high. On the last occasion the drift contained 1,600 saw logs, which floated from the Cuivre and its tributaries. The present bridge is a magnificent one, made mostly of iron. During the last year immense cribs of stone have been constructed in the river, above the bridge piers, to prevent the drift from striking them. It is believed that these cribs of stone will be sufficient to resist the pressure of any amount of drift that will be likely to collect in the future, and thus enable it to be broken and floated down between the piers without injury to the bridge.

MOSCOW.

Moscow (Moscow on the Cuivre) is situated on the western bank of the Cuivre River, and on the St. Louis & Hannibal (Short Line) Railroad, four miles southeast of Troy. It was laid out March 17, 1821, by John Geiger, Morgan Wright, James Duncan and Shapley Ross, the original proprietors. The plat was witnessed by Sylvanus Allison and Elijah Collard. The proprietors appointed C. K. Duncan, A. C. Woolfolk, Jeremiah Groshong, Andrew Miller and W. H. Robinson as a board of trustees of the town of Moscow to sell and convey lots. It was laid out as a competing point with Monroe, Troy, Alexandria and other places, for location of the county seat. Henry Martin was the first merchant of Moscow, having opened a stock of general merchandise soon after the town was laid out. He continued in business several years and made considerable money, after which he died and was buried there. At the time Martin did business at Moscow, Adolphus Foster and Thomas McCune also carried on a small business. William Hammer was the next settler in the town and he also engaged in merchandising. He was the first postmaster the town ever had, having been appointed as a Republican. He remained in business until 1884, when he retired. Next came A. M. Bouldin, who opened a grocery store, and C. & L. Branders and James Anderson, who opened general stores. All these were doing business at Moscow in 1885. A saloon was established there some three years ago by John Horton. He was soon succeeded by Thomas Stuart, and he by Hammer, who continued the business until the Downing law went into effect. Next came James Cunningham, who continued the business for a time.

The grist and saw mill owned by Wing & Son has always been one of the greatest factors of Moscow's success. It was established about the year 1820, by Jeremiah Groshong. He sold it to John Geiger, and he to Henry Martin, who died while in possession of it. The heirs of Martin sold it to Thomas Multon, who sold it to John Foster. The latter sold it to James and Ed. Leach, and in 1868 they sold it to Frederick Wing, the senior member of the firm of Wing & Son, its present owners. There is a large grain elevator attached to the mills. A bridge was built across the Cuivre River at Moscow in 1852. It fell in 1860, having been undermined by the strong current of water. The following is a list of the business of Moscow as it was written up and published in 1885: General stores, C. & L. Brandes and J. H. Anderson; grocery, A. M. Bouldin; saloon, J. C. Cunningham; hotel, Frank Hill; blacksmith, Louis Schroeder; Wing & Son, millers and dealers in grain; Fritz Durand, blacksmith and wheelwright. Several beautiful residences, a union church and a schoolhouse.

In 1870, when the prospect for a railroad at Moscow was good, the proprietors of the vacant lots had the town re-surveyed, preparatory to selling them. The old corners, to some extent, had been lost, and in order to re-establish them the deposition of Joseph H. Shelton, who had personal knowledge of their location, was taken on the 16th day of September, before James D. Shelton and Wilson T. Harris, justices of the peace. With the information thus obtained, John C. Downing, surveyor of Lincoln County, made a complete re-survey of the town, beginning at the northwest corner of Lot 4 in Block 12, where he perpetuated the corner by placing a stone in it 26x9x4 inches in size. John Franklin and S. G. Wright were the chain carriers in making this re-survey. The town, as thus surveyed, contains nine blocks of four lots each, and fifteen blocks of eight lots each, the lots being 128x65 feet, except in Blocks 1 to 4 inclusive, where they are of the same width but greater length. Jacob Voepel's addition to the town of Moscow was surveyed and platted in June, 1882, by J. F. Wilson, the county surveyor.

The contract for the bridge recently built across the Cuivre, at Moscow, was let by the county court to Raymond & Campbell, of the Council Bluffs' Bridge Company, for $3,825; $3,000 to be paid by the county, and the balance by the citizens of Moscow and vicinity. The bridge is a substantial iron structure.

About 1879 a colored man by the name of Cavello Sydnor went over the dam in a skiff. Three days later his body was found one mile below. Soon after that fatal accident Miss Acsah Shultz, sister to the nurseryman, was trying to ford the river, when her horse became frightened and threw her off. She was swept by the current into deep water, where she was drowned. Her body was recovered about two hours later. The next case of drowning at Moscow was that of Pat Carney, which occurred about four years ago. He was supposed to have gone into the river bathing while in a state of intoxication. His body was found by the use of dynamite. It is no wonder that the people of Moscow were anxious for a good bridge across the Cuivre.

MILLWOOD

Is situated in the western part of Section 14 and the eastern part of Section 15, in Township 50 north, Range 2 west, and is about twelve miles northwest of Troy. In 1843 an effort was made for the establishment of a postoffice near where Millwood now stands, and Dr. Hilary P. Mudd, who became the first postmaster, selected and forwarded to the department at Washington the name of Fairview for the new office; but there being already a postoffice in the State of that name it could not be adopted. He then sent on the name of Millward, after the name of the Federal marshal of the Eastern District of Pennsylvania, who was at that time a prominent Whig politician. The postoffice department mistook the last syllable, "ward," for "wood," hence the name "Millwood." Joseph S. Wells built the first house in the village in 1851, and used it as a store and dwelling house. The second store was opened by William F. Elder. In 1853 Dr. H. P. and Judge H. T. Mudd formed a partnership, opened a store and continued the business together until about 1859, when the former retired. The latter, Judge Mudd, then continued the business alone until 1885, when he took in his son Daniel as a partner, comprising the firm of H. T. Mudd & Son, and they still continue in the business and keep a general stock of everything needed by the people. (They also have a general store and lumber yard at Silex.)

At present the village contains the general store above mentioned and two drug stores, kept respectively by Drs. H. B. Wommack and J. D. Mudd. The former, in 1871, established the first drug store ever kept in the place. The physicians of Millwood are the druggists here mentioned. Since the village was founded other business enterprises have existed. In 1866 William R. Mattingly commenced the business of wagon-making and blacksmithing, and in 1876 R. M. Elder opened a boot and shoe shop, and for a time J. Emmet Cummings sold drygoods and farm implements. Millwood has two schools, public and select. The latter is a high school wherein instruction in the higher branches is given. Prof. C. B. M. Thurmond, the efficient principal, has just closed the high school for the last year, and has given good satisfaction to his patrons. With the exception of a few years during the excitement of the war period, the postoffice has remained in the hands of the Mudds. Dr. H.

P. Mudd, the first postmaster, held the office at his dwelling house until some time during the war, when he was succeeded by William F. Elder. The latter was succeeded by James E. Mudd and he by Daniel H. Mudd, the present incumbent. Millwood is surrounded with a very good farming country, but being situated as it is within three and one-half miles of Silex, a leading shipping point on the railroad, it is destined to continue only a small village. A few things will remain with it, among which may be mentioned the large general store of Judge Mudd & Son, and the Roman Catholic Church and the convent school. The church and school will be mentioned elsewhere in this work.

The history of Millwood would not be complete without a personal mention of its founder, Joseph S. Wells, who was one of the pioneer settlers of the county, and who taught the first schools in the Millwood neighborhood. After leaving Millwood he went to Olney, and founded that village. He became a Baptist minister, did much good in the cause of Christianity, and was well liked by all who knew him. His wife was a Miss Sands, whom he married about the year 1844. After completing a period of very useful citizenship in this county, he moved to Texas, where he remained until his death.

NEW HOPE.

New Hope, a small village in Hurricane Township, was surveyed January 16, 1837, on land of Charles Cox, being the south part of the east half of the southeast quarter of Section 35, Township 51 north, Range 1 east. The plat was acknowledged before Francis Parker, clerk of the circuit court. Being surrounded with an excellent farming country, it was formerly a place of considerable business importance. It is now only a post hamlet, containing a general store, postoffice, a couple of churches, and a few residences. Andrew Cochran was the first merchant at New Hope, and kept a store there during the thirties. It was then a wilderness all the way from there to what is now Elsberry.

NEW SALEM.

New Salem is a small hamlet, situated on Section 16, Township 49 north, Range 2 east. It contains New Salem Lodge No.

270, A. F. & A. M., which was instituted in 1867, and chartered in that or the following year. The lodge had seventeen charter members. The first officers were W. H. Crenshaw, W. M.; Dr. William H. Wise, S. W.; J. H. Dryden, J. W.; Beverly Duey, S. D.; D. T. Killam, J. D.; B. F. Hardesty, Secy.; William Magruder, Treas.; John Bell, Tyler. The lodge owns a hall, which is the second-story of a dwelling house. The hall cost about $400. The present membership of the lodge is sixty-four. Its financial condition is good, and it is doing good work.

OLNEY

Is situated in the southwest corner of Section 22, Township 50 north, Range 3 west. It lies west northwest of Troy, and about fifteen miles distant on a straight line, and one mile east of the western boundary of the county. It is surrounded by a beautiful and fertile prairie country, the surface of which is slightly rolling, with here and there a visible grove of timber, which makes the landscape exceedingly picturesque. The town was founded in 1855 by Joseph S. Wells, who, in that year, built the first house but gave no name to the place. A few years later a post-office was established there by the name of Lost Branch, the name of the creek on which the town is located. This name originated, according to tradition, from the fact that on one occasion, when the old pioneer settler, John Hudson, was hunting near the source of the creek, and near the present site of Olney, he became lost, and had to lie out over night, "and would have frozen to death but for his faithful dogs, that lay on and around him, and kept him warm until daylight appeared, and he again discovered his bearings." For many years the town was regularly called Nineveh, but on the 17th of May, 1875, it was surveyed and platted by Surveyor John C. Downing for John C. Wells and the other proprietors, and was named Olney. As surveyed, it contained seventy-five lots of various sizes.

The first store in the place was opened by its founder, Joseph S. Wells, and continued until it was closed on account of the Civil War, after which it was again opened. Samuel Green opened a general store in 1876, and conducted it alone until 1881, when he took in M. P. Smith as a partner, comprising the firm of Samuel Green & Co., with a capital of about $10,000. Afterward, Higginbotham & Reed kept a general store, with a like amount of capital. The town has grown so that at the present (June, 1888) it contains two large general stores, kept respectively by Samuel Green and Mason, Duvel & Co.; the well-filled drug store of Dr. Theron Ives, which he established in 1874; the hardware and agricultural implement store of William C. Logan; the furniture and undertaking store of A. L. Orr; the millinery store of Mrs. Kate Green; the millinery and dressmaking establishment of Mrs. Annie Jones; the blacksmith shops of F. C. Stroker and J. W. Williams; the extensive manufactory of wagons, buggies, plows, cultivators, etc., of F. C. Stroker; the grist and saw mill of Joseph Palmer, run by N. G. Cornelius; the Olney Hotel, erected in 1885, and since kept by the accommodating landlord, E. G. Dehart, and his lady. The physicians of the town are W. L. Northcut, Charles G. Moseley and Theron Ives. Dr. H. W. Sperry, an old practitioner, having practiced about forty years, now retired, is a resident of the place. Rev. J. J. Smiley, of the Methodist Episcopal Church, is also a resident. Olney contains two church edifices, the Cumberland Presbyterian and the Methodist Episcopal Church South. It also contains the following societies: Nineveh Lodge No. 472, A. F. & A. M., chartered October 15, 1874, with J. S. R. Gregory W. M.; A. S. Morris, S. W. and Joseph Myers, J. W.; present membership, thirty-one. The hall occupied by this lodge was erected in 1873 by a joint stock company. It is a two-story frame building, the lower story being used as a wareroom. Olney Lodge No. 190, A. O. U. W., chartered May 31, 1880, has fifty-four members, and meets on the second and fourth Saturdays of each month. Olney Lodge No. 18, Triple Alliance, chartered April 16, 1883, meets occasionally. Olney has a district school, and about eighty-five children of school age.

Olney Institute.—At the fall term, 1885, of the Lincoln County Circuit Court, the following petition was presented:

" *To the Honorable Elijah Robinson, Judge of the Third Judicial Circuit of Missouri:*

" We, the undersigned stockholders, herewith submit to your

honor our constitution and by-laws, together with a list of the stockholders, praying your honor to grant us incorporation.

"J. L. DUNCAN, *President.*
"BEN. F. REED, *Secretary.*
"SAMUEL GREEN, *Treasurer.*"

Then followed the names of over forty stockholders, and also a copy of the constitution and by-laws, and the following is a copy of the record of the decree of the Court:

"In the matter of the Olney Institute. Now at this day comes J. L. Duncan, president; B. F. Reed, secretary; and Samuel Green, treasurer of said Olney Institute, and submit to the Court the articles of association, together with a petition praying for a *pro forma* decree in manner provided by law, and it appearing to the Court that said petition has remained on file in the clerk's office of said court at least three days since same was presented to the Court, and the Court having duly examined said articles of association, and the purposes of the association as herein expressed come properly within the purview of Article 10, Chapter 21 of the revised statutes of Missouri, of 1879, entitled 'Benevolent, Scientific, Educational and Miscellaneous Associations,' and amendments thereto, approved April 2, 1885, and not inconsistent with the laws of the United States or the State of Missouri. It is therefore adjudged and decreed by the Court that the prayer of the petition be granted and that said petitioners pay the costs in this suit expended."

Prior to its formal incorporation the association had organized and purchased a lot containing two acres, beautifully located on the north side of the village of Olney, and had erected thereon a handsome two story brick building, containing two schoolrooms on each floor, those on the second or upper floor being separated by folding doors so arranged as to throw them into one room when occasion required. The building cost $3,500, and was completed in time for school to commence about the date of the incorporation of the association. The first school therein was opened by Prof. Nichols, who taught and superintended the school for two years, and succeeded in giving it a good reputation. The third year of the school was taught and superintended by the present able and efficient principal, Elijah Ford, B. S. His assistants were Miss Carrie Alloway, Prof. A. J. Marshall and Miss Margie Connell.

The course of study, expenses, etc., as copied from the published catalogue, is as follows:

Preparatory Department.—Reading, spelling, writing, geography, map drawing, English grammar (primary), mental arithmetic, written arithmetic, United States history, voice culture, compositions and declamations.

High School Department.—First year—English grammar, familiar science, natural philosophy, physiology, physical geography, higher arithmetic, civil government, elements of algebra, essays and orations. Second year—Rhetoric, elocution, universal history, word analysis, political economy, mental philosophy, moral philosophy, higher algebra, geometry, essays and orations, Latin and Greek. Third year—Astronomy, chemistry, botany, geology, zoölogy, methods of teaching, trigonometry, navigation and surveying, essays and orations, Latin, Greek.

EXPENSES.

Preparatory department, per term	$ 9 00
High School " " "	15 00
Contingent " "	1 00
Instrumental music, per lesson	50
Use of instrument, per month	50
Portraiture in crayon, per scholar	10 00

Vocal Music free.
Good board from $2 to $3 per week.
Tuition must be paid in advance.

Students pay tuition from time of entrance to close of term unless special arrangements are made.

No "family tickets" are issued.

No student's time will be counted on that of another.

No deduction for absence, unless caused by protracted sickness.

Departments.—Olney Institute is divided into four departments; Preparatory, High School, Musical and Art.

Preparatory.—The aim in this department is to give the student a good common school education, and to lay well the foundation for a more advanced course.

High School.—This department embraces a thorough English, mathematical and scientific course.

The following is the announcement of Prof. Ford for the forthcoming school year:

The fourth scholastic year of this institution will begin September 19, 1888, and continue nine months. Preparations have been made to accommodate a large attendance next year.

Miss Jennie Baker, of Danville, Mo., has been employed as teacher of English language and literature. Miss Baker is a regular graduate of the Danville Academy, receiving the degree of Mistress of Arts. She has taught successfully in the St. Louis public schools and in St. Charles' College.

Dr. W. L. Northcutt has consented to deliver lectures on special subjects in physiology and hygiene. His knowledge and experience in his profession eminently qualify him for this important feature of the work.

Mr. George Thomas will assist in the mathematical department during the second term.

Mr. Walter Barbee will have charge of the department of vocal music. He is a very successful teacher and has a wide reputation as such.

Miss Mattie E. Smiley will give lessons in instrumental music. She has received instructions from one of the best graduates of the St. Louis Musical Conservatory, and comes very highly recommended.

Mr. Robert Stephenson will conduct the art department. His work speaks for itself.

Miss Margie Connell will have charge of the preparatory department. She is not a stranger, but a tried and faithful teacher. Her work in the school last year was highly satisfactory to all concerned.

Olney Institute has a well-selected library containing nearly one hundred volumes.

OWEN,

Or Owen Station, is situated on the St. Louis & Hannibal (Short Line) Railway, four miles southeast of Moscow. It was laid out and platted in January, 1884, on lands owned by James W. Owen and S. P. Hill, and named in honor of the former. Madison Wommack opened the first store at this place, and in February, 1884, he sold it to Capt. Martin V. Moseley, who still continues in the business, it being the only store there. Mr. Moseley is also the postmaster.

SILEX,

A village containing nearly 300 inhabitants, is situated on the St. Louis & Keokuk Railroad, twelve miles northwest of Troy. In 1880 George P. Smith was engaged in the mercantile business at a point called Cave City, just beyond the rock-cut north of where Silex now stands, and when the railroad was completed to the site of Silex he moved his stock of goods there and opened the first store in the town. Mr. Smith continued in business and boarded the railroad hands until 1882, and was then succeeded by L. C. Kimbler, who continued in business until March, 1885, when his property was destroyed by fire. He received $2,000 insurance and afterward rebuilt. The town was laid out and platted in 1882, by Portus B. Weare.

The second store in Silex was opened by the Jameson Bros., in a building which stood upon stilt legs, as it were, but in the fall of 1882 they built and moved into another building. This was all of the town up to 1884, when the Moseley Hotel was begun. This hotel is a very large, three and a half story frame building, with business rooms on the first floor, and hotel rooms above. The erection of this hotel seemed to give an impetus to the further building of the town, and in the fall of 1885 the business directory was as follows: General merchandise, Porter & Crider; drugs, J. T. Henry & Co.; hardware, F. B. Martin, Mudd & Gift; hotel, Andrew Teague; boarding-house, Frank Dyer; livery, Frank Dyer; lumber, Porter & Crider; saloon, T. J. Mattingly; builder and contractor, W. S. Henry; saw mill, W. C. Freeman; jewelry, S. E. Cruzen; general merchandise, W. D. Jameson & Co.; millinery and dressmaking, Miss S. E. Hudson; wagon and blacksmith shop, J. N. Mudd; physician, Dr. Slaughter.

Since then the business of Silex has undergone some changes. At the present writing, Porter & Crider occupy four business rooms on the first floor of the Moseley Hotel building, with their immense stock of general merchandise. Judge H. T. Mudd &

Son keep a general store, and also a lumber-yard. The other business of the town is as follows: Hardware, J. S. Donaldson; grocery, J. B. Henry; furniture and undertaking goods, W. S. Henry; drugs, Dr. G. P. Smiley; grocery and restaurant, L. C. Kimbler; blacksmithing, H. W. King; harness and shoemaker, Samuel Wirz; hotel, T. J. Mattingly; millinery, Miss Bettie Hudson; agricultural implements, J. E. Cummins; livery, Walker & Hall; hardware and blacksmithing, J. N. Mudd; grain dealers, H. T. Mudd & Son, and J. Overstreet; postmaster, L. C. Kimbler; corn mill, T. B. Duncan; wool-carding mill, Gus Elder. On the railroad stands a neat and convenient passenger and freight depot, the water-tank and a large grain warehouse. There is also one church (Baptist) and a public schoolhouse. Silex is situated on a beautiful, level site in the valley of the Cuivre, about half a mile from the big iron bridge on the road leading to Millwood and Olney. It is the principal outlet for a large tract of good agricultural lands, especially in the western part of the county, and consequently will remain a permanent business place, and improve with the country around it.

STERLING.

Sterling is a landing on the west bank of the Mississippi River. It was laid off November 9, 1836, on a Spanish grant of 800 arpents, confirmed by Congress to Louis Brazeau, being Survey 1679, Township 50 north, Range 3 east, on lands of Francis Withington and Joseph Cochran. The plat was acknowledged before Lawrence B. Sitton, justice of the peace. Like the other landing on the river in Lincoln County, Sterling has become, since the building of the railroads, a place only in name.

TROY.

Troy, the county seat of Lincoln County, is situated on the St. Louis & Hannibal (Short Line) Railway, 68.4 miles south from Hannibal, and fifty-seven miles northwest from St. Louis. It lies one mile north and the same distance west of the southeast corner of Township 49 north, Range 1 west. It was surveyed and laid out September 16, 1819, by Deacon Joseph Cottle, Lee F. T. Cottle and Zadock Woods, the original proprietors.

The survey was made on an angle of thirty-one degrees west of North Main Street, on which nearly all the business of the town is located. Main and Monroe Streets were surveyed sixty feet wide, those running parallel with Main fifty, and the cross streets thirty-three feet wide. It is hard to conceive why such intelligent men as the original proprietors of Troy should lay out a town, prospectively, as they did, for the county seat, with such narrow streets, the cross streets (running north fifty-nine degrees east) being less in width than ordinary country highways. The insufficient width of the streets detracts very much from the appearance of the town. It might have been made much more attractive had the streets been given sufficient width. The original town contained 200 lots. The spring on the west side of Main Street and a small tract of ground surrounding it were donated to the public when the town was laid out by Joseph Cottle and Azubah, his wife.

Additions to Troy.—In October, 1825, J. N. Robbins, E. Collard, J. Ruland and Samuel Wells laid out an addition to Troy, adjoining the original town to the westward, and lying between Boone and Collier Streets. It appears on the map of Troy in the county atlas as a part of Woods' addition. Collier's addition, adjoining the latter on the northward, was laid out in 1837 by George Collier, the original proprietor. It was surveyed by John M. Hopkins. The block where the jail stands is the southeast corner block of this addition. The schoolhouse is also on this addition. Brown's addition was laid out on February 29, 1872, by James D. Brown and wife. It contains lots numbered 401 to 424, inclusive, all being 90x100 feet in size except Nos. 401 and 402, which are 100 feet square. It lies on the right hand of the street leading to the railroad depot. Perkins' addition, in the extreme western part of Troy, was laid out in April, 1875, by Walton Perkins. Avery's addition, adjoining the original plat to the eastward, was laid out in May, 1882, by Samuel W. Avery. Woolfolk's addition, joining Avery's on the east, was laid out in November, 1881, by Shapleigh R. Woolfolk. It was surveyed by John F. Wilson, county surveyor. Bonfils' addition, adjoining the original plat on the south, was laid out in June, 1882, by E. N. Bonfils. Some other tracts have been platted and added to the original town.

The first house in Troy was a log cabin, erected about the year 1801 by Deacon Joseph Cottle. It stood a short distance south of the public spring. Soon thereafter a corn mill, operated by horse-power, was erected by Mr. Cottle near his residence, it being on the property now occupied by Mrs. Sedlacek. Afterward Col. David Bailey erected a distillery on the spring branch at the southeast corner of the lot occupied by the fine residence of Henry Havercamp. He also erected a horse-power corn mill on the same lot, the latter within the inclosed yard just east of Mr. Havercamp's house, and between the distillery and the street. Zadock Woods erected a double log house (on the present burnt district) just in front of the dwelling house on the lot known as the Miller or Nichols property, and about thirty-five yards north of the spring. It was in this house where he kept the first tavern in the place, and where the officers first met and organized the county of Lincoln.

Woods' Fort.—This fort, of which mention is made elsewhere in this work, in connection with the War of 1812–15, consisted of a stockade made of strong oak timbers, set in the ground and extending perpendicularly a sufficient height above to afford protection from the Indians. In the stockade thus constructed, port-holes were made, through which the brave pioneers and soldiers could fire when attacked. The line of the stockade extended from a point near the southeast corner of the present spring park, being the corner of the brick building now standing on Lot 166 (according to the original plat of Troy), and extended up what is now Main Street to a point about fifteen feet south of the brick block owned by Mr. Buchanan and now occupied by T. W. Simonds with a grocery store; thence westerly and parallel with the south wall of the said brick block to the Miller or Nichols property; thence in a southerly direction, passing in front of the Methodist Church, and extending far enough to inclose Joseph Cottle's house; and thence in an easterly direction to the place of beginning. Thus it will be seen that the stockade inclosed the spring, the residence of Joseph Cottle, and the residence and tavern of Zadock Woods. Small block-houses stood on each corner of the stockade, and a larger one stood in the center of the inclosure near the spring.

Several cabins were built within the stockade for the occupancy of the early settlers who were compelled to take refuge therein during the war. This was the most extensive fort erected in the territory now included in Lincoln County. Capt. Callaway, Jonathan Riggs and a son of the famous Daniel Boone were among the officers stationed in this fort during the war, Capt. Callaway being mostly in command. Lieut. Zachariah Taylor (afterward President Taylor) was also in this fort with his command for a time during the war. At that time all that part of Troy west of the fort had been recently cleared and was under cultivation. While some worked in the fields others stood guard. "The boys would watch for the gates to be opened and would then slip out to get slippery-elm bark to appease the cravings of hunger." Quite frequently during the War of 1812-15 the settlers in this fort were in a continual state of siege. Farming was almost entirely abandoned, thus making provisions very scarce, and the inmates of the fort suffered much with hunger. These facts pertaining to the fort have been mostly obtained from John S. Null, who was with his father's family in the fort.

After the war closed and the fort was no longer needed for protection, it was abandoned for that purpose, but some of the cabins continued to be occupied for some years thereafter. Walton Perkins, who published some reminiscences a few years ago said with reference to the time that he settled with his parents near Troy, in 1818, that "there were quite a number of cabins around the spring lot—mostly grog-shops. J. R. Robbins was the only merchant and Zadock Woods kept hotel. People came here to mill from all parts of the county. Us boys were delighted at an opportunity to go to Mr. Cottle's mill. Often the patrons would give us a quarter to put our horse in and grind their grist—and a quarter was then considered no small amount of money."

In 1819 Woods' Fort was still standing, or at least portions of it, and Mr. Robbins kept the only store in Troy. Opposite this store, across Main Street, was a blacksmith shop. At the December term of the circuit court, in 1819, Benjamin Cottle was licensed "to keep a tavern in the town of Troy for twelve months," the fee being $10. From this time forward until 1829, when Troy became the permanent seat of justice of Lincoln County, it remained a rather insignificant trading point for the pioneer settlers. Having secured the county seat it then became a place of central importance to the people of the county, but on account of its being so far inland from that great line of transportation—the Mississippi River—it continued to grow slowly.

In 1830 Troy contained two general stores, kept respectively by J. N. Robbins (the first merchant of the place) and Emanuel Block; two hatter's shops, kept respectively by Perry G. Burrows and B. G. Martin; two tailor shops, kept respectively by John S. Besser and Jordan S. Sallee; and two "dram-shops," as they were called in those days, kept by Philander Powers and Thomas Park. Andrew Monroe, the noted and highly respected pioneer Methodist preacher, kept a hotel in the brick building on Main Street, at the southeast corner of the spring lot. There were also two blacksmith shops, kept by John Goodrich and William Howdeshell. Horace B. Wing, father of Frederick Wing, now living near Moscow, then owned and managed the tannery, which had been previously established on the spring branch, on the east side of the street, and nearly opposite the present Christian Church edifice. He also manufactured boots and shoes in connection with the tannery business, and did an extensive business in both lines. The hats then manufactured in Troy were peddled and sold to the southward, nearly down to the Arkansas line. The Bailey corn mill and distillery before mentioned were then managed by John B. Stone, but neither of them did much business, and were discontinued soon thereafter. The Presbyterians and Christians both had church organizations at that time, but no church buildings. They worshiped in the courthouse.

In 1840 Troy contained two general stores, kept, respectively, by Block Bros. (Emanuel and Eleazer) and Snethen & Wells. About this time, and some years later, Walton Perkins kept the hotel formerly kept by Rev. Andrew Monroe, and in 1848 or 1849 he engaged in mercantile business with Frederick Wing. The town had grown a little during the decade of the thirties, so that there was some more business in it in 1840 than in 1830.

About this period (1840) all religious denominations in Troy worshiped in the courthouse, and all worshiped together. They were not so allied to sectarianism as they have been latterly. It is said that nearly as many people attended divine services in Troy at that time as at present. If this be true, the whole population, or nearly the whole, must have attended. There is no doubt that a larger percentage of the people attended divine services in the pioneer days than at present.

The following is a list of current prices at Troy in 1840: Pork, $2 per hundred; milch cows, $6 to $8; horses, $30 to $50; butter, 6 cents per pound; corn, 1 "bit" per bushel; calico, 35 to 40 cents per yard; coffee, 30 cents per pound; axes, 25 cents; coarse boots, $5. An old citizen, who gave these prices through the medium of the Troy *Herald* some years ago, said that at that time "Troy contained five or six saloons, no city council, and only a piece of a jail." Troy then had a tri-weekly mail from St. Louis. It is also said that Troy had many pretty girls in those days. It has more now, and is noted for the beauty of its women.

The following facts pertaining to Troy in 1855 are taken from a copy of the Lincoln *Gazette*, Vol. 1, No. 31, of that year. The paper contained a notice of the public exercises of the Lincoln Academy, to be held at the Presbyterian Church, February 14 and 15, 1855. The faculty of the academy was then as follows: C. G. Jones, principal; Miss Sarah Kittredge, preceptress; Miss C. C. Adams, teacher of music; Sallie Bird, assistant preceptress; James E. Hutton, assistant teacher. The paper also contained the business cards of the following parties: Merchants, Britton, Woolfolk & Co., D. W. Smiley, Snethen & Wells and Kouns & Murray; lawyers, William Porter, J. L. Blannerhassett and W. H. Merriwether; physicians, Drs. Wells & Johnson, Dr. Shadburn and C. M. Edson. The paper also stated that the North Missouri Railroad (now the Wabash) was nearly finished from St. Louis to St. Charles.

The following is a list of advertisements which appeared in a Troy newspaper in 1860: Troy Seminary, G. G. Jones, principal; Miss Mary J. Strong, preceptress; Miss Blanche Hughes, teacher of primary; Miss Emily M. Hudson, teacher of music; board of trustees, J. S. Salle, president; William Young, secretary; Fred. Wing, treasurer; C. W. Parker, Hon. T. R. Cornick, J. M. Heady, Col. Thomas G. Hutt, John W. Sydnor, Gen. David Stewart, S. R. Woolfolk, Rev. E. P. Noel, Gen. E. J. Peers. Merchants, D. C. Russell, stoves and tinware; Britton, Woolfolk & Co., general merchandise; Vance & Hawey, forwarding and commission merchants at Cap-au-Gris; Moritz & Love, cabinet shop; William Mohr & Co., carriage and wagon shop; Isaac Springston & William Crouch, carpenter, blacksmith and wagon shop; physicians, H. E. Jones, Douglas Morrison; dentist, A. E. Noel. It must not be inferred that this constituted all the business of Troy in 1860, but that which was advertised only. Like nearly all other Missouri towns, the business of Troy was much depressed during the period of the Civil War. However, Troy was not destroyed, neither was it sacked by either of the contending armies. It recovered from the depressing effects of that period as soon as could be expected.

The following is a list of the business houses of Troy in 1873, as published in the *Herald* of July 9, of that year: Cake & Rogers' Tannery. This extensive manufactory had been established about forty years before, by Horace B. Wing, and was in 1873 the most extensive business in the town, and gave employment to the greatest number of men. In connection with it the proprietors had a large boot and shoe, saddle and harness manufactory. Few towns in the west could boast of better hotels. The Laclede was built in the summer of 1870 by Thornhill & Buswell, its proprietors, at a cost of from $8,000 to $10,000. In 1872 a large addition was erected, making it one of the most complete and convenient of modern hotels, a good bar and billiard room being in the basement story. The Planters' House, formerly a frame building, was replaced, early in the seventies, by its proprietor, J. F. Brown, with a large three-story brick. A bar was kept in the basement story. and the accommodations throughout were first class. Farmers' and Mechanics' Bank, Walton Perkins, president; J. R. Knox, vice-president; E. N. Bonfils, cashier; Parker, Crews & Co., with a large stock of merchandise in a commodious brick building. A very old house, the firm name of which had been frequently changed—Norton,

Harlan & Norton, in a large brick building on the east side of Main Street; Crump & Wing, with a fair stock of goods; Joseph Hart, with an immense stock in a large brick building on the east side of Main Street, and Walter S. Cooper. These houses under head of merchandise, kept a general stock of dry goods, groceries, etc. There were three stores which kept groceries principally, F. S. Sweeney, G. W. Mohr and M. T. Britton. The latter had a bakery connected with his establishment; J. P. Lynott, with one of the largest stores of hardware outside of the cities; Henry & Bro., with a large store and manufactory of boots and shoes; F. M. Brickey with a boot and shoe shop; Thomas W. Withrow, successor to his father in saddles, harness, trunks, etc., who established the business many years before in a little frame building; L. Wolfgram, with an extensive stock of jewelry and watches; Woolfolk & Co., and Dr. S. T. East, drugs; Miss S. J. Tentem and Mrs. M. Sadlacek, millinery; Mrs. Ogden and Mrs. Ward, dressmaking; H. W. Kemper, a very large furniture store; F. W. Harbaum, wagon factory; William Swan, A. Kuhne and T. H. Stephens, blacksmith shops.

The following is a business directory of Troy, including the school and professions, on the 1st day of January, 1882: High and graded school, Prof. R. B. D. Simonson, principal; Miss Mary Buchanan, assistant principal; Mrs. W. S. Hutt, teacher of intermediate department; Miss Pinkie Woolfolk, second primary; Mrs. Walter McKay, first primary; Farmers' and Mechanics' Bank, Walton Perkins, president; H. W. Perkins, cashier; dry goods, W. L. Sturgeon, James A. Jackson, Charles M. Hamilton, Bragg Bros. & Co. and Joseph Hart; drugs, Dr. R. L. Robinson, J. J. and J. H. Alexander; hardware, Russell & Miller and E. N. Bonfils; groceries, J. W. Pilcher, F. S. Pilcher, F. S. Sweeney, Mrs. Ida Hellriegel, George Mohr and John A. Trail; jewelry, Henry Havercamp; furniture and coffins, H. W. Kemper; wagon manufactory, F. W. Harbaum; saddles and harness, Thomas W. Withrow and M. Sadlacek; millinery, Mrs. M. Sadlacek, Mrs. J. S. Thornhill and Mrs. T. M. Stephens; tailor shops, George O. Brickey, John Sykora and Jordan S. Sallee; boot and shoe store, Henry & Brother; hotels, "Laclede," by O. F. Buswell, "Planters' House," by J. S.

Shannon, "College Street Boarding House," by Capt. William Coose; livery, Birkhead & Son, proprietors of the Laclede Livery Stable, and Kabler & Kennedy, proprietors of Transfer Stable; lumber-yards, Baxter Crawford and S. R. Woolfolk; Troy Mills, William M. Norton; blacksmith shops, Thomas M. Stephens, Augustus Kuhne and William Swann; meat markets, Avery & Stratton and Capt. William Coose; saloons, R. A. Trail and John Worsham; cigar manufactory, J. J. Cheeley; barbers, I. W. Clark and Frank Wulf; physicians, M. H. McFarland, D. W. Tice, A. H. Chenowerth, James A. Ward, R. L. Robinson and T. N. Bragg; dentist, E. L. Sydnor; lawyers, R. H. Norton, Charles Martin, Nat. C. Dryden, A. V. McKee, O. H. Avery, G. T. Dunn, George W. Colbert, Howard S. Parker, Jeptha Wells, James M. McLellan, Josiah Creech, R. D. Walton and J. B. Allen; ministers, Elder D. M. Grandfield, of the Christian Church, Rev. C. R. Dudley, Presbyterian, Rev. J. N. B. Helper, Methodist Episcopal South, Rev. C. W. Carter, colored Methodist, Rev. Benjamin Guthrie, colored Baptist; wool-carding, Lewis Vertrees; ice and dairy, E. G. Hammond; brick-yard, Hammond & Krebs; newspapers, *Herald*, by W. T. Thurmond, and *Free Press*, by Ward & Childers.

The business of Troy, at the present writing, July, 1888, consists of the following: Dry goods and clothing, James A. Jackson; general merchandise, Joseph Hart; groceries, John E. Worsham, Augustus Kuhne, George W. Mohr, J. W. Ruenzi, F. W. Simonds, John W. Pilcher, F. S. Sweeney, George B. Kempf, Nicholas Ebert; drugs, Hutchison & Perkins, Dr. R. L. Robinson, Avery Bros.; hardware, Stanza & Carter, W. R. Holmes, D. C. Russell & Son; harness and saddles, Thomas W. Withrow, J. J. Hechler; millinery, Mrs. Mary Sedlacek, Miss Delia Cottle and Miss Emma Duey; furniture and coffins, H. W. Kemper; jewelry, Henry Havercamp; tailor-shops, John Sykora, M. Kaphan; cigar manufactory, Cheeley & Trail; hotel, Colbert Hotel, by Capt. William Colbert; restaurants, Fred. Meyer, Frank Wulf, Thomas U. Wright; boots and shoes, Henry Bros.; barber-shops, I. W. Clark, Frank Wulf; meat-shop, Robert Schuchmann; blacksmith and manufacturer of wagons, plows, etc., F. W. Harbaum; blacksmith-shops, A. B. Ellis, William H. Swann; transfer and feed stable, Kabler & Shumate; livery stable, Duff & Brown; Troy Flouring mills, Elias Norton; lumber-yards, Thomas M. Fisher, D. Duback & Co.; grain dealers, Hart & Son, Jackson & Barley; dealer and shipper of live stock, Samuel W. Avery. In addition to the foregoing there are two parties who supply the town with ice, and two that supply it with milk. There are also several boarding-houses in the town.

The physicians of Troy are James A. Ward, D. W. Tice, C. D. Avery, T. N. Bragg and R. L. Robinson. The dentists are E. Sydnor and C. W. Knox.

The resident ministers are C. Van Oostenbrugge, of the Presbyterian Church, Dennis Grandfield and J. W. Bouvee, of the Christian Church, O. B. Holliday, of the Methodist Church South, and Max Schroedel, of the Evangelical Zion's Church; also J. W. Cravens and Henry Bragg, of the colored Methodist Church.

The newspapers are the Troy *Herald*, by W. T. Thurmond, and the *Free Press*, by Boulton & Townsend.

The Farmers' and Mechanics' Savings Bank of Troy was organized May 21, 1873, through the efforts of Walton Perkins, William Colbert, J. W. Welch, John R. Knox, F. C. Cake, E. N. Bonfils, John R. Britton, Judge C. W. Martin, W. M. Norton, M. R. Watts and Douglas Wyatt. At a meeting of the stockholders, the following officers were chosen: Walton Perkins, president; John R. Knox, vice-president; E. N. Bonfils, cashier; R. H. Norton, attorney. Directors—Walton Perkins, William Colbert, James W. Welch, J. R. Knox, F. C. Cake, E. N. Bonfils, John R. Britton, Charles W. Martin, W. M. Norton, M. R. Watts and Douglas Wyatt. On the death of Walton Perkins, in 1885, William Colbert was chosen president. After serving as cashier for a few months, E. N. Bonfils was succeeded by H. W. Perkins, son of the first president of the bank. The names of the present officers are as follows: William Colbert, president; Charles Martin, vice-president; H. W. Perkins, cashier; R. H. Norton, attorney. Board of directors—William Colbert, Charles Martin, R. H. Norton, Elias Norton, J. W. Welch, J. M. McLellan and H. W. Perkins.

The bank has a paid-up capital of $10,000, backed by $70,000 of subscribed capital. It is a fact worthy of note, that during the fourteen years in which the present cashier has conducted the business of the bank, not a dollar has been lost by it. This is a very useful and necessary institution to the business interests of Lincoln County.

Incorporation of Troy.—At the November term, 1825, of the county court, Troy was incorporated upon petition of its citizens, and Joseph Cottle, John Chandler, Elisha Perkins, Edward J. Peers and Thomas Dozier, were appointed trustees of the corporation. The corporate limits were made to include the original plat, and the plat known as Woods' addition. The town was again incorporated in May, 1870, upon a petition of one hundred of its citizens. The order of incorporation provided that the town should be incorporated under the name and style of " The Inhabitants of the Town of Troy," and to have all rights and privileges of the bodies politic and corporate, except the right to purchase and own burial grounds and cemeteries. The corporate limits were described as follows: " Beginning at the center of the public spring, thence due north, south, east and west, one thousand yards in each direction to points; thence to form a square upon said points, of two thousand yards upon each side thereof." The court then appointed Charles W. Parker, Eugene N. Bonfils, William Frazier, John McDonald and James M. McLellan, a board of trustees for the town thus incorporated.

Afterward, on the 15th day of May, 1877, a petition signed by E. N. Bonfils, George W. Colbert, A. B. Ellis and 110 others, was presented to the Court, asking for the incorporation of the town of Troy, with the following metes and bounds: "Beginning at the center of the public spring in said town of Troy; thence due north, south, east and west six hundred yards in each direction from said spring to points; thence to form a square upon said points of twelve hundred upon each side of said square." After considering this petition, the Court made the following entry upon the record of its proceedings: " And it appearing to the satisfaction of the Court that two-thirds of the taxable inhabitants of said town have signed said petition, and that the prayer of the petitioners is reasonable, and that no tracts of land containing forty acres or more, which are needed exclusively for agricultural or grazing purposes, and which have not been laid out or platted as town property, are included within the proposed corporate limits, it is therefore considered, adjudged and decreed by the court that the said inhabitants within the metes and bounds aforesaid, shall be a body corporate and politic, by the name and style of 'The Inhabitants of the Town of Troy,' and by that name they and their successors shall be known in law, have perpetual succession unless disincorporated, sue and be sued, plead and be impleaded, defend and be defended in all courts, and in all actions, pleas and matters whatever; may grant, purchase, hold and receive property, real and personal, within said town, and burial grounds and cemeteries outside of said town, and may lease, sell and dispose of the same for the benefit of the town, and may have a common seal, and make, break and alter the same at pleasure, and in general may have and enjoy all and singular, the rights and provisions specified and contained in an act of the General Assembly approved March 30, 1874, and Chapter 41, general statutes of Missouri, 1865. And it further appearing to the satisfaction of the Court that the number of inhabitants of said town of Troy is less than 2,500, the Court doth thereupon appoint George W. Colbert, Oscar T. Buswell, Charles Martin, Jr., W. W. Birkhead and John M. Ellis, a board of trustees in and for the incorporation of the town of Troy.

In 1881 Troy was incorporated as a city of the fourth class and some changes in the boundary lines were made so as to exclude certain farming lands from within the corporate limits. The change in the boundary line of the city was proposed in July, 1881, and afterward submitted to a vote of the electors, who were almost unanimously in favor of making the change. The present officers of the city of Troy are George W. Colbert, mayor; H. F. Childers, clerk; Preston Creech, marshal; Jesse Swinney, collector; J. A. Jackson, treasurer. Board of aldermen, J. R. Witt, D. C. Russell, R. A. Trail and W. H. Hutchison.

The population of Troy in 1880, as given in the United States Census, was 839. It will probably reach about 1,200 at this time (1888).

Societies.—Troy Lodge No. 34, A. F. & A. M., was chartered October 7, 1841, and is consequently the oldest lodge in Troy. The first meeting under the charter was held October 13, 1841, at which time Brothers Thomas G. Hutt, R. H. Woolfolk and James M. Zimmerman were appointed a committee to make arrangements for the installation of the officers. Emanuel Block was appointed a committee on music, and E. J. Peers was appointed marshal for the occasion. The installation took place at the courthouse on the 3d day of November following, when the first officers were installed as follows: Francis Parker, W. M.; Eleazer Block, S. W.; E. J. Peers, J. W.; Emanuel Block, Treas.; J. P. Fuller, Sec'y; William Porter, S. D.; J. Davis, J. D.; L. Robinson, Tyler. There were twenty-three members of the lodge, and thirteen visiting brothers present, and a large number of ladies and gentlemen in attendance at the installation services. Prominent among those present were James H. Britton, Philander Draper, A. H. Martin, A. S. Buchanan, Col. Thomas G. Hutt and John W. Sydnor. Of the original members of the lodge A. S. Buchanan, James H. Britton, J. W. Sydnor and Col. Thomas G. Hutt are the only ones now living. Philander Draper was the first man made a Mason under the charter of this lodge. Many of the most prominent men of Lincoln County were initiated and became members of the Masonic fraternity in this lodge. Many, after becoming members, moved away and were demitted, and others have departed to join the lodge of the Grand Master of the Universe. The membership of the lodge at present is about forty-five, and the officers are Jesse J. Shaw, W. M.; R. H. Norton, S. W.; John E. Richards, J. W.; J. A. Jackson, Treas.; T. H. Harris, Secy.; George W. Colbert, S. D.; G. T. Dunn, J. D.; and D. C. Russell, Tyler.

The walls of the Masonic Hall building were erected about the year 1837, by Col. David Bailey, and the building stood in an unfinished condition until 1851 or 1852, and was then sold to the trustees of the Universalist Church, and the trustees of the Masonic lodge. These societies finished the building and owned it in partnership; the Masons occupying the upper story and the church the lower. Some time between 1855 and 1860 the church became disorganized, and then followed some trouble about the ownership of the building, and about the payment of the taxes thereon. Finally the property was sold for taxes, the Masonic lodge becoming the purchaser. The building is now a substantial two-story brick structure, and the lower story is used as a store-room. It stands at the east side of Main Street, on Lot 114, original plat of Troy. Prior to the completion of this building the lodge held its meetings in the courthouse. The money for the purchase of the building in its unfinished state was raised by subscription, some parties contributing on behalf of the church, some on the part of the lodge, and some for both.

Troy Royal Arch Chapter No. 85, was chartered October 7, 1875, just thirty-four years to the day after Troy Lodge No. 34, A. F. & A. M., was chartered. The dispensation, however, had been granted on the 13th day of the previous March. The first principal officers were J. J. McElwee, High Priest; Marcus H. McFarland, King; J. P. Blanton, Scribe. The chapter has about thirty-five members at this writing, and the officers are Thomas H. Harris, High Priest; J. M. Wilson, King; W. A. Woodson, Scribe; George W. Colbert, Captain of Host; J. H. Alexander, P. S.; J. J. Shaw, R. A. C. The chapter, by paying half of the expense of repairs, is entitled to the use of the Masonic hall, where it holds its meetings.

Troy Lodge No. 68, I. O. O. F., was instituted in 1853, upon the application to the Grand Lodge of the State, made by Gen. John B. Henderson and four other members of Louisiana Lodge No. 28. The first meeting of Troy Lodge was held November 14, 1853. John W. Sydnor was the first Noble Grand, and S. R. Woolfolk first Secretary. After this lodge was fully in working order and a fair membership was secured, an exodus of its members to California took place, whereby it became so reduced in numbers that it was compelled to suspend operations, the date of its last meeting being December 29, 1857. The Noble Grand at that time was A. V. McKee, and the Secretary, Lewis C. Wright. The latter was the Noble Grand-elect, but was not installed on account of the suspension of the lodge. Troy Lodge No. 68, of this order, was reinstated upon the petition of Lewis C. Wright, A. V. McKee, Dr. James A. Ward, Thomas M. Carter and Samuel Shirkey, and a new charter was granted, bearing date of June 10, 1873. The lodge was reorganized by J. W. Pilcher, P. G. of Lodge No. 5 in St. Louis. The present officers of Troy Lodge are John D. Carter, N. G.; William A. Jackson, V. G.;

R. P. Boulton, Secretary; Samuel E. Kribs, Permanent Secretary, and Lewis C. Wright, Treasurer. The present membership of the lodge is forty-five. They rent a hall, where they meet, in the second story of the Withrow Building. The lodge is out of debt, and has money out on interest.

Troy Lodge No. 109, A. O. U. W., was chartered February 20, 1879, with twenty original members, including the following first officers, viz.: B. W. Wheeler, M. W.; Rev. W. B. Y. Wilkie, P. M. W.; Josiah Creech, G. F.; George S. Hutt, Overseer; Newell Ackerman, Recorder; John A. Knott, Financier; H. W. Perkins, Receiver; E. G. Hammond, Guide; William Coose, I. W.; Jacob Metz, O. W.; Dr. William S. Hutt, Med. Ex. This society does not own a hall, but rents one in which to meet. Of the foregoing officers, two, Newell Ackerman and Dr. William S. Hutt, have since died. The present officers of the lodge are James Linahan, M. W.; L. J. Henry, P. M. W.; George S. Hutt, Foreman; William Coose, Overseer; B. W. Wheeler, Recorder; George W. Mohr, F.; H. W. Perkins, Receiver; Stephen Cottle, Guide; William A. Ellis, I. W.; Charles Shumate, O. W.; Drs. D. W. Tice and Charles D. Avery, Medical Examiners. The present membership of this lodge is forty-nine.

Maj. A. Bartlett Post No. 289, Grand Army of the Republic, was chartered October 13, 1886, with the following charter members, viz.: John W. Moore, J. W. East, L. Carter, J. Altman, M. Dalton, William Colbert, L. B. Sitton, F. A. Colbert, N. Dunard, J. J. Mallan, D. H. Cannon, James Murphy, W. B. Seay, J. W. Hunter, P. Herbel, L. Howell, F. Wirshing, W. P. Gladson, Joe Page, W. J. Cook, F. M. Howell and F. M. Campbell. At this writing the post has forty members.

This order has no parallel. It is composed of men who lived at a certain time, were soldiers of a certain army, and who have been honorably discharged therefrom. As a class the survivors of that army are on the downhill side of life, rapidly approaching the end of the journey; consequently the society cannot be perpetuated like those that have existed for ages, and their memberships passed away with the succeeding generations, and whose future members are yet unborn. The G. A. R. must pass away entire; it cannot long survive the present century. Those young men who, at the age of twenty-one, entered the army when first organized to put down the Rebellion, will, at the close of this century, if living, be sixty years of age, while the average age of soldiers, who will then survive, will be between sixty-five and seventy years. Thus it is demonstrated that the G. A. R. cannot long survive the present century.

The Temperance Benevolent Association, located in Troy, Lincoln County, was incorporated on the 27th day of September, 1884. The incorporators were Joseph B. Allen, Thomas H. Harris and A. H. Chenoweth, all residents of Troy. The object of this association is to promote the cause of temperance by restricting and prohibiting the sale of intoxicating liquors, and to provide for its members in case of death or disability, upon the cheapest and most equitable plan of assessments, where the temperate take no part of the risk of the intemperate. These objects are proposed to be obtained by organizing State associations and local aid societies, which by moral and instructive lectures, and by teaching the principles of the association, to promote the moral and social advancement of the members, and encourage them in the performance of the duties of good citizenship, and which will enable them to secure, by organized efforts, the fullest and most preferable considerations for themselves and their interest at the hands of the public generally.

To promote the cause of temperance by uniting all opposition to the licensed sale of all intoxicants as a beverage.

To encourage each other in business, and to assist each other in obtaining employment.

To further promote, incidentally, benevolence and charity, by establishing a charity fund for the temporary relief of indigent or suffering members and their families, and to provide for the aid and relief of the families, widows or orphans, or other dependents of their deceased members, and for assisting such of its members as may be sick or disabled, from the proceeds of assessments as authorized and provided by law.

Mr. Allen, one of the incorporators, devised and formulated the plan, with the view of blending a contract of a pecuniary and moral character, so as to make it to the financial interest of all who unite with the association to comply with the rules, and not to violate their pledge and agreements. His experience in the temperance work had taught him that men would readily agree to be temperate, but were easily led to violate the agreement, but if he was stimulated to keep the vows he had made by a valuable consideration, that he would be less liable to break them. This it is proposed to accomplish by issuing certificates of "benefits," wherein it is agreed they are to become void if the holders are found to use intoxicants as a beverage or to sign a petition for the sale of the same.

The association has made considerable progress, and found favor with the temperance workers of the State. It has been enabled to meet all its obligations, and has the advantage in pushing its work, in that it does not force its workers to pass the hat for means to pay expenses, its beneficiary department having an income sufficient to pay all expenses incurred in the prosecution of its work. The beneficiary department is managed by a board of trustees, consisting of a president, vice-president, secretary and treasurer. The president, secretary and treasurer are elected once in three years. The vice-president is the president of the State Association, elected annually by the State conventions. The constitution provides that all presidents of State Associations, when organized, are to become *ex-officio* members of the board of trustees. The State conventions, to be composed of delegates sent from the local societies, have the power to appoint committees to examine the books and records of the beneficiary department, and make a report of their condition to the members of the convention. The first convention was held in Troy, Mo., November 17, 1886, at which time W. A. Monroe, of Memphis, Mo., was elected president, and D. M. Grandfield, of Troy, Mo., vice-president; Joseph J. Brown, of Monroe City, secretary; C. E. Cummings, of Canton, Mo., treasurer; Thomas H. Harris, of Troy, Mo., assistant treasurer, and George H. Adams, of Piedmont, Mo., chaplain. A State constitution, and constitution and by-laws for local societies, were formulated and adopted.

The Secretary of the board of trustees reported $5,806.19 as collected and disbursed to date, and total membership 4,000. The incorporators of this association, like all various benevolent associations of the State, deemed their plan of issuing certificates of benefits to be within the purview of the law of the State of Missouri, and it was so considered by the court that issued the decree of incorporation, but the commissioner of insurance claimed that their work was a violation of the insurance laws of the State, and brought suit against this association and several others. The Legislature passed a law in 1887 that was so framed that all benevolent asssociations could comply with its requirements. This association immediately arranged their plan so that it would, in every respect, conform to this new law, and thereby, as far as they were concerned, stopped the controversy. They now have a guaranty deposit, as required by law, in interest-bearing bonds, deposited with the commissioner of insurance.

The association makes annual reports to the department, and is licensed to do a life insurance business. Dr. A. H. Chenoweth, the treasurer and medical director, died November 28, 1887. [See biography elsewhere in this work.] His death created a vacancy in the board of trustees, and left them without a medical adviser. Ben. F. Reed, clerk of the circuit court of Lincoln County, was elected treasurer, and Dr. James A. Ward, medical director. Biographical sketches of these gentlemen are given elsewhere in this work.

The association has made considerable progress since it arranged to conform its business to the insurance laws of the State. There is no longer any doubt about its having authority to do business, and that the business is done under the supervision of the insurance department of the State, which gives assurance that it must be conducted in a fair, as well as lawful manner, and that all moneys collected must be applied to the objects for which it is collected. Dr. W. A. Monroe, the president of the State Association, moved to Washington Territory in 1887, at which time he resigned as the president of the association. Mr. D. M. Grandfield, the vice-president, has acted as president, and is a member of the board of trustees. In 1886 Dr. John A. Brooks, president of the Temperance Benefit Union of Kansas City, made application to officers of the Temperance Benevolent Association for membership for members of the Temperance Benefit Union. It was agreed to admit all who could pass a satisfactory medical examination. A number availed themselves of the offer. The business of life insurance is transacted largely through the mails, which adds largely to the income of the postoffice department, and the business of this association, and of the Triple Alliance, also located in Troy, has made the postoffice at Troy a presidential office. The printing is also quite an item, and the amount of work furnished the local printers is considerable, as all this work is done at home.

Casualties.—Like all other towns, Troy has had its usual amount of casualties, the destruction of property by fire, etc., but during the last year it has suffered an extraordinary amount of loss from conflagrations. In January, 1876, an out-house belonging to William Worrick, in the southern part of town, and in which Aunt Minnie Cottle, colored, the oldest person in the county, was sleeping, was consumed by fire. All that was left of the body of the unfortunate woman was a few charred bones. Her age was not definitely known, but was not far from one hundred years. On the 8th day of December, 1885, before daylight, the large three-story frame building, with a basement story under it, the whole containing twenty-two rooms, owned and used at the time by Mrs. Hutt as a boarding-house, was consumed by fire. This house stood on College Street, near the schoolhouse. It was erected in 1867, at a cost of $8,000. At the time of its burning it was insured for $4,000, and the furniture within for $2,000. The boarders lost some property on which there was no insurance.

Troy has suffered great loss by fire within the last year. On September 1, 1887, the Jackson property, consisting of a wooden building, with two business fronts and a dwelling in the rear, located on the west side of Main Street, was consumed by fire. The loss on the building was about $2,500, and the insurance thereon was $1,250. The loss on Holmes' hardware stock in one of the rooms was $2,500, on which there was $1,200 of insurance. The loss of a millinery stock in the other business room was about $200, which was fully insured. The loss of the household goods of Mrs. Brickey, who occupied the dwelling, was total, there being no insurance.

The Laclede Hotel, owned by O. F. Buswell, was burned

down in February, 1888. The loss of property was about $10,000, and the insurance thereon was about $9,000. It stood on the east side of Main Street, opposite the Colbert Hotel.

The following is the *Free Press* account of the last fire in Troy up to this writing, it having occurred June 17, 1888:

Tom C. Thornhill, George Jackson, Vilray Tice and John Ellis were awakened about half past two o'clock Sunday morning, in the front room over T. C. Thornhill & Co.'s, by a dense smoke that came up from the rear of the lower story. They at once began a hasty exit by way of the front windows and the awning to the street. On examination they found the flames had made considerable headway in the rear of the lower story, and the whole store was too full of smoke and heat to make it possible for them to save anything. The alarm was given by shouting fire, discharging firearms and ringing bells. At once a large company gathered, but too late to do more than turn their attention to the work of saving the adjacent buildings. The brick store of Joseph Hart, across the street north, was not in immediate danger, but the frame building of F. S. Sweeney was only about twenty feet away, and without great effort would be ignited by the immense heat. Several dozen buckets were obtained from George Pratt's store, and a brigade began carrying water from the city reservoir in the park. The roof and the north side of Mr. Sweeney's house were kept wet until the flames had consumed the Thornhill house.

The firm of T. C. Thornhill & Co. lost their entire stock of goods and all their store fixtures, amounting to about $11,000, and bearing insurance as follows: In the North American Insurance Company $2,000, and $1,500 in the Phœnix, of London, for which companies O. H. Avery is agent, and $4,000 in companies represented by Josiah Creech. The building was a total loss. It was owned by A. E. and H. W. Bryant, of Hebron, Ind., and insured with O. H. Avery for $2,300.

The firm of T. C. Thornhill & Co., started in business this spring, and by square dealing and low prices had built up an excellent trade. The *Free Press* is glad to say that the probabilities are the same men will put a new stock of goods into another house and resume their business here at no distant day.

Cholera.—When cholera visited this country in 1849, there were a few deaths from it in and about Troy, but they were so isolated that but little alarm was created. In the latter part of June, 1873, the alarm was sounded that cholera was approaching. The council met and appointed a sanitary committee, consisting of James D. Brown, George W. Colbert and John McDonald, and ordered the town marshal to notify all maintainers of nuisances to abate them at once. The Troy *Herald*, in its issue of July 2, announced that "cholera is in our midst," the first case, which was fatal, having been reported June 24, and another one on the 25th. After these deaths a few people left the town. During the week following June 28 two more deaths occurred, and on Monday, July 7, three deaths occurred. The exodus of the population then began in earnest, and in a very short time half the people had left the town. The mortality was unchecked, and during that week eight deaths occurred. On the 15th of July the sanitary committee reported as follows:

"First. That the town has been thoroughly cleansed and disinfected, and that they have caused to be burned upon the streets 200 bushels of stove coal, besides a large amount of wood. They also desire to state that the citizens generally have responded to the orders of the committee in cleaning and disinfecting their premises.

"Second. That there has been thirteen deaths from cholera in the past fifteen days; no deaths within the last four days, and no new cases to report.

"Third. That thirty-four families and a considerable number without families left town, but fortunately, however, but one physician, and his place is now ably filled by Dr. McFarland, of Clarksville. * * We trust and believe that cholera has taken its leave from us.

"JOHN McDONALD,
"G. W. COLBERT, *Committee.*"
"JAMES D. BROWN,

After the date of this report only one death occurred from the fatal disease within the corporate limits. On the 23d of July the sanitary committee made their final report, as follows:

"The town has been thoroughly cleansed of all filth and nuisances, and the general health is better at present than usual for this season. There have been fifteen deaths in the town limits, and five in the near vicinity, from cholera. The committee apprehends no further danger, and is satisfied that those who have fled to the country can return in safety. Many have already done so.

"JOHN McDONALD,
"G. W. COLBERT, } *Committee.*"
"JAMES D. BROWN,

The first death that occurred in the town on this occasion, from cholera, was that of a negro, and the second was that of Samuel Shirkey, the first white man that died. Among others who fell victims to the fatal scourge were Mrs. Mary A. Martin, Miss Josephine Martin, Cyrenius Lay, Mrs. William Frazier, Miss Fannie Carter, a child of Mrs. Arcelia Frazier, a Mr. Rogers, Mrs. Joseph Hart and two children, Mrs. Thomas Sydnor and Mrs. C. Graff.

The Press.—The first newspaper printed and published in Lincoln County was the Troy *Gazette*, established by Ellis & Edrington, in July, 1854. It was the official paper of this, Warren and Montgomery Counties. The first editor was Judge E. N. Bonfils, who was succeeded, after a few weeks' service, by Henry B. Ellis, one of the proprietors. The first number of the second volume appeared with Maj. George W. Huston as editor. In a short time he was succeeded by Mr. Ellis, who again took charge of the editorial department. In January following Ellis & Edrington sold the paper to A. V. McKee and H. W. Perkins. In March following Mr. Perkins sold his interest to Henry A. Bragg, and Mr. McKee continued, as he had been, the editor. June 13, 1856, they changed the name of the paper to the *State Rights Advocate*, and April 16, 1857, sold it to Edmund J. Ellis, by whom it was conducted two or three years. During the presidential campaign of 1860 he published the *Tribune* and Henry B. Ellis the *Independent*. During most of the war period there was no regular paper published in the county.

At the close of the war, Edmund J. Ellis established the *Lin-*

coln County *Herald.* Theodore D. Fisher bought a half-interest, May 31, 1867, and the next year the remaining half. Dr. Joseph A. Mudd established the Troy *Dispatch,* April 8, 1871. The two papers were consolidated June 11, 1873, under the name of the Troy *Herald.* William T. Thurmond, the present proprietor of the *Herald,* purchased Dr. Mudd's interest December 13, 1876, and Mr. Fisher's interest October 23, 1878, and has continued to publish the paper ever since he became its sole proprietor. The Troy *Free Press* was established in July, 1878, by W. J. and J. A. Knott. Early in 1881, the latter sold his interest to C. H. Ward, and in the fall of that year, the former sold his interest to H. F. Childers, who a few months later purchased the interest of Mr. Ward, and became sole proprietor, and sold out entire to George S. Townsend, on January 1, 1888. The *News* was established August 28, 1885, by J. A. Knott and H. M. Cornick. In 1887 Mr. Cornick purchased his partner's interest, and in November of the same year he sold a half interest to R. P. Boulton. On the 3d of February, 1888, the *News* was consolidated with the *Free Press,* Mr. Cornick retiring from the business. The *Free Press* has since been published by Boulton & Townsend, its present proprietors. The *Herald* and *Free Press* are both good county papers, each having a large circulation, and both advocate Democratic principles.

Troy Schools.—On the 8th day of May, 1837, George Collier, of St. Louis, sold and conveyed for the consideration of $1, to Richard H. Woolfolk, David Bailey, Emanuel Block, Horace B. Wing, Valentine J. Peers, Cary K. Duncan and Francis Parker, trustees of Lincoln Academy, Lots 338, 339, 348 and 349, in Collier's addition to Troy, for the express purpose of having an academy erected and maintained thereon. The Lincoln Academy existed for a number of years, and was generally under the supervision of able instructors. The property was sold to C. G. Jones, who, in 1856, erected the present school-building on the old academy grounds. It is a large three-story brick structure, with three rooms and a hall and stairway on the first floor, four schoolrooms on the second floor, and one large room on the third floor. Mr. Jones opened a private school in his new building, had able assistants, and for a series of years following taught an excellent school. In 1867 he conveyed the property to the trustees of the Troy Christian Institute, by which body a school was opened and conducted for a few years. On the 4th day of March, 1874, the property was conveyed to the board of education for School District No. 4, in School Township No. 13, it being the Troy Public School District, and since that time it has been used for the public school.

The teachers employed for the school year of 1888-89 are G. A. Y. Reeds, principal, Mrs. C. S. McKee, Miss Lizzie Hutt, Miss Ella Garrett, Miss Willie Coose and Miss Carrie Alloway. The school commences in September and continues eight months. It is thoroughly graded, and the higher branches, making it equivalent to an academy, are taught. In another part of the town is the colored district school, and the teachers employed for the ensuing year are George T. Neal, principal, and J. W. Cravens, assistant. The Troy school board consists of Josiah Creech, president, George W. Colvert, Levi J. Garrett and W. A. Jackson, the latter being secretary. Pupils from abroad are charged from $2 to $3 tuition per month, but such pupils are not solicited, as there are pupils enough in the district to occupy the rooms, and to constitute a good school.

TRUXTON.

Truxton is situated in the southwest corner of Lincoln County, one mile from the Montgomery line, and three-fourths of a mile from the Warren County line, being on Section 22, Township 49 north, Range 3 west. It is very pleasantly located on an elevated plateau just in the northern edge of the prairie. The view of the surrounding country, except to the northward, is splendid. The lands in the vicinity are rich and productive, and well adapted to the raising of nearly all kinds of grain, grass and live stock. Robert B. Allen, the founder of Truxton, was born in Virginia, October 6, 1808. He settled in Lincoln County in 1840, and three years later built the first house in Truxton. In June, 1852, he procured the services of James Reid, the county surveyor, and with his assistance laid out and platted the town of Truxton; and two years later he platted an addition thereto. Mr. Allen became a permanent resident of the village, and lived there until his death, in 1875. He was prominently identified with the place, the church and schools, and his excellent wife assisted in all his good works. The village was named in honor of Capt. Truxton, a noted naval officer in the Revolutionary War. [A partial history of this officer can be found on pages 326–27, of Quackenbos' History of the United States.] Rev. J. B. Allen, of Troy, was the first child born in Truxton.

For a number of years before the late Civil War Truxton had a large and well-regulated seminary of learning, with an able corps of teachers, and it was well patronized. In 1860 F. T. Williams was principal, W. Cunningham, assistant, and Miss M. C. Williams, teacher of the primary department. The school was closed during the war, and has never since been opened. The old building is still standing. The school of Truxton is now managed in another building erected for the purpose, under the village act for organizing schools in connection with the free school system. Truxton being situated as it is, in a good agricultural country, has always been a place of considerable trade. Its business at present consists of the following: General stores, Jarot Ingram & Son, Thomas Aydelott & Sons, H. L. Ross and William Hoech. Aydelott & Sons established their business in September, 1880; Ross established his business in 1885, and William Hoech in 1881. Mr. Ingram established his business about sixteen years ago.

Besides the above Truxton has a livery and hack line to Jonesburg, run by H. S. Owens; hotel and livery, Henderson Branstetter; blacksmiths, Lansche & Korth; carpenter, wagon-maker and blacksmith, J. H. Hoech; millinery and dressmaking, Mrs. Bettie Pennington, Mrs. Annie Holder and Miss Sallie Branstetter; harness, saddles, boots and shoes, D. K. Jennings and Ed. Temmer; boots and shoes, B. F. Jennings; grist mill and saw mill, Joseph Holder. In addition Crockett & Ritter run a hack and carry the mail to and from Jonesburg. The physicians are Benjamin Perkins, G. R. Spreckelmeyer and — Martinek. Dr. Spreckelmeyer also keeps a small drug store. William S. Pennington is a notary public and justice of the peace. The grist mill of Joseph Holder is one of the oldest mills standing in the county. The merchants of Truxton purchase a vast amount of

HISTORY OF LINCOLN COUNTY. 453

light produce, such as poultry, eggs and butter, of which all is hauled to the Wabash Railroad for shipment. The poultry is said to pay a larger per cent on investment than any other product of the vicinity. Many of the families buy all their goods at the stores with poultry, eggs and butter. Formerly there was a commodious church edifice at Truxton, but there are none at present. The following denominations: Methodist Episcopal, Missionary and Regular Baptist, and Christian, hold services alternately at the schoolhouse.

Societies.—Levi F. Pennington Post No. 347, Grand Army of the Republic, was chartered August 1, 1878. Mr. Pennington, after whom the post was named, was a private in Company A, Forty-ninth Regiment, Missouri Infantry Volunteers. He died from disease during the war. The charter members of this post were Benjamin Perkins, Reuben W. Colbert, W. S. Pennington, Fred. Hoekried, Fred. Dedert, H. C. Pennington, Benj. F. Jennings, J. W. Delventhal, James S. Strather and William N. Morris. At present writing the three principal officers are J. W. Delventhal, C.; Joseph Goodwin, S. V. C., and William N. Morris, J. V. C. The post contains fifteen survivors of the Union army.

About three miles east of Truxton, on the Troy road, are the extensive mills known as the Dutch Mills, consisting of a grist and saw mill combined, and owned by Koelling, Pettig & Co. These mills are located in the beautiful valley of Camp Creek, and are large and expensive in structure. They are run by steam power.

WINFIELD.

Winfield is situated on the St. Louis, Keokuk & Northwestern Railroad, forty-eight miles from the city of St. Louis. The business portion and some of the residences of the town lie on a level plateau at the foot of the bluffs, on the western side of the Mississippi bottoms, while the finest residences are located on the bluffs nearly 100 feet higher. From these bluffs a grand view of the valley, and of the towering heights and rounded hills on the Illinois side of the great river, is obtained. The town was surveyed and platted in October, 1879. John Wise, the first merchant in Winfield, began business in general merchandising in 1880, and after continuing for a time, retired. Next came Col. Parker with a general store, and also Baxter Crawford, with a stock of furniture and a supply of lumber. About 1885 Col. Parker quit business and left the place. After these business houses had been established, the large frame flouring mill, with a stone engine-house attached, was erected in 1883, by a joint stock company known as the Winfield Milling Company, with a capital stock of $10,000. For several years after this mill was erected it did a good business, and a large quantity of flour and meal was shipped both north and south from it, but not having the roller apparatus connected with its machinery, it had to suspend operations when that method of making flour came into general use. There is prospect, however, that the roller apparatus will be put in and the mill again put into operation. About the year 1884 the Story Bros. opened a drug store in Winfield. They were succeeded by Hewitt & Son, who were burned out by the destructive fires in the winter of 1884-85. They soon rebuilt and continued their business. After this drug store was established, DePue & Thomasson opened a general store. Soon thereafter they took in as a partner D. T. Killam, and the firm then became DePue, Thomasson & Co. Some time after this house was established, Birkhead Bros. opened a grocery store. They soon sold out to Birkhead & Argent, they to Magruder & Bro., who were victims of the fire and did not afterward resume business. Next in order after DePue, Thomasson & Co. came W. A. Woodson & Co., who opened a general store and also handled farm implements.

In addition to the foregoing there were, in 1885, the following business houses: Hardware, T. D. Hardesty; saddles and harness, John Kumbera; millinery and dressmaking, Mesdames Neville, Thompson and Steele; hotel, C. W. Ricks; saloons, Patrick Hyland and Guion & Archer; livery, Guion & Archer; barber, C. N. Forbush; restaurant, same; wagon-maker, H. J. Muth. The following is a directory of the business of Winfield at the present writing (1888): General stores, A. C. De Pue and C. H. Stephenson; drug store, F. Hewitt & Bro.; drugs and groceries, T. B. Martin; farm implements, F. W. Rohland; blacksmith and wagon-maker, H. Schierbaum and H. J. Muth;

dealer in grain, D. F. Killam, who has a grain-elevater attached to the flouring mill; dealer in live stock, John W. Thompson; hardware, F. D. Hardesty; millinery, Mrs. M. F. Nevelle; furniture and lumber, B. Crawford; restaurant, Mrs. Fannie Sanders; farm implements, Gus. Thomasson; hotel, Mrs. Mary Cook; physicians, R. H. Talbott and D. E. Hewitt. The town also contains two church edifices, Missionary Baptist and Methodist Episcopal South; also a frame schoolhouse containing three rooms. Winfield was incorporated February 14, 1882, under the corporate name of "The Inhabitants of the Town of Winfield." Its first board of trustees were F. D. Hardesty, A. C. De Pue, B. Crawford, D. T. Killam and J. A. Mudd. The town has a population of nearly 300. It is a prosperous village, and will continue to grow as the country improves.

A few years ago a party of St. Louis gentlemen constructed a commodious club-house on the margin of King's Lake, near Winfield. It has become famous as a summer resort for the city gentry and their families. Boat-riding and fishing are the principal sports indulged in.

WHITESIDE.

Whiteside, named after its proprietor, William Whiteside, is a village on the St. Louis & Keokuk (Short Line) Railroad, situated in the central part of Township 51 north, Range 1 west, and about fourteen miles on a direct line from Troy. When the railroad was completed, in 1882, Mr. Whiteside, in order to secure the erection of a depot on his farm, donated to the railroad company one-half of six acres of land for a town site, and a judgment in his favor for $500, and also built the depot. The company accepted the donation, and laid out the town. The first houses in the town were erected by Dayton Moxley and Benjamin Miles. These were frame dwelling-houses. The first merchants were Dayton Moxley and W. Hull, under the firm name of Moxley & Hull, who kept a grocery. The first general store was opened by Moxley & Bainbridge. When the postoffice was established, Dayton Moxley was made postmaster, and continues to hold the office. The Missionary Baptists have just completed a frame church 35x48 feet in size. The following is a directory of the present business of the village: General stores, Luck Bros. and Pogue & Moxley; hardware, furniture and undertaking goods, Elias Magruder; drugs, Dr. A. W. Slaughter; blacksmithing, Henry Elliott; boarding-house, William Parks. Dr. Slaughter is the practicing physician. The village contains from eighty to a hundred inhabitants. It is situated in a good agricultural region, and, consequently, will always be a good shipping point, its growth keeping pace with the development of the country. Miss Emma Keightley taught the first school in Whiteside in 1886.

POSTOFFICES.

The following is a list of the postoffices and postmasters in Lincoln County in 1888:

Apex, H. H. Morris; Argentville, O. Argent; Auburn, J. M. Terrell; Bals, George Bals; Brevator, Jacob Eisenstein; Briscoe, Cyrus Finley; Brussells, Joseph Dryden; Burr Oak Valley, Lee Frank; Chain of Rocks, Stephen Reller; Chantilla, Alfred Filsinger; Corso, J. C. Williams; Dameron, J. W. Jenkins; Davis, William Owen; Early, Robert Howell; Elsberry, J. W. Bibb; Famous, Logan Howell; Foley, ——; Hawk Point, Alexander Kennedy; Hines, F. M. Cole; Linn's Mills, F. W. Graue, Louisville, T. J. Higginbotham; Mackville, S. R. McKay; Moscow Mills, J. H. Anderson; Millwood, Daniel Mudd; New Hope, ——; Okete, ——; Old Monroe, W. T. Cambron; Olney, Theron Ives; Owen, J. V. Moseley; Silex, L. C. Kimler; Troy, George W. Mohr; Truxton, H. L. Ross; Whiteside, J. V. Moxley; Winfield, C. H. Stephenson.

Fairview postoffice has recently been taken up, and there being so many in the county, it is probable that a few more of the country offices, not on the line of the railroads, may be discontinued. Those at the stations on the railroads, and in the larger villages, will remain permanent, but the postmasters usually change with every change of administration; some of them, however, are retained through several presidential administrations, irrespective of their political preferences.

CHAPTER XIV.

EDUCATIONAL INTERESTS.

In common with the pioneers of all newly settled countries, the early settlers of Lincoln County were deprived of educational advantages for their children. As soon, however, as a sufficient number of pupils was found to exist in any particular locality, the parents, or guardians thereof, assembled and erected one of the old-fashioned log schoolhouses, with puncheon floor, open fireplace, with its stick and mud chimney, and furnished with hewed plank benches for seats, and rough boards resting on pins driven into the logs, for writing desks. These were the early schoolhouses in which the children of the first settlers received the rudiments of their education. These schools were known as "subscription schools," the teachers being paid by the parents or guardians of the pupils, in proportion to their numbers. No superior education was required of teachers in those days. It was the custom with some men to contract to teach "reading, writing and arithmetic to the rule of three," and nothing more. Occasionally a well-educated man could be employed.

Samuel Groshon (or Groshong) probably taught school in Lincoln County before the War of 1812, as an account is given of his riding out one day near one of the forts (perhaps Clark's) when he was espied by some Indians, one of whom shot him in the shoulder. He then put spurs to his horse and ran for life, and when about 300 yards from the fort his horse fell dead. His comrades in the fort then ran out and carried him safely in. The narrator of this incident spoke of Mr. Groshon as a school teacher; hence the conclusion that he had previously taught school in the vicinity. The first school teacher in the vicinity of Auburn was Philip Orr, and the others were James Wilson and James Reid. Mr. Wilson taught the first school in his neighborhood where he settled, about three miles northeast of Auburn. He still survives, lives at Auburn, and is ninety four years of age. In 1829 Clayton Alcom taught school in a log cabin near Mill Creek, and Ariel Knapp taught the first three years at Mill Creek. He taught almost continuously, and received from $12 to $15 per month. Joseph E. Wells was the first teacher in the vicinity of Millwood. He was well educated and was an excellent teacher. Richard H. Hill, brother of the Hon. Clem Hill, of Lebanon, Ky., settled on the branch between Millwood and Silex, and pre-empted his claim, and was very poor. He had four children. He taught school with great success as a teacher, but with poor success to himself financially. His brother Clem furnished him some land warrants, which he located on 280 acres of land near the line of the Wabash Railroad. He sold this land for $2,500, then went to Texas, where he became quite wealthy, raised ten children, and at last account, he and his wife were both living at the age of about eighty years. Another early school teacher in the vicinity of Millwood, was Athanasius Mudd, a graduate of the College of Georgetown, D. C., both in literature and law. The first school near Elsberry was taught about the year 1833, by William Watts. An old settler of that vicinity remembers a fight that took place at the raising of the log schoolhouse in which Watts taught, between one William Vance and one Mellon.

PUBLIC SCHOOL SYSTEM.

Missouri has had a public school system ever since it became a State, but for many years it was considered as an institution of charity for the benefit of the poor, and, consequently, was not patronized nor encouraged by the more wealthy classes. The original incentive to the creation of the school system was the donation, made by the General Government to the State, of the sixteenth section of land in each and every congressional township, for the purpose of raising a fund to maintain free schools. The first step preparatory to the establishment of such schools in Lincoln County was taken in April, 1821, by the county court, by appointing Samuel Howland, Daniel Draper, Andrew Miller, Thomas Blanton and Benjamin Allen as "school land trustees of Lincoln County." The duties of these trustees, however, were merely to oversee and protect the school lands from spoliation. In August, 1823, the court appointed two commissioners of school lands for each township, as follows: Bedford, Cary K. Duncan and John Griffee; Union, Samuel Smiley and Philip Sitton;

Hurricane, Alfred Gordon and William Hammock; Monroe, John Lindsey and —— Webb. In November of the following year Duncan and Griffee, commissioners for Bedford Township, leased Section 16, in Township 48 north, Range 1 west, to Alambe Williams, for a term of five years, for the consideration of making certain specified improvements on the land. This was the first lease of school lands made in the county.

An act of the General Assembly of the State, approved January 17, 1825, required the tribunal holding court, at its first session, in 1825, and every two years thereafter, to appoint three respectable householders in each municipal township as commissioners of school lands, their duties being to care for and manage the school lands, etc. The act provided that each congressional township, or fractional township, having not less than 100 acres of school land, should compose a school district, to be numbered and recorded; and that the rents and profits of the school lands should be appropriated to the support of the common school in such district. The school trustees were given the power to determine what number of children and what children should be educated, and for what length of time each year. The act further provided that there should be taught in all common schools, reading, writing, arithmetic and English grammar; and that the school trustees might levy a *per capita* tax on the children attending the schools, to make up any deficiency in the funds for paying teachers. This was the first provision for helping to support the schools by a tax. It was not, however, a direct tax on property, but simply a *per capita* tax on those belonging to the schools, as designated by the trustees. In May, 1826, Henry Watts, Nicholas Wells and Thomas Wells were appointed commissioners of school lands in the newly formed municipal township of Waverly. In November following these commissioners reported their first lease, the northwest quarter of Section 16, Township 51 north, Range 2 west, to Henry Watts, and another lease to Nicholas Wells for the northeast quarter of the same section. In August, 1827, Cary K. Duncan, Alexander Hill and Walter Wright were appointed the first commissioners of school lands for the newly organized municipal township of Clark.

The fractional townships along the Mississippi, and some

other townships partially covered with Spanish grants, contained no section numbered sixteen, and consequently had no school lands. To provide for this deficiency, Congress passed an act which was approved May 20, 1826, providing for the selection of other public lands to be donated to the inhabitants of such townships in lieu of Section 16. To fractional townships a proportionate share of school land only was donated. In February, 1828, the county court appointed Henry Watts as commissioner for the county, for the purpose of making selections and locations of lands granted by the above mentioned act of Congress. At the following August term of the court, Commissioner Watts reported that he had selected lands at the Palmyra land office, as follows: Town 51 north, Range 2 east—The southeast quarter of Section 30, containing 160 acres; the southeast quarter of Section 31, containing 160 acres; the east half of the northeast quarter of Section 31, containing 80 acres; Lot No. 1, of the southwest quarter of Section 31, containing 80 acres; and the southwest quarter of Section 32, containing 160 acres. Town 49 north, Range 3 east—The southwest quarter of Section 19, containing 160 acres. Town 51 north, Range 1 west— The west half of Section 11, containing 320 acres; the northwest quarter of Section 14, containing 160 acres; the southeast quarter of Section 14, containing 160 acres, making a total of 1,440 acres selected at the Palmyra office. He also reported that he had selected from the St. Louis land office (as shown by the record) Section 16, in Town 48 north, Ranges 1 and 2 west; and Section 16, in Town 48 north, Ranges 1 and 2 east; and the northeast quarter of the southeast quarter, and the southwest quarter of Section 29, Fractional Township 48 north, Range 3 east. The query arises here, why he should report the selection of lands already donated by Congress. This needs an explanation which the records do not show. In 1831 the court appointed Gabriel Reeds commissioner or agent for the school lands of the county. In November following the first petition for the school lands was presented to the court, coming from Township 51 north, Range 2 west (Waverly).

An act of the General Assembly of the State, approved March 19, 1835, provided that all congressional townships having fifteen free white householders should have the right to sell the school lands thereof, upon petition to the county court, the sheriff to be ordered to sell them; and that whenever school lands in a township were sold to the amount of $800, the county court could incorporate the inhabitants thereof into as many school districts, not exceeding four, as they might require. The act also provided that the trustees should employ a teacher and keep up a school in each incorporated school district at least six months in every year, in which school all white children between the ages of six and eighteen years, permanently residing in the district, should be free to enter as scholars; and that in all schools established under the act "reading, writing, geography, English grammar, and such other branches of education (theology excepted) as the funds might justify," should be taught; and if the annual income from the school lands was not sufficient to sustain the school six months, the trustees should apportion the deficiency among those who sent to school, in proportion to the number sent by each patron. The act also contained other provisions not necessary here to mention.

ORGANIZATION OF SCHOOL DISTRICTS.

In February, 1837, the county court incorporated the inhabitants of Township 50 north, Range 1 east, into two school districts, the eastern half being designated as No. 1, and the western half as No. 2. Elijah Myers, Alexander Martin and James Stoddard were appointed trustees of District No. 1, and Thomas S. Reid, James Finley and Harrison D. Allen, of No. 2. At the same time the inhabitants of Township 48 north, Range 1 west, were incorporated into four school districts, the northeast quarter of the township constituting No. 1, the northwest quarter No. 2, the southwest quarter No. 3, and the southeast quarter No. 4. The trustees appointed for the four districts were as follows: No. 1, Andrew Brown, William Vaughan and Benjamin Bowen; No. 2, Silas M. Davis, Robert Hammond and Allen Jameson; No. 3, John Thurman, B. F. Blanton and David Boyd; No. 4, John M. Faulkner, Marvin Ross and A. Cohall.

At the following August term of the court, the inhabitants of Township 51 north, Range 2 east, having derived over $800 from the sale of their school lands, were incorporated into one school district, and Rawleigh Mayes, Samuel M. Davis and Samuel Cannon were appointed trustees thereof. At the same time the inhabitants of Township 51 north, Range 2 west, were incorporated into three school districts, the first being composed of Sections 4 to 9 inclusive, and 16 to 21 inclusive; the second, of Sections 1 to 3 inclusive, 10 to 15 inclusive and 22 to 24 inclusive, and the third of Sections 25 to 36 inclusive. Gabriel Reeds, Nicholas Wells and O. N. Coffey were appointed trustees of the First District; David Stewart, William Jameson and Jacob Copenhaver of the Second, and Abraham Estis, William B. Sitton and William Uptegrove, of the Third. Also at the same time, the inhabitants of Township 50 north, Range 2 west, were incorporated into four school districts, the first being composed of Sections 1, 2, 3, 10, 11, 12, and the north half of Sections 13, 14 and 15; the second, of Sections 4, 5, 6, 7, 8, 9, 16, 17 and 18; the third, of Sections 19, 20, 21, 28, 29, 30, 31, 32, 33 and the west half of 22, 27 and 34, and the fourth of Sections 23, 24, 25, 26, 35, 36 and the south half of 13, 14, 15 and the east half of 22, 27 and 34. William Hammock, Guion G. Wilson and Perry Park were appointed trustees of the First District; Lot Terence, Edward Chasen and John Yale of the Second; Bethuel Sharr, Robert Mudd and Robert Salmond of the Third, and George Sand, George Jameson and Lewis Mudd, of the Fourth.

In February, 1841, the inhabitants of Township 51 north, Range 1 west, were incorporated into two school districts, the First being composed of the south two-thirds of the township, and the Second of the north one-third. James Wilson, Alexander Williams and James Reid were appointed trustees of the First District, and Fountain Merriwether, James Clark and Daniel Lyles of the Second. At the same time the inhabitants of Township 49 north, Range 2 east, were incorporated into one school district, and A. B. Birkhead, William Overall and John Argent were appointed trustees thereof. In May, 1841, the county court, on application under the new school law then recently passed, appointed June 21 as the time for the inhabitants of Township 51 north, Range 1 west, to meet at the house of Samuel Smiley, to take preliminary steps for organizing the township for school purposes.

James Wilson was appointed commissioner of common schools, and James Clark and James Reid school directors of the township. In August following, the inhabitants of Township 50 north, Range 2 east, were incorporated into two school districts, the First being composed of the west half of the township, and the Second of the east half thereof. Joseph McIntosh, Hiram Wommack and Jacob Coffey were appointed trustees of the First District, and E. Allen, Francis Riffle and John Galloway of the Second. In February, 1842, Township 51 north, Range 2 west, was organized under the new law for school purposes, and the inhabitants were ordered to meet at Louisville on the first Monday of April following, to take such steps as the law required, pertaining to the schools. David Stewart was appointed commissioner, and Solomon R. Moxley and O. N. Coffey as inspectors and directors of the schools of the townships. Afterward, from time to time, the organization of school districts was continued until all parts of the county were embraced.

TUITION AND TOWNSHIP SCHOOL FUNDS.

In August, 1841, the county court ordered that school funds consisting of the interest collected on the principal derived from the sale of school lands, and the income leased lands, should be paid to certain school districts, as follows:

First District, Township 51 north, Range 2 east	$161 17
First District, Township 50 north, Range 1 east	41 80
Second District, Township 50 north, Range 1 east	25 95
First District, Township 51 north, Range 2 west	61 00
Second District, Township 51 north, Range 2 west	65 00
First District, Township 50 north, Range 2 west	52 00
Fourth District, Township 50 north, Range 2 west	34 00

From the foregoing it will be seen that while the first district received an ample fund, and others a fund sufficient to sustain a school three or four months, some of them did not receive an amount sufficient to support a free school for more than one or two months. This proves that the income from the school lands was very unequal and insufficient, as a whole, to support the common schools. Rate bills of course had to be made out and collected in order to make up deficiencies. At this term of the county court Charles Wheeler, treasurer of the county, made his annual settlement in regard to the school funds of the several townships, whereby it appeared that the funds derived from the sale of the school lands in the following townships, including interest, and excluding expenses, were as follows:

Township 50 north, Range 1 east	$1,206 02
Township 51 north, Range 2 west	1,879 82
Township 50 north, Range 2 east	1,000 56
Township 49 north, Range 1 west	1,383 68
Township 51 north, Range 2 east	1,938 39
Township 48 north, Range 1 west	2,642 30
Township 49 north, Range 2 east	311 40
Township 49 north, Range 2 west	586 11
Township 51 north, Range 1 west	2,743 66
Township 50 north, Range 1 west	376 14
Township 49 north, Range 1 east	490 81
Township 50 north, Range 2 west	1,911 11

The foregoing does not include all the townships of the county, which is evidence that the school lands in several of the townships had not at that date been sold.

The following is a statement of the principal accrued from the sale of the school lands in the several townships up to May 3, 1842, as officially reported to the county court, in June of that year:

Township 50 north, Range 1 east	$1,104 13
Township 51 north, Range 2 west	1,677 17
Township 50 north, Range 2 east	913 95
Township 49 north, Range 1 west	1,313 07
Township 51 north, Range 2 east	1,778 21
Township 49 north, Range 2 east	586 41
Township 49 north, Range 2 west	561 59
Township 51 north, Range 1 west	2,546 98
Township 50 north, Range 1 west	414 91
Township 49 north, Range 1 east	577 70
Township 50 north, Range 2 west	1,996 98
Township 48 north, Range 1 west	2,723 17

This table gives the principal of the funds without including the interest, while the preceding one gave both.

In March, 1843, William Young, the county treasurer, reported to the county court that the township funds, including the interest and excluding the expenses up to January 1st of that year, were as follows:

Township 51 north, Range 2 west.....................$1,720 24
Township 50 north, Range 2 west..................... 2,104 64
Township 48 north, Range 1 west..................... 2,816 74
Township 49 north, Range 1 west..................... 1,221 17
Township 49 north, Range 2 west.....................   599 05
Township 49 north, Range 2 east.....................   599 85
Township 51 north, Range 2 east..................... 1,863 38
Township 49 north, Range 1 east.....................   612 56
Township 50 north, Range 1 west.....................   735 78
Township 51 north, Range 1 west..................... 2,651 86
Township 50 north, Range 2 east..................... 1,088 34
Township 50 north, Range 1 east..................... 1,142 97

Passing on to 1846, the record shows that William Young, the county treasurer, had in his hands on the first day of January of that year the township's school funds, including the accrued interest thereon, after deducting payments to school commissioners and money lost on loans, as follows:

Township 50 north, Range 1 east.....................$1,429 49
Township 51 north, Range 2 west..................... 1,952 46
Township 49 north, Range 1 west..................... 1,235 20
Township 51 north, Range 2 east..................... 2,061 09
Township 49 north, Range 2 east.....................   698 54
Township 51 north, Range 1 west..................... 2,830 98
Township 50 north, Range 1 west.....................   973 81
Township 49 north, Range 2 west.....................   823 33
Township 49 north, Range 1 east.....................   695 99
Township 50 north, Range 2 west..................... 2,350 39
Township 48 north, Range 1 west..................... 3,014 62
Township 50 north, Range 2 east..................... 1,324 61
Township 49 north, Range 3 west.....................   625 49

This table shows that school lands had now been sold in one additional township, being Township 49 north, Range 3 west.

In 1850 the amount of principal belonging to each congressional township in which school lands had been sold was as follows:

Township 50 north, Range 1 east.....................$1,300 64
Township 51 north, Range 2 west..................... 1,775 99
Township 50 north, Range 2 east..................... 1,204 80
Township 49 north, Range 1 west..................... 1,226 25
Township 51 north, Range 2 east..................... 1,890 77
Township 48 north, Range 1 west..................... 2,737 20
Township 49 north, Range 2 east.....................   685 13
Township 49 north, Range 2 west.....................   557 23
Township 51 north, Range 1 west..................... 2,571 01
Township 50 north, Range 1 west.....................   886 03

Township 49 north, Range 1 east	731 98
Township 50 north, Range 2 west	2,144 94
Township 49 north, Range 3 west	817 92
Total amount	$18,529 89

To observe the increase of the principal of the township fund, compare this table with the one reported in June, 1842, and with the following, which shows the amount of the principal of the fund in the several townships in which school lands had been sold up to the year 1860:

Township 48 north, Range 1 east	$ 331 78
Township 48 north, Range 2 east	157 25
Township 49 north, Range 1 east	871 87
Township 49 north, Range 2 east	1,033 18
Township 49 north, Range 3 east	33 24
Township 50 north, Range 1 east	1,339 94
Township 50 north, Range 2 east	1,451 07
Township 50 north, Range 3 east	7 89
Township 51 north, Range 1 east	1,508 04
Township 51 north, Range 2 east	1,890 74
Township 48 north, Range 1 west	2,737 20
Township 48 north, Range 2 west	1,209 96
Township 49 north, Range 1 west	1,383 46
Township 49 north, Range 2 west	1,367 73
Township 49 north, Range 3 west	1,608 23
Township 50 north, Range 1 west	896 52
Township 50 north, Range 2 west	2,144 93
Township 50 north, Range 3 west	1,136 49
Township 51 north, Range 1 west	2,608 78
Township 51 north, Range 2 west	1,775 98
Total amount	$25,494 28

The following is a statement of the principal of the township school fund belonging to each congressional township, as shown by official records, July 1, 1888:

Township 48 north, Range 1 east	$ 426 94
Township 48 north, Range 2 east	229 19
Township 49 north, Range 1 east	1,493 80
Township 49 north, Range 2 east	1,080 75
Township 49 north, Range 3 east	33 24
Township 50 north, Range 1 east	874 94
Township 50 north, Range 2 east	1,322 80
Township 50 north, Range 3 east	7 89
Township 51 north, Range 1 east	1,693 84
Township 51 north, Range 2 east	1,238 12

Township 48 north, Range 1 west.................. 2,204 11
Township 48 north, Range 2 west.................. 1,151 84
Township 49 north, Range 1 west.................. 1,561 86
Township 49 north, Range 2 west.................. 1,439 43
Township 49 north, Range 3 west.................. 1,206 16
Township 50 north, Range 1 west.................. 1,207 75
Township 50 north, Range 2 west.................. 1,662 30
Township 50 north, Range 3 west.................. 1,133 71
Township 51 north, Range 1 west.................. 2,669 53
Township 51 north, Range 2 west.................. 1,866 64

Total amount........ ....$24,504 84

By comparing this table with the one for 1860, it will be seen that additions have been made to the fund in Township 48 north, Ranges 1 and 2 east; Township 49 north, Ranges 1 and 2 east; Township 51 north, Range 1 east; Township 49 north, Ranges 1 and 2 west; Township 50 north, Range 1 west, and Township 51 north, Ranges 1 and 2 west; while the fund has sustained losses in Township 50 north, Ranges 1 and 2 east; Township 51 north, Range 2 east; Township 48 north, Ranges 1 and 2 west; Township 49 north, Range 3 west, and Township 50 north, Ranges 2 and 3 west, and in the other townships the fund remained the same in amount. It will also be observed that the losses exceeded the gains, and that the aggregate of the principal of the township fund is now $989.44 less than it was in the year 1860. It is claimed that the losses occurred principally during the war period, on loans made with insufficient securities. The principal of this fund is loaned to individual borrowers, and the interest thereon is collected annually, and distributed to the school districts for the support of the schools. The school lands of the county are all sold, except about 160 acres in Township 49 north, Range 3 east. The township fund can be increased by whatever may be realized from the sale of this tract of land, after which it will remain a permanent and perpetual fund, which can never be increased, but may be decreased by mismanagement. It is proper, however, here to say that in loaning this fund the law now requires both real and personal security, instead of personal security only, as was formerly required, and consequently it is not liable to sustain further loss, if proper care is exercised in its management.

THE STATE SCHOOL FUND.

This fund was created by an act of the General Assembly of the State of Missouri, approved December 12, 1855, the first three sections of which read as follows:

"SECTION 1. There is hereby created and established a fund for the support of common schools within this State, to be called and known as 'The State School Fund,' which shall consist of: First, All moneys heretofore deposited, or which shall hereafter be deposited with this State according to an act of Congress entitled, 'An act to regulate the deposit of public monies,' passed June 23, 1836. Second, The proceeds of all lands now or hereafter belonging to the State, known as the Saline Lands, and of all lands now or hereafter vested in this State by escheat, or purchase, or forfeiture for taxes.

"SEC. 2. The funds hereby created shall be and remain a permanent fund for the support of common schools.

"SEC. 3. The interest, dividends, proceeds and profits of such school fund shall be denominated, 'State School Money,' and shall be distributed annually for the support of the common schools throughout the State."

Other sections of the act provided for the establishment of the office of "superintendent of common schools," and defined the duties of the incumbent thereof, one of which was that he should, in the month of May each year, apportion the State school money, that is the interest and proceeds of the State school fund, to the several counties in the State, in proportion to the number of white children above the age of five, and under the age of twenty years; and that the same should be apportioned in like manner in the counties to the several townships. The act also provided that twenty-five per centum of the State revenue should be annually set apart, and become State school money.* It further provided that the proceeds of the sale of the school lands should constitute a "township school fund," and it authorized the school districts to elect three trustees, and to levy a direct tax to raise funds for the purchase of or erection of schoolhouses, purchase grounds, etc.

The money deposited with the State under the act of Con-

---

* The law now provides that one-third or thirty-three and one-third per centum of the State revenue shall be set apart and become State school money.

gress, as mentioned in Section 1, of the aforesaid act, was the surplus revenue which had then accumulated in the National Treasury, and bore the same relation to the people of the United States as the surplus in the National Treasury bears at the present time. To relieve an over-loaded treasury, the surplus was then distributed to the several States of the Union, and has become a part of the permanent school fund of each. The famous Blair Bill now proposes to relieve the treasury in a similar manner. The amount of the State school fund created by the act of the General Assembly of Missouri as above mentioned, and augmented by subsequent laws, has reached, according to the last published report of W. E. Coleman, State superintendent of public schools, the enormous amount of $3,135,906.74. There is also another State school fund managed by the State officers, known as the "University or Seminary Fund," which was derived from the sale of certain lands donated by Congress to the State for educational purposes. This fund, as shown by the above mentioned report, amounts to $519,095.08. These funds are a permanent and perpetual principal, loaned by the State officers.

The annual interest thereon is collected and distributed to the several counties composing the State. The reader should bear in mind that the "State school fund" and the "University or seminary fund" are principals or capital, and that the interest and proceeds of these funds are "State school money."

COUNTY PUBLIC SCHOOL FUND.

This fund consists of the accumulations in the county treasury of "the net proceeds from the sale of estrays; also the clear proceeds of all penalties and forfeitures, and of all fines collected in the several counties for any breach of the penal or military laws of this State; and of moneys which shall be paid by persons as an equivalent for exemption from military duty." A portion of the proceeds arising from the sale of the "swamp or overflowed lands" also augment this fund. [See Public Lands elsewhere in this work.] But as Lincoln County failed to select her swamp and overflowed lands, and receive them from the General Government, no part of her "county public school fund" came from that source, and this failure accounts in a great measure for the small amount of this fund now controlled by the county, which is $8,560.47.

RECAPITULATION OF SCHOOL FUNDS.

The entire amount of the school funds of Missouri, including that controlled both by State and county officers, as shown by the last report of the State superintendent of public schools, is as follows:

State school fund	$3,135,906 74
University or seminary fund	519,095 08
County public school fund	3,386,201 66
Township public school fund	3,331,490 74
Special public school fund	68,734 99
Fines, penalties, forfeitures, etc.	120,525 05
Total school fund of Missouri	$10,561,954 26

The State funds can be increased only by "grant, gift, or devise," notary fees or appropriations by the General Assembly.

The county public school fund is annually increased by the "net proceeds of fines, penalties, forfeitures, and sale of estrays."

The township public school fund can only be increased by the sale of school lands remaining unsold.

Special funds are such as have been secured by grant, gift, devise or special legislation to school districts.

The following is a recapitulation of the permanent school funds of Lincoln County:

Township school fund	$24,504 84
County school fund	8,560 47
Total	$33,065 31

This amount is loaned under the supervision of the county court, some at 8 per cent, and some at 10 per cent.

The following is a statement of the receipts and expenditures of school moneys in Lincoln County for the school year commencing July 1, 1887, and ending June 30, 1888:

RECEIPTS.

Interest from State school funds	$ 5,435 50
Interest from county fund	1,687 13

Interest from township fund	1,942 38
From tax on railroads	1,188 36
From direct taxation	15,271 39
Total receipts during the year	$25,524 76
Add amount on hand July 1, 1887	5,735 66
Amount for distribution	$31,260 42
Total expenditures during the year	24,372 67
Balance on hand July 1, 1888	$ 6,887 75

The State school law was radically changed soon after the close of the Civil War, an almost entirely new system being inaugurated, and it has been changed and improved from time to time until the present efficient educational system has become established. During the existence of slavery there were no schools for the benefit of the children of the colored people, nor were they allowed in any way to become educated. But those times have passed away, and the curse of slavery is no longer a blot on America's free soil. A revolution has taken place, and now the children of all classes, rich or poor, white or black, are provided with free public schools. The law of Missouri makes the following provision for the establishment of schools for colored children:

SEC. 7052, General School Law. "Boards of education and the trustees and directors of schools, or other officers having authority in the premises, in each city, incorporated village or district, shall be and they are hereby authorized and required to establish, within their respective jurisdictions, one or more separate schools for colored children, when the whole number, by enumeration, exceeds fifteen, so as to afford them the advantages and privileges of a common school education, and all such schools so established for colored children shall be under the control and management of the board of education or other school officers, who have in charge the educational interest of the other schools. But in case the average number of colored children in attendance shall be less than ten for any one month, it shall be the duty of said board of education or other school officers to discontinue said school or schools for any period not exceeding six months at any one time; and if the number of colored children shall be less than ten the board of education shall reserve the money raised on the number of said colored children, and the money so reserved shall be appropriated, as they may deem proper, for the education of such colored children. In all other respects the terms and advantages of said schools shall be equal to others of the same grade in their respective districts, cities and villages: provided, that when the number of colored children in any district shall be less than sixteen, they shall have the privilege of attending school in any district in the township where a school is maintained for colored children, and the board of directors of the district in which such children are enumerated shall transfer to the credit of the teachers' fund of the district in which such children may have attended school, an amount equal to the *pro rata* expense of such attendance, the same to be pro-rated according to the amount paid for teacher's wages during such school term." The law further provides for the establishment of joint schools for the colored children in two or more adjoining districts when their combined number is sufficient. To show the practical working of the school system in Lincoln County the following statistics are taken from the last published report of the State superintendent of public schools, it being for the school year ending June 30, 1887:

Scholastic Population.—White: male, 2,738; female, 2,559; total, 5,297. Colored: male, 374; female, 350; total, 724. Total white and black, 6,021.

Number Enrolled in the Schools.—White: males, 2,054; females, 1,739; total, 3,793. Colored: males, 153; females, 159; total, 312. Total white and black, 4,105. Average days attendance, 61.

Number of colored schools	9
Number of white schools	91
Number of rooms occupied	100
Seating capacity	4,906
Number of teachers employed	109
Value of school property	$39,445 00
Average salary of teachers per month	32 14
Paid for repairs and rent	693 19
Paid for sites, building and furnishing	730 45
Paid for district clerks	478 15
Paid for incidentals	2,776 80
Paid teachers	19,788 75

By reference to the scholastic population and the number enrolled in the public schools, it will be seen that between seventy-one and seventy-two per cent of the white children enumerated in the county attend the public schools, and that only a fraction over forty-three per cent of the colored children enumerated attend the public schools. The reason for the small percentage of colored children attending the public schools is because many of them reside too far from the colored schools to attend them.

CHAPTER XV.

ECCLESIASTICAL.

As mentioned elsewhere the date of organized efforts in behalf of church organizations in Lincoln County is closely allied to the early settlement of the country. In these worthy movements pioneer ministers bore an important part.

Among these pioneer ministers of Lincoln County were Andrew Monroe, David Hubbard, Bethuel Riggs, Hugh R. Smith, Abraham Welty, Darius Bainbridge and Benjamin S. Ashby, all of whom solemnized marriages, as shown by the record of marriage certificates prior to 1830. And, commencing with 1830, the record shows the following: 1830, James W. Campbell and Thomas Bowen; 1832, Elder Thomas McBride of the Christian Church and Rev. Samuel Findley of the Presbyterian Church; 1833, Nicholas C. Kabler of the Methodist Episcopal Church; 1834, John S. Pall of the Presbyterian Church, Jacob Lanius of the Methodist Episcopal Church, Sandy E. Jones of the Christian Church, John M. Hopkins and Robert Gilmore of the Baptist Church, and Fred B. Leach; 1835, Hugh L. Dodds of the Methodist Episcopal Church, and J. H. Hughes of the Christian Church; 1836, Ephraim Davis and Ezekiel Downing of the Cumberland Presbyterian Church; Peter P. Lefever of the Catholic Church, and S. G. Patterson of the Methodist Episcopal Church; 1837, Robert L. McAfee and Lewis Duncan; 1838, F. B.

McElroy and William Patton of the Methodist Episcopal Church, and Nathan Woodsworth. Some signed their names as "ministers of the gospel," and others as ministers of the churches to which they belonged.

BAPTIST CHURCHES.

Fee Fee Creek Baptist Church was organized with about seventeen members in 1807, by Elder Thomas R. Musick. It is located in a beautiful country, about fifteen miles northwest of St. Louis, and was the second Baptist Church organized in what is now the State of Missouri. Soon thereafter followed the organizations of Coldwater, Boeuf, Negro Fork, Upper Cuivre and Femme Osage Baptist Churches. These churches were organized, in 1817, into the "Missouri Association," which is now the "St. Louis Association." Fee Fee Creek Church, having stood from the beginning, is now the oldest Baptist Church in the State. Of the Upper Cuivre, Rev. R. S. Duncan, author of the "History of the Baptists in Missouri," says: "This pioneer community was located several miles southwest of Troy, the county seat of Lincoln County; was gathered and formed by we know not whom, in about the year 1815 or 1816, and after an existence of some twenty years, dissolved." It was probably located near the present line of Lincoln and Warren Counties.

Stout's Settlement (now New Hope) Baptist Church was organized June 16, 1821, by Elders Bethuel Riggs and Jesse Sitton, the latter of whom is supposed to have been the pastor until 1828, when he was dismissed by letter, and left the State. Elder David Hubbard succeeded him, and continued pastor for some years.

In February, 1830, a serious difficulty was brought into the church, growing out of the marriage of a young sister to a man who had a living wife. On an investigation the sister was acquitted. The minority were dissatisfied with the decision of the majority, and asked that a council be called, which was granted. Sulphur Lick, Troy and Little Bethel Churches each sent three members, who sat as a council, and, after hearing the case, advised that the sister be excluded, and, the majority refusing to do so, the minority withdrew from the church in June, 1830, and

Henry T. Mudd
LINCOLN COUNTY.

formed the Bryant's Creek Church, in the same neighborhood. In August, 1831, the name of the church was changed from Stout's Settlement to that of Union, and about the year 1836 a log meeting-house was built, 46x20 feet, about two miles north of New Hope. Elder Ephraim Davis became pastor in May, 1835. During this pastorate the church adopted " a resolution refusing correspondence with any society of Christians who hold to the present benevolent institutions of the day." Elder Davis, who was a good man, and much beloved by the church, died in October, 1851, and left the church much divided on doctrine and the subject of missions. Finally, in 1852, a majority called Elder A. Mitchell as pastor. Being dissatisfied with this action, the minority withdrew, some getting letters and some not, most of whom united with Bryant's Creek Church (anti-mission). Soon after this the church rescinded all her acts and resolutions in opposition to missions, and, under the ministry of Elder Mitchell, gradually grew in numerical and moral strength, and in 1857 the place of meeting was moved to New Hope, the church having built a commodious frame house in that town 40x60 feet, which it now occupies. By resolution the name was changed from Union to New Hope in July, 1867.

Sulphur Lick Baptist Church.—Dr. Mudd says, in his history, that Rev. Bethuel Riggs organized the Sulphur Lick Baptist Church, in 1813, but this is evidently a mistake as to time, and most likely a mistake of the printer, as the sequel will show. At that date the few settlers and their families were confined in the forts, on account of the hostilities of the Indians during the War of 1812–15. A definite account of the organization of this church is given by Rev. R. S. Duncan, as follows: "This church is in Lincoln County, eight or nine miles northwest of Troy, the county seat. It was organized by Elder Bethuel Riggs, in his own private house, near a large spring, called Sulphur Lick, close to the north fork of Cuivre, four miles east of the present site, in the year 1823, of four members, viz.: Bethuel Riggs, Nancy Riggs, his wife, Armstrong Kennedy and Polly, his wife. John Cox and his wife, Polly, were received by experience the same day of the organization, and were baptized by Elder Riggs. In 1826 or 1827 it moved to its present location, and a few years after erected a substantial brick house, which was replaced by its present frame building, in 1856. This church has been a fruitful vine in days that are past, but is now in a feeble state, having passed its semi-centennial. It is an ecclesiastical grandmother, and had in 1881 only nineteen members."

Cuivre and Troy Baptist Churches were organized some time prior to the year 1828.

New Salem Baptist Church was organized in 1843. In 1882 it numbered 161 members, with J. Reid as pastor.

Bethlehem Baptist Church (now Fairview) was organized in 1845, and for many years worshiped in a log house, with a dirt floor. It has now a substantial frame church building.

Cottonwood Baptist Church was organized in October, 1852.

Mill Creek Baptist Church, located about three miles southeast of the village of Whiteside, was organized in 1851, by Elders Albert Mitchell and James Smith. Among the constituent members were John Cannon and wife, Jacob Whiteside and wife, Duncan Ellis and wife, William Ackers and wife, and Mrs. Hannah Ellis. The present frame church was built in 1853, at a cost of about $1,100. It was dedicated by Rev. James Smith. Rev. Albert Mitchell was pastor of the church twenty-five years. He was followed by William Mitchell, W. M. Modisett and Patrick —the latter having served eleven years.

Corner-Stone Baptist Church was organized about the year 1874. It is located about two-and-a-half miles west of Whiteside, and was organized by Revs. Marcellus S. Whiteside, William Bibbs and Thomas Sanderson. Its constituent members were J. R. Gibson and wife, Hiram Hall and wife, Adam Hall, Robert Chasten, wife and daughter, Elijah Stephens, wife and daughter. A frame house, still in use, was built in 1876, at a cost of about $1,100 outside of work donated on the building. It was dedicated by Rev. Burnham. The pastors have been Revs. William Bibb, M. S. Mitchell, James Reid, F. M. Birkhead, J. N. P. Helper and William Tipton, the latter being the present pastor. This church has a membership of about eighty.

Ebenezer Baptist Church, situated in Township 51 north, Range 1 east, some seven miles north of New Hope, was organized about the year 1869, by Elder M. S. Whiteside, with eight members. They first worshiped in the Methodist Episcopal Church building, and at Smith's schoolhouse, for about three years. The present house in which they worship was erected in 1876, at a cost of $600. It is 36x40 feet in size. It was dedicated by Rev. Pope Yeaman, D. D. The pastors of this church have been M. S. Whiteside, William Mitchell, W. H. Burnham, J. D. Robnett, M. P. Matheny, C. A. Mitchell, Bland Beauchamp, William Tipton and W. N. Maupin, the latter being the present pastor. The present membership of this church is about 100.

Star Hope Baptist Church was organized at Reid's schoolhouse in May, 1867, with nine members, by Elder W. F. Luck. The first pastor was Elder M. S. Whiteside; Elder W. H. Burnham was his successor. In 1882 this church had 126 members.

The names of the other Baptist Church organizations in the county at this writing are Oak Ridge, Winfield, Highland, Silex, Mt. Gilead and Harmony Grove.

The Baptist Church at Elsberry was organized October 27, 1883, by Elder W. A. Bibb. The constituent members were J. R. Cannon and wife, J. W. Waters and wife, Landy Waters, R. D. Waters, Lena Waters, G. L. Gennie and wife, Mrs. Ada Mays, Mrs. Annie Powell and J. W. Taliaferro. C. A. Mitchell was pastor from 1885 to 1886, and J. D. Hacker, the present pastor, has served since 1887.

Bethuel Riggs, a pioneer preacher of Lincoln and adjoining counties, was born about 1760 in the colony or State of New Jersey. Not much is known of his very early life, he having spent more than half his life out of Missouri. At the age of seventeen years, while but a youth, young Riggs enlisted as a soldier in the War of the American Revolution, and for the services rendered therein he afterward received a pension. He married in early life. His wife was Nancy Lee, sister of a celebrated preacher by the name of James Lee, who used to preach under the trees with his gun by his side, apprehending an attack from Indians. At the age of eighteen years, Bethuel Riggs was converted to Christ and became a Baptist, and soon after moved to North Carolina and subsequently to Georgia, where he lived some years, and here he not only began his ministry but traveled and preached somewhat extensively. * * * While still a comparatively young man, he, in company with a large colony, came across the Indian country to Kentucky. This trip was made during the early Indian wars. Mr. Riggs settled in that part of Kentucky opposite Cincinnati. In the year 1809 he came to Missouri and first settled on Dardenne Creek, in St. Charles County, where he lived some eight years. He then moved higher up the country and settled north of Troy by the Sulpher Lick Spring. Here he organized the Sulphur Lick Church and spent much of his time itinerating. He preached over large portions of Lincoln and adjoining counties. Subsequently he moved to Monroe County, and from there to Illinois, thence to Ohio and back again to Missouri, where he died and was buried by the side of his faithful wife, the companion of both his youth and his old age.*

David Hubbard was also a pioneer minister of the gospel in Lincoln County. He was born in the year 1796, in the State of Kentucky, near where the celebrated Daniel Boone first settled. His father, Charles Hubbard, was a native of Virginia, and after spending several years in Kentucky, he moved to and settled in St. Louis County, Mo., in 1809, when David was a small boy. Charles Hubbard was an influential Baptist, and while he lived in St. Louis County, filled the office of deacon in the old Fee Fee Baptist Church. David Hubbard grew up in the Territory of Missouri, in an age when schools were almost unknown so far west. He therefore secured few advantages from this source; but possessing a strong, active mind, he made the best use of his limited opportunities. He, however, never secured what would be called a good, common school education.

At the age of twenty-three he professed conversion, and was baptized by Elder Charles Collard, while he was a resident of Gasconade County. Soon after this he moved to Warren County, and about this time (1821 or 1822) commenced preaching, and was ordained by Little Bethel Church in 1824. After spending a short time in Warren County he moved to Lincoln, and settled about ten or twelve miles west of Troy. In 1829 he moved to the

---
*Duncan.

neighborhood of New Hope, where he lived some ten or twelve years; thence he moved to Pike County, Ill., where he lived until he moved to Oregon, about the year 1853. He was popular in the pulpit and out of it. Wherever his name was known in Eastern Missouri he could get a congregation week-day or Sunday. As a pastor he labored industriously with the Sulphur Lick, Bryant's Creek and Union (New Hope) Churches, all in Lincoln County. He was almost all the time pastor of four churches. He died at his home in Oregon, June 14, 1868.

Darius Bainbridge was a native of Kentucky, and son of Rev. Absalom Bainbridge, M. D. He moved to Missouri and settled in St. Charles County, about 1822. He was married in Kentucky to Miss Mary Wright, sister of Elder Thomas J. Wright. Darius Bainbridge commenced preaching as early as 1824, labored in Missouri twelve years, moved to Wisconsin, thence back to Missouri, and settled in Clay County in 1847, where he spent the remnant of his days. He was chosen moderator of Cuivre Association in 1828, and was re-elected for eight consecutive years. He died in Clay County about the year 1862.*

Rev. William Healey, a Baptist preacher, was an Englishman, who left his native country and went to Texas, and from there he came to Lincoln County, and did missionary work during the fifties, traveling on foot from place to place. John Snethen, taking pity on the man, bought a horse and gave it to him. He died at Snethen's house.

Robert Gilmore, a pioneer preacher in Lincoln County, was born in 1792, in the State of Virginia, and subsequently moved to the State of Kentucky, where, in 1818, he married Mary Hansford. In 1819 he immigrated to Missouri, and settled in St. Charles County, where he remained for a brief period, then moved to Lincoln County, and settled in the neighborhood of Old Sulphur Lick Church. Not long after his settlement in Lincoln County he professed religion, and became a member of the Baptist denomination, having been baptized by the old pioneer, Bethuel Riggs. He began preaching before 1830, but was not ordained until 1841. He was a most excellent man, had only a limited education, and was a real, old-fashioned preacher of the gospel.

---
*Duncan.

His labors in the ministry were confined chiefly to Lincoln and Montgomery Counties. In the spring of 1849 he, with his family and many others from his adopted State, started across the plains for California. The cholera broke out among the emigrants, and many were made its victims. Elder Gilmore, his faithful wife and one son, were among the sufferers. He died at the head of Sweet Water, on the 25th of June, 1849.

METHODIST EPISCOPAL CHURCHES.

The Missouri Conference of the Methodist Church was organized in 1816, by the General Conference, while in session at Baltimore, Md. The first session of the Missouri Conference was held at Shiloh meeting-house, near the city of Belleview, in Illinois, commencing September 23, 1816. At this time there were two circuits only, in the territory of Missouri—Belleview and Saline—the former lying southward and the latter northward, and both together including all the settlements west of the Mississippi. The dividing line between these circuits was some distance south of St. Louis. At the first conference above mentioned, John C. Harbison and Joseph Reeder were appointed "circuit riders" for these two circuits. The second session of the Missouri Conference was held at Goshen settlement, in Illinois, commencing October 6, 1817. At this session Rev. Thomas Wright was appointed circuit rider of the Belleview and Saline Circuits. The third conference was held at Bethel meeting-house, at the place of the meeting of the previous session in Illinois. At this session Thomas Wright and Joseph Piggott were appointed to the Missouri Circuits. The fourth session of the Missouri Conference, and the first one held west of the Mississippi, was held at McKendree's Chapel, in Cape Girardeau County, beginning September 14, 1819. John Piggott and John McFarland were appointed to the Missouri Circuits.

The fifth session of the Missouri Conference was held at Shiloh meeting-house, St. Clair County, Ill., commencing September 13, 1820, and a new circuit, called St. Francois, was formed in Missouri. John Harris was appointed to Belleview Circuit, and Samuel Bassett to Saline and St. Francois.

The sixth session of the Missouri Conference was held at

McKendree Chapel, in Cape Girardeau County, commencing October 17, 1821, and the seventh session was held it St. Louis, commencing in October, 1822. About this time the territory east of the Mississippi was cut off from the Missouri Conference, and thereafter the sessions continued to be held in the newly admitted State of Missouri.

New Liberty Methodist Episcopal Church was organized in 1818, at some private house (probably that of the father of Judge S. T. Ingram), near Corso, in the northwestern part of the county. It is believed that it was organized by Rev. John Scrips. The Ingrams, Owings and Hudsons were some of its constituent members. No church building was constructed until 1848, when a log chapel was erected.

The present frame building was erected in 1874, at a cost of $850. It was dedicated in July, 1875, by Rev. N. Shumate. It is located on Section 1, Township 50 north, Range 3 west. Among the pastors have been Revs. Henderson, Alderman, Hyde, Anderson, Thompson, McMaster, Shumate and Ferell. This is the oldest Methodist Episcopal Church in Lincoln County, and probably the first one organized therein. It is also among the first Methodist Episcopal Churches organized in Missouri Territory. In the division of the Methodist Episcopal Church, which took place in 1844 and 1845, only about four members of New Liberty Church withdrew and went with their Southern brethren into the Methodist Episcopal Church South. The rest all remained true to the old church, but, after the division, owing to the many persecutions of the adherents of slavery, this church did not prosper well until after the Civil War closed, and slavery, the cause of the division, was abolished. At the close of the war she had about sixteen members—at the present time she has about fifty.

There is but one other organization of the Methodist Episcopal Church in Lincoln County, and that is at the village of Truxton, where they have no church edifice, but worship in the schoolhouse. Rev. Smiley, probably the only resident minister of the Methodist Episcopal Church in Lincoln County, resides at Olney, at this writing. He preaches at Truxton, in this county; at Pin Oak, in Warren County, and at Union Chapel, in

Montgomery County. Prior to 1845 there were other Methodist Episcopal Churches in Lincoln County, which lost their identity when the division took place, their members going mostly in a body into the newly-organized Methodist Episcopal Church South.

METHODIST EPISCOPAL CHURCH SOUTH.

This church had its origin in name, as has been stated, when the people composing it withdrew from the old church. It has been fairly prosperous in Lincoln County, but owing to the large German population, among whom other churches have been organized, it has not become as strong as in some other portions of the country. The records not having been kept, it is not possible to give the dates and particulars of the several individual church organizations.

The Troy and Wentzville Circuit embraces a church each at Troy, Moscow and Slaven's Chapel, in Lincoln County, and at Wentzville, in St. Charles County. The membership of the circuit, not including Wentzville, is 175. These are very old organizations. The church edifice in Troy, known as Monroe Chapel, was erected in 1859. It is a commodious brick building, and is well preserved. Brussells Circuit lies wholly within Lincoln County, and has organizations at Brussells, Old Alexandria, Fairview, Winfield and New Church, the latter being about four miles east of Troy. This circuit has 380 members, according to the last conference minutes. Rev. O. B. Holiday is the pastor of the Troy and Wentzville Circuit, and Rev. W. J. Blakey of the Brussells Circuit.

Smith's Chapel, Methodist Episcopal Church South, is situated on Survey 1743, in Hurricane Township, and it belongs to the Clarksville Circuit. It was organized, in 1869, by Rev. Thomas B. King, with twenty-nine members. It now has about 160 members. The pastors have been Revs. Thomas B. King, I. A. M. Thompson, J. M. O'Brien, Henry Kay, Jesse Sutton, S. D. Barnett, M. Williams, H. D. Groves and J. W. Ramsey, the latter being the present pastor. W. W. Jamison has been secretary of the church ever since its organization. The frame church building, in which this organization now worships, is 32x40 feet in size, and was erected in the year 1871, at a cost of $1,200. It was dedicated in the same year by Rev. William A. Tarwater. The church at this place had formerly been Methodist Episcopal, organized in a very early day, and lost its identity after the trouble in 1844 and 1845, and before the late war. When originally organized, services were held at the residences of the old pioneers, James Smith and Judge Pepators, who, with their wives, were constituent members.

The Methodist Episcopal Church South at Elsberry also belongs to the Clarksville Circuit. Another Methodist Episcopal Church South, located about two miles northeast of Auburn, belongs to the Prairieville Circuit, and the Olney Methodist Episcopal Church South belongs to the Ashley Circuit. The circuits of this denomination in Lincoln County belong to the conference district of St. Charles. An account of the proceedings of the last session (the twenty-second) of the conference of this district, held in the last week of April, 1888, was given in the Troy *Free Press*, as follows:

"The Troy Methodist Church had the pleasure of entertaining the members of the St. Charles District Conference of the Methodist Episcopal Church South last week. The session of the conference began Thursday evening, April 26. Rev. S. L. Woody, of St. Charles, preached a most excellent sermon.

"The conference met for a business session at 9 o'clock, Friday morning, Bishop Hendrix presiding. P. P. Ellis, of New Florence, Montgomery County, was chosen secretary. The usual committees were appointed, namely: on church records, on Sunday-schools and on church finance.

"The next matter taken up was the reports from the management of the church schools of the district. St. Charles College, under the able management of President Meyers, was reported as having four teachers employed in giving instruction to 160 students. Prof. R. H. Pitman, principal of Woodlawn Seminary, at O'Fallon, reported his charge to be in a most encouraging condition. The school has four teachers, is giving full courses in art and music, and has matriculated fifty students the present session, that being all that it can accommodate.

"The conference then heard from the different churches in the district, which is composed of twelve circuits, in the counties of

St. Charles, Warren, Pike, Lincoln, Callaway and Montgomery. There was in these reports great cause for rejoicing among those who have at heart the interest of the church. The church membership has had a steady growth, the Sunday-schools are flourishing, and the communicants show increased zeal in good works.

"Friday evening Bishop Hendrix preached a grand sermon on church growth. The auditorium of the Methodist Church was crowded, and all felt repaid for the ill conveniences of a packed house by the eloquence and logic of the Bishop.

"Conference met Saturday forenoon at 9 o'clock. After the reading of the minutes of Friday's meeting, W. O. Gray opened the discussion of the qualifications of a steward. A good number of members of the conference followed him in a very interesting and instructive treatment of the subject. The rest of the time before the hour for preaching was occupied by a discussion of the material interests of the church, led by Rev. S. L. Woody, of St. Charles, and participated in by Rev. H. M. Meyers and others. Rev. J. W. Ramsey, at 11 o'clock, preached an effective and pointed sermon on Christian service, when an adjournment was taken till 2:30 P. M.

"The afternoon session was opened with religious services, conducted by Rev. J. M. L. Hogan, after which Rev. J. W. Ramsey made a report on the spiritual interests of the church.

"St. Charles was chosen as the next place of meeting. The next order of business was the choice of lay delegates to the annual conference, resulting in the election of O. H. Avery, of Troy, Rev. J. D. Vincil, of St. Louis, D. K. Pitman, of O'Fallon, and P. P. Ellis, of New Florence, with M. L. Cape, of Jonesburg, and W. O. Gray, of Louisiana, as alternates.

"Resolutions of thanks to the people of Troy for hospitalities extended, and to the members of the Christian Church for the use of their place of worship Sunday, were passed. Conference then adjourned, to meet at St. Charles on the call of the presiding elder.

"Every one in attendance seemed to enjoy the session of conference and his stay in Troy, and pronounced it one of the most useful meetings ever held in the history of the district conference. One of the veterans of the cross expressed his appreciation by saying that the only drawback he witnessed was the fact that he could not accept all the hospitable invitations extended to him.

"Saturday evening Rev. J. M. O'Brien, of Shelbina, preached to a large audience at the Methodist Church, taking for his theme the missionary interests of the church. Dr. John D. Vincil's sermon on the crucifixion was heard by a delighted audience at the Methodist Church Sunday forenoon, as was the discourse of Rev. H. M. Meyers at the Christian Church, and Rev. H. H. Craig at the Colored Church. The Methodist Church was filled Sunday evening by listeners to the last discourse of the conference, that of Prof. J. M. Gibson, of St. Charles."

PRESBYTERIAN CHURCHES.

The First Presbyterian Church of Troy was organized November 26, 1831, by Revs. William S. Lacy and John S. Ball, the former the father of Rev. B. F. Lacy, and the latter the father-in-law of Gov. Frederick Bates. There were ten constituent members, and Francis Parker and Horatio S. Linn were elected and ordained ruling elders. Occasional services were held, with Rev. William Ball as minister, up till 1834; from that time till 1846, by Rev. James Gallaher; from 1848 to 1850 Rev. David Dimond had charge of the church; from 1850 to 1864, Rev. E. P. Noel; from 1864 to 1868, Rev. J. V. Parks; during part of the time from 1860 to 1870, Revs. C. P. B. Martin and James Rosamond; 1871-73, Rev. O. C. Thompson; from 1873 to 1888, Revs. W. B. Y. Wilkie, A. A. Pfansteihl and the present minister, C. Van Oostenbrugg, in the order here named. After the organization, until 1848, the congregation worshiped in the courthouse. On the 16th of September, 1847, the cornerstone of a brick building, on Court Street, was laid, and on the 23d of January, 1848, it was dedicated as a church. It cost $1,600. In 1868 the new and handsome edifice on Boone Street was taken in hand, and was finally completed in 1874, but not being wholly out of debt the dedication was deferred until after the debt was provided for. It was dedicated on a Sunday in July, 1875, by Rev. Dr. Brookes, of St. Louis, his text being the second verse of the first chapter of Joshua. The building cost nearly $17,000. This society has received many members from time to time, and has lost many by dismissals and deaths, and now has a membership of seventy-five. It belongs to the St. Louis Presbytery. A session of this body was held in Troy in the first week of May, 1888, and the following is the Troy *Herald's* account of its proceedings:

"The presbytery met at the Presbyterian Church in Troy, Wednesday, and organized with J. G. Carr, of St. Louis, moderator, and J. A. Smith, of St. Louis, clerk. Rev. T. Payton Walton was received from the Palmyra Presbytery. Grand Avenue Presbyterian Church, in St. Louis, was allowed permission to call Rev. Dr. Strickler, of Atlanta, Ga., as pastor. J. Addison Smith and Rev. Dr. William N. McPheeters were chosen commissioners to the general assembly, with Dr. R. G. Brank and Thomas M. Barrow as alternates. Rev. Claggett, Palmyra, was allowed to work outside the bounds of the presbytery. Report of Rev. Oostenbrugg, from committee on bills and overtures, recommending no change in the book of church order, concerning union with other bodies, adopted. Interesting talk by Rev. Wright, agent of the American Bible Society, who leaves the employ of the society in July, after a service of twenty-five years. Rev. T. P. Walton substituted for Dr. Hollifield on education committee. Resignation of Rev. Thomas Watson as pastor of Dardenne Church accepted, and Dr. R. P. Farris appointed in his place. Report of J. J. Johns and George Penn, Jr., committee to audit treasurer's report, accepted. Dr. Farris and J. H. Wear appointed standing committee on the report of the treasurer. Statement of Mr. Boyd, of Hickory Grove Congregational Church, heard. He will put his letter in a Presbyterian church, and be taken under care of St. Louis Presbytery.

"Decided to ask presbyterial committee of the home missions committee for $200 to finish the church at South Dardenne.

"Joseph Alexander, of St. Charles, was chosen superintendent of Sunday-schools of the presbytery.

"Rev. J. Addison Smith preached an able sermon at 8 o'clock in the evening on the Christian evidences.

"The committee on Sunday-schools reported in favor of the

use of lesson leaves and books of the church in the Sunday-schools.

"Dr. R. P. Farris reported that the state of religion among the churches was healthy, and the attendance on worship is very encouraging; also that there has been a gratifying growth in the membership of the churches. He condemned the purchase and reading of Sunday newspapers, as encouragement of the worst use of money and the most potent instrument of vice.

"The request of Rev. John W. Stagg, to be relieved from this presbytery and allowed to put himself under the care of the Nashville Presbytery, was granted.

"An interesting free conversation on the state of the churches was held, and showed an encouraging condition of affairs.

"The following resolution by Rev. J. A. Smith was unanimously adopted:

"*Resolved*, That this body tender its manifold thanks to the good people of Troy for their elegant hospitality and for the sweet communion around their firesides. Judging the past by the present, we wonder not at the siege of Troy as told in classic story: Troy was worth the siege. We invoke upon the pastor, his family and his people the enriching tokens of the Divine favor."

"Presbytery adjourned to Thursday, September 20, at 11 A. M., at Joachim Church, Jefferson County."

The Cumberland Presbyterian Church at Olney was organized in the fifties at Mount Vernon schoolhouse, and was afterward moved to Olney. The first members were Charles Hudson, Hiram Hendrix, John H. Downing, Thomas Hammett and their wives. The present frame edifice, 34x54 feet, was erected in 1879, and cost $1,400. It was dedicated in 1880 by Rev. Ephraim Pharr, assisted by Rev. Taylor Bernard, who held a revival at Olney, resulting in the acquisition of thirty new members, and through whose efforts, mainly, the church building was erected. Capt. John H. Downing was the leader in building it, and was the principal contributor in furnishing the funds for that purpose. The pastors, since the organization moved to Olney, have been Revs. Taylor Bernard, Ephraim Pharr, J. W. Duval, Henson McGee and H. P. Ingram. The present pastor is W. H. Jones. The membership is sixty-five. There is another church of this denomination located at Auburn, and preaching by its ministers is had at some other points.

There is an organization some miles northeast of Troy, called the "Reformed Presbyterian Church."

CHRISTIAN CHURCH.

The oldest organizations of the Christian Church in Lincoln County are located at Louisville and Auburn. The Troy Christian Church was organized in July, 1856. The following is a copy of the proceedings pertaining to its organization, viz.: "On the 6th (Lord's Day) of July, A. D. 1856, M. A. Crump, Ann E. Wing, Joannah Null, Elizabeth Hunter, persons who, under the preaching of Elders J. J. Errett and Timothy Ford, have confessed their faith in our Lord and Saviour Jesus Christ, and by baptism put Him on, and Benedict Crump, John S. Null, Mary Wing, Sarah Sheets and Elizabeth Shipp (by Mary Wing, proxy), and Eliza Null and Frederick Wing, persons known to each other as former members of the Church of Christ, met at the Universalist Church in Troy, Mo., and resolved to live together in the capacity of a church, to be known as the Church of Christ in Troy, Mo., taking the Scriptures of truth in their own statements and communications as their only rule of faith and practice. And, in accordance with said resolution, F. Wing was chosen a clerk of said body, for the purpose of keeping a strict and impartial record of their proceedings. James Ellis, Fidelia Ellis and Harrott Fisher, persons known to all of the above mentioned individuals as former members in good standing in the Church of Christ, and who were unable to attend the meeting mentioned, did, at the next meeting of said body, join in the same resolutions and purposes. F. WING, *Clerk*."

This organization continued to worship in the Universalist Church, known now as the Masonic Building, until the present commodious brick church edifice was erected in the year 1859. The pastors of this church have been Elders J. J. Errett, from the organization to 1859; then the church was supplied with preaching by different elders until 1866, when Elders William Frazier and E. V. Rice were chosen. The pulpit was then filled by Elder Rice until 1868. In July, 1869, James A. Wing took charge of the church as pastor, but soon resigned on account of financial difficulties. Since 1874 the pastors have been Elders W. A. Meloan, to 1876; W. B. Gallagher, 1876-78; William Errett, 1878-79; Robert L. McHatton, 1880-81; D. M. Grandfield, 1881-84; S. W. Martin, 1884-86; J. M. Bovee, present pastor, since June, 1888. The membership at this writing is seventy-seven.

Lynn Knoll Christian Church on Survey 1743, Hurricane Township, was organized in July, 1885, by Elders Jeptha Jeans and D. M. Grandfield, with forty members. Elder Jeans has been pastor from its organization to the present time (July, 1888). The building in which they worship is a frame 32x40 feet in size, and was erected in the winter of 1885-86. It was dedicated the first Sunday of May, 1886, by Elder D. M. Grandfield. It cost about $1,000. Sunday-school, consisting of forty to fifty pupils, is taught in this house during the summer months. A. R. Barton, Sunday-school superintendent, has served since the spring of 1887.

The Corinth Christian Church, situated about one and a half miles north of the village of Foley, was organized in 1848, at the house of Frank Riffles, and in 1871 the frame church building, in which the society now worships, was built.

Elm Grove Christian Church, near Mackville, was organized in 1860, under the ministry of Elder T. Ford. The present church edifice used by this society was dedicated August 25, 1875, by Elder J. J. Errett, assisted by Elder J. H. Thomas. The text used by Elder Errett consisted of the first six verses of the sixth chapter of Second Chronicles. Following the sermon, $262.60 were collected to pay off all the indebtedness of the new church. It was built by Pendleton, of Clarksville, at a cost of $2,000.

Other organizations of the Christian Church exist in Lincoln County at the following places: New Hope, Highland Prairie, near Chain of Rocks; Old Alexandria, Wilson's schoolhouse, four miles east of Troy; Winfield, Sulphur Lick, Louisville and Hawk Point. The present brick church at Louisville was erected in 1847. Christian ministers also preach at some other points.

Considering the many points covered, it is clear that this is one of the strongest churches in Lincoln County.

CATHOLIC CHURCHES.

Saint Alphonsus' Church.—Judge Henry T. Mudd, who settled at Millwood in 1839, was the first Roman Catholic to enter the lands in the northwest part of Lincoln County. During the years 1840 and 1841 services of his church were occasionally held at his house by Father Walters. In 1842 a log church, costing about $300, was erected and fitted up for services, and continued to be used until about the year 1850, when a brick edifice, costing $6,000, was erected in its stead. This fine church, together with its $800 organ, was caught in a cyclone in 1876, and completely destroyed. Soon thereafter the present frame church building, 34x76 feet in size, and 20 feet in height, with organ and side galleries, was erected at a cost of $4,000. It was dedicated, when completed, by Peter Richard Kenrick, archbishop of St. Louis. In the ministry of this church Father Walters was followed by Father Murphy, of Monroe County, who held services twice a month during the years of 1842 and 1843. He was followed by Father Robert Wheeler, of St. Louis, who located at Millwood and took entire charge of the church for two or three years. Following him, and up to 1849, one or two others officiated temporarily. In 1849 Father Daniel Lyne located at Millwood, and officiated until 1858, when he left. He built the brick church in 1850. He was succeeded by Fathers Healey, O'Reagan, O'Hanlon and Cummings,* who filled the remaining space of time up to 1863, and since that time Father Thomas Cleary, the present priest, has officiated, having been a resident of Millwood all the while. This church has about 130 familes in membership, and averages about fifty baptisms and twelve weddings a year. In connection with this church a fine two-story frame building 18x60 feet in size, with a one-story wing 18x30 feet attached, has just been completed for a convent school. It stands on a beautiful lot, adjoining the church on the north. Father Daniel Lyne is said to have been as talented a minister as ever filled a country pulpit. He once preached

---

*Perhaps these four are not named in exact order.

a sermon in Washington, with Daniel Webster as an attentive listener, and was one of the two delegates who represented Missouri in the Buffalo Immigration Convention early in the fifties. He died in Ireland about the year 1870.

After leaving Millwood Father Cummings located at Louisiana in Pike County, Mo. The Drake Constitution provided that every priest, preacher and teacher, as well as every officer or voter, should take the "iron-clad oath." This Archbishop Kenrick forbade his clergy to do, as such an interference with church matters was contrary to the constitution of the United States. In obedience to the Archbishop's commands, and, no doubt, in accordance with the dictates of his own conscience, Father Cummings refused, as generally did the Catholic priesthood in Missouri, to take the "test oath of loyalty," as it was called, but continued to perform his ministerial duties. Accordingly, he was arrested, and, refusing to give bond for his appearance at court, he was placed in jail. About the same time other Catholic priests in Missouri were arrested, but their cases were continued with the understanding that Father Cummings' should be made a test case. This case was taken to the supreme court of the United States, where a decision was rendered in favor of the defendant, and against the validity of the so-called test oath, and thus ended all such cases in Missouri.

The Church of the Immaculate Conception, parsonage and schoolhouse, are situated on an eminence midway between Chain of Rocks and Old Monroe. Holy services were held in the parsonage as early as 1860, and were first celebrated by Father C. Tintrup, of St. Paul, Mo. The present frame and log church edifice was erected in 1867, at a cost of $4,000, and was dedicated by Father P. Gerard. The pastors have been Fathers C. Tintrup, of St. Paul, Mo.; Nicholas Standinger, of St. Peters, Mo.; George Fuersterberg and J. G. Sudeik. The latter, the present pastor, has served ever since August 19, 1875. The membership of this church consists of seventy-two families.

The corner-stone of the schoolhouse was laid August 22, 1879, and the blessings of the school were given in December of that year by Rev. Father H. Muehlsiejun, vicar-general of the Most Rev. Archbishop Peter Richard Kenrick, D. D., of St.

Louis. This building is of brick, and is 28x40 feet in size, the upper part being the dwelling of the Sisters having charge of the school.

EVANGELICAL CHURCHES.

St. Paul's German Evangelical Church stands on an eminence midway between Chain of Rocks and Winfield. It was erected on its present site in 1859 of logs, and was replaced in 1881 by the present fine brick edifice, which was built by subscription at a cost of $3,400. Forty-five families, numbering about 225 souls included in the church, have services every Sunday. They have about twelve baptisms per year. Rev. Philip Albert is now, and for many years has been, pastor of this church. The school in connection with the church was organized about sixteen years ago, and for the last six or seven years has been under the immediate control of Rev. Albert.

Evangelical Zion Church at Troy, was organized July 24, 1887, by Rev. Philip Albert, with sixteen constituent members. The fine brick church edifice, standing prominently on a mound-like hill in the northeastern part of the town, was erected in 1887, and was dedicated on Thanksgiving Day of that year. It cost $2,000. This society, as yet, has not increased its membership. There are two other organizations of this denomination in the county, located at Moscow and Big Creek.

SUNDAY-SCHOOLS.

Nearly all the churches situated in the towns and villages of Lincoln County support and maintain Sunday-schools in their respective edifices, and in sôme of the country churches, but not in all, Sunday-schools are taught, except during that portion of the year when the roads are almost impassable. In April, 1880, a Union Sunday-school organization was formed at the Methodist Episcopal Church South, in Troy, and the following officers were selected: W. J. Knott, president; S. R. Woolfolk, P. G. Shelton and W. A. Woodson, vice-presidents; T. J. Nally, treasurer; and O. H. Avery, secretary. In July, 1888, a Sunday-school convention was held in the Christian Church at Troy, for the purpose of encouraging more thorough organization in Sunday-school work, and, if possible, to provide Sunday-school facilities for the many children in the county that are deprived of such privileges.

CHAPTER XVI.

MISCELLANEOUS.

The following, from the Troy *Free Press* of July 20, 1888, will be read with interest:

"ART LOAN EXHIBITION.—A GRANDLY SUCCESSFUL ENTERPRISE.

"One of the most interesting and deservedly successful church affairs ever given in Troy was the Art Loan Exhibition, held this week by the ladies of the Presbyterian Church. The rooms in the basement of the church were just full of beautiful things, costly things, unique things, things ancient, modern, rare and quaint. Space would not permit a full list of even the articles that are more than ordinarily interesting, so the chronicler will have to content himself with a recital of the ancient articles, and those that attract by reason of their association.

"Beginning in the pastor's study, the visitor sees a little blue salt stand, one hundred and fifty years old, the property of Mrs. Geiger. Mrs. P. G. Shelton's contribution to the exhibition embraces many ancient articles. Among them are hand made tapestries that were in existence during the Revolutionary War, a silver cup used by Augustine Claiborne during the same period, and Masonic regalia worn by Mr. Shelton's ancestors before the voice of Patrick Henry incited the colonists to fight for the rights of independent States.

"Mrs. D. C. Russell exhibits a specimen of taxidermy in the shape of a squirrel mounted in England one hundred years ago, and a decorated powder horn upon which a prisoner whiled away many hours during the late war.

"Mrs. A. S. Buchanan exhibits a strongly made chair of plantation manufacture that saw the stirring events of the dawn of the century, and a piece of continental money bearing a date about that of Washington's commission as general of the American armies.

"A pitcher one hundred years old is another antiquity in this room; also a silver spoon one hundred and fifty years old, now the property of Mrs. Anna Farmer.

"Mrs. S. R. Woolfolk has on display a china tea set one hundred years old, and oil portraits of her grandfather, Henry Bragg, and her great uncle, Allen Bragg, that were painted before the Revolution.

"Among the really historic relics on exhibition are several displayed by Mrs. Blennerhassett, being the property of the once famous Blennerhassett of the Island. They are a pistol case, spectacles, snuff box and match box.

"In the same case was a small gold seal ring from the finger of a man who fell at the battle of Waterloo.

"Mrs. Jane Wheeler contributed a pin and needle case one hundred and fifty years old, the epaulettes worn by Capt. Wheeler in the Black Hawk war, a stiletto made from the ship 'St. Lawrence.'

"J. W. Pilcher exhibits a fox and geese board that was once the property of the Duke of Wellington, and a brass hammer and scales two hundred years old.

"Table linen made in Germany long years ago is contributed by Mrs. Rosa Hart.

"In other parts of the rooms the visitor saw Indian hatchets, wooden shoes, a razor used in 1788, and an elegant old clock more than a half century old. A large show case full of geological specimens, and containing a small bundle of wheat bound by the first self-binder, was the property of T. C. Wilson. In another corner was a flower grotto made in very artistic style by Mesdames Tice and Carter. There were several beautiful displays by merchants of town, and a number of samples of needle work and painting that would do great credit to any exposition.

"The exposition was open Tuesday and Wednesday evenings and Wednesday afternoon."

LOCAL OPTION.

Prior to the August term, 1887, of the county court, in Lincoln County, a petition on behalf of the cause of temperance was circulated throughout the county, and the several sheets of legal cap paper on which it was circulated, and on which the names of the petitioners were written, when pasted together, making one continuous petition, measured twenty-five feet in length. This enormously large petition was presented to the county court on August 10, 1887, and the following is a copy of the record of the proceedings relating thereto:

"*In the matter of Local Option in and for Lincoln County, Missouri:*

"And now at this day comes Thomas H. Harris, A. H. Chenoweth and 837 others, and file their petition with this court, which said petition is in words and figures as follows, to wit:

"*To the Honorable the County Court of Lincoln County, Mo.:* We, the undersigned, qualified voters of said county of Lincoln, hereby petition and ask that an order be made causing an election to be held in said county, to determine whether or not spirituous and intoxicating liquors, including wine and beer, shall be sold within the limits of said county, in pursuance of and in all respects as provided in and by what is known as the local option law, enacted by the General Assembly of the State of Missouri, approved April 5, A. D. 1887, and, it appearing to the satisfaction of the Court that said petition contains the names of more than one-tenth of the qualified voters of said county of Lincoln, and is in conformity with Section 1 of said act, it is therefore ordered by the Court, that a special election be held in said county of Lincoln, at the usual voting precincts thereof, on Saturday, the 17th day of September, 1887, so that the question of whether or not spirituous and intoxicating liquors, including wine and beer, shall be sold within the limits of Lincoln County, may be submitted to the qualified voters of said county. Said election shall be conducted, the returns thereof made, and the result thereof ascertained and determined, in accordance in all respects with the laws of this State governing general elections for county officers. It being deemed expedient, it is ordered by the Court that there shall be written or printed on each ballot voted at said election the following sentences:

"'Against the sale of intoxicating liquors.' 'For the sale of intoxicating liquors,' with the further instruction printed on such ticket or ballot: 'Erase the clause you do not want.' And it is further ordered by the Court that a copy of this order be inserted in some public newspaper published in the county for four consecutive weeks, and the last insertion shall be within ten days next before said election."

In accordance with the foregoing order of the court Jesse J. Shaw, the county court clerk, published a certified copy thereof as required, in the Troy *Herald*, the last publication of the order being on the 7th day of September. No active canvass was entered into by and between those opposed to and those in favor of the sale of intoxicating liquors. The election was accordingly held, and the following table shows the result in each election precinct:

VOTING PRECINCT.	Votes Cast Against Sale of Liquors.	Votes For Sale of Liquors.
Chain of Rocks	19	119
Chantilla	79	24
Winfield	95	72
Burr Oak Valley	113	14
Brussells	104	12
New Hope	125	16
Elsberry	175	61
Smith's Schoolhouse	35	18
Auburn	62	12
Louisville	88	59
Olney	73	56
Millwood	55	62
Truxton	66	52
Snow Hill	41	44
Hubbard's Schoolhouse	34	138
Troy	288	134
Richardson's Mill	24	18
Whiteside	85	18
Silex	66	22
Total	1,622	951

On the 22d day of September following the election, the county court made the following entries on the record of its proceedings:

"It appearing to the satisfaction of the Court from the returns on file in the office of the county clerk, and from the official count made by said county clerk and two justices of the peace, and filed in this court, that at the special election held in the county on the 17th day of September, 1887, a majority was given against the the sale of intoxicating liquors in said county, it is therefore ordered by the Court that the following notice be inserted in the Troy *Herald* and the Elsberry *Advance* for four consecutive weeks:

"STATE OF MISSOURI, } ss.
COUNTY OF LINCOLN.

"This is to certify that at a special election held in Lincoln County, State of Missouri, on Saturday, September 17, 1887, in accordance with an act of the General Assembly of the State of Missouri, entitled 'Local Option,' approved April 5, 1887, to determine whether intoxicating liquors, including wine and beer, shall be sold in said county, there were 1,622 votes cast against the sale of liquors, and 951 votes cast for the sale of intoxicating liquors. Majority vote against the sale of intoxicating liquors, 671."

Under this decision of the people of the county, the saloon-keepers made preparations to close out their business at the expiration of the time for which they had paid the license fee, and now there is not a saloon for the sale of intoxicating liquors in the county.

BIOGRAPHICAL APPENDIX.

William Achor, a worthy farmer of Lincoln County, is the son of Abram and Nancy (Ellis) Achor, who were born respectively in Virginia and Kentucky. They moved to Daviess County, Ind., and there died at a ripe old age. Their family consisted of eleven children, eight sons and three daughters. Both parents were members of the Missionary Baptist Church, and the father was a soldier in the War of 1812. Five of his sons served in the Union army during the late war, and were in service three years. The eldest son, William, was born in Shelby County, Ky., in September, 1824, was reared on a farm and received a limited education. At the age of twenty-one he began for himself as a farmer, and has continued that occupation ever since. In 1846 he married Miss Martha Sullenger, a native of Henry County, Ky., born in 1826. The same year of their marriage they moved to Lincoln County, Mo., and he has made that county his home since. To their marriage were born six children, of whom three are now living. Mr. Achor has been both school director and road overseer ever since coming to this county, with the exception of about two years. He was a Whig previous to the war, but now affiliates with the Democratic party. He has lived in this county for forty-two years, is accounted a good farmer and citizen, owns 260 acres of good land, and he and wife are members of the Missionary Baptist Church.

Reid Alexander, farmer and stock raiser of Lincoln County, Mo., was born in Shelby County, Ky., in 1827, and is a son of

John and Anna (Reid) Alexander, who were born in the same county and State as their son, and there lived until 1833, when they came to Lincoln County, Mo., and settled on a farm, where the father died soon after, it is supposed about 1835. His grandfather, James Alexander, was born in Virginia, and was of Scotch-Irish descent. His father, also named James, came from Ireland to America and located where Philadelphia now is. John Alexander, an uncle of our subject, was a soldier in the War of 1812, and his half brother, Archibald Alexander, was an eminent divine of Virginia, and was a man of great literary ability. Mrs. Anna Alexander died in 1851. Reid Alexander is the youngest of her five children, and his educational advantages were limited to the country schools. He was married in 1847 to Sarah J., a daughter of Cyrus and Jane Finley, of Kentucky, and by her became the father of six children: Jennie (deceased), Anna (wife of William Shannon), Bettie, Matie, Hadassah and Lou. He owns a good and well cultivated farm of 240 acres, and takes considerable interest in stock raising. He is a Democrat in politics and he and wife are members of the Associate Reformed Presbyterian Church of the South.

John J. Alexander is a cousin and son-in-law of Reid Alexander. He was born in Lincoln County, Mo., in 1832, and is a son of Samuel and Ann R. (Shannon) Alexander, who were born in Virginia and Tennessee, respectively, the former born in 1798, and the latter in 1800. He was married in Shelby County, Ky., about 1820, and in 1831 came to Lincoln County, Mo., where he died in 1854, and the mother in 1872. John J. is their only child that is living. He was educated in the common schools, and from 1879 until 1882 was in the drug business at Troy. Up to this time he was engaged in stock raising and trading, and is the owner of 526 acres of land, with 240 acres improved. In 1880 he took the census of Monroe Township. In 1882 he was married to Janie Alexander, who died in 1886, leaving two daughters, Estella and Jennie. Mr. Alexander is a Democrat and a member of the Associate Reformed Presbyterian Church.

Joshua H. Alexander, recorder of Lincoln County, Mo., was born in Lincoln County, August 30, 1846, and was educated in the district schools of his native county. Upon reaching manhood he began farming, but afterward turned his attention to merchandising, which occupation he followed for four years. In 1886 he ran for the office of recorder as the regular nominee of the Democratic party. In 1872 he married Miss Annie E. Nalley, a native of Lincoln County, and a member of the Christian Church. Mr. Alexander is a Democrat in his political views and is a member of the Masonic fraternity. His father, James Alexander, was born in Virginia, moved from that State to Kentucky and from there to Missouri. The mother, Julia A. (Dryden) Alexander, was born in Maryland, but when quite young moved to Lincoln County, where she married Mr. Alexander. Of seven children born to this union—five sons and two daughters—Joshua H. was the fourth. He has lived all his life in Lincoln County, and is well known and respected as a straightforward business man and a good citizen. His parents were both members of the Old School Presbyterian Church, and the father was a farmer and stock trader by occupation. He was also a Democrat in politics and died many years since. Mrs. Alexander is still living.

James H. Anderson, senior member of the firm of Anderson & Gear, of Moscow Mills, Mo., is a native of the county, born July 13, 1862, being a son of James and Mary (Eckstein) Anderson, who were born in Kentucky and Germany, respectively. The former came to Missouri in 1829, and the latter when about eighteen years of age. The father was a farmer by occupation and also kept a country store for some time. He was a Democrat, and died in 1881 at the age of seventy-six years. The mother still lives and is about forty-eight years old. The eldest of their five living children is James H., who was educated in the common schools and the schools of Troy. He farmed and also bought stock and grain until 1885, at which time he built a store-house at Moscow Mills and stocked it with general merchandise. The following year Mr. Gear became his partner in the business and their union has proved a fortunate one, as they have met with good and deserved success. They are wide awake business men, and are perfectly honest in all their dealings. In 1885 Mr. Anderson was appointed postmaster of Moscow Mills, which office he has since held. He is a Democrat and was a delegate to the Democratic State convention. He also belongs to the Masonic fraternity, and in 1885 was united in marriage to Mina J. Henry, a native of the county, by whom he has one child, Mary J.

S. W. Avery. Among the citizens who have assisted in building up Lincoln County should be mentioned the names of Samuel W. and Martha A. Avery. The former was born February 24, 1824, in Cincinnati, Ohio, and is the son of Samuel and Abigail (Fairchilds) Avery. Both parents came from the East, and located in Cincinnati, where the father followed carpentering. He died when Samuel W. was but three months old. Some years later the mother married again, and spent her last days in Yazoo City, Miss. Samuel W. Avery, the only survivor of a family of four sons born to the first marriage, went to live with an uncle, by marriage, at the age of four years. He was put to work in a paper mill when very young, and there he continued until seventeen years of age, never having attended school a day in his life. Seeing that the prospects for a rise in the world were not very flattering while he remained with his uncle, he determined to run away. This he did, and after roaming about for some time found himself in St. Louis. This was in 1843. With a keen appetite and nothing to satisfy it, he went in quest of a boarding place. A kind widow agreed to board him and wait until he could earn some money. He soon accumulated a few dollars, and with a little assistance purchased a horse and wagon. He then commenced peddling tinware. In 1844 he moved with his outfit to Lincoln County, Mo., and has made it his home ever since. In 1851 he married Miss Martha A. Sheets, who was born on June 29, 1833, in Callaway County, Mo., and who was the daughter of Charles Sheets, a native of Kentucky, born in 1796, though his parents were from Maryland. After reaching manhood Mr. Sheets married Sarah Edrington, a Kentucky lady, born in 1798. They moved to Callaway County, Mo., in 1830, and three years later to Lincoln County. He was a well-to-do farmer, a Whig and an active member of the Methodist Episcopal Church, as was also his wife. He died in 1868, and she July 3, 1888. Of their eleven children, nine lived to be grown. After marriage Mr. and Mrs. Avery settled on a farm. They became the parents of six children, only four now living, three sons and a daughter. One son, deceased, was a physician;

Omer H. is an attorney; Charles D., a physician; Samuel, a druggist, and Sallie is the wife of John E. Worsham, a grocer; all are located in Troy. Mr. Avery has always been a very liberal supporter of schools and churches. During the war he built, on his farm and at his own expense, a school-house at which were educated some of the able men of this part of the State. Before the war Mr. Avery was a Whig in politics, but since then he has been a Democrat. In 1881 he and family moved to Troy. He and wife are members of the Methodist Episcopal Church.

Omer H. Avery, attorney, and son of Samuel W. and Martha A. (Sheets) Avery, was born near Troy, April 3, 1854, and received his literary education in the district schools and in Troy. At the age of fifteen he began teaching, and followed this occupation for about eight years. He was principal of the schools at Auburn, Mo., for a time and also read law while there. In 1875 he entered the law department of the Missouri State University and graduated from the same two years later. Failing health deterred him from practice until 1879, when he began practicing with R. D. Walton, and was afterward a partner of Judge A. V. McKee, after whose death he formed a partnership with Charles Martin, which continues at the present. From 1880 to 1884 he was public administrator, and in 1881 he married Miss Kate Jefferson, of Montgomery County, and the daughter of Booker Jefferson. Three children were born to this union, only one, Clara, now living. Mr. Avery is a Democrat in politics, and he and wife are members of the Methodist Episcopal Church South. In 1888 Mr. Avery was the choice of the nominating convention for prosecuting attorney of Lincoln County. Competent judges pronounce the members of the firm of Martin & Avery as among the first lawyers of the Lincoln County bar.

Samuel M. Bailey, M. D., a practicing physician and surgeon and a furniture and harness dealer at Elsberry, Mo., was born in St. Louis County in 1849. He was educated in the public schools of St. Louis, and in 1873 graduated from the Washington University. He then began the study of medicine, and in 1876 received his diploma from the St. Louis Medical College, which institution he had been attending for some time. He entered upon the practice of his profession at Frankfort, Mo., where he remained about three years; thence to Southwest Missouri, and to Kansas City, where he practiced two years. In 1885 he came to Elsberry, and since then has been a successful practitioner of the county. Since 1887 he has been in the furniture and harness business. He is a Democrat and a member of the A. O. U. W., and in 1872 was married to Kate Powell, who died in 1884, leaving two children. The Doctor took for his second wife Sophia Banteen. His parents were Clifton and Mary (Walton) Bailey, and were natives respectively of Virginia and Missouri. The former died in 1851, and the latter in 1881.

William T. Baker, school commissioner of Lincoln County, is the son of David W. and Matilda P. (Fitzhugh) Baker. The father was a native of Virginia, and in boyhood was brought to this State by his parents, who settled in Montgomery County. The mother was born in Tennessee, and moved with her parents to the last named county while still an infant. She here married Mr. Baker and became the mother of ten children, seven now living. The father was a farmer, and was also a trader in live stock. He was a prominent man in the county, having held the office of judge of the county court, and had been representative of the county, and he and wife were members of the Methodist Episcopal Church. He died in 1865, but the mother is still living. William T. Baker was born January 16, 1849, in Montgomery County, Mo., and after attending the common schools and an academy, he entered Bryant & Stratton's Commercial College, at St. Louis, in 1870. After finishing his commercial course he came to Lincoln County, worked in the county clerk's office, kept books, studied, and was admitted as an attorney to practice law, and for about eleven years taught school in that county. He then went to the National Normal University at Lebanon, Ohio, and completed the teacher's course and a course in civil engineering. He then returned and taught mathematics and book-keeping in the Troy High School. In 1883 he was called to McCune College, Louisiana, Mo., where he taught mathematics and natural science, and the following year he became connected with the Farmers' & Mechanics' Savings Bank, at Troy, as assistant cashier and book-keeper. He is an Odd Fellow and a Mason, belonging to the Blue Lodge and the Chapter. He is a Democrat in his political views, and a good man. In 1885 he was appointed to serve an unexpired term as county school commissioner, and was elected to the same office in 1887. He is highly competent, both as an educator and a business man.

William H. Baskett is a native of Shelby County, Ky., where he was born in 1841, being the son of Horatio N. and Almeda (Griffith) Baskett. He is the second of eleven children, seven living, and was educated in the district schools. In 1870 he married Elizabeth F., daughter of William and Edna E. Sanders, natives of Virginia, but early residents of Kentucky and also of Lincoln County, Mo. Mr. Baskett is the father of three children: George V., Lemuel T. and Edna Effie. He rented land until 1877, and then purchased his present farm of ninety acres. In 1861 he joined Capt. Paul Penn's company of cavalry, Confederate States army, and was at the battle of Mount Zion. Since the war he has been a Democrat and is a member of the Masonic fraternity, New Hope Lodge No. 199. Mrs. Baskett's father died in 1858 and her mother in 1876.

Ex-Judge Horatio N. Baskett, father of William H. Baskett, was born in Shelby County, Ky., in 1809, and is the son of Job and Sarah (Mitchell) Baskett, both of whom were natives of Virginia. They were married in Kentucky in 1808, and the father spent the remainder of his days in Shelby County. He was a farmer and died in 1833. His wife moved to Missouri early in the fifties and died in Clark County in 1878, at the age of ninety years. The mother's father, Charles Mitchell, was a soldier in the Revolutionary War. Horatio N. is the eldest of eleven children, and was educated in the subscription schools. He was married in 1838 to Almeda Griffith, and their union resulted in the birth of eleven children, seven of whom are living. In 1841 they came to Lincoln County, Mo., and located on a farm near New Hope, where he lived until 1886, and since that time has resided in New Hope. In 1846 he was elected justice of the peace and served eight years. In 1854 he was elected associate county judge, serving four years, and was again elected, in 1874, for six years. He has been an earnest worker for the cause of education, and has substantially aided all enterprises for the public weal. He was formerly a Whig in politics, but is now a Democrat. He and wife have been members of the Missionary Baptist Church for many years.

William Berkley was born in Benton County, Mo., in 1849, and is the youngest of five children born to the marriage of Samuel Berkley and Martha Powers, who were born, reared and married in Pike County, Mo. They afterward removed to Benton County, and there the mother died about 1859. The father was a farmer, and in 1850 went to California and died soon after his arrival in that State. After his mother's death, William Berkley spent about two years with his uncle, Edward Powers, and then went to California; and, after remaining there some five months, went to Salt Lake City, where he spent nearly two years. He was in the military service there during 1864 and 1865, under Gen. Connor. After the close of the war he returned to Benton County, and in 1866 came to Lincoln County, where he married and has since lived. He owns a fertile and well cultivated farm of 260 acres, and in his political views is a supporter of Democratic principles. He belongs to the I. O. O. F. His marriage to Nancy J. Worthington occurred in 1879. She is a daughter of Francis and Catherine Worthington. The latter's death occurred in 1856. The father is living with his second wife and by her is the father of three children. Mr. and Mrs. Berkley are the parents of five children: William Francis, Charley, Katie, Mary J. and Rhoda.

Ludwell C. Bibb, a farmer of Lincoln County, is a native of Amherst County, Va., born in 1836, and is one of eight children in the family of William and Jane (Pryor) Bibb, who were also Virginians. The father was born in 1810, and in 1856 moved to Marshall County, Iowa, but later located in Pike County, Mo., and is now living in Lawrence County, keeping a hotel. He was formerly a farmer, and has been married three times. His first wife died about 1848. Ludwell C. was educated in the common schools of Virginia, and up to 1861 made his home with his father. At that date he came to Lincoln County, where he was married a year later to Mary E., a daughter of Tarplin R. Mitchell, who was formerly of Virginia, but an early settler of Lincoln County. To Mr. Bibb's marriage were born seven children, five of whom are living: Addie (wife of Guy Damron), Blanche,

Arthur, Iva and Lofton. Mr. Bibb has an excellent farm of 300 acres, which he has earned by his own efforts. He takes great interest in the cause of education, and votes the Democratic ticket. He and his wife have been members of the Baptist Church for over thirty years.

Elder Francis M. Birkhead was born in Lincoln County, Mo., in 1832, and is a son of Abraham B. and Joannah (Nixon) Birkhead, who were born in Loudoun County, Va., but were married in Nelson County, Ky., where they lived until 1830, when they came to Lincoln County, Mo., where they cleared a farm and spent the remainder of their days. The father died in Kentucky in 1849, aged about sixty-seven years. The mother died in 1873, aged nearly eighty years. The father was married twice, the first wife being a Miss Foreman, by whom he had four children. By his last wife he was the father of ten children, seven of whom are living. His son, Francis M., was educated in the primitive log school-houses of early times, only attending about three months during the year. He began farming for himself at the age of twenty, and was married in 1850 to Susan A., a daughter of William and Elizabeth Overall, natives of Nelson and Bullitt Counties, Ky., respectively, the former being of English and the latter of Dutch-Irish descent. Mrs. Birkhead was born in Bullitt County, Ky., in 1830, and made her home with her grandparents until eleven years of age, when she was brought to Lincoln County, Mo. She became the mother of eleven children, nine of whom are living: William N. (married to Eliza E. Nichols, September 24, 1879), John D., Joseph B., Euphemia J. (wife of John W. Crune), Albert H., Joel E., Eliza C., Emma L. and Joan M. Mr. Birkhead is residing on the old homestead, which consists of 260 acres, and has been a minister of the Missionary Baptist Church for fifteen years, and now fills four regular appointments. He was licensed in 1872, and ordained a year later. He has assisted in organizing a number of churches, and has done much to further the cause of Christianity. He is a Democrat in politics, and is a member of the Masonic fraternity.

Robert E. Black, a hardware dealer and lumber merchant of Elsberry, Mo., was born in Alleghany City, Penn., in 1846, and is the youngest of four children born to William and Margaret

(Elliott) Black, who were born in Scotland, where they were married about 1835. They came to America soon after, and located in Pennsylvania, where the mother died soon after Robert E. was born. Mr. Black was a contractor and builder, and was a large property holder. He died in Keokuk, Iowa, where he had gone on business. Robert E. Black was educated in the public schools of Alleghany City, and at an early day learned the carpenter's trade. He came to New Hope in 1864, but soon after returned to Pennsylvania, where he remained three years, when he again came to New Hope, and in 1869 married Lucy J., a daughter of J. Nicholas Dameron, and by her became the father of four sons and four daughters. Mr. Black lived at New Hope, where he followed contracting and building until 1880, when he came to Elsberry, and has since followed the same occupation here. He owns 413 acres of land near Elsberry, some fine town property, and 100 acres of land west of the town; he also owns about sixty vacant lots in Keokuk, Iowa. He takes a great interest in the cause of education, and was one of three men who erected a fine brick school-house at Elsberry. Mr. Black is a Mason, and a member of the Masonic and A. O. U. W. fraternities, and in his political views is a Democrat. His present business was established in 1880, and the firm name is Black & Luckett. Mr. Luckett was born in New Hope, and was there reared and educated, and also attended one session at Foggy Seminary in Pike County. He remained on the farm until 1882, and then became a partner of Mr. Black's, at Elsberry. He is a Democrat, and a son of W. S. and Mary (Cox) Luckett, who were born in Tennessee and Virginia, respectively. They were early settlers of Missouri, and are still residing at New Hope.

Samuel J. Blakely is a native of Christian County, Ky., born in 1816. He was brought to Howard County, Mo., when an infant and was reared here, but his educational advantages were very few. In 1839 he was united in marriage to Susan E. Myrtle, a native of Howard County, and seven children blessed their union, six of whom are living: Sally Ann (widow of Jesse Tate), Hannah Ramsie (deceased, wife of Julius F. Cox), Olivia (wife of James Sanders), John William (who is in a stock commission business with his brother-in-law, James Sanders, in St. Louis), Mary Susan (widow of Job B. Ballard), Cornelia (wife of Thomas Riley) and Addie Belle. Soon after his marriage Mr. Blakely removed to Macon County, but in 1866 came to Lincoln County, and located on a good farm near New Hope. He is a Democrat and a member of the Masonic fraternity. Mrs. Blakely and five of her daughters are members of the Christian Church, Mrs. Tate being a Presbyterian. Mr. Blakely's parents, John and Hannah (Hardin) Blakely, were born in Georgia and Kentucky, respectively, and were married in the latter State about 1817, and came to Howard County, Mo., where the mother died, before the war, and the father after, in 1866, at about seventy-eight years of age. He was of Irish descent.

Robert P. Boulton, editor-in-chief and one of the proprietors of the Troy *Free Press*, was born in Boone County, Mo., June 29, 1854, and is one of six children, five living, born to the marriage of Jesse A. and Clara D. (Perrine) Boulton, who were Kentuckians. The father was reared in his native State, and received a good education, and, after reaching a proper age, taught both public and private schools, and then turned his attention to farming. He was first married to Mary Smith, a Kentucky lady, with whom he came to Boone County, Mo., in 1840. Here the mother died, leaving two children. Mr. Boulton returned to Kentucky and married Miss Perrine, and came to Missouri in 1850, where he has since made his home. He was born May 19, 1817, and his wife, March 30, 1829. They are both members of the Christian Church, and he is a Democrat, and served as judge of Boone County two terms. Robert P. is their eldest child, and was reared on a farm. His early education was received in the public schools, and later he attended the Missouri State University, from which institution he graduated with the degree of B. L. in 1877. After pedagoguing in the public schools until 1880 he took a post-graduate course in his *alma mater* and received the degree of M. L. During the session of 1880-81 and 1881-82 he filled the chair of English literature and history in Christian University, at Canton, Mo., and the following year held a position on the staff of the chief clerk of the Missouri House of Representatives. In 1883-84 he was principal of the Hannibal Collegiate Institute, and in the latter year bought a third interest in the Hannibal *Morning Journal*, of which he became editor. Again, in 1885, he was on the staff of the clerk of the House of Representatives. In 1887 he sold his interest in the *Journal*, and purchased of H. M. Cornick a half interest in the *Lincoln County News*, and this he consolidated with the Troy *Free Press* the following year under the firm name of Boulton & Townsend. Mr. Boulton is a Democrat, and a member of the I. O. O. F., and is also a member of the Christian Church.

John J. Bradley is a Kentuckian, and was born in Bourbon County in 1815. He came to Missouri at the age of fifteen years, and lived successively in Pike, Ralls, Marion, Audrain and Lincoln Counties, locating in the latter county in 1863, where he has since been engaged in tilling the soil and raising stock. He was formerly a carpenter, but for some time has given his attention to farming, and is the owner of 160 acres of land. He is a Democrat, and a member of the Masonic fraternity. He was married in 1836 to Rhoda E. Bradley, who was born in Tennessee in 1819, and by her is the father of the following interesting family: James C. (living in Texas), Elizabeth Layton, (of Texas), John William, Henry H., Nancy J. (wife of John Wilburn), Virginia (wife of Thomas Smith), Margaret J. (wife of James Smith) and Mary (wife of Elmore Thompson). Mr. and Mrs. Bradley are members of the Baptist Church. His parents, Layton and Nancy (Delany) Bradley, were born in Culpeper County, Va., in 1779 and 1782, and died in Missouri in 1848 and 1841, respectively. They were married in 1802, and a year later located in Bourbon County, Ky., and about 1840 settled in Lincoln County, Mo. The father was of Irish-English extraction, and was a shoemaker by trade, but later followed the occupation of farming. His father was Augustine Bradley, and his grandfather was Lawrence Bradley. The latter came from England to America at a very early period, and participated in the French and Indian wars, and was with Braddock when he was defeated and killed.

Austin Bradley, farmer and stock raiser, of Lincoln County, is the youngest of nine children born to the marriage of Layton C. Bradley and Nancy Delany, who were born in Culpeper County, Va., about 1775 and 1780, respectively. They were married in their native State, and became residents of Bourbon County, Ky., previous to 1805. In the year 1830 they became residents of Missouri, and in 1841 came to Lincoln County. The father was a farmer and died in Ralls County. Austin Bradley was born in Bourbon County, Ky., in 1822, and was reared in the woods of Pike County, and at the age of eighteen years went to Wisconsin and worked in the lead mines for about a year, and after an interval of one year, spent six months more there. He then spent about one year traveling in the Southern States—Texas, Louisiana, Alabama and Arkansas. He was married in 1848 to Prudence Downing, and by her became the father of twelve children, six living: Martha Ann (wife of James A. Bradley), James Cooper, Ida L. (wife of B. F. Green), Owen W., John A. and Oscar D. The children have all received good educations, and are doing well for themselves. In 1850 Mr. Bradley crossed the plains to California, but was taken sick soon after his arrival there and was unable to work. He remained about fifteen months and then returned home, and since 1865 has been a resident of his present farm of 376 acres of land. He was formerly a Whig in politics, but is now a Democrat. He has been a member of the Masonic fraternity for about twenty-five years, and he and wife have been members of the Methodist Episcopal Church South for nearly forty years. Mrs. Bradley's parents, James and Martha Downing, were Kentuckians, and became residents of Missouri at an early day, and both died in Lincoln County. Mrs. Bradley was born here in 1830.

Dr. Talbot N. Bragg, physician and surgeon, is the son of Talbot and Elvira R. (Sydner) Bragg, both natives of Lincoln County, Mo. For a livelihood he followed mercantile pursuits, and for several years he was clerk in the land office at Jefferson City. He died in 1863 at the age of thirty, leaving a family of four children, three sons and one daughter. Two of the sons are professional men—Talbot N. and Kelly R., who is preparing for the dental profession. The former was born near Troy, Mo., January 14, 1860, and educated in the Troy schools. At the age of seventeen he began the study of medicine, and in 1878 he entered the Missouri Medical College at St. Louis, graduating from that institution in 1881. He then located at Troy, where he has since been engaged in the practice of his profession. He has been coroner two terms. In 1886 he married Miss Mary A. Pollard, a daughter of Dr. W. H. Pollard, of Pike County. Dr. Bragg has practiced for nearly eight years in Troy, and has secured a good class of patronage, and has met with very satisfactory success. He is a Democrat in his political views, is a member of the A. O. U. W., and he and wife are of the Episcopal faith.

William Brown, farmer and son of Levi and Mary (Oden) Brown, was born in Lincoln County, Mo., where he is now living, in June 1836. The father was born in Cocke County, Tenn., in 1796, and the mother in Barren County, Ky., she being a little older than her husband. He came to Lincoln County in 1815, and she to St. Charles County a few years before, and lived for some time in a fort. After their marriage, in 1829, they settled in Lincoln County, and here spent the balance of their days. He was a mechanic, making spinning wheels, coffins or whatever the early settlers needed, though at the same time he carried on farming. He died in 1881 and she in 1877. He was a Democrat previous to the war and afterwards a Republican. In their family were five children, of whom two sons and one daughter are now living. The grandfather, William Brown, fought in the Revolutionary War. William Brown, the subject of this sketch, was reared on a farm and received little or no education. He lived with and cared for his parents until their death. In 1858 he married Miss Nancy E. Williams, daughter of John P. and Mary (Hatfield) Williams, who were the parents of four daughters, of whom Mrs. Brown is the youngest. The fruits of Mr. Brown's marriage were two children, John L. (deceased) and Levi. Since his marriage Mr. Brown has lived on his fine farm, consisting of 222 acres all well cultivated; besides this he has ample means on interest. He has been a resident of Lincoln County for the past fifty-two years, and has never been on a train or a steamboat. For about three years during the war he belonged to the militia.

James W. Brown was born in Lincoln County, Mo., in 1841, and is a son of Andrew and Sarah (Miller) Brown, who were born in the "Old North State" (Carolina) and came to Missouri in 1826. The father was a farmer and died in 1863, and his wife in 1860. Their son, James W., assisted his parents on the farm, and in 1862 married Susan E. Owens, who bore him six children, and died in 1875. January 24, 1876, Mr. Brown married his second wife, Fannie G. Kemper, and by her is the father of three children. She was born in Kentucky, and died February 7, 1885. Bettie Lee Thompson became his wife in 1886, and two children blessed their union, but both died in infancy. Mr. Brown is a member of the Old School Baptist Church and also its clerk, and for the past fifteen years has been superintendent of the County Poor House and farm. He owns 220 acres of good land on which he has resided since March, 1887. Besides this he has two small farms in different tracts. In June, 1861, he enlisted in the Missouri State Guards, under Gen. Price, and served about six months. He is a stanch Democrat in politics, and on June 2, 1888, was nominated by the Democrats of Lincoln County for the office of public administrator, running ahead of his opponent's votes over two to one.

James H. Brown is a prosperous farmer of Lincoln County, Mo. He is a son of James and Abigail (Lindsey) Brown, who were born in Tennessee and Kentucky in 1803 and 1811, and died in Missouri in 1888 and 1882, respectively. They were married in Pike County, Mo., in 1836, whither the father had come in 1827. They became residents of Lincoln County in 1868, and were zealous members of the Missionary Baptist Church. He was a Whig in early days, but after the war became a Republican. Their family consisted of seven children, James H. Brown being the fourth in the family. He was born in Pike County, September 21, 1844, and spent his boyhood days on his father's farm, and in attending the common schools. In 1864 he enlisted in Company D, Third Missouri Cavalry United States army, and after serving about eight months, enlisted in Company C, Fourteenth Missouri Cavalry, serving until October, 1865, and participating in the battle of Pilot Knob. Since his return home he has followed the occupation of farming, and owns a good farm of 189 acres, on which he located in 1866. He is a member of the A. O. U. W., and is a Republican in politics. In 1870 he was wedded to Missouri C. Lovelace, who was born June 27, 1850, and is the mother of three living children. One child is dead.

Mr. and Mrs. Brown are members of the Missionary Baptist and Christian Churches, respectively.

Cornelius Brown is the son of John Brown, who was born in Virginia and came to Missouri with his parents when a boy, growing up on a farm. After attaining man's estate he took for his companion through life, Mary L. Gunn, who bore him one daughter. After her death he went to Dubuque, Iowa, and served the plasterer's trade, and from there, in 1849, started overland, with an ox team, for California, which he reached after a journey of six months, during which time he had a number of encounters and many narrow escapes from Indians. He was a successful gold miner for three years, and in 1852 returned home by water and subsequently was married in Pike County to Mary A. Hayden, soon after which he moved to Lincoln County and located on a farm. He was very prosperous in his chosen calling, and became one of the first farmers of the county. He was a Democrat, and died in 1877 at the age of fifty-seven years. His widow afterward married J. Bent. Henry, and died in 1881. She was the mother of four sons and one daughter by Mr. Brown, and three of her sons are living, the youngest of whom is Cornelius. He was born on the old home farm, which is now his, October 24, 1861, and there began his career as a farmer. He attended the common schools in boyhood, and at the age of eighteen years began to earn his own living. He worked at the carpenter's trade for some time as bridge carpenter on the St. Louis & Hannibal Railroad, but for the last few years has been living on and farming the old homestead, which consists of 200 acres, with 150 acres under cultivation. In 1886 he was married to Georgie B., a daughter of Abe Duff, and by her is the father of one son, Claude. Mr. Brown's political views are Democratic.

Manford Burley, agent and operator for the St. Louis, Keokuk & Northwestern Railroad, and agent for the American Express Company, at Elsberry, Mo., was born in Ontario, Canada, in 1843, and is the sixth of eight children born to Sylvester and Caroline (Jenkins) Burley, who were also subjects of Great Britain and spent their lives in Canada. The father was a farmer and was of English descent. He was born in 1800 and died in 1875. After his wife's death, which occurred in 1851 at the age of forty-two years, he married Susan Fox, their nuptials being celebrated about 1857. Both parents were members of the Society of Friends or Quakers. Manford Burley was educated in the common schools, and was a graduate of Eastman's Commercial College, at Poughkeepsie, N. Y., in 1865. Since that time very nearly all his attention has been given to railroading, and he has spent the most of the time in Illinois and Missouri, working for the Chicago & Alton Railroad in the former State, and for the St. Louis, Keokuk & Northwestern in the latter. He has been the efficient agent at Elsberry since 1881, and is a faithful and obliging employe. He has been quite successful in his business, and is the owner of a good farm of 250 acres near Elsberry. He is conservative in politics, is a Prohibitionist, and a member of the K. of H. and T. B. A. In 1873 he was married at Pleasant Hill, Ill., to Virginia A., daughter of Lawson Turner, who was a native of Virginia, and died in Illinois about 1877. His wife died in 1868. Mr. Burley is the father of three children: Russell Jay, Maud C. and Mabel Virginia. Mr. Burley is the only one of his family to locate in the United States.

Ephraim Cannon is the fourth of ten children born to John and Jane (Knox) Cannon, who were married in the "Blue Grass State" and became residents of Missouri, in 1818. They improved a good farm in Lincoln County, and there the father died in 1871. The mother's parents came from Ireland, and she was born three weeks after they landed on American soil. Her father, James Knox, came to Missouri at a very early day, and lived many years in Lincoln County. James Cannon, father of John, was probably born in South Carolina. He was a soldier in the Revolutionary War, and came to Lincoln County about 1818, and died when our subject was a young man. Ephraim Cannon was born near Troy, Mo., in 1821, and received a meager education in the old subscription schools of his boyhood days. September 30, 1845, he wedded Nancy A., a daughter of William and Lydia Elsberry, whose sketch appears elsewhere in this work. Their union has been blessed by the birth of ten children, all of whom are living: Sarah (wife of E. A. Cobb), George W., Elizabeth (wife of Israel R. Hinds), Lydia (wife of J. H. Larue), Susan (wife of Howard M. Moxley), John, Mary (wife of Henry

Nichols), Rebecca (wife of Samuel Elston), William F. and Benjamin E. Since his marriage Mr. Cannon has lived on the farm adjoining his old home and owns both places, 640 acres in all. He was in the State Militia a short time during the war. He was formerly a Whig in his political views but now votes the Democratic ticket. His wife died January 9, 1877. She was a consistent and worthy member of the Methodist Episcopal Church.

J. R. Cannon is a member of the dry goods and clothing firm of Cannon & Alloway, at Elsberry, Mo. The business was established in 1880 by Goodman, Cannon & Co., and existed under the firm names of Cannon Sons and Cannon Bros. until 1886, since which time the business has been carried on by the present firm. Their stock amounts to about $12,000, and their annual sales are between $35,000 and $45,000. Mr. Cannon was born in Lincoln County in 1856, and was reared on a farm and educated in the common country schools. He had always resided on a farm up to 1880. He was married in 1878 to Ida, a daughter of Edward and Serepha Whiteside, who were born in Lincoln County. Mrs. Cannon was also born here and is the mother of two children. Mr. Cannon is a Democrat and a member of the A. O. U. W., and he and wife are members of the Baptist Church. He is a son of Isaac, and a grandson of Samuel Cannon. The latter was one of the first white settlers of Lincoln County. His brother and all but one of his entire family were murdered by the Indians. Isaac Cannon was born in Lincoln County, and is now a farmer and stock raiser of Hurricane Township. He was married in 1855, to Lucy Wilkinson. M. S. Alloway, Mr. Cannon's partner in business, was born in Lincoln County, and was reared to an agricultural experience. His parents came originally from the "Blue Grass State," being early settlers of this locality. Mr. Alloway's educational advantages were such as the common schools afforded. Before entering into business at this place he was engaged for some time in merchandising at New Hope.

Joseph Cantriel is a native of Lincoln County, born April 1, 1834, and is the fourth of eight children born to the marriage of David Cantriel and Mary Presley, who were born in Kentucky and South Carolina in 1803 and 1804, and died in Missouri in 1853 and 1874, respectively. They were married in Missouri, and settled on a farm in Lincoln County. Both were members of the Primitive Baptist Church, and he was a supporter of Democratic principles. Young Joseph Cantriel spent the happy, uneventful life of the average farmer's boy, but only received about three months' schooling. By his own efforts, however, he has secured enough education to enable him to attend to his own business affairs. While hauling apples to Clarksville he took his arithmetic with him and learned the muliplication table while going backward and forward. In 1860 he went to Pike's Peak, where he mined for a short time and then returned home. He has a good farm of 240 acres of land, and is one of the prosperous farmers of the county. September 5, 1861, he married Ann Elizabeth Reid, who was born October 28, 1845, and their union has been blessed by the birth of three children, two of whom are living: Mary Elizabeth, born February 24, 1863 (wife of W. W. Broyles), and Richard Henry Walton, born October 12, 1882. Mr. Cantriel supports the principles of the Democratic party.

Thomas M. Carter, a prominent ex-county official, was born in the "Old Dominion," and came with his parents to Missouri in 1830, locating first in St. Charles County, and in 1852 in Lincoln County. He was engaged in the hotel business in the latter place until 1861, when he enlisted in the Confederate service as private, but was soon chosen captain, and before the close of the war rose to the rank of lieutenant-colonel. He was wounded as Elkhorn, Vicksburg and Franklin. At the close of the war he returned home, and in 1868 purchased the farm on which he now lives, consisting of 160 acres. He also gives considerable attention to stock raising. He is a Democrat, politically, and, from 1873 to 1877, served the people of Lincoln County as sheriff, and made an efficient and trustworthy officer. He was married in 1855 to Alabama, daughter of Col. Frank Henry, and by her is the father of two sons and two daughters. Mr. Carter was a soldier in the Mexican War about fifteen months, and his parents, C. L. and Mary (Sawyers) Carter, were both Virginians. The father was a saddler by trade, but in later years followed the occupation of farming and tobacco manufacturing. Both died in St. Charles County, Mo.

Alfred Hamlin Chenoweth, M. D. (deceased). One of the

ablest representatives of the medical profession with which Lincoln County has been blessed was Dr. Alfred Hamlin Chenoweth. Born of illustrious ancestry, he added the highest scholastic training. His father, Rev. Alfred G. Chenoweth, was born in Berkeley County, Va., in 1809, and was a lineal descendent of the fourth generation from Lord Baltimore, and of the third generation from Oliver Cromwell. He was a man of scholarly attainments and one of the shining lights in the Methodist Episcopal Church. While stationed at Greencastle, Ind., he was called to lay aside the burdens of life, dying in 1864. The Doctor's mother, Catherine A. (Peel) Chenoweth, has Rockingham County, Va., as the place of her nativity, and 1812 as the year of her birth. She lived to be sixty-nine, spending her last days in this county. Their family consisted of six children, three sons and three daughters. The oldest son, Bernard P., was a missionary to China, where he died while at the post of duty. William E. was a captain in the Federal army during the late war. The Doctor, the youngest son, was a native of Hampshire County, Va., born December 17, 1846. His literary education was acquired at Asbury University, of Greencastle, Ind., from which institution he graduated in early manhood. In 1863 he volunteered in Capt. Osborn's Company. He served until the close of the war, and after that struggle graduated from the medical department of the University of Virginia. About 1868 he came west, graduated at the St. Louis Medical College, and then located in Lincoln County, Mo. In 1869 he married Miss Ella, daughter of Jonathan and Leah J. (Dryden) Crume. She was born in this county in 1851, though her father was a native of Kentucky and her mother of Maryland. To Dr. and Mrs. Chenoweth were born seven children, four now living. The Doctor was a Mason and an active worker in the Methodist Episcopal Church, as is also his wife. He died November 28, 1887. He was a skillful physician and one pre-eminently fitted for that noble profession.

Francis B. Clare, farmer, is the son of Daniel and Jane (Hansford) Clare. The father was born in Virginia in 1791, although his ancestors were from Germany. He was young when his parents died and he was bound to his brother. At the age of eighteen he left for Keutucky, where he learned the tanner's trade, and at which he worked until coming to Missouri. While in Kentucky he married Miss Hansford, a native of that State, born in 1792. They moved to Lincoln County, Mo., in 1826, and there passed the remainder of their days. The father was a farmer and a soldier under Harrison in the War of 1812. The mother died about 1833, a consistent member of the Baptist Church. The father afterward married Mrs. Frances Cox, of Montgomery County. To the first marriage were born nine children, seven sons and two daughters, and by his second marriage was born one child, a son. Mr. Clare was an old Clay Whig, and he and last wife were members of the Christian Church. He died in 1843. Francis B. was the eldest child born to the first marriage, his birth occurring February 19, 1816, in Somerset, Ky. He attained his education in the country schools, having been reared on a farm, and of course this was limited. At the age of ten he came with his parents to Lincoln County, Mo., and there worked for his father until twenty-one years of age, when he began for himself in agricultural pursuits, making this his life-long work. In 1840 he married Miss Mary Gray, who was born in Kentucky, June 17, 1824. She lost her parents when about three years of age and was brought to this county and reared by her grandparents. To Mr. and Mrs. Clare were born ten children, nine now living, five sons and four daughters. In 1838 Mr. Clare began working on the place where he lives, which now consists of 678 acres in this and Montgomery County. As a farmer Mr. Clare has been quite successful, and his children, upon leaving home, all received a start. He has lived in this county for sixty-two years, and is much respected. He was a Whig but is now a Democrat, and he and wife are members of the Christian Church.

Rev. Father Thomas Cleary, the priest at Millwood, was born in County Tipperary, Ireland, in 1814. He received his literary education in the old country, where he taught school. In 1851 he sailed for America, and after teaching in South Carolina and Georgia, he was honored with the degree of LL. D. at St. Mary's College, S. C. He came to Missouri in 1857, and received his theological education at Carondelet, near St. Louis, and at Cape Girardeau. He was ordained in 1860, and four years later he came to his present charge, where he has continued ever since. Father Cleary is an estimable pastor, and is dearly beloved by all his members.

E. A. Cobb, farmer and stock raiser of Lincoln County, Mo., was born in Montgomery County, Mo., in 1846, and is a son of Henry and Rachel B. (Downing) Cobb. The father was a South Carolinian, and came with his mother and step-father to Missouri. He was married in Lincoln County, but made his home in Montgomery County, where he passed the remainder of his days, dying when our subject was an infant. His widow married again and lived in Lincoln County until her death, which occurred in 1884. Her second husband was George Elsberry. E. A. Cobb was the youngest of two children and was reared by his grandmother Downing, with whom he remained until about fourteen years of age, when at that early age he began farming for himself. Sarah Cannon became his wife in 1866. She is a daughter of Ephraim and Nancy Cannon, and is the mother of the following children: George, Nida, Gertie, Earl and John. Two children are dead. Mr. Cobb rented land until 1882, when he purchased his present farm of 126 acres, which is well situated and under good cultivation. He supports the principles of the Democratic party.

Osborn N. Coffey, an old and respected citizen and an early settler of Lincoln County, Mo., was born in Casey County, Ky., February 4, 1807, and is the son of Jesse and Elizabeth (Riffe) Coffey, both of whom were natives of Kentucky. Their ancestors were from Virginia and Pennsylvania, respectively. The father was an extensive dealer in hogs, which he used to drive to Richmond, Va., a distance of about five hundred miles. He was a colonel in the War of 1812, was for two terms a member in the State Legislature, and a member of the Constitutional Convention of Kentucky. Both were members of the Missionary Baptist Church, and lived to a good old age. They reared a large family of children, of whom Osborn N. is the second. While growing up he had very poor opportunities for schooling, though he aided himself very much in that direction after attaining his growth. At the age of eighteen he began for himself, and soon after engaged as clerk in a store, where he remained two years. In 1829 he married Miss Jane L. Bell, a native of Lincoln

County, Ky., and in their family were seven children who lived to be grown. One of the sons served in the Confederate army and was twice severely wounded. In 1831 Mr. Coffey moved to Missouri, and three years later to Lincoln County, where he opened a store at Louisville. At the same time he dealt in hogs and tobacco, but failing in this he purchased the place where he now lives, which consists of 363 acres of land. Both he and wife are members of the Presbyterian Church, and for many years he was a magistrate. He has done quite well, financially, though he has had many reverses and losses.

Capt. William Colbert, president of the Farmers' and Mechanics' Savings Bank at Troy, and proprietor of the Colbert House, was born June 22, 1827, his parents being Shelton and Elizabeth (Mabry) Colbert. The father was born in Kentucky, although his ancestors were natives of France, from which country they moved to Ireland and finally to America. The mother was born in North Carolina and was of English-Welsh descent. When a girl she moved to Kentucky, where she was afterward married to Mr. Colbert. In 1826 they came to Missouri, and located in Lincoln County, where a permanent home was made. He lived to be about forty-two years of age and she about seventy-six. He was a strong Democrat and she an active member of the Christian Church. In their family were nine children, four sons and five daughters. Capt. William Colbert attained his growth in Lincoln County, and received a very limited education. In 1848 he married Miss Margaret Brown, a native of North Carolina, who bore him seven children, three sons and four daughters. Having farmed until the breaking out of the late war, he organized Company B, of the Thirty-seventh Missouri Militia Cavalry, and was chosen captain of the same, serving in that capacity about a year. He then organized Company C, of the Second Provisional Regiment Cavalry, and held the captaincy of this until 1864, when he was commissioned second lieutenant of Company A, Forty-ninth Missouri Volunteer Infantry, and was elected captain on organization of that company. He was commissioned lieutenant-colonel of the Sixty-fourth Regiment of Missouri Militia, December 29, 1865. In 1869 he was appointed circuit court clerk of Lincoln County, and ex-officio recorder. Having filled that position two years by appointment, he was successfully elected four times to that office in the face of a strong Democratic majority, thus holding the office eighteen years, longer than any other man save one. Mr. Colbert was a Democrat before the war, a strong Union man during that time and has been a stanch Republican since. He began a poor boy and is now considered one of the wealthiest men of Lincoln County. Besides being president, he is also one of the directors of the bank. In 1866 his first wife died, and the following year he married Miss Mary Dregay, a native of St. Louis but of English extraction. Four children were born to this union, two sons and two daughters. Mr. Colbert is a member of the Christian Church, as were both of his wives. He is a member of the G. A. R. and is also an Odd Fellow.

Josiah Creech, attorney, of Troy, is the son of George W. and Parthena (Pollard) Creech, natives of Nashville, Tenn., and Lynchburg, Va., respectively. They came to Lincoln County, Mo., at an early day, and reared their family to honest toil. After attending the common schools, Josiah took an academic course as a foundation for the legal structure to be built thereon. Having taken a course of reading under Quigly & Bonfils, he was admitted to the Lincoln County bar in 1871. Four years later he was united in wedlock with Miss Marrie Brevator, a native of St. Louis, who bore him three children, two sons and a daughter. Mr. Creech has been called into active life somewhat; besides holding the offices of alderman and mayor, he has been public administrator of the county for eight years, and prosecuting attorney for two terms. In his political principles Mr. Creech affiliates with the Democratic party. He is a Royal Arch Mason, a third degree Odd Fellow and a much respected citizen.

Jonathan W. Crume was born in Nelson County, Ky., in 1821, and is a son of John and Jane (Kirkham) Crume, who were born in Virginia and Kentucky, respectively. The former was born in 1781 and when thirteen years of age went with his father, Philip Crume, to Kentucky, where he afterward married and, in 1830, removed to Lincoln County, Mo. He was a soldier in the War of 1812 and died in 1840. His wife was born in 1783 and died in 1856. The maternal grandfather, Michael Kirkham, was an Irishman. Jonathan W. Crume is the sixth of eight children, and received a limited early education. He was married in 1842 to Leah Jane, a daughter of Littleton Dryden, who came from Maryland to Lincoln County in 1836. He was a soldier in the War of 1812. To Mr. and Mrs. Crume were born eight children, two of whom are dead. He, at one time, had a good farm of 650 acres, and is a progressive and prosperous farmer. He was a Whig in politics previous to the war, but since that time has supported the principles of the Democratic party. He is a Mason and his wife is a member of the Methodist Church. Jesse S. Crume, the Democratic nominee for county sheriff, is the third child of Jonathan W. Crume, and was born in 1849. He received a limited education and at the age of twenty-three began doing for himself, engaging in the mercantile business at Cap-au-Gris in connection with an elder brother, continuing for two years. In 1873 he was married to Hettie, a daughter of Monroe and Susan Thomasson, who were formerly of Virginia and early settlers of Lincoln County. The father died in 1886 at the age of sixty-five years. Mr. and Mrs. Crume have six children: Arthur L., Minor M., Renie S., John L., Hubert J. and Ella G. Mr. Crume is quite extensively engaged in breeding fine horses and cattle. He is the present Democratic nominee for county sheriff, and, if elected, would prove a good officer. He is a Mason, belonging to Lodge No. 270, at New Salem.

Joseph D. Damron is a native of Nelson County, Va., born in 1827, and is a son of Druey C. and Charlotta (Martin) Damron, who were also born in Virginia, in 1802 and 1808, and died in 1887 and 1871, respectively. They came to Lincoln County in 1843 and here afterward made their home with the exception of 1846–47, which they spent in Pike County. They were members of the Baptist Church. Joseph D. is the second of their thirteen children, ten of whom lived to be grown, and in his boyhood days received a very limited education. At the age of eighteen years he began working for himself on a farm for $8 per month, and continued that occupation until 1857, when he went to California. In 1853 he made a trip to Vancouver's Island, but in 1859 returned to Missouri, and acted as overseer for the neighboring planters until the slaves were emancipated. March 1,

1861, he married Virginia Hall, who died in 1862. A year later he married Nannie B., a daughter of Richard and Mary J. Hall, and sister of his first wife, and by her is the father of three living children: Guy, Mollie (wife of L. D. Reynolds) and Charley. Mr. Damron owns a fertile farm of 136 acres, and is one of the county's prosperous farmers. He votes the Democratic ticket and he and Mrs. Damron are members of the Baptist Church.

James L. Dawson is the eldest of a family of six children, four of whom are living, and was born in Amherst County, Va., in 1828, to the union of Rev. Ludwell L. and Jane (Watt) Dawson, his grandfather being Rev. Lewis Dawson. The latter was a Methodist minister of Virginia for many years. The father was also a minister of that State and died in 1843, preceded by his wife in 1842. James L. Dawson was educated in the common schools and at the age of fourteen years began doing for himself. Subsequent to 1844 he and his youngest sister came to Lincoln County, Mo., and he was engaged in lead mining until 1850, when he began farming and has a fine farm of 330 acres, which he has managed in connection with stock raising up to the present time. He is a Democrat and Mason, and is Master of the lodge at New Hope. In 1850 he was married to Susan D. Harvey, and by her is the father of five living children, to whom he has taken great pains to give good educations. Mrs. Dawson's parents are Francis and Malinda Harvey, who were formerly of Virginia, but became residents of Missouri in 1831; six of their children were born in Virginia and ten in Missouri. The father died in 1860 and the mother eight years later. Mr. Dawson's only son, Francis L. Dawson, was born in Lincoln County, in 1857, and besides attending the common schools was a student at Clarksville High School for five years, and the Gainesville (Ark.) High School for two years. He then spent two terms at William Jewell College, Liberty, Mo., and after his return home assisted in tilling the farm and taught nine terms of school. October 16, 1885, he was married to Mollie J., a daughter of A. M. and Missouri Thomas, who were formerly from Kentucky and Tennessee, respectively. Both had been twice married, and died in 1883 and 1850, respectively. To Francis L. and Mrs. Dawson was born one child, Lillian. Mr. Dawson is living on the old homestead, which consists of 470 acres, and he is a Democrat in politics. He is a member of the A. O. U. W. and Triple Alliance, and also belongs to the Baptist Church.

Nathaniel N. Day is a son of James and Emily (Rochester) Day, and was born in Lincoln County, in 1840. He is the fourth of eight children, and was educated in the common schools. In 1861 he enlisted for six months under Col. Burbridge, of Price's army, and was in the battle of Lexington. In 1862 he was married to Mary, a daughter of Willett and Elizabeth Elston, who were formerly of Kentucky, but came to Lincoln County about 1839. The father died in 1873, but the mother is still living. Mrs. Day was born in 1840, and became the mother of nine children, eight of whom are living. Since his marriage Mr. Day has resided on his present farm of 100 acres. He is a Democrat in politics and his first presidential vote was cast for Breckinridge. He is a member of the Masonic fraternity, and he, wife and two children are members of the Baptist Church. His father was born in Kentucky in 1808, and came with his father, Francis Day, to Missouri in 1818. He was married in St. Charles County in 1832, and three years after came to Lincoln County, and became one of the well known farmers of the county. He has been a life-long Democrat. His wife was born in Virginia in 1815, and is still living. Francis Day, the grandfather, was of English-Welsh descent, and was born in Maryland. He was reared in Virginia, and was a soldier in the Revolutionary War under one of the Lees. He was an early settler of Kentucky, and also of Missouri, and died in the latter State about 1825 or 1826.

Thomas Diggs (deceased) was born in Bourbon County, Ky., in 1808, and in 1815 came with his parents, David M. and Susan Diggs, to St. Louis County, Mo., remaining there some three years and then coming, in 1817, to Lincoln County, being among its very earliest settlers. They located on Bryant's Creek on what is known as the Boone farm, lived there seven or eight years, then moved one mile east, and there the father spent the remainder of his days, dying in 1863 when about eighty-eight years of age. He and his son, Thomas, erected a saw and grist-mill on Bryant's Creek, which they managed for many years, it being probably the first water mill in Lincoln County.

The country was in a very wild state at that day, and the woods were full of Indians and wild animals. They had to seek shelter and safety a number of times in Clark's Fort, just below Troy, to protect themselves from the attacks of the former, who were very hostile at times. Thomas Diggs was an only child, and his early playmates were the Indian lads, with whom he would smoke, eat muskrat, coon and opossum. Owing to the primitive state of the country he received no educational advantages, but by his own endeavors became versed in the rudimentary branches. He always lived on the old home farm and was recognized as one of the most industrious and honest citizens of the county. He was a great hunter and sportsman, and at the time of his death, which occurred March 10, 1888, was well fixed financially. He was married in 1832 to Jane, daughter of William and Sarah McMillin, who were North Carolinians by birth, where Mrs. Diggs was born in 1812. They died in Missouri. To Mr. and Mrs. Diggs were born eight children, five of whom are living: William C., Henry H., Benjamin F., Thomas J. and Sarah E., wife of J. D. Tinder. Mr. Diggs took great interest in the cause of education and the general upbuilding of the country, and was noted for his hospitality and generosity, having reared and educated a number of orphan children. He was a Whig and a stanch Union man during the war, and later he became a Republican in politics. His son, David M., died in 1865, in the hospital at St. Louis, while serving his country, and Benjamin F. also served in the Union army. Mr. Diggs was a member of the Methodist Church and was strictly temperate in his habits.

Andrew J. Dixon, farmer, is a son of William H. and Hannah (Hensley) Dixon, who were born in Virginia and Kentucky, respectively. They were married in the latter State, and about 1837 moved to Monroe County, Ind., where they lived in a tent until the father could build him a house, which he, in time, succeeded in doing. It was a cabin of round poles, 16x16. Two other families spent the winter with them, and all lived in this house. The mother died in 1858, leaving five sons and four daughters to mourn her loss. The following year the father and four children came to Missouri, and in 1870 to Lincoln County. Here he spent the remainder of his days, being nearly eighty-two years old at the time of his death. He was a Democrat in politics and a millwright by trade, and in all respects was a worthy man. Andrew J. Dixon was born March 20, 1829, in Scott County, Va., but he was reared and educated in Indiana. At the age of sixteen he began working at the carpenter's trade, and also learned brick masonry and blacksmithing. In 1854 he wedded Elendar C. Cannon, who was born in North Carolina, and became an early resident of Indiana. They came to Adair County in 1858, and the following year to Lincoln County, where they have since lived. During the war he enlisted in Company D, Third Missouri State Militia, and served until April, 1865, and then helped organize the Enrolled Militia. He was commissioned captain of Company E, and was a participant in thirteen engagements, but was unhurt. Since the war he has been engaged in blacksmithing and selling farm implements. He was postmaster of Louisville from May, 1866, to February, 1885, and has been school director eighteen years and justice of the peace four years, and is now notary public. His wife belongs to the Christian Church, and he is a Mason, and in his political views is a Republican. He owns 100 acres of good land, and is a highly respected citizen. He and wife have three sons and two daughters.

Alexander Donaldson was born in Washington County, Penn., April 14, 1833, and is a son of James and Eliza (Crow) Donaldson. James came with his parents from Scotland to Quebec, Canada, when about fourteen years of age, and after residing there until after his father's death, he and the rest of the family located in Washington County, Penn., where he married and spent the remainder of his days. His wife was of Irish descent and died in 1847. The father died in Helena, Ark., while endeavoring to obtain his son's release from military duty, on account of being under age. He was a coal dealer and farmer, and a member of the Presbyterian Church. Alexander is the eldest of their five children. He attended the common schools of Greenfield, Penn., and at the age of fifteen years began clerking in a store, where he remained until 1852, at which date he went with his father to California, and was a successful miner. After sojourning in that State two years he returned home, and the following year was married to Mary Furnier, a native of Washington

County, born November 23, 1836. In 1856 he came West to look up a location, and the following year brought his family to Pike County, Mo., but since 1859 has made Lincoln County his home. He owns a fine farm of 286 acres, and has a pleasant and comfortable home. He suffered many privations incident to pioneer life, but overcame all those obstacles, and is now enjoying the fruits of his labor. He is a Republican in his political views, and during the war served in the Enrolled Militia. He also served one term as justice of the peace, and is a Master Mason. He became the father of nine children. His son, James S., was born in Lincoln County, June 7, 1864, and was reared on a farm, and educated in the common schools. He farmed until 1886, then built a commodious store room, and he put in a nice stock of hardware, stoves and tinware. He is doing a fairly prosperous business. He votes the Republican ticket.

Andrew F. Downing, an extensive farmer and stock raiser, and a native of Lincoln County, is a son of James and Martha (Cacy) Downing, and was born July 9, 1827. He received such education as could be obtained in the primitive schools of his day, and in 1848 was married to Nancy Tucker, who died in 1857, leaving four children. Six years later Mr. Downing wedded Emma A. Guthrie, who was born in Missouri, July 5, 1838. They also have four children. Mr. Downing and wife are members of the Cumberland Presbyterian Church, and in politics he was formerly a Whig, and later a Democrat, but for some years past has taken but little interest in politics. He was Master of the Masonic Lodge at Auburn for twelve years. He has a farm of 655 acres, and has a fine herd of short horned cattle, and is a prosperous and thrifty farmer. Mr. Downing's father was a hatter by trade, a Whig in politics, and he and wife were members of the Methodist Church. They both died in Missouri.

Ezekiel A. Downing, a farmer and stock raiser, is a native of Lincoln County, Mo., and was born in 1839. He is a son of Rev. Ezekiel and Margaret (Markle) Downing, who were born in the "Blue Grass State" in 1795 and 1796, respectively. The father became a resident of St. Charles County, Mo., when about eighteen years of age, and there married in 1815. They came to Lincoln County a year later, where they spent the remainder of their days. He was a thrifty farmer, and was a successful and prominent Presbyterian minister. After the mother removed from Kentucky she lived in Vincennes, Ind., for some time, and about 1802 removed to St. Charles County, Mo. She is still living and resides on the old home farm. Her father, David Markle, was born in Maryland and died in Lincoln County. Ezekiel A. Downing is the youngest of eleven children, and received his education in the old log school-houses of early days. In 1866 he was married to Mildred J., a daughter of Ichabod and Elizabeth Davis, formerly of Kentucky and Virginia. Mr. Downing has lived on a farm adjoining the old home place for a number of years. He owns ninety-two acres, all under fine cultivation and well improved. He is one of the first citizens of the county, and is trusted and esteemed by all who know him. He votes the Democratic ticket.

George J. Dryden was born in Hannibal, Mo., May 29, 1836, and is a son of Littleton and Eleanor P. (Johnson) Dryden, who were born in Maryland in 1797 and 1803, respectively. They came to Hannibal, Mo., in 1836, and soon after came to Lincoln County, where they both died in 1867, the former on the 16th of February, and the latter on the 14th. The father was a hatter by trade, and was a soldier in the War of 1812. George J. is the eighth of ten children, and after attending the common schools was a student one term at Troy. At the age of twenty years he began merchandising at Snow Hill, and then operated a steam saw and grist-mill for a number of years. Since 1867 he has followed farming, but has also taught several terms of school. March 1, 1860, he was married to Alice Wood, who died in 1869, leaving two children, one now living—Kate M. His second marriage was consummated in 1870, his wife's maiden name being Nancy Cunningham, who died in 1872. Two years later he married Lydia J. Hammock, and three of their six children are living: James L., Mary Lee and Georgia J. Mr. Dryden owns a fine farm of 200 acres, and in his political views is a Democrat. His wife belongs to the Methodist Church.

Beverly Duey, sheriff of Lincoln County, Mo., and a native of this county, born May 1, 1835, is the son of David and Mary G. (Harvey) Duey. When a mere child David Duey's parents parted and he was left with a couple who had no children. He moved with his foster-parents to St. Louis when six years of age, and was the only boy, with the exception of one, that spoke the English language in that city. After the death of his foster-father he came with the widow to Lincoln County, and tenderly cared for her all her life. In this county he married Miss Harvey, and the fruits of this union were nine children, eight sons and one daughter. He was a pioneer member of the Christian Church in this State, being a constant, zealous worker all his life, as was also his wife, and he was also a Democrat in politics. He died at the age of forty-eight and his wife at the age of sixty-three. Their second child, Beverly Duey, was educated in the old fashioned, puncheon floor school-houses, and at the age of twenty began his career as a farmer, and this has been his occupation through life. He has a fine farm of 300 acres, and has been successful. In 1857 he married Miss Dolly Crenshaw, a native of Lincoln County. Eight children were the results of this union, seven now living, four sons and three daughters. Both Mr. and Mrs. Duey are members of the Christian Church. In 1884 Mr. Duey was elected to the position of sheriff, and re-elected without opposition in 1886. In his political principles he affiliates with the Democratic party, and he is a member of the Masonic fraternity.

Joseph L. Duncan is a son of Rev. Lewis and Harriet (Kinniard) Duncan, and was born in Waverly Township, Lincoln Co., Mo., April 29, 1840. His early days were spent on the farm and in attending the district schools. At the age of twenty years he began farming for himself, and in 1861, after serving six months in the State service, he enlisted in Company A, First Missouri Infantry, Confederate States Army, which company was afterward known as Company B, Second Regiment. He served four years, and participated in the battles of Lexington, Pea Ridge, Corinth, Iuka, Franklin, and was before Sherman on the Georgia campaign from the beginning, as far south as Atlanta, Ga. He enlisted as a private, and six months later was chosen second lieutenant, and after another six months was chosen first lieutenant, which office he filled until the close of the war. He was slightly wounded three times, and at the battle of Franklin was taken prisoner, and held six months and seventeen days at Johnson's Island. Having been released at the close of the war he returned home, and has since followed the peaceful pursuit of farming, owning 647 acres of land in Lincoln County, on which is one of the finest dwelling houses in the county. On December 12, 1867, Kate, a daughter of Nathan and Patience (Bryant) Gillum, of Pike County, became his wife. She was born May 3, 1841, and is the mother of two sons and three daughters. Mr. Duncan is a Democrat, and belongs to the A. O. U. W., and he and wife are members of the Triple Alliance. Both also are members of the church, he belonging to the Missionary Baptist, and she to the Methodist. He has been president of the board of trustees of Olney Institute and also of the Stock Company since their foundation.

Hon. George T. Dunn, an able attorney of the Lincoln County bar, dates his birth March 26, 1840. Although Callaway is his native county, he has been identified with the people of Lincoln County most of his life. His father, William F., of Greenbrier County, W. Va., immigrated to Missouri at an early day, and became one of the substantial farmers of Callaway County. He was a man of considerable prominence, having been judge of the county court of that county for six years. He chose for his companion in life Miss Sarah H. Patton, who became the mother of our subject. George T. Dunn received, in addition to a common school education, training in a private school, sufficient to qualify him for the profession of teaching. Having followed this occupation for eight years, and having in the meantime read law, he was admitted to the Lincoln County bar in 1872. Four years later he was chosen prosecuting attorney of Lincoln County, which position he held for two years. In 1884 he was elected to represent Lincoln County, Mo., in the State legislature, and was re-elected in 1886. At the first session of the legislature he introduced four bills, which passed both houses of the legislature, and are now laws, the most important being one making homicide, committed in attempted robbery, burglary, arson, etc., murder in the first degree, instead of the second, as formerly. At the second session he prepared and introduced two bills, which also passed both houses of the legislature, and are laws of the State, one making it a punishable offense for railroads to furnish public officials with free passes. This supplements and enforces the State constitution which makes it punishable for public officials to receive free passes. The other defines a lawful fence, and virtually makes it obligatory for railroads to fence against all kinds of stock. In 1888 Mr. Dunn was returned to the legislature, thus showing how highly his services have been appreciated. He has always been a stanch Democrat, and is a member of the Masonic fraternity.

Frederick Duvel was born in Hanover, Germany, February 29, 1840, and is a son of Henry and Wilhelmina (Westfall) Duvel, and at the age of twelve years came with his parents to America, locating in Lincoln County, Mo., in 1852. The mother died in Warren County, Mo., in 1852, while on the way here, and the father died about two years later. Thus Frederick was left to fight his own way in the world. He worked for wages during the summer time, and in the winter attended school. He continued to work in this manner until twenty years of age, when he started out for himself as an independent farmer, and has succeeded well in his undertaking, being now the owner of 500 acres of land, and is a member of the merchandise firm of Mason, Duvel & Co., of Olney. Emma F. Owings became his wife December 27, 1850. She was born in Kentucky, and when a child was brought to Missouri. They became the parents of eight children, only seven of whom are living, and are members of the Missionary Baptist Church. Mr. Duvel's father was a carpenter and cabinet-maker by trade. When twenty-three years old he first married Hannah Albert, who died at the age of thirty-five years, leaving five children, and he afterward married Miss Westfall, and by her became the father of four sons and two daughters.

David A. Dyer is one of seven surviving members of a family of twelve children born to John S. and Martha A. (Bassett) Dyer, and was born in Monroe County, Mo., in 1844. The father and mother were born in Henry County, Va., in 1819 and 1818, respectively, were married in 1839, and in 1840 came to Missouri, locating first in St. Charles County, and later in Warren County, then in Monroe, and finally came to Lincoln County in 1852. The father was a farmer, and died in 1880, leaving his children well supplied with worldly goods. He was a brother of Col. D. P. Dyer, of St. Louis, who was once a Republican candidate for governor of Missouri, and served during the late war in Capt. Thomas Carter's company as second-lieutenant, and was a participant in the battle of Lexington. While on his way home he was captured and taken to St. Louis, where he was kept in prison about four months. He was a man of good business ability and an honest, upright citizen. David A. Dyer was educated in the common schools, and in 1864 joined Capt. Wood's Company, Shelby's Brigade, and operated in Arkansas and Texas until the close of the war. In 1869 Laura M. Wright became his wife. She is a daughter of Marion Wright, of Virginia, and became the mother of the following children: Hattie M., John, George, Nannie, Otis, Mattie, Alexander, Dadin and Shapley. Mr. Dyer owns 250 acres of land in different tracts, and in his political views supports the principles of the Democratic party. Mrs. Dyer's grandparents, John and Caroline (Ross) Geiger, were born in Kentucky, and came to Missouri in 1812, there being but three white families in the county at that time, and the woods were full of Indians.

Benjamin T. Elliott, farmer, is the son of Elisha and Sarah (Collins) Elliott, both natives of Albemarle County, Va. The mother had previously been married to a Mr. Eddings, who died in Virginia. After the death of her first husband she came to St. Charles County, Mo., where she and Mr. Elliott were married. Both died in that county. He was a farmer and a soldier in the War of 1812. In their family were four children, three sons and one daughter. The mother had three sons by her first marriage. Benjamin, the second child by her second marriage, was born in St. Charles County in 1834, and was about six years old when his parents died. He was reared by his grandfather Collins, received a limited education, and when about eighteen years of age started out for himself, farming and "baching." In 1856 he married Miss Susan E. Guthrie, a native of Virginia, born in 1834. To this union six children were born, three sons and three daughters: William James, George T., Josephine Lee, Ann Arrenah, Delana Othelo and Maud. Three years later they moved to Henry County, but soon returned on account of sickness, and settled in this county. In 1861 they went to Audrain, and in 1868 came to Lincoln County, Mo., where Mr. Elliott has farmed ever since. He owns 225 acres of land, of which about 150 are under cultivation. Although starting with a very small capital, he now owns one of the best farms in his community, the result of his own efforts. He occupies the farm once owned by his wife's father, Silas Guthrie, who moved here from Virginia, in 1837, and died in 1844. His widow remained on the farm until her death in 1885, aged seventy-five. Mr. Elliott purchased the farm in 1867, his mother-in-law finding a pleasant home with him the remainder of her life. He was a Whig in politics before the war, and since then has been a Democrat.

Isaac Ellis (deceased) was born in Shelby County, Ky., March 19, 1823, and when about twelve years of age he went with his parents to Indiana, but returned about six years later. After reaching manhood (1845), he married Miss Sarah A. N. Sullenger, who was also a native of Kentucky, born February 23, 1825. After their marriage they moved to central Indiana, and in 1850 came to Lincoln County, Mo., and here the father died, February 5, 1888. He was a hard-working farmer all his life, and when he first came to Lincoln County he had nothing. He set to work, cleared a fine farm in the woods, and gave all his children a good start. He was a member of the Masonic fraternity, and a good citizen. His wife, a member of the Missionary Baptist Church, is still living, and is in full possession of her accustomed vigor of body and mind. Their family consisted of seven children, three sons and four daughters, of whom all are married with the exception of Jefferson S., who lives with his mother and runs the farm. The old homestead consists of 230 acres, of which about 200 acres are tillable; this all falls to Jefferson S. Another son, Clark S. Ellis, was born in Lincoln County, Mo., September 16, 1853. He was reared on a farm, and received a common school education. After working for his father until twenty-one years of age he began for himself. In 1875 he married Miss Virginia McDowell, a native of St. Charles, Mo., who bore him three children, two sons and a daughter. In 1882 his wife died, and two years later he married Miss Virginia Wilson, a native of Montgomery County. One daughter was born to this last union. Mr. Ellis has met with success as a farmer. He purchased the farm where he now lives, which consists of 223 acres, in 1877. He is a Republican in politics, and he and wife are members of the Methodist Episcopal Church, as was also his first wife.

John A. Elmore was born in the "Old North State" on the 18th of September, 1809. His parents, John and Mary (Lee) Elmore, were born in North Carolina and Virginia, respectively. The latter moved to North Carolina when she was quite young, and there she afterward married Mr. Elmore. He was a tiller of the soil, and both were members of the Presbyterian Church and lived to a ripe old age. Of their three sons and five daughters, our subject is the only one now living. He received the education and rearing of the average farmer's boy, having to walk three and one-half miles to his first school. At his dying father's request he cared for the family until the youngest was of age. In 1834 he and Ann Eliza Roper united their fortunes, and four years later came to Lincoln County, Mo., where they entered land in 1840, and by industry and economy became the owners of 323 acres of land. In 1862 the wife died, having borne twelve children. His second marriage, with Permelia Thomas, was consummated in 1871, and their union has been blessed by the birth of five children. Mr. Elmore has been a Whig and Democrat in his political views.

Robert T. Elsberry is one of ten children—seven living—born to William N. and Lydia P. (Owen) Elsberry, who were born in Maryland and Kentucky, in 1792 and 1800, and died in Missouri in 1871 and 1882, respectively. The father was an early resident of Kentucky, and there married and lived, until 1837, when he became a resident of Lincoln County, Mo. He was a soldier in the War of 1812, and was an honest and upright citizen of the county. His eldest child, Robert T. Elsberry, was born in Bourbon County, Ky., in 1818, and was educated in the pioneer schools of that State. In 1839 he was married to Julia Ann, daughter of Thomas Buchanan, of Lincoln County, and after a happy married life of thirty-seven years, the mother died. In 1882 Mr. Elsberry married Mrs. Ella (Martin) Frazier. He is a prosperous farmer, and has accumulated a fair property by his industry and frugality. Since 1859 he has lived in the town of Elsberry, which was built on his land and was named in his honor. He owns about 300 acres of land, and is a strong advocate of prohibition. Town lots which he has disposed of have all been sold with the understanding that no liquor of any kind should be sold on them. Previous to the war he was a Whig, but since that time has been a supporter of Democratic principles. In 1880 he was one of the company who built a large flouring-mill at Elsberry, and since 1883 he has been a one-third owner of the same. Mr. Elsberry is very public spirited and may justly be considered one of the prominent and honored citizens of the county.

John A. Eversmeyer is a son of John A. and Anna M. (Schaper) Eversmeyer, who were born in Prussia September 25, 1829, and May 2, 1832, respectively. They were both brought to America when children, and were reared in Lincoln County, Mo., where they afterward married and lived. The father was an extensive agriculturist, and in politics endorsed and supported the principles of the Republican party, and he and wife worshipped in the Methodist Episcopal Church. He died February 8, 1888. Seven of his nine children are living, and John A. is the eldest son. He was born in Lincoln County on the 22d of October, 1856, and received the education and rearing of the average farmer's boy. After remaining with his parents until February 23, 1887, he, at that date, married Minnie P. Gillmore, a daughter of Judge J. T. Gillmore. She was born in the county August 17, 1865. John A. is a member of the Methodist Episcopal Church, and supports the Republican party. He owns 160 acres of fertile land and is a successful and wide-awake young farmer.

Sebastian Fares was born in Bavaria, Germany, in 1818, and is a son of Michael and Savannah Fares, who came to the United States in 1835 and settled near Dayton, Ohio, where they lived until their respective deaths, in 1846 and 1847. The father was a wealthy farmer, and had an uncle who was Chief Justice of Bavaria. Sebastian Fares is the fifth of eight children, and attended the common schools of his native country and also attended the night school of Cincinnati, Ohio, after locating in this country. For six years after coming to the United States he was employed on the Miami Canal, buying provisions, etc., for the employes. In 1843 he went to Cincinnati, where he clerked in a stove factory for eighteen years and then became one of the firm of Fares & Miller, and until 1876 was one of the prominent foundry men of that city. At that date he moved to Lincoln County, Mo., where he has since lived on his farm of 1,500 acres. He is a successful business man, and during his short residence in Lincoln County has made himself many friends, and is prominent among the leading men of the county. September 24, 1859, he was married to Alma, a daughter of Isaiah and Diana Bacon, who were born in Vermont, where the mother died when Mrs. Fares was a child. Mrs. Fares was born in Vermont, and when about twenty-three years of age went to Cincinnati, Ohio. Mr. Fares has been a life-long Democrat, and was formerly a member of the A. O. U. W. He and wife are members of the Congregational Church. Mr. Fares takes considerable interest in breeding short horned cattle and fine horses, and has one of the finest farms and one of the most beautiful residences in the county.

Andrew Finley, a well known farmer and stock raiser of Lincoln County, comes of a family whose name is a familiar one in connection with the early pioneers and representative citizens of this locality. His father, Cyrus Finley, was born in Virginia in 1799, but when a child, owing to the death of his parents, he was taken to Kentucky, where he continued to make his home for many years. While living in that State he met and subsequently married, in Shelby County, Miss Jane Shannon, a Kentuckian by birth, and some ten years younger than her husband. This happy union was blessed by the birth of ten children, eight of whom, six sons and two daughters, still survive. In 1829 Mr. Finley and wife left Kentucky and sought a home in the then thinly populated district of Lincoln County, Mo., where they continued to make their home until death, esteemed, respected members of society. The father died in 1861, his companion surviving him until 1887. Among their children is the subject of this sketch, a native-born resident of the county, whose birth occurred in Hurricane Township, January 20, 1833. While growing up he applied himself to the duties about the home farm, receiving a common school education, and about 1859 he and a brother purchased the farm of 220 acres which he still owns and cultivates. In 1869 he was married to Miss M. Jennie Finley, a daughter of Andrew Finley. She was born in Shelby County, Ky., April 8, 1835, and accompanied her brothers to this county in 1860. Their family consists of two children, Jane E. and Georgie S. Mrs. Finley is a member of the Associate Reformed Presbyterian Church. Mr. Finley is school director and road overseer, and politically is a Democrat. For fifty-five years he has made this county his home, gaining a reputation and success which account him a deserving citizen.

Cyrus Finley, a leading merchant of Briscoe, was born in Lincoln County, December 4, 1841, and is one of ten children, eight living, born to Cyrus and Jane (Shannon) Finley, whose births occurred in Virginia and Kentucky, in 1799 and 1809, and who died in Missouri in 1861 and 1887, respectively. The father's parents died when he was a child, and he was taken to Kentucky by an uncle. There he afterward met and married Miss Shannon, and in 1829 came to Lincoln County, Mo. Young Cyrus Finley attended the old subscription schools of Missouri, and assisted his parents in tilling the farm. After attaining his majority he began doing for himself, and farmed and followed mercantile pursuits in Illinois for some time; then returned to Missouri, where tilling the soil occupied his attention until 1883. At that date he erected his large store room at Briscoe, where he has since been in partnership with Mr. Broyles, the firm name being Finley & Broyles for some time, but is now Finley, Eversmeyer & Co. In 1884 he was married to Sarah M. Finley, who was born in the county, December 20, 1856. They have one daughter. Mr. Finley is a Democrat, and is post master of Briscoe. Mrs. Finley is a member of the Associate Reformed Presbyterian Church.

Walker Finley, farmer, of Lincoln County, Mo., and native of the same, was born in 1848, his parents being Cyrus and Jane (Shannon) Finley, who were born in Virginia and Kentucky in 1801 and 1809, and died in Missouri in 1862 and 1887 respectively. The father went to Kentucky when a young man, and was married in Shelby County in 1828, and the next year came to Lincoln County, Mo., where they cleared a large farm, and were among the prominent citizens of the county. Two of their ten children are dead. Walker Finley is the youngest of their children. He received such education as could be obtained in the schools of his day, and was married in 1876 to Mary Ann, a daughter of Gilmore Finley, of Kentucky. She was born in Lincoln County, and Cyrus Gilmore, Cynthia N., Justina May, Charles Walker and an infant are the children born to her union with Mr. Finley. The latter has always resided on the old home farm, and is the owner of 253 acres of good land. He supports the principles of the Democratic party, and his first presidential vote was cast for Horace Greeley. His wife is a member of the Associate Reformed Presbyterian Church.

Thomas M. Fisher, contractor, builder and lumber dealer, was born in Shelbyville, Ky., March 28, 1841, and is one of seven children born to Horace H. and Hannah M. (Eads, cousin of Capt. J. B. Eads, of world wide reputation) Fisher. The parents were natives of Baltimore, Md., and Simpsonville, Ky., respectively. They were married in Kentucky, and became the parents of two children, remaining in that State until 1842, when they moved to Troy. He was a watch-maker, a gold and silversmith, having served seven years as an apprentice. He died in 1857. The mother afterward married I. T. Nelson, a Virginian by birth, who had settled in Lincoln County, Mo., at an early date. Both are living, she seventy-eight years of age and he ninety-one. Grandfather Fisher was a soldier in the War of 1812. The mother was a member of the Christian Church, and the father was a life-long Democrat. When about a year old, our subject was brought to Troy, Mo., and educated in the town schools. At the age of sixteen he returned to Shelby County, Ky., and served three years as an apprentice. In 1861 he volunteered in Company A, Fifteenth Kentucky Infantry, United States Army, and served three and a half years. He participated in the following battles: Stone River, Chickamauga, the Atlanta Campaign, Resaca, and was discharged at Louisville, Ky., without a scratch, or having been taken prisoner. He worked in Shelbyville until 1865, when he moved to Lincoln County, Mo., and there has worked at his trade since. He has built some of the best business blocks and residences in Troy, also barns and residences in this county. In 1869 he married Miss Laura V. Nicklin, a native of Pennsylvania. Six children were born to this union, five now living, three sons and two daughters. He is a Democrat in politics, is a member of the I. O. O. F., and he and wife are members of the Christian Church. He has followed his trade all his life, and has by honest work gained the confidence of the people.

John Fleener, farmer, is the son of Nicholas and Nancy (Johnson) Fleener, who were born in Virginia and Indiana respectively. At an early day the father went to Indiana, was married there, and followed agricultural pursuits in that State until 1851, when they moved to Lincoln County, Mo., where the father died in 1872 at the age of eighty-one. He was a Democrat in politics, and an officer under Gen. Harrison. He was wounded at the battle of Tippecanoe, and drew a pension. His wife was a member of the Baptist Church, and died in 1884, at the age of eighty-three. In their family were fifteen children, twelve sons and three daughters. Their son, John Fleener, was born September 25, 1840, in Monroe County, Ind., was reared a farmer boy, and received a very limited education, being obliged to go five miles to secure any schooling. At the age of fifteen he began learning the bricklayer's trade, but soon turned his attention to carpentering. From that he went to giving entertainments in sleight of hand and ventriloquism, and was quite successful at this. In 1871 he married Miss Drucilla J. Murphy, who bore him seven children, two sons and five daughters, two of the daughters being twins. Mrs. Fleener died in 1883, and in 1885 he married Mrs. Margaret J. Cartwright, *nee* Skinner, daughter of Rev. William J. Skinner, of Jonesburg, and the widow of Rev. T. L. Cartwright, by whom she had no issue. Mr. and Mrs. Fleener are members of the Christian Church, and he is a Democrat in his political views. After marriage he settled upon his present property, which consists of 212 acres of good land; beside this he has eight lots in Louisville. He has a nice home just at the edge of town. He has been a resident of this county for thirty-seven years.

Lee Frank, postmaster and general merchant at Burr Oak Valley, Mo., was born in Bavaria, Germany, in 1846, and is a son of Gideon and Charlotte (Lippmann) Frank, who have spent their entire lives in their native country. Lee Frank is the youngest but one of eight children, and until thirteen years of age attended the common schools, and the following two years was a student at Furth Commercial College. He then learned the tailor's trade, and when eighteen years of age, to avoid military service, came to the United States, and located at Alexandria, Mo., where an elder brother was living. He remained here about two years, and after spending a short time in Warsaw, Ill., went to St. Louis, where he clerked for about two years. From that time until 1872 he clerked and peddled goods in different parts of the country, and then established his present business at Burr Oak Valley. He has also a store at Foley, Mo., and both his establishments are doing a large and profitable business. He also owns real estate at both of these places, and has a good farm of 225 acres near Burr Oak Valley. He is an energetic and persevering business man, and fully deserves the success that has attended his efforts. He affiliates with the Democratic party in his political views, and is a member of the I. O. O. F. His marriage to Emma Tiller took place in 1871. She was born in Lincoln County, and is the daughter of John Tiller, and the mother of three children: Anna, Sophia and Viennah. She is a member of the Christian Church.

Francis M. Gear is a member of the mercantile firm of Anderson & Gear, of Moscow Mills, Mo., and is the only living member of a family of fifteen children born to the marriage of John Gear and Rhoda Meardy, who were born, reared and married in Virginia, and there resided until 1836, when they came to Missouri, and after living a short time in St. Charles County, moved to Warren County, where they spent the remainder of their days. They were members of the Primitive Baptist Church, and both died about 1843. Francis M. Gear was born in Henry County, Va., September 20, 1833, and owing to the early death of his parents received but a limited education. Since ten years of age he has been the architect of his own fortune, and has proved himself to be an honest, industrious, and worthy citizen. In 1853 he drove an ox team through to California, and from that date until 1867 mined successfully in California, Idaho and

Montana. He then returned home, and turned his attention to farming, and by industry and economy became the possessor of 100 acres of good land, and is an equal partner in the firm of Anderson & Gear. In 1871 he was married to Mrs. Mary V. Gear, daughter of Thompson Shults, and widow of Joseph S. Gear. She was born in Rappahannock County, Va., January 12, 1831, and she and Mr. Gear became the parents of three children. By her first husband she was the mother of four children. Mr. Gear is a Democrat in his political views.

Rufus W. Gibson, farmer and stock raiser, is a native of Lincoln County, Mo., where he was born March 3, 1825. He was one of a family of four sons and four daughters born to the marriage of Joseph W. Gibson and Matilda Wright, both of whom had previously been married. The father was of Irish descent, and was born in the "Palmetto State." He was taken to Kentucky when quite young, and there married a Miss Houston, by whom he had six sons and seven daughters. Eighteen hundred and eighteen is the date of his arrival in Missouri. After his wife's death he married Rufus W.'s mother. She was born in Kentucky, and there had previously married a Mr. Cofher, by whom she had four children. She was of Scotch-Irish descent. Mr. Gibson was a soldier in War of 1812, and was justice of the peace for several years. Both were members of the Primitive Baptist Church. Rufus W., their oldest child, received the rearing and education incident to pioneer times. He remained with his father until 1845, when Sarah F. Sheets became his wife and he began doing for himself. They were in very limited circumstances for a number of years, but he is now doing well financially, and has a pleasant and comfortable home. They are quite extensive travelers, and have seen both the Atlantic and Pacific Oceans. They are members of the Primitive Baptist Church, and he has always been a stanch Democrat. Mrs. Gibson is a daughter of Charles and Sarah Sheets.

John M. Gibson. The firm of Gibson & Eastman, dealers in dry goods, clothing, boots and shoes, hats and caps, etc., at Elsberry, Mo., was established in February, 1885. Their stock amounts to about $10,000, and their sales are nearly $40,000 annually. Mr. Gibson was born in Lincoln County in 1855, and is the youngest of six children. He received the education and rearing of the average farmer's boy, and remained at home until about fourteen years of age, when he went to New Hope, and began earning his own living. In 1875 he engaged in the saloon business, continuing the same three years, and the two following years sold drugs at New Hope. He came to Elsberry in 1880, and after selling drugs for some time engaged in the grocery business, the firm being known as Gibson & Shipp until the present firm was established. He is a successful merchant, and is one of the honest and industrious citizens of the county. He is a Democrat, and a member of the I. O. O. F. He was married in 1878 to Ada B., daughter of John M. Hunter, and by her is the father of three children. Mr. Gibson's parents were Rufus E. and Nancy (Stallard) Gibson. They were born in Tennessee and Kentucky in 1820 and 1824, respectively. They came to Missouri when children, and were married about 1843. Mr. Gibson was a farmer, and was killed at a house raising about 1859. His father was John Gibson, one of the pioneer settlers of Lincoln County, where he was a prominent man in his day. Mrs. Nancy Gibson is still living. Her father, James Stallard, was also one of the early pioneers of Lincoln County, and, although a Democrat in politics, was a strong Union man during the war.

Benjamin A. Gililland is the son of Robert and Annie (Moore) Gililland, both natives of Kentucky, born in 1810 and 1809, respectively. The great-grandfather Gililland came from the boggy part of Ireland at an early day, and found a home in Kentucky. The mother's people were from Virginia, though of English descent. Robert Gililland and Miss Moore were married in Kentucky, where they lived until 1830, when they moved to Lincoln County, Mo. He was a blacksmith and gunsmith by trade, though he also carried on farming. During the Black Hawk War he enlisted, but peace was declared before he reached the scene of action. He was at one time a Whig, but after the dissolution of that party became a Democrat. He was a fine shot with a rifle, although he spent but little time in hunting. He lived to be sixty-six years of age. He was a member of the Missionary Baptist Church, as is also his wife, who is still living, and is in her eightieth year. The father was a stirring, energetic man, and, although landing in St. Louis with but one dollar, he soon became the owner of 250 acres of land. Of the ten children born to their marriage (seven now living), Benjamin A. was the eldest. He was born in Simpson County, Ky., May 27, 1830, and the same year was brought to Lincoln County. At the age of seventeen he learned to make fanning mills, which occupation he followed for about fourteen years. For a year he was boss of an extensive shop in Cooper County. He then returned home and he and his father put up a shop on Lead Creek. He then turned his attention to farming. In 1884 he opened a store on his farm, which he operated for four years. In 1853 he married Miss Margaret Grimmett, who was born in Pike County, Mo., and who died without issue. In 1882 Mr. Gililland married Miss Phemia Snethen, a native of Montgomery County, Mo., and the daughter of Dr. A. Snethen, who preached the first Baptist sermon in Troy. Four children were born to this union, two now living: Maggie E. and Benjamin Alie. In 1872 Mr. Gililland was elected justice of the peace, and held that position about fourteen years. He owns about 306 acres of good land, is a Mason, a Democrat in politics, and he and wife are members of the Missionary Baptist Church.

John T. Gilmore is the son of James and Elizabeth (Hammonds) Gilmore, the former of whom came from his native State of Kentucky to Missouri after reaching man's estate. They were married in the latter State, and soon after located on the farm where their son, John T., now resides. The father was a Whig in politics, and was a soldier in the War of 1812. He lived to be about thirty-one years of age. His widow afterward married Richard Wommack, and died at the age of sixty-six years. She had one child by her first husband and eight children by her second. John T. was born on the 1st of August, 1830, on the farm where he is at present residing. At the age of nineteen he began working for himself, at $8 per month, and some time after was spent in chopping and rafting logs down the Mississippi River to St. Louis. By industry and economy he has eventually become the owner of 460 acres of land, and is comfortably fixed financially. In 1851 he married Elizabeth Gililland, who died in 1870, leaving eight children. In 1871 he chose for his second wife Elizabeth Gililland, a niece of his first wife. This wife's death occurred in 1873. She left one child. The year of his marriage to his present wife, whose maiden name was Mattie Moore, was 1874. They have five children. Mr. Gilmore has always been a Democrat in politics, and from 1884 to 1886 held the office of county judge.

Taylor B. Green, farmer and fruit dealer, of Lincoln County, was born in Rappahannock County, Va., in 1828, and is a son of Moses and Harriet (Basye) Green, who were born in Virginia, and spent their entire lives in their native State. Moses Green's father was also a Virginian, and his father was born in England. Taylor B. Green is the seventh of sixteen children, and in his youth received a good common school education. He taught two terms in Virginia, and in 1854 came to Lincoln County, where he wielded the birch for some time. He followed merchandising and handling tobacco at Smith's Mill for some time, but the most of his life has been spent on his farm of 200 acres. Besides his farm work he has been quite extensively engaged in buying and shipping apples, handling, in the fall of 1886, 2,600 barrels. Soon after coming to Missouri he was licensed by the Methodist Episcopal Church to preach, but after following that calling for a number of years, was compelled to give it up owing to ill health, but has always taken a great interest in church work, and also the cause of temperance. During the winter of 1887 and 1888 he delivered some able and instructive lectures on the bible. His marriage to Elizabeth J. Smith took place in 1855. She is a daughter of James and Elizabeth Smith, natives respectively of Kentucky and Tennessee, and by Mr. Green is the mother of three children: Anna E. (wife of Elder Jeptha B. Jeans), Hattie (wife of E. Gibson), and James M. Mr. Green is a Democrat.

William W. Haines, farmer, and son of Dr. Mathias and Elizabeth (Brower) Haines, was born in Rising Sun, Ind., May 9, 1837. His parents were natives of New Hampshire and New York City, respectively. The Haines family was among the first permanent English settlers of New Hampshire. The Brower stock came from Holland. Mathias Haines came to Indiana about 1815, and the mother of our subject a few years later. They were married in Lawrenceburg, Ind., but afterward settled in Rising Sun of the same State. He was a graduate of medicine, and was in active service for about forty years. He served as assistant during the War of 1812. He was a Whig until the late war, after which he affiliated with the Republican party. He and wife were members of the New School Presbyterian Church. The father was born in 1785, and died in 1863; the mother was born in 1805 and died in 1873. Their family consisted of eleven children, eight of whom lived to be grown. Their eldest son, A. B., followed in the footsteps of his father, and practiced medicine successfully. The youngest but one, William W., received his education in the schools of his native town, and afterward spent a year at Wabash College. For two or three years he clerked in a store, and then with two companions, started for Kansas. Arriving there in 1857 he took an invoice of his means and found that he had the modest sum of 75 cents. Having secured a quarter section of land by pre-emption, he returned to his home in 1859. In June, 1861, he enlisted in the Second Indiana Battery Volunteers, United States Army, and served over three years. He participated in twenty-six battles during the war, and was never wounded or taken prisoner. He enlisted as a private, and arose step by step until he was first-lieutenant, which position he held about two years. He received his discharge at Indianapolis, in August, 1864. In 1866 he married Miss Jane S. Frank, a native of Henry County, Ky., born June 9, 1844. Their family consisted of eight children, six now living, three sons and three daughters. He was postmaster of his native town for about three years, and in 1870 he moved to Kentucky, and the same year to Lincoln County, Mo., settling where he now lives. For about four years he held the office of justice of the peace, but refused to serve longer. He is a Republican in politics, a member of the Masonic fraternity, and also a member of the A. O. U. W. He owns 469 acres of land as the reward of his own industry and good management. He is doing a great deal in the way of raising fine stock of all kinds. He has the first and only imported Percheron horse brought to Lincoln County. Mrs. Haines is a member of the Christian Church.

Jasper Hall, of the firm of Hall & Walker, liverymen, was

born in Lincoln County, Mo., January 30, 1853, and is the son of Nathan and Mildred (Parsons) Hall, both natives of Virginia. The father came to Lincoln County when about twenty-one, and the mother when a child. After marriage they settled near Troy, and there spent the balance of their lives. He lived to be about sixty-one, and she about forty-one. He was a Democrat in politics, and both were members of the Methodist Episcopal Church. Six children were born to their union, three now living, one son and two daughters. Jasper Hall attained his growth on the farm, and received a fair education in the common schools. At the age of nineteen he engaged in agricultural pursuits for himself, and thus continued until 1886, when he engaged in his present business at Silex, keeping twelve horses. In 1878 he married Miss Almadia Walker, a native of Lincoln County, and the daughter of James Walker. To this marriage were born four children, three sons and a daughter. He has lived in this county all his life, and is a well-respected citizen, and a stirring young business man. He owns a fine farm of 120 acres near Troy. He is Democratic in his political views, and he and wife are members of the Methodist Episcopal Church.

G. A. Hamilton, farmer, stockman, and a native of Lincoln County, Mo., was born in 1841, and is a son of Wilson and Catherine (Kring) Hamilton, who were born in Virginia, and were there reared and married. They came to Lincoln County, Mo., in 1831, and settled in the woods near Troy. They improved a good farm, and there the father died in 1843, and the mother in 1864. They were Presbyterians, and the parents of ten children. G. A. Hamilton is the ninth child, and was educated in the county schools. At the age of twenty-one years he began farming for himself and in 1867 was married to Virginia Hicks, a daughter of Milton L. and Paulina V. Lovell. She was born in Lincoln County, and is the mother of four children: Alla, Effie, Dona and Milton. Mr. and Mrs. Hamilton own a good farm of 420 acres about four miles from Troy, and are honest, upright citizens. He supports the principles of the Democratic party, and cast his first presidential vote for Seymour in 1868. His wife belongs to the Methodist Episcopal Church South, and his eldest daughter is a member of the Presbyterian Church.

Elder Benjamin F. Hardesty, minister of the Old School Baptist Church, was born in Burr Oak Township, Lincoln Co., Mo., April 9, 1842, and is a son of George W. and Sarah (Taylor) Hardesty, who were born in Kentucky and Virginia in 1811 and 1806, respectively. They were married in Shelby County, Ky., in 1833, and came to Lincoln County three years later, settling in what is now Snow Hill Township, where they improved a good farm. Both are members of the church, and are still living. They reared seven of their eight children, and Benjamin F. is the fifth. He received but little schooling until after attaining his majority, and then spent a short time at Auburn, and afterward taught school for several years. Eveline Overall became his wife in 1865, and their union resulted in the birth of twelve children, eleven of whom lived to majority: Sarah Lizzie, Annie M., Tully O., Nora E., Lucy E., Riley R., Susie F., George M., Willis B., Joseph W. and John F. Mr. Hardesty owns 400 acres of land, on which he has resided since 1866. At the age of fourteen years he was converted to Christianity, and in 1867 was ordained by the Missionary Baptist Church to preach the Gospel, which calling he followed for several years. In 1876 he united with the Old School Baptists, and was ordained a minister by that order, and since his early conversion has been an active and earnest worker for the noble cause of Christianity. In his political views he is a Democrat. Grandfather Capt. William Hardesty was born in Maryland, and was a captain in the early Indian wars. He died in Shelby County, Ky., and his wife died in Lincoln County, Mo., in 1863. The maternal grandparents, John and Nancy Taylor, were born in Ireland, and both died in Shelby County, Ky., of the cholera, in 1832.

Francis M. Harlan, farmer, was born in Scott County, Ind., April 2, 1831, and is the second of ten children, three now living, born to Joseph and Sarah (Kempton) Harlan. The father was a native of Kentucky, and moved to Indiana in 1818. The mother was born in South Carolina, and her parents moved to Indiana when she was but a child. Here Mr. and Mrs. Harlan were married, and afterward settled in Scott County, where they spent the remainder of their days. He was a painter and chair maker by trade, and both lived to be about seventy-three years old. Their son, Francis M., was educated in the common schools, and at the age of sixteen began for himself by writing in the circuit clerk's office, of Scott County, and there remained three years. He then began clerking in a store, and in 1854 he engaged in the mercantile business for himself. After running the store for about six years he engaged in the mill business. In 1856 he married Miss Mary Oldfield, a native of Indiana. Eight children were born to this union, three sons and five daughters. In 1867 they moved to Lincoln County, Mo., and here Mr. Harlan engaged in the mercantile business in Troy, where he continued until 1881. He is at present interested in farming and stock raising, owning 222 acres of land. He was deputy collector for four years, and is a stanch Democrat, politically. Mrs. Harlan is a member of the Methodist Episcopal Church.

George L. Harness, a successful farmer and stock raiser of Lincoln County, Mo., is a son of John L. and Elizabeth (Beswick) Harness, both of whom were born in the "Buckeye" State. There they married and lived until 1850, when they came to Missouri and settled in Pike County, where the father still resides. The mother's death occurred there in 1881. Their family consisted of seven children—five sons and two daughters—only four of whom are living. The eldest child, George L., was born June 9, 1850, and was reared and educated in Pike County. He made his home with his father until 1879, when he was married to Lucinda Strother, who was born in the "Old Dominion" and came to Pike County, Mo., in 1854. Three children blessed their union and are named in the order of their births: Nellie, Harry and Reuben. Since his marriage Mr. Harness has resided on his present farm of 280 acres, which is well improved. He is neutral in politics and his father is a Republican. His wife belongs to the Methodist Church South.

Nicholas A. Harvey was born in Nelson County, Va., in 1823, and is a son of Francis and Malinda (Damron) Harvey, who were natives of Orange and Albemarle Counties, Va., respectively. The father came to Missouri in 1829, and in 1831 brought his family here. He became a wealthy land owner and had 400 acres under cultivation at the time of his death. He died in 1860, aged about seventy years, and his wife in 1878, aged seventy-seven years. They were members of the Baptist Church, and were the parents of fifteen children, ten of whom are living. Nicholas A. was educated in the common schools and by his own effort secured a good practical education. In 1845 he went to Wisconsin for his health, and after clerking for two years engaged in the mercantile business, which he continued until 1850, when he returned to Lincoln County and followed the same occupation at New Hope for eight years. From that time until 1863 he was a merchant at Cape au Gris, and the following five years was traveling salesman for a Philadelphia clothing house. Since 1870 he has been residing on a fine farm of over 400 acres, and is one of the successful farmers of the county. He was married in 1854 to Amy J. Reid, and by her is the father of four living children: James, George R., Lucy M. (deceased), Caroline (deceased), Alex. R. (deceased), Lucy R. (wife of William P. Starks), Andrew, and Fannie F. (deceased). Mr. Harvey is a Democrat, and a member of the Masonic and I. O. O. F. fraternities. Mrs. Harvey's parents were James and Lucy Reid. They were formerly of Shelby County, Ky., and located on the farm where Mr. Harvey now lives in 1830. They were born in 1799 and 1808, and died in 1871 and 1886, respectively. They were among the early and prominent settlers of the county, and were members of the Associate Reformed Presbyterian Church. Mr. James Reid was surveyor of Lincoln County for a number of years, and also did a great deal of surveying for the government.

Henry Haverkamp, jeweler, of Troy, was born in Prussia, January 5, 1848, and his education was confined to the common schools. At the age of fourteen he began learning the watchmaker's trade under an uncle, worked for him four years without pay and boarded himself. In 1866 he immigrated to America to escape military duty, and for seven years after reaching this country he worked for one man in St. Louis. He then went to Quincy, Ill., and here remained for two years. In 1876 he came to Troy, Mo., and after working for some time for different parties, in 1879 bought out his employer and has since conducted the business and is doing well. He carries as good a stock of jewelry as will be found in any town of the size of Troy. In 1881 he married Miss Aida Wright, a native of Lincoln County, and the daughter of L. C. Wright. This union resulted in the birth of three children, two sons and a daughter. Mr. Haverkamp began business a poor boy, but by persistent effort has risen to a place among the first business men of Troy. Politically he is a supporter of Democratic principles. His father, Frederick Haverkamp, was a native of Prussia, and in boyhood learned the shoemaker's trade, at which he worked until he was sixty-seven years of age. His mother, Lina Koch, was also a native of Prussia. Their marriage was solemnized in the old country, where all the children were born, two sons and a daughter. The other son came to America in 1867 and the rest of the family in 1871. The father died in 1886 and the mother is still living and is seventy-six years of age.

J. Bent. Henry, dealer in groceries, queensware, etc., was born in Millwood Township, September 7, 1841, and is the son of Simeon B. and Mildred (Roberts) Henry, born respectively in Virginia and Kentucky. After marriage they moved to Lincoln County, Mo., at an early day, and here the father followed farming. He was a Democrat in politics and lived a quiet, irreproachable life. They were both members of the Methodist Episcopal Church. Their family consisted of eight children, six sons and two daughters. The fourth child, J. Bent. Henry, was reared on a farm and received a good common school education. Having left home he began clerking at Millwood, and this continued until 1886, when he moved to Silex and opened his present stock of goods, having the only exclusive grocery and queensware house in town. In 1871 he married Miss Martha R. Mudd, of Monroe County, Mo., who died at the end of eighteen months. Mr. Henry then married Mrs. Mary A. Brown, a daughter of Dr. Hayden, of Pike County. She only lived about two years. Mr. Henry is a Democrat in his political views and is a man well respected.

Don E. Hewitt, M. D. and druggist at Winfield, Mo., was born in Audrian County in 1857, and is a son of Elkana and Mary J. (Hawes) Hewitt, who were born in Oneida County, N. Y., and West Plains, Tenn., in 1812 and 1817, respectively. The father received a good common school education, and at the age of nineteen went to Monroe County, where he taught school for several years, and was married in that county in 1840. At the end of ten years he went to California, where he followed mining for about six years, and also sold goods. After his return to Missouri he located in Audrain County, where he purchased a farm and began tilling the soil. He was the father of six children, five of whom are living, and Dr. Don E. Hewitt is the youngest of the family. The latter attended the common schools until nearly grown, and then spent three years in the State University at Columbia, Mo. In 1881 he graduated from the Missouri Medical College of St. Louis, and then came to Winfield, which was then just laid out, and here has since resided. He was in partnership with Dr. J. A. Mudd until 1833, but since that time has practiced alone. In connection with his practice he has been in the drug business since 1882, first in partnership with his father, and now with his brother, the firm name being F. L. Hewitt & Bro. He was married on the 2d of April, 1884, to Lucy C., a daughter of Harvey and Hannah M. Bassett, natives, respectively, of Connecticut and New York. They were married in Ohio, and the father yet resides in Cuyahoga County. The mother is dead. Mrs. Hewitt was educated in Youngstown and Oberlin, Ohio, and was married in her native State. She is a member of the Methodist Church, and the Doctor is a Democrat, and belongs to the I. O. O. F.

Henry H. Higginbotham, merchant of Louisville, is the son of Rufus A. and Sarah E. (Hargrove) Higginbotham, both of whom were natives of Virginia. The Higginbotham family came from Scotland in an early day, and settled on the James River, where they owned great possessions. The mother's people were connected with the Randolph family of Virginia. The father was an extensive planter, was a Whig in politics, and a member of the Methodist Episcopal Church South. He died in Virginia, where the mother is now living. In their family were eleven children, eight of whom still survive, five sons and three daughters. Three of the sons were in the Confederate service, and one of them, Pitt A., was killed in the skirmishing around Richmond, Va. Henry H. was the second child born to his parents, his birth occurring in Amherst County, Va., February 25, 1841. He was reared on a farm and received an academic education.

At the age of seventeen he began merchandising as salesman, and in 1861 he enlisted in the Confederate army, Stewart's Cavalry, where he served until the close of the war, participating in many of the leading battles. After the war he returned home, where he remained a year, and in 1866 he came to Clarksville, Mo. Here he clerked until the following year, when he moved to Louisville, Lincoln Co., Mo., opened a store, and, with the exception of three years, has been engaged in the mercantile business in that town. Several times the firm has changed hands, but he has always been the senior member, except the three years from October, 1882, to October, 1885. In 1885 he and his brother, Thomas J., bought out their brother J. W. They have one of the largest stocks in the county, and are now occupying three rooms with a fifty-two foot front, besides rear rooms and upstairs. In connection with this he owns about 800 acres of land. As a business man he has been quite successful, having landed in Missouri with $1.50 in his pocket. He is now one of the heavy tax payers of Waverly Township. In 1875 he married Miss Mary F. Bilbro, a native of Lincoln County, Mo., though she was reared in Pike County, and is a daughter of James C. Bilbro, a Virginian by birth. Mr. Higginbotham is a Democrat in politics, and is a K. T. in the Masonic Lodge. He has been a resident of this county for twenty-one years. Mrs. Higginbotham is a member of the Christian Church.

Israel R. Hinds was born in Wayne County, W. Va., in 1847, and is a son of William L. and Catherine Ann (Brumfield) Hinds, who were born in the same county and State. The former's birth occurred in 1821 and the latter's in 1824. They were married in 1841, and about 1857 removed to Platte County, Mo. After the close of the war they resided in their native State for about eighteen months, but then returned to Missouri, where they afterward made their home. Here the father still lives. In his younger days he was for some years a pilot and engineer of a steamer, plying on the Ohio River, but the most of his life has been spent in farming. His father, Elias Hinds, was born in New Jersey and died in Wayne County, W. Va. He was a farmer and millwright. Mrs. Hinds died soon after her return to Missouri. Her father, William Brumfield, was a captain in one of the early wars. Israel R. Hinds is the third of eight children. His early education was limited to a few months, and what education he has has been acquired by his own efforts. He came to Missouri with his parents, and was married in Lincoln County to Elizabeth, a daughter of Ephraim and Nancy Cannon, and by her became the father of seven children: William Ezra, Helen A., Walter E., Edgar F., Gracie, Alva and Cleveland. Since 1883 Mr. Hinds has lived on his farm of 238 acres of land one mile and a half from Auburn. When young he spent about eighteen months rafting on the Ohio River, but of late years has given his attention to farming. He is a Democrat in politics, and is a member of the Triple Alliance, and his wife belongs to the Baptist Church.

Louis H. Hisey is one of twelve children born to Philip and Nancy (Pine) Hisey, who were born in Pennsylvania and Virginia, respectively. The father was a steamboat captain, and in 1838 he and family moved to St. Louis, where he operated a mill, and ten years later came to Lincoln County and farmed the rest of his days. Both lived to a ripe old age, and both were church members. Louis H., their son and the subject of this sketch, was born September 14, 1844, and was reared on a farm in Lincoln County. His father died when he was eleven years old, and he was obliged to assist in maintaining the family, consequently his educational advantages were few and far between. He cared for his mother until her death, and in 1873 was married to Elizabeth Reed, a daughter of James A. Reed. She was born on the farm of 180 acres where she and Mr. Hisey reside, May 8, 1853. Their family consists of two sons and two daughters. Mr. Hisey is a Democrat, a member of the A. O. U. W., and he and wife belong to the Cumberland Presbyterian Church.

George W. Huff, farmer and stock raiser, of Lincoln County, is the fourth of eleven children in the family of Calvin and Lavina (Raines) Huff, and was born in Arkansas, February 14, 1844. The father and mother were born in Kentucky and Indiana, respectively, and were married in the latter State. About 1844 they moved to Arkansas and five years later to Missouri, and are still residents of Lincoln County, he being seventy-eight years of age and she sixty-eight. The former is a blacksmith and farmer, and both are members of the Presbyterian Church. George W. Huff received but little early education, but has since acquired a good practical education through his own earnest endeavors. He has followed the occupation of farming through life, and although $120 in debt at the time of his marriage (1863) he has now a well located and fertile farm of 329 acres and is out of debt. His wife's maiden name was Nancy E. Morris. She is a native of the county, and became the mother of eleven children, six of whom are living, all daughters. Mrs. Huff is a member of the Missionary Baptist Church, and Mr. Huff's political ideas coincide with the Democratic party.

William H. Hutchison, senior member of the firm of Hutchison & Perkins, dealers in drugs and medicines, was born in Warren County, Mo., October 29, 1862, and is the son of John and Lydia J. (Yeater) Hutchison, both natives of this State. The father was a farmer by occupation, a Democrat in politics, and his wife was a member of the Christian Church. He died in 1866, but the mother is still living and is sixty-four years of age. Their only child, William H., received his education in Watson Seminary, Pike County, Mo., and afterward clerked for four years in a drug store. He then went to Troy and engaged in the drug business with Dr. A. H. Chenoweth, and later with R. S. Shelton, and in 1888 H. W. Perkins bought Mr. Shelton's interest. They have a good stock and an excellent trade. In 1882 Mr. Hutchison married Miss Carrie E. Logan, a native of Virginia, who bore him two children, William H., Jr., and Lulu S. Mr. Hutchison began business on a small capital, and is now ranked among the wide-awake business men of Troy. He is a member of the Masonic fraternity, and is a Democrat in politics. His wife is a member of the Methodist Episcopal Church.

Jarot Ingram, of the firm of J. Ingram & Son, dealers in general merchandise at Truxton, Mo., was born in Warren County, Mo., in 1833, and is a son of John and Huldah (Oden) Ingram. The former was born in Logan County, Ky., in 1811, and in 1818 came with his father, Jarot Ingram, to Pike County, Mo., he being one of the first white settlers of Northeast Missouri, where he was one of the first teachers of that district. John married and settled in Warren County, where he lived until 1853, with the exception of a short time spent in Lincoln County. He then removed to Montgomery County, where he died in 1888. He was a soldier in the Black Hawk War, and from 1864 to 1868 was assessor of Montgomery County, and was a well-to-do farmer. His wife was born in St. Charles County, and died in 1855. Mr. Ingram was married twice. Jarot Ingram is the eldest of nine children, and was educated in the common schools of Lincoln and Warren counties. He was married in 1859 to Sarah A., a daughter of H. R. and Mary Sitton, who were formerly of Tennessee, but were early settlers of Lincoln County. Four children were born to their union, three of whom are living. Mr. Ingram farmed in Montgomery County until 1880, when he removed to Truxton and engaged in the merchandise business in connection with William T. Aydelott and William Owings, but at the end of three years Mr. Owings retired, and in March, 1888, Mr. Ingram became the sole proprietor, and the firm became known as Ingram & Son. Since the war Mr. Ingram has been a Republican in his political views, and while in Montgomery County served for some time as justice of the peace. During the war he served in Capt. William Colbert's Company of Enrolled Missouri Militia. Mrs. Ingram has been a member of the Methodist Episcopal Church since her youth.

Theron Ives, druggist at Olney, Mo., was born in Westfield, Mass., January 13, 1834, and when some eight years of age was taken to Rochester, N. Y., where he received a fair education. At the age of sixteen years he engaged as salesman in a wholesale house at Rochester, but at the end of three years took charge of his father's business. The latter was a manufacturer of gloves, mittens and whips, and Theron remained in the store until 1854, when he came to Pike County, Mo., and began running the engine of a saw-mill, and after a short time bought an interest in the same, which he continued until 1860. When the war broke out he took a strong stand for the Union, and after doing some service in his home neighborhood he enlisted in Company K, Col. Fagg's Regiment, Missouri State Guards, serving until 1862, when he took a trip to Idaho, where he remained (mining) until 1868. He then returned to Missouri and opened a drug store at

New Harmony two years later. Since 1874 he has resided in Olney. In 1871 he was married to Julia A. Branstetter, who died in 1880, having borne three children, two living. In 1882 Mr. Ives married Theresa Stephenson. She was reared by a Methodist minister, and is a member of the Methodist Episcopal Church South. Mr. Ives is a Unitarian in faith, and in his political views is independent. He is a Mason and has been secretary of his lodge for ten years. He also belongs to the K. of H., A. O. U. W. and Triple Alliance, and has been postmaster of Olney for thirteen years. His father, Theron Ives, was born in Massachusetts, and was of English and Scotch descent. His father was a prominent lawyer of Massachusetts and served several times in the State Legislature. Mary A. (King) Ives, the mother of our subject, was also born in Massachusetts, and was of English descent. She and the father made their home principally in the East, although they spent a few years in Missouri. The father died at the age of sixty years in Springfield, Mass., but the mother is still residing there, aged seventy-four.

James A. Jackson, dealer in general merchandise at Troy, Lincoln Co., Mo., was born in that county September 10, 1844, and is the son of Early and Isabella A. (Irven) Jackson. The father was born in Kentucky in 1814, and the mother in North Carolina in 1814 also. When a boy Early Jackson moved to Missouri with his father, and, after living in Cape Girardeau County for some time, moved to Lincoln County. The mother came to Lincoln County, Mo., when a child, and after her marriage to Mr. Jackson they settled near Troy. He was a stirring farmer and a highly respected citizen. He died in 1876, but she is still living and is seventy-four years of age. Their family consisted of seven children, five now living. James A. was reared a farmer boy, receiving a limited education, not attending school after he was sixteen years of age. Upon reaching years of maturity he engaged in agricultural pursuits, but abandoned this to engage in merchandising, under the firm title of Hand & Jackson. Three years later he purchased his partner's interest and is now engaged in business by himself. He does business in a large, two-story brick, 100x25, with both stories filled to the ceiling. In connection with this Mr. Jackson handles a great deal of grain. In 1878 he married Miss Fredonia Dyer, a native of Warren County, and to them was born one child—Floy. Both Mr. and Mrs. Jackson are members of the Methodist Episcopal Church. Mr. Jackson is a Mason, a Democrat in politics, and as a business man has been quite successful.

John W. Jameson, a representative farmer and stock raiser, is the son of William and Mahala (Bruce) Jameson. The father was born in a fort where Mount Sterling, Montgomery Co., Ky., is now situated, in 1789. About 1620 the Jameson family emigrated from Scotland to America, and settled in Culpeper County, Va. From there they found their way to Kentucky, and built the above mentioned fort. The mother was born in 1804, in Garrard County, Ky. The Bruce family were descendants of Robert Bruce, and emigrated from Scotland about 1820. They settled in Albemarle County, Va., and from there a branch of the family became the pioneers of Kentucky. The father of our subject was a soldier in the War of 1812; after that struggle he followed contracting and building, largely building up Mount Sterling. For two years he was engaged in dredging the Ohio, taking out sawyers, planters and snags. For ten years he assisted Grandfather Bruce, who was very wealthy, in running Kinnicanick Salt Works, in Lewis County, Ky., and while there nearly all his negroes ran away into Ohio. He here failed in business, but being proud in spirit, he refused to stay and see his property sold. So, with his family, he boarded an emigrant boat and moved to Clarksville, Pike Co., Mo., in 1831, with $65 in his pocket. The same year they settled near the Northern line of this county. For about ten years he was justice of the peace in Lincoln County, and was assessor for four years. Having gone back to Kentucky, to serve as a witness, he took cold, and died in 1846, leaving a wife and ten children, of whom John W. was the eldest, and twenty-three years of age. The mother died in 1876. The father was an Old School Baptist in early life, but upon hearing Alexander Campbell, he planted his faith in the Christian Church, and assisted in organizing the first Christian Church in Northeast Missouri (1832) at the house of Cumberland Kilbey, in Pike County. He was a Jacksonian Democrat in politics. His son, John W., was born November 19, 1823, at the old Kinnicanick Salt Works. Owing to the scarcity of schools when his parents first moved to Missouri, he received a very limited education, and at the age of twenty-one he could not write his name. He afterward attended school a sufficient length of time to be enabled to transact all common business. In 1847 he married Miss Levicy Stephens, and two years later went to California, leaving his wife, who died in June of the same year, though he heard nothing of this until February, 1850. He returned in 1852, came by water, and while in the harbor at Acapulco, Mexico, the ship went down with 900 passengers, none being lost, however. After returning he attended school, and there met and married Miss Susan Clare, to whom he was married in 1853. She died in 1859, leaving two children, as did his first wife. At the same school was a little girl of about twelve, who afterward became the wife of Mr. Jameson. She was Miss Mary E. Fentem, and her father, Richard Fentem, came from England. By her he became the father of five children, four daughters and a son. Mr. and Mrs. Jameson are members of the Christian Church, as was also his second wife, but not his first wife, who was a member of the Missionary Baptist Church. He has been justice of the peace of Millwood Township for about twenty-four years, and has often been solicited to run for important offices, but does not seek public notice. Since 1852 he has lived on his present farm, which consists of 230 acres. He has practiced law to a limited degree, having been admitted to the bar about fourteen years ago.

William Wesley Jamison, farmer, stock raiser and a native of Lincoln County, was born in 1838, and is a son of Joseph and Catherine Jamison, who were natives of Cabarrus County, N. C. The father came with his parents to Pike County, Mo., in 1820, and was married about 1833. After living for a short time in Wisconsin, they came to Lincoln County, and located on the farm now owned by F. L. Dawson, where the father farmed and operated a saw-mill until 1843, after which he returned to the lead mines of Wisconsin, where he was engaged in mining until his death, which occurred in December, 1845. His wife died in 1859. William W. Jamison is the third of five children, and received a good common school education. As a means of earning a livelihood he taught school for several years in Pike and Lincoln Counties, and was a successful pedagogue. He also worked at the carpenter's trade to some extent. At the breaking out of the war he was enrolled in Company C, Forty-ninth Enrolled Missouri Militia, and served as scout. He was married in 1862 to Harriet E., daughter of William and Susannah (Steele) Jamison, and by her is the father of the following children: Joseph Lee, a graduate of Paynesville Institute; Luetta, a teacher in Texas and a graduate of Paynesville Institute; Maud and Delphine. Mr. Jamison has a good farm of 180 acres, and is an energetic and successful farmer. He was a Union man during the war, and is a Democrat in politics. He is a member of a temperance organization and is a member of the Triple Alliance, and he and wife are members of the Methodist Episcopal Church South. Mrs. Jamison's parents were born in North Carolina, and the father died in Lincoln County in 1881.

Joseph Jones, farmer, of Lincoln County, Mo., was born in Halifax County, Va., in 1816, and is a son of Absalom and Polly (Adams) Jones, who were also born in Halifax County, Va., where the mother died when Joseph was quite small. The father was married a second time and spent his entire life in his native county. Joseph Jones is the fourth of six children, and never received any schooling. He remained with his father until 1836, when he came with an old gentlemen, Tommy Sydnor, to Lincoln County, Mo., and worked as a farm hand, or at such work as could be obtained, until 1842, when he married Lucinda J. Highsmith, a daughter of William Highsmith, who was a Georgian. Mrs. Jones came with her parents to Missouri and located in Lincoln County, being among the first white settlers. Out of a family of nine children born to Mr. Jones, only three are living: John William, Joseph Absalom and George W. By industry and good management Mr. Jones has become the owner of a fine farm of 205 acres, and is an honest and industrious citizen. Feeling the need of an education himself, he has spared no pains to give his children good educations. He has been a life-long Democrat, and has been a member of the Masonic fraternity for over twenty years.

James R. Kabler, of the firm of Kabler & Shumate, was born in Franklin County, Mo., May 28, 1846, though reared principally in St. Charles County, and is the son of William A. and Jane (Pendleton) Kabler, both natives of Virginia. They both moved to Missouri when young, were married in Warren County of this State, and both were members of the Methodist Episcopal Church. The father was agent for the Wabash Railroad for about ten or twelve years, and previous to this he was engaged in merchandising for some time. The mother died in 1880 at the age of fifty-three, but the father is still living and is sixty-five years of age; he is a Democrat in politics. The oldest child now living of the six born to their union, James R., received a limited education, and when about fourteen years of age hired out to assist in supporting the family. On reaching manhood he engaged in agricultural pursuits. In 1870 he married Miss Louisa Igo, who was born June 24, 1847, in Pike County, Mo., and who bore him one child, a daughter named Oro. In 1877 Mr. Kabler started a freighting line from Wright City to Troy, and continued until the railroad was built to Troy. In 1881 he came to that city and began the feed and transfer business. The firm had changed hands several times, when, in 1886, Mr. Shumate joined him; they run from four to six teams, doing a good business. Mr. Kabler is a member of the I. O. O. F., being the Noble Grand of his lodge. He is a Democrat in politics. Besides the above business this firm also handles considerable timber.

Henry W. Kemper, the only furniture dealer in Troy, was born in Prussia, Germany, May 25, 1835, and while growing up learned the cabinet-maker's trade, at which he worked until 1854, when he came to America. He then worked at different places until 1869, when he came to Troy, and opened a furniture store in a little wooden building that is still standing on Main Street. In 1876 he built a large two-story brick building, 62x22, where he now does business. In 1886 he added another brick, three stories high, 75x24. His stock fills the first building and the second and third stories of the second, being the largest store of the kind in the county. In 1857 he married Miss Louisa Wintker, also a native of Germany. To this marriage were born thirteen children, seven sons and six daughters. Mr. Kemper is a Republican in politics, and during the late war served a short time in the militia. He and wife are members of the Methodist

Episcopal Church. His father, Henry Kemper, was also a cabinet-maker, and his mother was Mary (Brinkhof) Kemper. Both were born in Prussia, and came to America about five or six years after our subject. They brought seven children with them; two of the boys were cabinet-makers, as are also two of his sons. Mr. Kemper is one of the board of directors of the Farmers' and Mechanics' Savings Bank.

Alexander Kennedy, merchant at Hawk Point, Mo., is one of five sons and five daughters born to the marriage of Armstrong Kennedy and Mary Richey, who were of Irish and Scotch lineage. The former was born in Sumner County, Tenn., in 1786, and after his marriage made his home in Tennessee, in 1816, when they moved to St. Charles County, Mo., and four years later to Lincoln County, where the father followed farming and gunsmithing. He was gunsmith for the army during the Florida War, and in his political views affiliated with the Democratic party. He died in 1856, and his wife in 1853. Their son Alexander, who is the third child, was born September 13, 1824, in Lincoln County. He received such education as the district schools afforded and, like a dutiful son, assisted his mother on the farm until twenty-four years of age. In 1848 he married Sarah Howell, a native of Lincoln County, and by her became the father of seven children, who lived to be grown, only one of whom is now living. His wife died in 1866, at the age of thirty-eight years. The following year he married Mary Howell, a sister of his first wife, who died in 1882, having borne one son and two daughters. After living two years a widower he wedded Mrs. Rhoda (Devis) Williams. The family are members of the Christian Church. Mr. Kennedy gave his exclusive attention to farming until 1860, when he began merchandising at Hawk Point, and has followed both occupations up to the present time. He has been postmaster at the latter place for twenty-eight years. He is a Democrat and held the office of justice of the peace for three years. He ran on the Independent ticket for representative, but was defeated, though he made a strong race.

Armstrong L. Kennedy, retired farmer, a native of the county, was born March 11, 1827, and was reared on a farm and educated in the old subscription schools. He remained with his mother until her death, and in 1853 went to Oregon, where he mined gold successfully for two years. After his return home he betook himself to farming, and after his marriage, which occurred in 1861, he located on the old homestead near Hawk Point, where he lived until September, 1887, when he moved to Olney to educate his children and secure rest after a life of toil. He owns 786 acres of land which he has earned by his industry and good management. Farming and stock raising have been his chief occupations through life, although he also followed merchandising for about four years. He has always been a Democrat in politics, and during the war was a strong Union man. He served for some time in the militia, and after another call for troops was made he sent a substitute and moved to Illinois, where he spent the remaining years of the war. His wife's maiden name was Mildred Garret. She was born in Virginia in 1833, and was brought to Missouri when two years old by her parents, Jesse and Z. (Jones) Garret. Three of her four children are living, one son and two daughters. Mr. Kennedy's parents were Armstrong and Mary (Richey) Kennedy.

Charles W. Kimler is a son of Daniel and Elizabeth (Brewer) Kimler, who were born in Loudoun and Prince William Counties, Va., in 1789 and 1787, respectively. They were married in their native state and there lived until 1837, when they came to Lincoln County, Mo., and settled in Waverly Township. Daniel Kimler was a blacksmith and farmer, and was a soldier in the War of 1812. He was a Democrat, and lived to be over eighty-seven years of age. His wife lived to be about eighty years old. There were ten children in their family, four sons and six daughters. The sixth child and subject of this sketch, was born February 13, 1824, in Loudoun County, Va., and spent his boyhood days on a farm. In 1848 he married Mildred A. Duncan, a native of Lincoln County, born April 5, 1830. Seven children have blessed their union, one son and six daughters. Mr. Kimler and wife are members of the Missionary Baptist Chnrch, and since the dissolution of the Whig party he has been a believer in the principles of the Democratic party. During the late war he and family resided in Central America for some time, but subsequently returned to Missouri. He owns 120 acres of land, the greater part of which he has earned by his own industry.

Claudius F. Kimler may be mentioned as one of the successful and worthy farmers of Lincoln County. He was born in the county July 2, 1847, and his boyhood days were spent in assisting his parents on the farm, and in attending the common schools of his district. He spent two years at Blackburn College, Carlinville, Ill., and after returning home taught one term of school, but not liking this occupation turned his attention to farming, and is now the possessor of 260 acres of tillable and fertile land. His marriage with Katie E. Corley was celebrated in 1873. She was born in the "Empire State," March 20, 1850, and became the mother of four children. Her death occurred in 1885, and the following year Mr. Kimler married Alice C., a daughter of Zachariah Callaway; she was born in Lincoln County, November 12, 1861, and is a member of the Christian Church. Mr. Kimler's parents, John T. and Sophronia (Hammonds) Kimler, were born in Virginia and Kentucky in 1813 and 1827, respectively. Both parents were early residents of Lincoln County, and the father was a tiller of the soil all his life. He affiliated with the Democratic party, and died in 1880. His widow still survives.

Joseph A. Knox, M. D., was born near New Hope, Lincoln County, Mo., August 21, 1839, and is one of nine children born to Henry and Lucinda (Hunter) Knox, who were born in Tennessee and Missouri in 1806 and 1811, respectively. They were married in 1830. The father was a farmer and Democrat, and died in 1885. The mother is still living, and is the oldest native citizen of Lincoln County. The Knox family trace their origin to John Knox, the Presbyterian reformer of Scotland. James Knox, the father of Henry Knox, was a nephew of General Knox of the Revolution, and came to America about the close of the Revolution, first locating in South Carolina, and later near Knoxville, Tenn., where his son Henry was born. At a later period he moved to Christian County, Ky., and in 1818 to Lincoln County, Mo. His wife was Jane McElroy, whom he married in Ireland. Joseph A. Knox, whose name heads this sketch, remained on the farm and attended the old subscription schools until he was seventeen years of age, when he entered the Missouri State University and attended two sessions. In 1860 he began the study of medicine under his brother, and in 1863 entered the St. Louis Medical College, and was graduated from the same in 1865. Almost immediately he located at Auburn, and has enjoyed a liberal patronage ever since. He is interested in farming, and in connection with his practice oversees his farm of 330 acres. He was married in 1872 to Sarah A. Cochran, a daughter of Andrew Cochran, one of the early settlers of Auburn. She was born in this town August 21, 1852, and is the mother of three daughters. The Doctor supports the principles of the Democratic party, and is a Master Mason. His mother's people, the Hunters, came from Virginia to Kentucky, thence to Lincoln County, Mo., about 1804.

Edward H. Lawrence is a son of Richard D. and Rebecca (Williams) Lawrence, who were born in Maryland and Kentucky in 1820 and 1824, respectively. The father came to Lincoln County, Mo., at the age of sixteen years, and followed the occupation of farming through life, and was married in 1841. He became the father of two sons by this marriage. After his wife died he was married a second time, and to this marriage eight children were born. The father died at the age of forty-six years. Edward H. Lawrence was born in Lincoln County November 3, 1844, and was reared on a farm and educated in the common schools. In 1861 he enlisted in Company B, Second Missouri Infantry, C. S. A., and served over four years, being a participant in the following battles: Pea Ridge, Boonville, Lexington, Springfield, Carthage, Vicksburg, Corinth, Iuka, Holly Springs, Boston Mountain and Guntown. He was severely wounded at Pea Ridge. After the war he returned home and in 1867 was married to Mrs. Martha (Bilbro) Gillum, who was born in Lincoln County, Mo., March 14, 1842. She had one daughter by her first marriage and three sons and one daughter by her second marriage. Both Mr. Lawrence and wife are members of the Christian Church, and he is a successful farmer of the county and the present owner of 160 acres. He is a Democrat in his political views and served four years as Justice of the Peace. He belongs to the Masonic fraternity.

William Lindsey was born in Christian County, Ky., in 1813, and is a son of John and Margaret (Carr) Lindsey, who were born in North Carolina and Kentucky, respectively. John Lindsey started for Kentucky with his parents when quite small, but the father was killed by the Indians while en route and only he, his mother and brothers and sisters, ever reached the "Blue Grass State." John clerked in a store in Dover, Tenn., for a number of years, and was married in Kentucky about 1809. In 1818 he and family came to Pike County, Mo., of which he became a prominent and influential citizen. He was the second sheriff of Pike County, served twelve years, and was at one time coroner of the county. In 1840 he was elected to represent the county in the State Legislature, and proved to be an able and efficient representative. He was a descendant of one of five brothers who came from England to America before the Revolution, and many of his descendants reside in Pike County. He died in 1856. His wife died in 1855, and both she and the father were for many years members of the Baptist Church. William Lindsey, the subject of this sketch, is the second of eleven children, and was educated in the common country schools. He attended school three months after he was twenty-three years of age, which schooling did him more good than all his previous attendance. He served as deputy collector and sheriff of Pike County, Mo., during the last term, and in 1838 was married to Harriet Humphrey, who died in 1840, leaving one child, James D. His second marriage was consummated in 1855, his wife being Lucinda Humphrey. She died in 1862, also leaving one child, Elizabeth, wife of George Long. Annarah Day became his wife in 1863, and their union was blessed by the birth of six children, four of whom are living: Andrew Johnson, Jennie Lee, Albert J. and Liberty Day. Mr. Lindsey is a Democrat in politics, and served in the Mexican War under Gen. Sterling Price. In 1850 he crossed the plains to California, and after spending about three years in mining and stock trading he returned home, and in 1854 came to Lincoln County, but since 1865 has resided on his present farm of 310 acres.

William C. Logan, dealer in hardware, stoves, tinware and agricultural implements at Olney, Mo., was born in Yadkin County, N. C., July 2, 1838, and is a son of George and Mary (Uptegrove) Logan, who were born in the same county and State, and were there married and became the parents of five sons and two daughters. The father was a farmer and Democrat, and died in 1866 at the age of sixty-six years. The following year William C. and his mother came to Lincoln County, Mo., where the latter died in 1873, being seventy-six years of age at the time of her death. William C. Logan was reared a farmer's boy and received a limited education. Soon after coming to Missouri he located in Montgomery County, where he was engaged in tilling the soil. Sarah M. Henton, a native of Lincoln County, became his wife in 1873, and by her he became the father of eight children, seven of whom are living. In 1878 Mr. Logan returned to Lincoln County, and in partnership with a brother ran the Olney grist and saw-mill for one year. He then engaged in his present business. For about two years he hired a tinner and learned the trade of him. Now he makes all kinds of tinware with the skill of an old tradesman. He is a Democrat, and for six years has held the office of justice of the peace and for about seven years has been school director. He is a member of the Masonic order and A. O. U. W., and he and wife are members of the Missionary Baptist Church. Mr. Logan also belongs to the Temperance Benevolent Association of Troy.

Llewellyn Z. Long, farmer, is a son of William H. and Sarah (Williams) Long, who were born in Maryland and Kentucky in 1815 and 1822, respectively. They were married in the latter State, and in 1836 came to Lincoln County, Mo. The father was a finely educated man and was a school teacher by profession. At the time of his death, which occurred when he was about thirty-six years of age, he was preparing to publish an arithmetic and grammar. He was a Henry Clay Whig, and after his death the mother married L. D. Liles. She was the mother of five children by Mr. Long and six children by Mr. Liles. Her eldest child, Llewellyn Z. Long, was born in Lincoln County, March 12, 1837. He was reared on a farm and received but very meager educational advantages. At the age of twenty years he began learning the carpenter's trade, but becoming disgusted with his insufficient education, he gave up this work and attended school. After teaching school two years he commenced tilling the soil, and in 1861 was married to Virdilla Ferry, who was born in Lincoln County, October 17, 1839, and died in 1864, having borne one son. Mr. Long then married Eulala Robertson, and by her became the father of six children. She was born in Lincoln County, August 14, 1848. Mr. Long is a Democrat, and is the owner of 187 acres of land. He is a Mason.

Dr. James Long was born in Pike County, Mo., in 1838, and is a son of John and Eliza (Grimes) Long, who were born in Montgomery and Bourbon Counties, Ky., in 1804 and 1808, respectively, and were married in Missouri in 1830. In 1827 the father went to St. Louis, where he built the old Missouri Hotel, but soon after went to Pike County, where he afterward spent the major part of his days. He was a farmer and millwright by trade, but gave the most of his attention to farming. His death occurred in 1881. His widow is still living, and is an earnest member of the Christian Church. Dr. James Long was educated in the common schools, and was reared on his father's farm. After attaining his majority he began the study of medicine with Drs. Hawkins and Bankhead at Paynesville, and graduated from the St. Louis Medical College in 1861. He practiced in New Hope and then in Troy, remaining in the latter place until 1867. He then spent five years in St. Charles County, and, after taking another course of lectures, returned to New Hope, but soon after located in Elsberry, and after residing there until 1879, located on his present farm of 1,100 acres of fine land. The Doctor is a Democrat, and was married March 1, 1862, to Mary A. Jenkins, who died in 1872, leaving one child. His second marriage took place in 1875. His wife, Isiaetta Carter, is a daughter of John C. and Margaret (Coleman) Carter, who were born in Virginia, and became residents of Pike County, Mo., in 1852. At the time of their respective deaths they owned the tract of land on which the Doctor now lives. Dr. and Mrs. Long have two daughters and two sons, and are members of the Christian and Episcopal Churches, respectively. He is a member of the A. O. U. W.

William H. Long is a son of William H. and Sarah (Williams) Long [see sketch of Llewellyn Z. Long] and was born in Pike County, Mo., October 12, 1840, but was reared on a farm in Lincoln County. He attended the district schools and the school near Paynesville, Pike County, Mo., but at the death of his stepfather was obliged to leave school and assist his mother in obtaining a livelihood. Virginia F. Mitchell became his wife in 1864. She was born in Lincoln County, June 9, 1846, and to her marriage with Mr. Long were born ten children, five sons and five daughters. Mr. and Mrs. Long are members of the Missionary Baptist Church, and he is a supporter of Democratic principles. He has lived on his present farm of 290 acres since 1870. He has been prosperous in his business enterprises, and his property has been acquired through his good management and industry. He has been a Mason for twenty-four years.

Richard O. Long, farmer and stock raiser, of Lincoln County, was born in Hurricane Township of that county, November 30, 1842. At the early age of six years he was put to work on the farm and his education was limited to the district schools. When nineteen years of age he began fighting the battle of life for himself by splitting rails at sixty-five cents per 100, and at a later period began tilling the soil. This occupation he has continued up to the present time, and is now the owner of over 102 acres of land, though he annually tills over 400 acres. His wife, who was formerly Martha Mitchell, is a daughter of Rev. A. G. Mitchell, and was born in Lincoln County. They were married in 1867, and are the parents of five sons. Mr. Long is a Democrat and belongs to the Masonic and K. of H. fraternities, and he and wife are members of the Missionary Baptist Church. He has given his children good educational advantages, and is one of the representative citizens and farmers of the county.

Henry L. Luck is a son of Joel T. and Nicy L. (Terrell) Luck, who were born in Virginia and followed the occupation of farming. They were members of the Missionary Baptist Church, and he was a Democrat and died in 1876. The mother is still living and is hale and hearty. Henry L. is the eldest of their six children, and was born in Caroline County, Va., May 11, 1836. His early days were spent in tilling the home farm and in attending the district school. When seventeen years of age he began clerking in a store, but owing to ill health was obliged to abandon this occupation and began tilling the soil as a more healthful occupation. He came to Missouri in 1857, and in 1858 Odessa A. Robertson became his wife. She was born in Shelby County,

Ky., October 12, 1839, but came while young to this county with her parents. She has borne nine children, seven of whom are living. After trying different parts of the county, Mr. Luck, in 1866, located on his present farm of about 200 acres, which he has earned by his own industry and economy. Mr. Luck is a Democrat, and is a worthy and upright citizen of the county.

James Lyons, farmer, and son of Philip and Elizabeth (Whalen) Lyons, was born in Ireland in 1837, his parents both being natives of Ireland, and there the mother died when the subject of this sketch was but a child. After her death the father was twice married. By his first marriage were born five children, four sons and one daughter, of whom three sons are now living. By his second marriage there are no children living. By the third marriage were born two sons and a daughter; one son and daughter are now living. In 1851 all came to America, and settled in New Jersey, where the father died in 1860. He was a farmer by occupation. The third son born to the first marriage was James Lyons. He received only three years' schooling, though, by self-study, he has become a well-informed man. He cared for his father and aided in rearing the other children. In 1860 he came to Lincoln County, Mo., where he has farmed ever since. During the late war he served in the militia. In 1864 he married Mrs. Mary A. Corcoran, a native of Ireland, who came to St. Louis, Mo., when a baby. By this union were born ten children, five now living, a son and four daughters. Mrs. Lyons has a daughter by a previous marriage. Mr. Lyons owns 320 acres of good land, and has lived in this county twenty-eight years, being accounted a successful farmer and a highly respected citizen. He is a Democrat in politics, is a member of the C. K. of A., and he and wife are members of the Catholic Church.

Solomon R. McKay, M. D., is the eldest of four children —three of whom are living—born to the marriage of Dr. S. H. McKay and Lucy A. Moxley, who were born, respectively, in Kentucky and Virginia. Both came to Missouri when young, and married in Lincoln County, and were earnest and devoted members of the Missionary Baptist Church. The father was a graduate of the St. Louis Medical College, and during the war was appointed examining surgeon for several drafts. In 1867 he moved to Pike County, where he died in 1876. His wife's death occurred in 1872. Their son, Solomon R., was born in Auburn, Mo., March 4, 1855, and was educated in the district schools and the high school of Clarksville. After studying medicine with his father for some time, he entered the St. Louis Medical College, and was graduated from that institution in 1876, and soon after located at Mackville, where he has met with good success in the practice of his profession. He is a Republican in politics, and has been a delegate to the State convention the last two times. He belongs to the A. O. U. W., and in 1877 was married to Julia Alexander, and their union has been blessed by the birth of two sons and two daughters. Mrs. McKay was born in Washington County, and is a member of the Catholic Church.

James Martin McLellan, an extensive farmer and stock raiser of Lincoln County, Mo., was born in Clay County, Mo., December 22, 1839, and is the son of Dr. William E. and Emaline (Miller) McLellan, natives of Smith County, Tenn., and Windom, Vt., respectively. In early life the father graduated from a medical college in Cincinnati, Ohio, and while in that State he married Miss Miller, who came with her parents to that locality in 1815. For many years Dr. McLellan practiced successfully in Ohio, Pennsylvania, Illinois, Michigan, Iowa and Missouri, where he passed his last days, dying at Independence, where the mother still lives at the age of seventy-eight; though so far advanced in years she does her own work. Their family consisted of six children, only two now living—one son and a daughter. James Martin McLellan learned the printer's trade while growing up, serving an apprenticeship of about two and one-half years. His higher education was received at Geauga Seminary, Chester, Ohio, and at Western Reserve Teachers' Seminary, Kirkland, Ohio. He then went to Michigan, taught school a short time, and while there read law under William Newton, of Flint, Mich., being admitted to the bar in 1860. In the year 1862 he came to Troy, Lincoln Co., Mo., and accepted the position of deputy county clerk, which office he held continuously until 1875.

During the war he served a time as captain of Company A, Sixty-seventh Missouri State Militia. While acting as deputy clerk he also practiced his chosen profession, and after leaving that position gave his entire attention to law. He was county school commissioner for thirteen years, and organized and put into working order the public schools of the county. In 1880 failing health drove him from the practice of law, and he then engaged in farming and the raising of short-horned cattle and Percheron horses. He owns a fine farm of 500 acres adjoining the town of Troy, besides other lands. In 1865 he married Miss Martha W. Cummings, a native of Indiana. Nine children were born to this union, six now living. Mrs. McLellan is a member of the Presbyterian Church. Mr. McLellan is a Democrat in politics, and is a Knight Templar in Masonry. During the sale of railroad bonds of Lincoln County, Mr. McLellan was appointed agent for the county, and $150,000 worth of bonds were given him to dispose of, the court not requiring him to give bond. While this was contrary to all business principles, it showed unbounded confidence in him, which was not betrayed.

David M. Magruder was born in Henry County, Ky., October 9, 1831, and is of Scotch ancestry. His parents, Alpheus and Sarah (Martinie) Magruder, were born in Maryland and Kentucky in 1803 and 1812, and died in Lincoln County, Mo., in 1858 and 1886, respectively. When the family first came to America they spelled their name McGregor, but to escape the prosecutions of the English they changed the name to Magruder. The parents were married in Kentucky, and in 1852 came to Lincoln County, where they spent the remainder of their days. David M. is the eldest of their nine children. He was reared on a farm and educated in the common schools. After remaining with his parents until twenty-three years of age, he engaged in farming on his own responsibility, and by industry and economy has secured a farm of 610 acres. Previous to the war he was a member of the old Whig party, but since that time has voted the Democratic ticket. He was married in 1855 to Letitia A. Magruder, of Kentucky. She bore him five sons and died in 1872. Five years later he married Mrs. Phœbe (Estes) Day, and by her is the father of two daughters. Both husband and wife are members of the Missionary Baptist Church.

Elias Magruder, dealer in hardware, furniture, agricultural implements and also undertaker's goods, in Whiteside, was born February 20, 1833, in Henry County, Ky., and is the son of Alpheus and Sallie (Martinie) Magruder, whose sketch appears in that of David Magruder. Elias was the second child born to his parents. He received his education in the old subscription schools, and came to Lincoln County with his parents. In 1856 he married Miss Nancy Hardesty, a native of this county, and to this union were born four children, three sons and one daughter. After marriage Mr. Magruder moved to his present farm, where he has resided ever since. In 1884 he was chosen business manager of the Grange Store at Argentville, and held the position two years. In 1886 he opened his present store, being one of the leading merchants of Whiteside. Beside this he owns 176 acres of good land. He is a Democrat, though not an active politician, and has been a peace-loving man all his life, never having a law-suit and was but once on the witness stand. He and wife are members of the Baptist Church.

Thomas G. Martin was born in Rutherford County, Tenn., in 1820, and is a son of Louis and Balinda (Rucker) Martin, who were born in Henry County, Va. In 1818 the former came with a brother to Tennessee, where the mother died in 1832. The father came to Lincoln County, Mo., in 1840, and there died in 1877. He was a soldier in the War of 1812, and his father was a Revolutionary soldier, and died in Virginia. Thomas G. Martin is one of two living members of a family of seven children, and was educated in the common schools of Tennessee. At the age of seventeen years he came on horseback and alone from his native state to Lincoln County, Mo., and made his home with an uncle, and that fall and winter attended the schools of Troy. He then went to work on a farm, and in 1840 was married to Georgia Ann, a daughter of Dabney and Mary M. Carr, who were born in Albermarle County, Va., in 1793 and 1799, respectively. They were married in 1818, and in 1831 removed to Pike County, Mo., where they reared a family of five children. The father died in 1872 and the mother in 1877, the former being a soldier in the War of 1812. His father, Gideon Carr, was a Virginian, of English descent, and was a Revolutionary soldier. He died near

Nashville, Tenn., aged one hundred and six years. Thomas G. Martin has a good farm of 220 acres near Brussells. He is a Democrat, and he and wife are church members. They became the parents of two children, Thomas Dabney (deceased) and William L. Thomas Dabney was married in 1869 to Susie F. Hayes, and died in 1882, leaving three children: Lottie A., Louis C. and George Thomas Dabney. In 1884 his brother, William L., married his widow. They have two children, Rubie L. B. and Birdie Lee. William L. lives on the farm where he was born. His wife was born in St. Louis, and is a member of the Methodist Church. Grandfather Gen. Joseph Martin was captured by the Indians in one of the Indian wars and afterward married a Cherokee squaw, by whom he had two children, whose supposed descendants, the Rosses, are prominent among the Cherokee Indians to-day. He was sentenced to be executed by the Indians, but owing to the intercession of his wife was spared, and succeeded in making his escape.

William R. Mattingly, a blacksmith and wagon-maker of Millwood, is a son of Philip and Elizabeth (Mudd) Mattingly. The father had been previously married, and after his first wife's death he married Miss Mudd. The father died in Kentucky, and in 1848 she and six children moved to Lincoln County, Mo. William R. was the fourth child, and was born in Washington County, Ky., January 2, 1839, and when nine years of age was brought to this county. Being the eldest son he had to help support the family, and therefore received a very limited education. At the age of fourteen he began learning the blacksmith and wagon-maker's trade, and worked at this until after the war, when he opened a shop at Millwood and there has since remained. He has a large shop, well furnished, and does first-class work. In 1868 he married Miss Anna Mudd, a daughter of Luke Mudd. To this union were born five children, one son and four daughters. Mr. Mattingly has met with good success as a tradesman, and has one of the best shops in this county. He takes an active part in all things pertaining to education, and has been director in his district a number of times. He and wife are members of the Catholic Church, and he is a Democrat and a member of the Catholic Knights of America.

Thomas J. Mattingly, proprietor of the Mosely Hotel, is the son of Stephen J. and Sarah E. (Mudd) Mattingly. The father was born in Kentucky in 1819, and the mother was a native of the same State. They were married here, and two of their children were born in this State. In 1847 they moved to Lincoln County, Mo., settling in Waverly Township, and here the father followed farming and coopering. Both he and wife were members of the Catholic Church. He was a Democrat in politics, and died July 2, 1878. The mother died August 2, 1862. Their family consisted of ten children, Thomas J. being the eldest son. He was born March 30, 1848, in Waverly Township, was reared on a farm, and received a very limited education in the district schools. At the age of twenty he could scarcely write his own name, but he worked out, and with the money thus obtained attended school in St. Charles County, and also attended Blackburn University, at Carlinville, Ill. Returning, he clerked for about two years in the town of St. Charles, and then worked for his father on the farm for about two years. He afterward clerked for H. T. Mudd, of Millwood, and followed this occupation for about three years, a part of the time carrying on a farm. He then engaged in business for himself. In 1878 he married Miss Lucy Hagan, of Hannibal, Mo., and to them were born four children, three living, two sons and a daughter. In 1880 Mr. Mattingly was elected constable of Millwood Township, and has held that position since, four years by election and two years by deputyship. In 1888 he moved to Silex, and took charge of the Mosley Hotel. He has just fitted up a nice store-room, and filled it with drugs and groceries. He has been quite successful in all business transactions, having commenced in life worse off than nothing, being in debt. He is a Democrat in politics, and he and wife are members of the Catholic Church. He is a member of the Catholic Knights of America, and belongs to Branch No. 108, at Hannibal, Mo.

Charles J. Meriwether is a son of Dr. Fountain and Adeline (Miller) Meriwether, who were born, reared and married in Virginia. They came to Lincoln County, Mo., in 1836, where the father, for about forty years, practiced medicine, and also carried on farming. He was a Democrat, and lived to be sixty-five years of age. His wife lived to be a few years older. Six sons and four daughters blessed their union. The fourth child, Charles J., was born in the "Old Dominion" February 3, 1830, and received the education and rearing of the average farmer's boy. When eighteen years of age he hired out as overseer, and as soon as he had accumulated sufficient money, purchased a piece of land, and has added to the same from time to time until he now has a fine farm of 330 acres. For fifty-two years he has been a resident of Lincoln County, and has proved himself a good neighbor, and a successful farmer. In his younger days he was a great lover of hunting, and was considered a fine shot with a rifle. He was accidentally shot, while out hunting, by a friend, and the sight of the left eye was totally destroyed. For a companion through life he chose Lydia Wells, a native of Albemarle County, Va. She was brought to Missouri when two years old by her widowed mother, and she and Mr. Meriwether became the parents of five sons and two daughters. She is a member of the Episcopal Church, and he is a Democrat.

John Meuth, farmer and stock raiser, was born in Nassau, Prussia, on the Rhine, May 3, 1830, and is one of eight children, seven sons and one daughter, born to John and Sophia (Wagoner) Meuth, both natives of the same place as our subject. The father was a fine cabinet-maker and house-carpenter, and in connection therewith ran a farm. Four of his sons learned trades. The youngest, John Meuth, received a good education in the German language, and when fourteen years of age began learning the shoemaker's trade. He was only about six years old when his father died, and when he was about sixteen his mother also died. Having received his property he left it in the hands of his guardian, and in 1849 he started for America. For several years he worked at his trade, chopped cord-wood, etc., and in 1854 he married Miss Ellen Gleson, a native of Ireland. Now was the time to send for his money, and he proceeded to do so, but found that his guardian had made way with the whole of it. In 1856 he moved to Lincoln County, Mo. Here his wife died, and the following year he married Miss Margaret Kaster, a native of Hanover, Germany. Nine children were the fruits of this union, eight now living, four sons and four daughters. For twenty-six years Mr. Meuth has lived on his present homestead, which consists of 620 acres. He is a Democrat in politics, and he and wife are members of the Catholic Church. His first wife was also a member of the same church.

Capt. William Miller was born in Lincoln County, N. C., in 1812, and at the age of six years was brought by his parents, Andrew and Jane (Wilson) Miller, to Missouri. They settled near the mouth of Crooked Creek, in the woods among the Indians and wild animals, and there cleared a good farm. The father died on the 30th of December, 1826. The mother was born near Philadelphia, Pa., and when quite small moved with her people to North Carolina, where they lived during the Revolutionary War, her father, Thomas Wilson, furnishing supplies to the army. He was born in Ireland, and was a weaver by occupation. The grandfather Miller was of Scotch-Irish descent, and his son Andrew was a soldier in the War of 1812, and was captain of militia at an early day. He was instrumental in establishing towns in Lincoln County, and aided to a great degree in settling the county. At the time of his death he weighed 355 pounds, although in his young days he was of ordinary weight. They reared a family of nine children, William being the youngest in the family. He was reared in the wilds of Lincoln County, and received very poor educational advantages, being compelled to walk three miles to school through the woods, which were at that time inhabited by wolves and panthers. His marriage to Emily Foster took place in 1832. She was born in North Carolina, and died in 1854, leaving six children. His second marriage was to Sarah Shults in 1855. She was a daughter of Thompson Shults. Their six children are all grown and married. Mr. Miller has lived on his present farm for seventy years. It consists of about 600 acres, and lies near Moscow Mills. He gave about 400 acres to his children. He served as justice of the peace for nearly fifteen years, and has been prominently identified with the churches and schools in his community. He has been a life-long Democrat, and his first Presidential vote was cast for Jackson. His children by his first wife are: James A.; Lizzie, wife of William Wright, and Josephine, wife of T. H. Harris. By his second wife are:

Alvina Alice, wife of Alex. Miller; Sarah Emma, wife of E. B. Wilson; Lucy Margaret, wife of T. A. Cooper; Martha L., wife of C. M. Wells; Katie, wife of John Carter, and Ida Clay, wife of Hugh Geiger.

Thomas N. Mitchell, a farmer, stock raiser and a native of Lincoln County, Mo., was born in 1848, and is the fifth of ten children. He was reared on his father's farm, educated in the common schools, and at the age of twenty began earning his own living. In 1868 he was united in marriage to Martha J., a daughter of William S. and Mary Luckett, and by her is the father of five children: Maggie, Walter, Mary, Cora and Helen. Mr. Mitchell has a good farm of 240 acres, and makes a specialty of breeding Clydesdale horses, and has a fine imported horse of that breed. He sympathizes with the Democratic party, and he and wife are members of the Baptist Church. His parents, Elder Albert G. and Amanda Jane (Davis) Mitchell, were natives of Amherst County, Va., the former being born in 1813. He became a member of the church in 1842, was licensed to preach, and soon after began his ministerial duties. He was married in 1833, and in 1845 came to Lincoln County, locating on a farm near Auburn. From there he moved to Pike County, thence to St. Charles County, and about 1883 moved to Montgomery City, where he still resides. He was ordained an elder in his church in 1847, and since his conversion has been an earnest worker for the cause of Christianity. His wife was an earnest and faithful member of the Baptist Church, and died in 1860. Mr. Mitchell took for his second wife Helen Carr. He had a brother, W. W. Mitchell, who was also licensed to preach, and after coming to Missouri was ordained, and became pastor of a number of different churches in Missouri and Illinois. He died in the latter State in 1879. The grandfather of our subject, Tarplin Mitchell, was a Virginian of English descent, and at an early day came to Missouri. His wife, Polly C., died in 1881, at the advanced age of ninety-five years. He died several years previously.

George W. Mohr, postmaster at Troy, is a native of Hesse Darmstadt, Prussia, born November 6, 1836, and is the son of J. Leonard and Barbara Mohr, who were both born in Hesse Darmstadt, Prussia. The father followed agricultural pursuits all his life, and in 1848 they emigrated to America, settling in New York, and three years later moved to Monroe County, Ill., where both passed the remainder of their lives, he at the age of sixty-six and she at the age of fifty-eight. Of their family of eight children, five sons and three daughters, all were born in Prussia. Their son, George W., received a good common education in both the English and German. He learned wagon-making and the carriage business while at Belleville, Ill., and this he followed for sixteen years, three at Belleville and eleven at Troy. In 1856 he came to Troy, and the following year he married Miss Mary C. Marsh, a native of Kentucky, who bore him nine children, five sons and four daughters. After working at his trade in Troy until 1870 he opened a bakery, grocery and restaurant, and three years later he was appointed postmaster at a salary of $420 per year. He has held this position fifteen years. In 1884 this office became one under presidential appointment with a salary of $1,000 per year. He is one of the few who has held over under Democratic administration, though a stanch Republican. The office now pays $1,200, and his last commission runs from 1884 to 1888. This office was made a money order office July 1, 1879, for which additional pay is received. Mr. Mohr is a member of the A. O. U. W., being financier of his lodge. He has been trustee of the public schools and trustee of Troy. In connection with his official position Mr. Mohr carries on the general merchandise business. He and wife are members of the Presbyterian Church.

William Moore, collector of Lincoln County, Mo., and a native of this county, was born July 9, 1840, and is the son of John L. and Agnes (Trail) Moore, both of whom were of Southern birth. They came to this county when young, were married here and are still residents of this county. The father was an old line Whig before the war and is now a Democrat. Both are members of the Missionary Baptist Church. Of the eleven children born to their marriage, ten now living, William Moore was the eldest. He was educated in the district and Troy schools, and at the age of nineteen began for himself by teaching school in the winter seasons and farming during the summer. For about sixteen years he "wielded the birch," and then abandoned this and turned his attention to stock dealing, which he continued until 1886, at which date he was elected collector. In 1869 he married Miss Alcinda F. Sanders, who bore him two children, a son and daughter, the former only, living. After the death of his wife Mr. Moore married Mrs. Ella R. Ransdell, *nee* Sydnor. He is deeply interested in farming, and is now the owner of 280 acres of good land. He started in life with little or nothing, and has made what he has by his own efforts. He is a member of the A. O. U. W., and is a Democrat in politics.

James Y. Morriss is a son of Yovel and Ursula (Thornley) Morriss, both of whom were born in the "Old Dominion." They were married in their native State and resided there until their respective deaths. The father was quite an extensive planter and was a soldier in the War of 1812. He was twice married, and was the father of four sons by his first marriage. James Y. Morriss is the youngest of seven children, and was born January 3, 1818, in Spottsylvania County, Va. In 1836 he came to Pike County, Mo., and the following year to Lincoln County. Here he has resided and farmed ever since. In 1843 he was married to Judith B. Stewart, a daughter of Gen. David and Margaret (Jameson) Stewart. Mrs. Morriss was born in Montgomery County, Ky., May 28, 1826, and is the mother of eight sons and four daughters. Mr. Morriss is a Democrat, and is the owner of 220 acres of land, and he and wife are members of the Christian Church. Mrs. Morriss' parents were natives of Kentucky, and came to Missouri in 1829, settling in Marion County, on the Muldrew farm (now the city of Palmyra), moving a year later to Lincoln County. They were the parents of ten children, and were members of the Christian Church. The father was previously a Whig, but later a Democrat, and was for many years prominently identified with the business affairs of Lincoln County, holding a number of responsible offices. He represented his county in the State Legislature. His first wife died in 1848, and in 1850 he married Mary McFarland, by whom he had one child. While he and wife were going to church in 1871 their horse ran away, throwing them from the buggy, killing her instantly, and he died from the effects of his injuries in about an hour.

John E. Moseley is one of sixteen children born to the marriage of Guerrant and Elizabeth F. (Smith) Moseley, who were born and raised in Jessamine County, Ky. The former's birth occurred in 1802 and the latter's in 1811. They came to Missouri in 1830, and in 1867 came to Lincoln County, where the father died in 1886. He was a farmer and Democrat. John E. Moseley was born in Marion County, March 18, 1831, and was reared on a farm. At the age of twenty he began working for himself and earned enough money to take him through two years at a higher school. For twenty-five years he farmed during the summer months and taught school during the winter. During the war he spent the most of his time in Illinois, and there in 1860 married Ellen G. Boyd, who died in 1876, leaving three sons. In 1878 he married Susan A. Parsons, who was born in Pike County, Mo., November 22, 1842, and is a daughter of Lewis and Louisa (Moore) Parsons, who came to Pike County, Mo., about 1827. A daughter has been been born to Mr. Moseley and wife. Since 1867 he has been a resident of Lincoln County, where he owns 300 acres of fertile land. Previous to the war he was a Whig, but since that time he has been a Democrat. In 1886 he was elected justice of the peace, and June 2, 1888, was the regular nominee of the Democratic party for associate county judge of the second district. He is a Mason and a member of the A. O. U. W.

Capt. Martin V. Mosley, postmaster and general merchant at Owen, Mo., was born in St. Louis County, Mo., January 1, 1840, and is a son of John and Martha (Arnold) Mosley, who were born, reared and married in Scott County, Ky., and about 1826 came to St. Louis County, the father dying in Montgomery County in 1876, and the mother in Texas two years later. They were of Scotch-Irish and German descent, respectively. Martin V. is the eighth of eleven children who lived to be grown. His education was obtained in the common schools and at Des Peres College in St. Louis County, after leaving which he began a military experience, which is deserving of more extended mention than the limits of this work will allow. About the breaking out of the war he joined a company at Truxton, Mo., and was subsequently made captain of Company E of Hull's Battalion. The second day after reaching Price's army, and at the battle of Lexington, he was wounded in the left shoulder and disabled for six months. On the day that Beauregard left the forts of Memphis on his retreat to Tupelo, Miss., Capt. Mosley rejoined Price and remained with a part of his old command in Col. Cockrill's regiment for six weeks. He was then persuaded by Col. Burbridge to return to the Western Department to recruit and organize troops in Missouri, his efforts in this direction in the northern part of the State proving fairly successful. In the spring of 1863, while attempting to gather recruits from several counties into the cedar hills of Callaway County, he was captured near Danville and kept in close confinement at Gratiot Street Prison, St. Louis, wearing a ball and chain for five months, at the expiration of which time he was tried as a spy. He was sentenced to hard labor at Alton Prison (Ill.) during the remainder of the war, but in seven months succeeded in making his escape with others, one of the latter being killed and two again taken prisoners. Thirteen of these fleeing prisoners crossed the Missouri River at Clarksville, an undertaking attended with great danger, but which was successfully accomplished, owing to a mistake of the encamped Federal forces that they were militia-men. After pushing on through the country without any serious obstacle, though of course constantly liable to capture, Chain of Rocks was reached, and the next night, to insure greater safety, the little company was disbanded into squads of two and three. Capt. Mosley finally gathered part of his men together and recrossed the Missouri, resting a few days near the site of his old home, and then, well equipped, starting again for the sunny South. In Reynolds County Col. Douglas, direct from Price's army, was met on his march to Pilot Knob, where Capt. Mosley organized a company and once more joined Price's command at Jefferson City. After that some serious hardships were experienced before Texas was reached, concerning which it is hardly necessary to speak in this connection. He surrendered at Shreveport, La., as officer of the day and first lieutenant of Pindall's Battalion of Sharpshooters. Following this Capt. Mosley lived with his parents on the old homestead for two years, then farmed on shares a while, bought the Carr farm in 1869 and kept bachelor's hall until his marriage, November 23, 1875, to

Miss Mary Newton McCarty, of New Jersey. In 1884 they located upon their present place in this county, consisting of 180 acres, near Owen. Capt. Mosley is a Democrat politically, and is a member of the Masonic fraternity. His wife belongs to the Methodist Church.

Ezekiel A. Mounce is a son of Henry and Ann E. (Downing) Mounce. The former was born in Montgomery County, Ky., in 1811, and after reaching manhood came with his widowed mother and sisters to St. Louis County, Mo., where he was married to Edith Davidson, who died leaving two children. He located in Lincoln County in 1844, where he married Miss L. Sitton, who died soon after marriage. He chose Miss Downing for his third wife, and by her became the father of eight children, only two of whom are living. The mother was born in Lincoln County in 1825, and died in her sixty-third year. The father died at the age of seventy years. They were members of the Cumberland Presbyterian Church, and he is a Democrat in politics. Their son, Ezekiel A., was born in the county where he now resides, July 29, 1848. Like a dutiful son he assisted his parents on the farm until twenty-one years of age, when he was united in marriage to Mary, daughter of Calisthenes Sanford, who was quite an early and influential settler of the county. She was born in 1849, and became the mother of six children, five of whom are living, four sons and one daughter. They located on their present farm of 160 acres in 1881, and are considered worthy citizens and good farmers. Mr. Mounce belongs to the Cumberland Presbyterian Church, and is a member of the A. O. U. W., and supports the principles of the Democratic party.

Solomon R. Moxley was born in Virginia September 2, 1803, and was educated in the old field schools. In 1830 he married Mary V. Bowley, and in 1836 came to Lincoln County, Mo., where the mother died in 1837, and the following year the father married Maria L. Verdier, who was also a native of Virginia. Two children were born to his first marriage, and seven to the last. With the exception of three years Mr. Moxley has lived in this county for forty-two years. He was county judge for many years, and was the first probate judge of Lincoln County, and has followed the occupation of farming through life, and owns 232 acres of land. His parents were James J. and Hannah (Robinson) Moxley, both of whom were born in Westmoreland County, Va. They were the parents of two children, and after the father's death, which occurred in 1804, his widow married again, and became the mother of seven children. The father had previously been married, and two children were the result of that union. James V. Moxley is a son of Solomon and Maria (Verdier) Moxley, and was born in the house where he now resides September, 18, 1839. He was educated in the district schools, and was reared on his father's farm. At the age of twenty-one he began studying medicine under Dr. S. H. McKay, and was preparing to take a course of lectures when the war broke out, and his plans had to be given up. In 1862 his marriage with Emma Rodifer was consummated. She was born in Lincoln County in January, 1846, and she and Mr. Moxley became the parents of eight children. They own 133 acres of land, and he affiliates with the Democratic party in his political views.

Judge Henry Thomas Mudd. Among those who have taken a prominent and active part in the growth and advancement of Lincoln County, stands the name of Judge Henry Thomas Mudd. We have been kindly permitted the perusal of his diary, a well bound book of some 300 pages, in which is found a great amount and variety of valuable and interesting matter that will doubtless be prized very highly by his descendants hereafter. Among the matter is a well written history of the Mudd family; a copy of the patent to the old homestead of his ancestors in Charles County, Md.; the will of his father, grandfather and great-grandfather; also many articles written by him and published in the county papers in reference to the Lincoln County railroad bonds, and various other matters of interest and amusement; from all of which and other sources we glean the following facts and information: The name of Mudd is very familiar to the people of Lincoln County, and not uncommon to the people throughout the States. Family tradition says that three brothers of that name came over from England with Lord Baltimore and his Catholic colony to America, and settled in Maryland in the year 1634. Only one of these brothers married, whose given name has not been preserved. His son, Thomas, procured a tract of land, containing about 900 acres, equal distance between the Potomac and Patuxent Rivers, patented to him under Lord Baltimore, which has remained continuously a family possession for 240 years, descending from Thomas to his eldest son Henry Thomas, and from Henry Thomas to his eldest son Henry, and from Henry to his eldest son Theodore, and would have descended to his eldest son, the subject of this sketch, but for the abolishment of the old English law of inheritance. This family has become very numerous, from the fact, as found from the copy of the wills in the diary, that the Judge's father, grandfather and great-grandfather, each reared a family of twelve children. Of the Mudd family, in its various branches, many have become skillful physicians and not a few eminent lawyers. The father of the subject of this sketch, Theodore Mudd, was born on the old homestead in Maryland, and was a man of good sense and irreproachable character. He was colonel of a regiment of the State Militia and member of the Maryland Legislature. His mother, Dorothy Dyer, was also a native of Charles County, Md., and was of a highly respectable family, also of twelve children; she died in Maryland at the age of sixty-six. His father spent his last days in Lincoln County, Mo., and was eighty-four years old at the time of his death. Their eldest son, Henry Thomas, was born September 23, 1816, also on the old homestead, where he obtained his growth and received his education in the common country schools of that day. At the age of seventeen he went to Washington, D. C., and for about two years was clerk and collector for the mercantile house of Semmes & Shepherd, both from Charles County, Md., the former the father of Captain Raphael Semmes, of the Confederate Navy, a very intelligent boy about ten years of age at that time and afterwards a graduate at the old Catholic College of Georgetown, D. C. His experience in Washington during those two years has been of much practical benefit to him in his after business life. In his collecting tours he had frequent opportunity to spend half hours in the galleries of the United States Senate whilst Jackson was President and Martin Van Buren Vice-President, and to witness some of the debates of the great Clay, Webster, Calhoun and Benton, the renowned Senators of their day and generation. In the year 1837 he married Miss Elizabeth E. Dyer, a native also of Charles County, Md., and to them were born ten children; only two are now living. In 1839, with his wife, one child and a few servants, he moved to St. Charles County, Mo., and the following year located at Millwood, where he devoted himself to agricultural pursuits. Two years later he was chosen assessor of that county, which position he held for four years. From 1847 to 1849 he held the office of sheriff, discharging his duties in a fearless and satisfactory manner. His mercantile career dates from 1853, when he opened a store at Millwood, and has continued in the same business ever since. In June, 1855, he lost his first wife and in June of the following year married Miss Mary O'Brien, an educated lady, born in Ireland of most respectable parents; she came to this country with her father and mother when about six years of age, and was reared and educated in Washington County, Mo. To this union eight children were born, five of whom are living, all sons. Two of his sons graduated in medicine, Dr. George Alton Mudd, in the St. Louis Medical College, and Dr. James Theodore Mudd, at the University of Maryland, in Baltimore. The rest of his sons are farmers and business men. Daniel H. is a legal partner of his father in the store at Millwood, and also in the store and lumber yard at Silex, being a wide-awake young business man, with a good prospects of success. In 1875 Mr. Mudd was elected county court judge, and for six years held that position with exceptional ability. We find that during his term of service in the court a compromise was offered by the railroad bond holders, which he and his associates in the court at that time most earnestly recommended to be accepted, and had such a course been pursued and accepted by the people of the county and the committee of their appointment, many thousand dollars, as well as much trouble, litigation and cost, would have been saved to the people of Lincoln County. He always held that the county should pay its just debts the same as an individual, and although at that time the majority of the people stood against him, and he was unable to carry out his views for the benefit of the people, all now acknowledge the righteousness of them. The Judge was a Whig until the dissolution of that party, and since then has been a firm and consistent Democrat. He is one of the founders and main-stays of the Catholic Church at Millwood, and a liberal supporter of all worthy and charitable enterprises. He has been successful as a business man, having the full confidence of the people, and is one among the larger tax payers of the county. His means, however, have been accumulated by no miserly course through life, but he believes most firmly in the scriptural injunction that it is more blessed to give than to receive.

Robert Mudd, another successful farmer of Lincoln County, was born in Washington County, Ky., October 9, 1817, and is the son of Nicholas and Martha (Janes) Mudd. The father was a native of Maryland, and when a boy went with his parents to Kentucky, where he married Miss Janes, a native of Kentucky, though her parents came from Maryland. The father was a farmer, and died in Kentucky at a good old age. He was a Whig in politics and a member of the Catholic Church, as was also his wife. She died in Lincoln County, Mo., when quite old. Their son, Robert, who was the eldest of a family of seven children, five now living, was reared on a farm and educated in the old field schools. In September, 1835, he married Miss Eliza Mudd, a native of the same county as himself, born July 11, 1816. Her ancestors, however, came from Maryland. By their union Mr. and Mrs. Mudd became the parents of eleven children, six of whom are now living, two sons and four daughters. After farming in Kentucky until 1843, they moved to Lincoln County, Mo., settling near Millwood, where they have lived ever since. In 1845 they moved to their present property which consists of 290 acres, and here he has since resided. He has been quite successful, as when he landed in Lincoln County he had only an old horse and $25 in money. For about eight or ten years he served as constable of Millwood Township. He and wife are members of the Catholic Church and he is a Democrat, although a Whig until the dissolution of that party.

Benjamin S. Mudd, farmer and son of Francis L. and Emily A. (Berry) Mudd, was born in Charles County, Md., March 4, 1825. His parents were both natives of Maryland, where they were married and where ten children were born to them. After farming in that state until 1835, they moved to Pike County,

Mo., and seven years later to Lincoln County of the same State, where they passed the remainder of their lives. The father was a lieutenant under Gen. Barney in the war of 1812, was a Democrat in politics, a member of the Catholic Church, and lived to be sixty-six years of age. His wife was also a member of the Catholic Church. Their son, Benjamin F., was about ten years old when his parents moved to Missouri. He grew up on the farm, received a very limited education, and when about twenty-one years of age he began for himself, by working for Judge H. T. Mudd at $85 a year. After farming for some time he began learning the carpenter trade, and thus made a start. Having saved about $800 he purchased the farm where he now lives. In 1854 he married Miss Mary Hammonds, a native of Lincoln County, born April 24, 1838, being the daughter of William Hammonds, one of the early settlers of the county. The result of this marriage was the birth of one daughter, who is now the wife of J. E. Mudd. Mr. Mudd now owns 200 acres of good land and has made all his property by his own industry and good management. He is a Democrat in his political views, and he and Mrs. Mudd are members of the Catholic Church.

A. N. Mudd, farmer and stock raiser, was born in Marion County, Mo., March 12, 1841, and is the fifth of eight children born to Atha N., Sr., and Priscilla N. (Jamison) Mudd, both of whom were natives of Maryland, where they attained their growth, married and lived until 1839, when they moved to Missouri and located in Marion County. Ten years later they moved to Lincoln County, Mo. The father followed merchandising in Maryland, and after coming to Missouri taught school. He was a man of delicate health, and died in the prime of life. He was well educated, was a graduate from a law school, but never practiced. He was a Whig in politics, and he and wife were members of the Catholic Church. Their son, Atha N., attained his growth on the farm and received a limited education. Being the eldest son, and his parents poor, he had to aid in supporting the family, and remained at home until twenty-four years of age. In 1865 he went to California, and after working by the month on a farm for about two years he began farming for himself, following this occupation successfully for seven years. In 1873 he returned, purchased a farm, and in February of the same year he married Miss Sophia Dyer, a native of Lincoln County, and daughter of George Dyer. This union resulted in the birth of seven children, four now living. In 1883 Mr. Mudd located where he now lives and is the owner of 450 acres of land. He is a Democrat in his political views, and he and wife are members of the Catholic Church. He is a good citizen.

James Edwin Mudd, stock breeder and farmer, and son of Judge H. T. Mudd, was born near Millwood, May 13, 1844. He was reared chiefly in his father's store, and educated in the common schools. He worked for his father, receiving wages for the same, until thirty-two years of age, and in 1876 he married Miss Hester E. Mudd, daughter of Benjamin S. Mudd. She was born in Lincoln County, Mo., in 1860, and by her marriage became the mother of five children, two sons and three daughters. Soon after marriage Mr. Mudd began farming and keeping breeding horses. In 1878 he moved to his present farm, which consists of 160 acres. He has, perhaps, done more than any other man in this county to improve the horses thereof. He owns three fine horses—a Percheron and Clydesdale, a Morgan and Englishshire, and a Clydesdale. Besides these he owns three jacks. He is accounted an enterprising, wide-awake young man, and although he has met with misfortune in the loss of stock, and in the destruction of his house by fire, with undaunted courage is still working away. He is a Democrat in politics, a member of the Catholic Knights of America, and he and wife are members of the Catholic Church.

James P. Mudd, another successful farmer of that name, was born in Lincoln County, Mo., January 27, 1848, and is the eldest of six children, four sons and two daughters, born to Thomas W. and Mary (Mattingly) Mudd. The father was born in Kentucky in 1809, although his ancestors were from the old Maryland stock of Mudds. The mother was also a native of Kentucky, born in 1807. They were born in Washington County, Ky., where they lived until 1847, when they came to Lincoln County, Mo., and located near Silex, on a farm. The father was a Whig until the dissolution of that party, when he advocated the principles of the Democratic party. He died in 1864, and his wife in

1870. Both were members of the Catholic Church. James P. Mudd was reared on a farm and educated in the district schools. He was but sixteen years old when his father died, and he thus became the main dependence of the family, and managed with the skill of a man. In 1878 he married Miss Alice Hammonds, a native of this county, and the daughter of William and Rose Ann (Wells) Hammonds, both natives of Kentucky, born in 1808 and 1818, respectively. They came to Lincoln County when quite young, were married here, and here the father followed the occupation of a brick-mason and farmer. He died in 1872, but the mother is still living, and is a member of the Christian Church. To Mr. and Mrs. Mudd were born three children, all daughters. Mr. Mudd is a Democrat in his political principles, is a member of the Catholic Church, and of the C. K. of A. He owns a good, although a rather small farm, and is accounted a successful farmer. He has made this county his home all his life, and has won a place of high esteem among his neighbors.

Alphonsus H. Mudd, farmer, is the son of Dr. Hillery P. and Clare (Mudd) Mudd, who were both born in Maryland, where they grew up and were married. The father had been previously married to a Miss Mudd, by whom he had one child. After her death he married the mother of our subject, who was a sister of Judge H. F. Mudd. In 1839 the father and mother moved to Missouri, locating near Millwood, and here the Doctor practiced medicine, farmed, and was also engaged in merchandising. He and a partner kept the first store in Millwood, secured the first post-office, named it Millwood, and Mr. Mudd was the first postmaster. He was a Democrat in politics, and he and wife were members of the Catholic Church. To his second marriage were born eight children, all of whom lived to be grown, and Dr. Joseph A., who wrote a brief history of Lincoln County for the county atlas, is one of his sons. Alphonsus H. Mudd, another son, and the subject of this sketch, was born in Millwood, September 11, 1849, attained his growth on the farm, and received his education in the common schools. After reaching manhood he taught school for about two terms, although his chief calling has been farming. In 1877 he married Miss Mary E. O'Brien, a native of Lincoln County. To this marriage have been born four children, two now living, and both daughters. Mr. Mudd has lived in this county all his life, and owns a good farm of 160 acres.

William Murphy, an enterprising farmer of Lincoln County, Mo., was born in County Wexford, Ireland, April 12, 1819, and is the eldest of a family of seven children born to Garret and Mary (Roster) Murphy. The parents were both born in County Wexford, Ireland, about 1788. After marriage the father engaged in the dairy business for many years, and then tilled the soil until 1849, when he set sail for America, the voyage taking seven weeks. They landed at New Orleans, and came by steamer to St. Louis, which they reached New Year's day, 1850. They then came to Lincoln County, and here the remainder of their days were passed. Both lived to be seventy-five years old, and both were members of the Catholic Church. The father was a Democrat in politics. Their son, William Murphy, came to St. Louis with his parents, and there met Judge H. T. Mudd, to whom he hired out for a year, at the rate of $95 per year. Soon he pre-empted a piece of land, and has added to this until he now owns 425 acres. In 1854 he married Miss Ann Murphy, also a native of Ireland, who came here a short time after her future husband. To them were born four children, all of whom lived to be grown, but only three now living, one son and two daughters: Mary (wife of Michael Dunn, a farmer), Michael (also a farmer, married to Miss Georgie Roby), and Josephine (wife of Beuford Shocklee). Mr. and Mrs. Murphy are members of the Catholic Church, and he is a Democrat in politics.

Clinton T. Nash is one of three sons and six daughters born to the marriage of William M. and Naomi M. (Menifee) Nash, who were natives, respectively, of Virginia and Kentucky. The father was a saddler by trade, and a very wealthy man. In his political views he was an old line Whig, and was a soldier in the War of 1812. Both parents died in Kentucky, leaving their children well provided for. Clinton T. Nash was born in Georgetown, Ky., January 16, 1826. Not liking the idea of being compelled to go to school, he ran away from home in 1844, and taking a boat went down the Ohio and up the Mississippi River, until he came to Clarksville. Here he kept bar on a boat for some time, and also a confectionery store opposite the Planters' House, in St. Louis. He afterward returned to Kentucky, and engaged in the grocery business at Great Crossings, but in a few months sold out his interest and returned to Lincoln County, Mo. He loaned out his money and worked on a farm for wages, then went to New Hope, in Lincoln County, where he opened a grocery store and managed it for some time. In 1854 he began dealing in apples, his trade extending up and down nearly all the tributaries of the Mississippi River. After a time he turned his attention to farming which occupation he has continued up to the present time. In 1858 he married Martha J. Haislip. She was born in Lincoln County, June 23, 1839, and became the mother of three sons and one daughter. Two children are living: Susie S. (Mrs T. M. Rose) and Clinton T. Mr. and Mrs. Nash are members of the Christian Church, and he is a Democrat in politics. He has been a Mason since 1849. Mrs. Nash's parents were R. W. and Susan S. Haislip, who came from Virginia to Lincoln County at an early day. The father was accidentally killed, and the mother died in 1876.

Richard H. Norton, one of the leading attorneys of Troy, and son of Elias and Mary (McConnell) Norton, and grandson of William and Sarah (Harlan) Norton, was born in Troy, November 6, 1849. The grandparents moved from Kentucky to Scott County, Ind., at an early day and were there married. The grandfather was a cabinet-maker by occupation, and was for a number of years county judge. He was a Democrat in politics, and both he and wife lived to a good old age, dying in Indiana. In their family were two sons, both of whom found their way to Lincoln County, Mo. The only one now living is Elias Norton, father of our subject. He was born in Scott County, Ind., August 1, 1820, and while growing up worked a short time in his father's shop, after which he went to school, but only for a few months. In 1842 he came to Lincoln County, Mo., drove the stage for some time, and then turned his attention to hotel keeping. In 1860 he was chosen sheriff and collector of this county, which position he held until the breaking out of the late war. He took no part in this, except to save a company of Germans from slaughter, and thereby prevented retaliation on his own community. For about fourteen years after the war he was engaged in merchandising, but retired in 1883. Many years previous, in 1844, he married Miss Mary McConnell, a native of Virginia. By this union he became the father of three sons. After the death of his first wife Mr. Norton married Miss Carrie Williams, a native of Pennsylvania. She lived but six weeks. In 1871 Mr. Norton married Miss Ella Turner, a native of Pike County, Mo., and to this union were born five children, all sons. His first wife was a Methodist, the second an Episcopalian, and his present wife is a Presbyterian. He is a Democrat, and one of the board of directors of the Farmers' and Mechanics' Savings Bank. When he came to Lincoln County he had a little over a dollar and, notwithstanding the fact that he has lost about $30,000, he now owns between 8,000 and 10,000 acres of land. On this he has a fine prospect for coal, though, as yet, it has not been developed. His son, Richard H. Norton, was educated in the Troy schools and St. Louis University. At the age of twenty he began reading law under A. V. McKee, and graduated from the law department of the Washington University in 1870, after which he located at Troy, where he has practiced ever since. In 1874 he married Miss Annie Ward, daughter of Dr. James A. Ward, by whom he has a daughter. Mr. Norton is a member of the Masonic fraternity, the A. O. U. W., and is also a member of the I. O. O. F. He is also one of the board of directors of the Farmers' and Mechanics' Savings Bank of Troy. and has always been a Democrat in politics. In 1884 he ran for the nomination as Representative in Congress from the Seventh District. Several candidates were in the field, of whom he and Elijah Robinson, of Pike County, were the strong candidates, too strong indeed, for either to be elected. Again, in 1886, when the race for the nomination to the same office was made, he and Mr. Robinson found themselves pitted against each other. The nomination again fell to an obscure candidate, scarcely known in the race, but like Hector and Achilles, neither would succumb, and the friends of each did their utmost to have their favorites nominated in August, Mr. Norton proving to be the successful candidate. He is accounted one of the leading lawyers of this section.

John A. Overall, farmer and stock raiser, of Lincoln County, of which he is a native, was born in 1838, and is the seventh of ten children born to William O. and Elizabeth (Crenshaw) Overall. They were born in Nelson and Bullitt Counties, Ky., and were reared and married in their native State. They came to Lincoln County, Mo., about 1837, and here spent the remainder of their days, dying in 1869 and 1877, respectively. John A. Overall, their son, attended the district schools of his county in boyhood, and remained with his parents until he attained his majority, when he began farming for himself, and in 1868 was married to Ellen Argent, and by her became the father of seven children, six living: John William, Ida E., Albert S., Rolly H., Francis M. and Jessie B. Mr. Overall has spent his entire life on the farm of his birth, and now has over 1,000 acres in different tracts. He takes great interest in raising fine cattle, hogs and sheep, and is one of the extensive and prosperous farmers of the county. He votes the Democratic ticket, and his first presidential vote was cast for Breckinridge in 1860. His wife died in 1881. She was a member of the Baptist Church, and was an earnest Christian, and devoted mother and wife. Her parents, John and Nancy Argent, were born in England and Maryland, respectively. The father's birth occurred in 1808 near London, and at the age of twelve years he came with a married sister to the United States, settling in St. Louis, and later in Troy. He was married in St. Charles County, and was twice married after his first wife's death. He died in 1871.

James Wiley Owen was born in Halifax County, of the "Old North State," in 1843, and is the eldest of three children born to William H. and Lucy A. (Jones) Owen, also North Carolinians, where they resided until 1847, when they came to Lincoln County, Mo. Here the mother died two years later, and the father in 1850. Sheridan Owen the grandfather, served as a colonel in the Revolutionary War, and James Wiley Jones, the other grandfather, was also a Revolutionary soldier. James Wiley, the subject of this sketch, was educated in the common schools, and after his parents' death lived with Joel Blanks until he was twenty-two years of age, but had worked for himself after he had attained his nineteenth year. He was married in 1866 to Sarah C., a daughter of Lorenze D. and Mary Ann Hill, natives of Missouri. Mr. and Mrs. Owen have one daughter living, Clara

Belle, and three children dead, W. H., L. A. and T. Owen. Mr. Owen has a well-cultivated farm of 326 acres of land, and in connection with farming he is quite an extensive stock dealer, and has a fine herd of short-horned cattle. He has been a Democrat in his political views all his life, and is a member of the Masonic fraternity. When Owen Station was established it was named in his honor.

Richard H. Owings is one of the firm of Mason, Dubel & Co., of Olney and was born in Warren County, Mo., March 2, 1844. His parents, George W. and Mary O. (Willnot) Owings, were born, reared and married in Kentucky, and there resided until about 1837, when they moved to Warren County, Mo., and settled on a farm, where they yet live. The father is a Democrat, and has held the office of justice of the peace for many years. Both parents are members of the Missionary Baptist Church. Richard H. Owings is the fifth of eight children, and received very limited educational advantages in his youth. He assisted his parents on the farm until nineteen years of age, and then went to Nevada, where he remained until 1867, when he returned and located in Warren County, and in 1874 came to Lincoln County. Here he has a fine farm of 357 acres of land, and is well fixed financially. Addie Eams, a native of this county, became his wife in 1870. She has borne him seven daughters, the last two being twins. Mr. Owings is a Democrat, and a member of the A. O. U. W., and he and wife are members of the Missionary Baptist Church.

Frederick W. Page is a native of Orange County, Vt., where he was born in 1831. He is a son of Ephraim Page and Miranda (Tillottson) Page, who were natives of Vermont. The former was born in 1806, and in 1840 came with his family to Ogle County, Ill., where the mother died. In 1856 he came to Lincoln County, Mo., and in 1864 died in St. Louis while serving his country. He was of Scotch descent, and his father, Reuben Page, was a soldier in the War of 1812. Frederick W. Page received a common school education, and was married in Illinois, in 1856, to Susan Kauffman, who died in 1859, leaving two children. Ten years later Mr. Page married Lydia Cannon. He owns 536 acres of land, and his wife owns eighty acres. From fifteen to twenty-three years of age Mr. Page followed the sea, and made one trip to Havre de Grace and one to Rio Janeiro. In 1862 he joined Company A, Third Missouri Cavalry, State Militia, and served until the close of the war, and since that time has been engaged in farming and stock raising. He is a Republican in his political views, but was formerly a Democrat. His wife belongs to the Christian Church and he is a member of the Methodist Episcopal Church. His only son, Frederick Ephraim, is married, and lives on the old farm.

Joseph N. Palmer is a son of Henry and Mary A. (Flood) Palmer. The father was born in Virginia in 1814, and when about ten years of age moved with his parents to Kentucky. In 1830 he came to Pike County, Mo., where he married Nancy E. McGowen, who bore him one son and two daughters. After her death he returned to Kentucky and married Mary A. Flood, and by her became the father of three sons and three daughters. After his second marriage he returned to Missouri, and in 1848 located in Lincoln County. In 1871 his second wife died, and two years later he wedded Mrs. Lydia J. Hutchison, *nee* Yeater, who is a member of the Christian Church. Mr. Palmer has been quite successful in his business ventures through life, and has become a man of wealth and influence. Joseph N. Palmer was born in Ralls County, Mo., March 28, 1846, and spent his early days on a farm. He worked for his father until twenty-one years of age, and then began fighting the battle of life for himself, as a farmer. In 1870, the same year he was married, he located on his present farm of 236 acres of land. He is a member of the Missionary Baptist Church, and in his political views is a Democrat. His wife's maiden name was Nancy E. Giles. She was born in Lincoln County, April 9, 1847, and is a daughter of Williamson C. Giles. She became the mother of two sons and two daughters. She is a member of the Christian Church.

Joseph W. Park, blacksmith and wood workman at Corso, Mo., is a son of Josiah W. and Barbara (Ingram) Park, who were early settlers of Lincoln County. The father was a farmer and chair maker, and both he and his wife were members of the Methodist Episcopal Church. He was a Whig and died in the prime of life. The mother was born in Logan County, Ky., and immigrated to Missouri when quite small. She became a widow at the age of forty-six years, and was left in very moderate circumstances, but the husband, in his wisdom, bequeathed to her the little homestead, and by judicious management and indomitable perseverance on her part, she brought her children up to manhood and womanhood and won for herself the admiration of all who knew her. She lived to a good old age. Their family consisted of ten children, six sons and four daughters. Their fifth son, Joseph W., was born in Lincoln County, Mo., March 13, 1850, and was reared on the home farm and educated in the common schools. At the age of eighteen he began working for himself, and in 1872 was married to Sarah E. Abbott, a native of Ohio, and by her became the father of two children, Minnie B. and Sadie G. In 1876 Mr. Park began working at the carpenter's trade, which he continued some four years, and at the end of that time began working at the blacksmith's trade and has continued the same up to the present time. By close application to business (unaided by a tutor) and fair dealing with the public, he has become a good workman, and has the good will of all that know him. He has a good shop and a profitable business, and is the owner of forty-three acres of land. He supports the principals of the Republican party, and is a member of the A. O. U. W. He and his wife are members of the Methodist Episcopal Church.

Caswell P. Paxton, farmer and stock trader, is a son of Luke and Mary E. (Prewitt) Paxton, both of whom were born in Kentucky. Tradition gives the origin of the Paxton family in the United States, thus: Three brothers came from the highlands of Scotland and settled in Virginia. One of the brothers became separated from the other two and in time spelled his name Paxson. The other two retained the old Scottish way of spelling the name. Later generations found their way into Kentucky, and when young, the parents of Caswell P. Paxton came to Lincoln County, Mo., and were here married. The father was a merchant in Louisville, Mo., and erected the best store building the town has ever had. Both he and wife were members of the Christian Church, and he was a Whig until the extinction of that party, and was afterward a Democrat. He lived to be forty-five years of age. His widow still survives. Of their ten children nine are living—seven sons and two daughters. Caswell P. Paxton, the eighth child, was born in Louisville, Mo., June 14, 1859. His early days were spent on his father's farm, but his educational advantages were limited. He has, however, acquired a good education through his own efforts. When about twenty-two years of age he began trading in stock and has carried on that business up to the present time. In 1886 he was married to Bettie N. Vaughan, a native of Pike County, Mo. She is a member of the Cumberland Presbyterian Church, and he belongs to the Christian Church and is a Democrat in politics.

Henry W. Perkins, cashier of the Farmers' and Mechanics' Bank of Troy, Mo., is the son of Walton and Louisiana (Green) Perkins. The father was born in Lincoln County, N. C., November 26, 1807, and when eleven years of age came to this county with his parents, who settled about two miles south of Troy, where they purchased a tract of land from the government. To make a payment on this young Walton was sent to St. Louis with the money sewed in his jacket pocket. This thirteen year old boy made the trip, paid over the money and returned—a triumph of boyhood! He remained on the farm until seventeen years of age, when he came to Troy and learned the tanner's trade under "Boss" Wing, with whom he remained until the last day of his minority. As he put aside his apron, at the close of the first day, he whispered to it confidentially—earnestly—"Now lie there!" With a capital of $63 he purchased a horse, and started for the lead mines of Galena, Ill., where he arrived with a lone dollar in his pocket. He mined a while with ill success, then sold his horse and came on a flat-boat to Clarksville, after which he walked to Troy. In 1834 he married Miss Green, who bore him one child, Henry W. With the exception of a short time spent in California, Mr. Perkins made Lincoln County his home, and made farming and trading in stock his chief business, although he followed mercantile pursuits and kept hotel several years. In 1873 he, with associates, organized the Farmers' and Mechanics' Savings Bank, of which he was president until his death, which occurred in 1885. His son, Henry W., was born in Troy, Lincoln County, Mo., April 21, 1835, and received his literary education in the Troy High School and in the State University. He received his business education in Jones' Commercial College, St. Louis. After his return he engaged as clerk and book-keeper, being the first to keep a double entry set of books. His chief occupation in life has been farming and banking, having carried on the former quite extensively. In 1874 he was chosen cashier of the above-named bank, and has been in that capacity since. Early in 1888 he was appointed to fill a vacancy in the county treasurer's office, made by the resignation of W. S. Bragg. Mr. Perkins, however, had been custodian of this county's available funds for the last fifteen years. In 1860 he married Miss Georgie Ritner, a native of Virginia, though reared in St. Louis County, Mo. She is an active member of the Presbyterian Church. To them were born seven children, four now living, one son and three daughters. Mr. Perkins is a stanch Democrat in politics, is a member of the A. O. U. W., and is also a member of the Masonic Fraternity, having gone as high as the K. T. degree.

James F. Pogue, of the firm of Pogue & Moxley, was born at White Sulphur Springs, Va., June 27, 1850, and is the son of William H. and Sarah E. (Brown) Pogue, natives of Virginia, where they grew up and were married. The father was a teacher and also a merchant. In 1858 they moved to Ralls County, Mo., and in 1870 to Callaway County, where they are still living on a farm. For about eight years he was justice of the peace of Callaway County. Both he and wife are members of the Old School Presbyterian Church. Five children were born to their marriage, the oldest being James F. He was educated in the public schools, also at Westminster College, of Callaway County, and at New London Institute he took the prize for making the most advancement in all studies in a department of about sixty. He then read medicine for some time, after which he engaged in teaching, being then nineteen years of age, and this occupation continued for nine years with good success. In 1878 he opened a family grocery in Wellsville, Montgomery County. In 1884 he moved to Whiteside and opened a drug store, but two years later took to general merchandising. In 1887 he was joined in business by John A. Moxley, and they carry the largest stock of goods in town, and are stirring business men. While teaching in Lincoln County he married Miss Maggie A., daughter of Judge S. R. Hoxley. This union resulted in the birth of four children, two sons and two daughters. Mr. Pogue commenced in the world a poor boy, and has made all he has by his own efforts. He is a Democrat in politics and is a member of the Triple Alliance. His wife is a member of the Baptist Church.

George W. Pollard was born in Pittsylvania County, Va., in 1823, and is a son of John and Judith (Bortel) Pollard, and a grandson of George Pollard, who was of Scotch descent and died in Missouri. Grandfather Bortel was born in Virginia, and served seven years during the Revolutionary War. He died in Virginia. John Pollard is a Virginian, born in 1790, and was married at about nineteen years of age. In 1831 he located in St. Charles County, Mo., and some time after in Lincoln County, where he cleared a large farm. He was a soldier in the War of 1812, and died in 1870, being over seventy-nine years of age. His wife died in 1869 over seventy-five years of age, and both were consistent members of the church. George W. Pollard, the immediate subject of this sketch, was the fifth of eleven children, and received no early educational advantages. He began farming for himself at the age of twenty-one, and in 1846 was married to Serepta B., a daughter of James Blanks, of Virginia, who became a resident of Lincoln County, Mo. in 1831 or 1832. Mr. Pollard has lived on his farm of 230 acres since his marriage, and in his political views has been a life-long Democrat. His children are William Jasper, who is a traveling salesman for a St. Louis house; John N., a druggist at Springfield, Mo.; Benjamin W., a farmer; Jennie B., wife of J. F. Hall, a farmer; Permelia, wife of W. H. True, also a farmer; Laura L., unmarried; G. S. Pollard, a teacher, and Douglas M., who is a farmer and lives at home. Mr. Pollard and wife, and all but two children are members of the Christian Church.

John W. Pollard is a brother of George W. Pollard, whose sketch precedes this, and was born in Pittsylvania County, Va., in 1830, being the seventh of the family. He was brought to Missouri when an infant, and in his boyhood days received but little schooling. After attaining his majority he began farming on his own responsibility, and followed this occupation exclusively until 1877, at which time he began merchandising at Chain of Rocks, Mo., the firm being known as John N. Pollard & Co., but two years later changed to Rellen & Pollard, and has continued the same up to the present time. They carry a stock of merchandise valued at about $4,000, with a good annual profit. Mr. Pollard was married in 1875 to Virginia Hamilton, who was born in Lincoln County, and became the mother of three children—George O. M., Edward and an infant. Since his marriage he has lived in the vicinity of Chain of Rocks, and owns over 500 acres of land, all of which he has made by his own efforts. He has been a life-long Democrat, and is a member of the Masonic fraternity. His wife belongs to the Christian Church and is a daughter of Aaron Hamilton, a Virginian.

James and Lydia K. (Sitton) Porter are among the oldest settlers of Lincoln County, Mo. The former was born in Williamson County, Tenn., August 10, 1807, and is the son of David and Elizabeth (Hopkins) Porter, who were natives of Virginia and South Carolina, respectively. In early life the parents moved to Tennessee, where the mother died when James was about nine days old. He was taken by his grandparents and remained with them until about ten years of age. The father married again and moved to Missouri about 1810, where they made a settlement on Big Creek, within the present limits of Lincoln County. In 1836 they moved to Pike County, Ill., and here the stepmother died at the age of eighty-two. Her husband in 1849 started for California, and at Fort Hall dropped dead; he was sixty-nine years of age. He was of English-Scotch extraction, was a blacksmith and farmer by occupation, was a ranger in the war of 1812, and was a man of infinite jest. At the age of ten James was brought to Lincoln County, Mo., where he had almost no advantages for an education; six months in all would cover his schooling. At the age of seventeen he was apprenticed to "Boss" Wing, of Troy, to learn the tanner's trade, served his time, laid aside his apron and engaged in agricultural pursuits. March 17, 1829, he married Miss Lydia K. Sitton, who was born near Nashville, Tenn.,

January 24, 1807, and who was the daughter of Lawrence B. and Rachel S. (Gibson) Sitton. Her father was born in 1785, in North Carolina, and her mother in South Carolina in 1776. They immigrated to Davidson County, Tenn., were married there and afterward moved to Warren County in 1811, and moved to their farm on Big Creek in 1812. The war coming on, Mr. Sitton left that place, secured a home within one and three-fourth miles of Kennedy's Fort, Warren County, and then enlisted in Capt. Callaway's company, serving fourteen months. After returning from the war he built a house near Auburn in 1816, and moved there the following year. He was a farmer all his life. The mother died in 1824 and he in 1863. He was magistrate for about twenty-four years. After marriage Mr. and Mrs. Porter made a settlement in what is now Monroe County, and in 1835 they returned to Lincoln County, where they have resided ever since. To their marriage were born five sons: James C., a farmer of Reno County, Kas.; William C., a farmer of Lincoln County; David D., a merchant of Paris, Tex.; John L., deceased, and George W., a farmer of Lincoln County. All the sons, with the exception of the one in Texas, are Republicans, and four of them were in the late war. George W. was captain in the Union army; David D. was captain in the Confederate army; William C. was orderly sergeant in the Union army, and James C. was a private in the State militia. Mr. and Mrs. Porter are members of the Cumberland Presbyterian Church. When they were first married he had a horse and a cow, and she had a cow and a bed. They have seen almost every side of the wheel of fortune. Having giving their children a good start in life they still have enough to keep them in their old age. Mr. Porter cast his first presidential vote for John Q. Adams, was a Whig in politics, then a Know-Nothing, and is now a Republican. When he first settled in Monroe County he had to go twenty-two miles to get his ax re-set.

Hon. Charles U. Porter, an early settler, is the son of William, Sr., and Mary A. (Duncanson) Porter, both natives of Fredericksburg, Va., born respectively in 1770 and 1777. In early life the father engaged in merchandising in Fredericksburg, and later purchased a farm in Culpeper County, which he cultivated until 1835, when he and family came to Lincoln County, Mo., locating on the bluffs of the Mississippi, but sickness of the family caused them to move further back into the county. In 1840 the father died, and the mother survived him fifteen years. While in Virginia the father was judge of the court of his native town. Both were Episcopalians, though they joined the Presbyterian Church in the absence of the church of their choice. He was a Whig in politics. In their family were six children, three sons and three daughters; of these four survive. Charles U. was the third child born to this union, his birth occurring in Fredericksburg, Va., October 2, 1815. He was reared on a farm and secured a good common school education. He came to Lincoln County with his parents, and has since made this his home. In 1849 he was chosen to represent Lincoln County in the Legislature, and filled the office for one term. He and his colleague went to Jefferson City in a carriage, and at that session the grants were made to the Hannibal, St. Joe & Southern Pacific Railroad. In 1878 he was chosen county judge, and held the office four years. He was a Whig previous to the war, but since then has been a Democrat. Although a slave holder he was always a Union man. Mr. Porter taught school for some time, though his chief business has been farming. He owns 440 acres, and has made this county his home for fifty-three years. He is accounted a good citizen and a kind neighbor. He is a single gentleman, and a member of the Presbyterian Church.

Norman Porter, senior member of the firm of Porter & Crider, was born in Lancaster, Garrett Co., Ky., October 8, 1837, and is the son of William and Sallie (Richardson) Porter, who were born respectively in Kentucky and Tennessee. The father was a blacksmith by trade, and is now a resident of Lincoln County, Mo. He is living on a farm, and is in his eightieth year. The mother is in her seventy-fourth year. He was a Whig in politics, then a "Know-Nothing," and is now a Republican. Both he and wife are members of the Christian Church. Norman Porter was the third son of nine children born to his parents. He was educated in the common schools, and at the age of eighteen he started out for himself, working on a farm, and with the proceeds thus obtained schooled himself. In 1859 he came to Lincoln

County, Mo., and there, for ten winters, taught school. From 1865 to 1870 he engaged in farming, and in 1873 he opened a stock of goods at Olney, Lincoln Co., where he continued until 1883. The following year he came to Silex and opened the largest stock of goods in the place. In 1869 and 1870 he was assessor. In 1884 he married Mrs. Martha J. Gilbert, *nee* Jones, daughter of Rev. William M. Jones, a Baptist minister. She is a native of Montgomery County, and by her marriage became the mother of one child, Charles T. Porter. Mr. Porter is a Republican in politics, is a member of the Christian Church, and is a highly respected citizen. Besides the store the firm deals quite extensively in grain. Mrs. Porter is a member of the Baptist Church.

J. W. Powell and R. H. Womack are the proprietors of the Elsberry *Advance*, which paper was established in 1880. Mr. Powell was born near Troy in 1855, and is a son of Watson and Sarah W. (Zimmerman) Powell, who were born in Halifax County, Va., and Lincoln County, Mo., in 1821 and 1837, respectively. They were married in Lincoln County in 1852, and there the father still lives, a well-to-do farmer. The mother died in 1870. J. W. Powell attended the common schools and the schools of Troy, and in 1878 began the study of law, and was admitted to the bar a year later. He became a member of the law firm of Walton, Avery & Powell, and later of the firm of McKee, Avery & Powell. In 1880 he came to Elsberry, and the following year purchased an interest in the Elsberry *Advance*, with which paper he has since been connected. He also continues his law practice and has met with good success. In 1881 he was married to Annie, a daughter of Isaac and Mary Whiteside, and two children have blessed their union. Mr. Powell is a supporter of the principles of the Democratic party, and is a member of the I. O. O. F. and A. O. U. W.

R. H. Womack was born in Mansfield, La., October 31, 1853, and is a son of H. H. and Jane A. (Carr) Womack, who were native Virginians. They were married in Alabama, but spent the greater part of their lives in Louisiana. H. H. Womack was a successful lawyer, and was for some time sheriff of De Soto Parish, La. He served in the Confederate army, and died about the year 1874; he is buried at Mansfield. The mother is still living and resides at Houston, Tex. R. H. Womack was educated at private schools, and learned the printer's trade at New Orleans, at which he worked in different parts of the country for some time. For the past eight years he has been engaged as an editorial writer on Missouri newspapers, and is a stanch Democrat in principle. He bought into the Elsberry *Advance* in July, 1887, since which time he has, jointly with Mr. Powell, edited and published that paper. Mr. Womack was married in 1880 to Susie E. Megown, daughter of Judge John Megown, of New London, Ralls County, and by her he is the father of three children, two boys and one girl.

George Pratt, grocer, of Troy, was born in Callaway County, Mo., February 9, 1852, and was reared to agricultural pursuits, being educated in the log school-houses. At the age of seventeen he began clerking, and continued this occupation for seven years. He then opened a general store at Medora, Osage County, Mo., but only remained there until 1879, when he moved to Troy, and has since been engaged in the grocery business, meeting with fair success. Mr. Pratt started a poor boy, and by his own efforts has made all he has. He is well respected by all who know him, and is scrupulously honest in all his dealings. In 1885 he married Miss Clara Sedlack, daughter of Martin and Mary (Cassidy) Sedlack, who are natives of Bohemia and Ireland, respectively, and who left their native country and immigrated to America when young. To Mr. and Mrs. Pratt was born one daughter, who was named Lillian. Mr. Pratt is a Democrat in his political views.

Robert Chandler Prewitt, M. D., is a son of Robert C. and Elizabeth M. (Elgin) Prewitt, who were born in Virginia and Maryland, respectively. They were early residents of Kentucky, and there the father first married a Miss Garth, who bore him a son. After her death he married Miss Elgin, and by her became the father of eight children, five sons and three daughters. He was a farmer and a soldier in the War of 1812, and in his political views was a Democrat. He became a resident of Lincoln County, in 1835. He died in 1850. His wife lived to be nearly ninety years of age. Dr. Robert Prewitt is their second child.

He was born in Fayette County, Ky., April 27, 1821, and was reared on a farm. In 1844 he began the study of medicine under Dr. Isaac Lee, and in 1845-46 took a course of medical lectures at the Medical College of St. Louis, and since that time has been a successful practitioner of Louisville, Mo. He graduated from the college in 1852. In 1850 he was married to Lucy E. Shaw, who died in 1858, leaving two children, one daughter now living. In 1860 he married Mary E. Elgin, a native of Georgetown, Ky., and by her became the father of five children, three of whom are living, one son and two daughters. In connection with his practice the Doctor is interested in farming and is the owner of 250 acres of land. He is a Mason, and is well known throughout the county as a successful practitioner.

Benjamin F. Reed, clerk of the circuit court of Lincoln County, Mo., was born in Lincoln County, Mo., April 10, 1851, and is the son of James A. and Emily C. (Cobb) Reed, natives of Tennessee and North Carolina, respectively. They were married in Pike County, Mo., in 1838, and soon after came to Lincoln County, Mo., and here made their home. The father was of Scotch-Irish and German descent, was a farmer by occupation, and was a member of the Methodist Episcopal Church South. He was a Democrat in politics. His wife was a member of the Cumberland Presbyterian Church. Their family consisted of five children, three sons and two daughters. The father died in 1858 at the age of forty years, but the mother still lives and is now in her sixty-ninth year. Benjamin F. Reed was the third child born to this union. He received a meager education in the public schools of his native county, having to work hard on the farm to support his widowed mother and orphan sisters; but after arriving at the age of eighteen years he determined to have a liberal education, to which object he bent all his energies for the ensuing ten years. Being almost entirely without means, he worked on the farm and attended school, alternately, until he became competent to teach, when he continued to teach and attend school alternately, putting in one year at Westminster College, Fulton, Mo., and three years at the Missouri University, the last year having been devoted to the study of law. Failing health, however, caused him to abandon his profession, and in the spring of 1880 he returned home and entered a dry goods store as clerk, where he continued—in 1882 becoming a partner—until December, 1886. In March, 1882, he was married to Miss Nancy J. Motley, a native of Lincoln County, who bore him three children, two living, a son and a daughter. The same year Mr. Reed made the race for the office he now holds, but was defeated by 125 votes. In 1886, however, he was more successful, and entered upon the discharge of his present position January 1, 1887. He is a Democrat in politics. He was a delegate to the State convention at St. Louis in 1884, to select delegates to the National convention, and also, the same year, was a delegate to the State convention at Jefferson City, to nominate the State ticket. He is a member of the A. O. U. W., being a Past Master, and is also a member of the Temperance Benevolent Association, of which he is now the Grand Treasurer, and was one of the original incorporators of Olney Institute.

John M. Reid, farmer, stock raiser, and a native of Lincoln County, Mo., was born in 1837, and is a son of John and Matilda (Wallace) Reid, natives, respectively, of Shelby and Garrett Counties, Ky. They were both born in 1801, and after their marriage came first to St. Louis County, Mo., and in 1832 located in Lincoln County, where they spent the remainder of their days. The father died in 1856, and the mother in 1863. Both were members of the Associate Reformed Presbyterian Church. John M. Reid is the second of four children who lived to be grown. He was educated in the old subscription schools, and in 1866 was married to Martha E., daughter of James and Julia A. Alexander, who were born in Kentucky and Maryland, respectively, and came to Lincoln County in 1832. Mr. Reid and wife are the parents of seven children, and own a fertile farm of 200 acres near Brussells. Mr. Reid supports all laudable enterprises. Previous to the war he was a Whig in politics, later became a Democrat, and now affiliates with the Greenback party. He and wife are members of the Associate Reformed Presbyterian Church. Grandfather Reid was a member of the county court for some time while in Kentucky, and was also a member of the State Legislature. He died in Lincoln County in 1836.

Judge William W. Reid was born in the house where he now

lives, in 1842, and is the son of Hon. Alexander and Elizabeth (Duff) Reid. The former was born in Shelby County, Ky., in 1797, and he was there reared and was first married to Mary Shannon, who died a few years after, leaving one child. After her death Mr. Reid came to Missouri and purchased a farm, and then returned to Kentucky and married Miss Duff, who was born in Madison County, Ky. He then returned to Missouri, where he spent the remainder of his days, dying in January, 1851, at Jefferson City, while a member of the State Legislature. He was an honest, upright citizen and an able and conscientious official. His remains were interred in the cemetery at Jefferson City. His widow spent the remainder of her days on the old homestead, and died in 1884 at the age of seventy-six years. Both were members of the Associate Reformed Presbyterian Church. Judge Reid is their only child. He has spent his entire life on the farm where he was born, and in his boyhood days received such education as the schools of that day afforded. Elizabeth Finley became his wife in 1866. She was born and married in Shelby County, Ky. Her parents, Andrew and Icyphena Finley, lived and died in Kentucky, but several of her brothers and sisters came to Lincoln County. Mr. Reid owns one of the best farms in the county, consisting of 230 acres, and is a successful agriculturist. He is a Democrat, and in 1886 was elected associate judge of Lincoln County. His wife belongs to the Associate Reformed Presbyterian Church.

John E. Richards is a native of St. Charles County, Mo., where he was born in 1846. His parents, Charles and Louisa (Eddens) Richards, were born in the "Old Dominion," but were married in Missouri in 1844, and there reared a family of three sons. The father was a farmer and tobacco manufacturer, and was a prosperous business man. His death occurred May 3, 1855, followed by his wife's death March 30, 1875. At the breaking out of the war John E. Richards enlisted in the Confederate army, but only served a short time when he was captured and paroled. He returned home at the first opportunity, again enlisting in the Confederate service. This was, however, the latter part of the war. Mr. Richards has resided on his present farm of 400 acres since 1876. His property is well improved and situated about seven miles from the county seat. Besides his residence property he has another farm of 200 acres. In 1874 he was married to Ida A. Carter, who was born in Lincoln County in 1856, and is the mother of three daughters and one son. One daughter died when about one year old. Mrs. Richards is a daughter of Col. Thomas M. Carter.

James Riley is one of the successful farmers and stock raisers of Lincoln County, and was born in the "Emerald Isle" about 1829, being one of seven children born to Patrick and Rose (Teffe) Riley. The father lived and died in the old country, where he had followed the life of an agriculturist, but the mother came with her children to the United States, and from 1848 to 1849 were residents of New Orleans. At the latter date they moved to St. Louis, where the mother and two sisters died of cholera the same year. James Riley received but little schooling in his youth, and during the time he should have been attending school, he served on board a boat that plied on the lower Mississippi, as dish-washer. From that he arose to the position of watchman. At the end of thirteen years he gave up this life and began farming, and succeeded beyond his expectations, being now the owner of 150 acres of fertile land, besides assisting his son in many ways. He was married in 1856 to Bridget Costillo, who was also born in Ireland. They have two children, Rose and Thomas. The family worship in the Catholic Church, and Mr. Riley is in sympathy with the Democratic party.

Benjamin F. Robertson, farmer, stock dealer and merchant, of Lincoln County, Mo., was born in Shelby County, Ky., in 1823, and is the sixth of nine children born to Horatio and Nancy (Gill) Robertson. Both parents were born in Virginia and removed to Kentucky with their parents when quite young, and were married in Shelby County, after reaching maturity. They came to Lincoln County about 1826, where the father died in 1840. The mother then went back to Union City, Ky., where her death occurred in 1860. Mills Robertson, grandfather of Benjamin F., was also a Virginian, and Thomas Gill, the maternal grandfather, was an Englishman. Benjamin F. obtained his education in the old log school-houses of early times, and at the age of seventeen years began working for himself and learned the carpenter's and cabinet-maker's trade. In 1854 he married Mary Elizabeth Gilham. She is a daughter of Tandy and Mary Gilham, of Virginia, and was born in Pike County of that State. She is the mother of four children: George (a hardware merchant at Montgomery City), Ardena T. (wife of C. C. Williams, a broker at Nevada, Mo.), Alice (wife of Samuel Marks, a merchant at Foley), and Martha E. (wife of Joseph Varnum, a merchant at Montgomery City). In 1857 Mr. Robertson settled on his present farm of 306 acres, in Lincoln County. He owns considerable property at Foley, which town he established, and since 1879 has had a store there. Soon after locating on his farm he erected a steam saw and flour-mill which he ran for fifteen or sixteen years. He was engaged in the agricultural implement business from 1872 to 1876, and is counted one of the prominent citizens of the the county. He is a Democrat, and he and wife are members of the Methodist Episcopal Church.

Owen C. Robinson, retired farmer, is the son of Benjamin and Rebecca (Lakin) Robinson, natives of Maryland and Pennsylvania, respectively. After marriage they settled in Maryland. In early life the father was a sailor, but in later years he followed farming. From Maryland they moved to Virginia, and in 1840 to Pike County, Mo., where they both died, he at the age of sixty-eight, and she also about the same age. The mother was a member of the Methodist Episcopal Church, and the father was an old line Whig in politics. Their family consisted of nine children, three now living. Owen C. was born August 4, 1814, in Alleghany County, Md., and when about nine years of age was taken to Virginia, and to this State about 1840. He received a limited education, and when in Virginia he assisted his father in running a stage line. After coming to Missouri he followed agricultural pursuits chiefly. He remained with his father until twenty-eight years of age, when, in 1843, he came to this county and located on a farm in the northern part of Lincoln County. In 1848 he married Miss Elizabeth Salmonds, a native of Lincoln County. The result of this marriage was the birth of five children, three now living, two sons and a daughter. Their son Elijah is one of the ablest lawyers of this section of the State. He is now making his third race for Congress. Mr.

Robinson has been a resident of this county for forty-five years, and has always been a peace-loving and highly respected citizen.

Dr. Robert L. Robinson, physician and druggist at Troy, is the son of Owen C. and Elizabeth (Salmonds) Robinson. [For sketch of parents see above.] The Doctor was born April 14, 1854, in Lincoln County, Mo., and was the second child born to his parents. He remained on the farm until about sixteen years of age, and secured a good education in Watson Seminary and McGee College, near Macon City, Mo. He then spent some time in Bryant & Stratton's Commercial College, at St. Louis. Having studied medicine under Dr. W. S. Hutt, of Troy, he entered the St. Louis Medical College, graduating from the same in 1876. He then began practicing at Troy, and continued in active business until 1881, when he purchased a stock of drugs, and has since had an office practice. Dr. Robinson has made this county his home all his life, and is one of Troy's useful, stirring business men. He is a member of the I. O. O. F., and is a Democrat in politics. He is a single gentleman.

Judge William Webb Shaw is a son of William and Martha (Webb) Shaw, who were born in Virginia in 1784 and 1793, respectively. After their marriage, which occurred in 1811, they lived in their native State until 1833, when they came to Missouri and located in Pike County, where they spent the remainder of their days. The father was quite skillful in the use of tools, and found plenty of work to do, at that early day, in making furniture and shoes for his own and the neighboring families. He was an extensive farmer, and had twenty-one tobacco barns on his farm. He was a Democrat, and died while visiting in Virginia in 1846. The mother died in Pike County in 1845. Judge William Shaw is the eighth of their ten children. He was born in Bedford County, Va., November 14, 1830, and his early days were spent on the farm and in the district and select schools. At the age of sixteen he was left alone in the world, and two years later taught his first school, and continued to teach the "young idea" during the winter months for ten years. When out of the school room he farmed and handled stock. He has been quite successful in his business ventures, and owns 320 acres of land, and deals extensively in stock. He is a member of the Masonic fraternity and the A. O. U. W., and supports the principles of the Democratic party. He served two years as justice of the peace, and in 1860 was chosen judge of the county court, being, perhaps, the youngest judge the county has ever had. From 1872 until 1875 he served as collector of Lincoln County, and, as an official, has given the best satisfaction. He is now filling the office of notary public, and is a wide-awake and highly respected citizen.

Jesse J. Shaw, county court clerk, is the son of William W. and Mary J. (Stewart) Shaw. The father was born in Bedford County, Va., in 1830, and when three years of age was brought to Pike County, Mo. In 1847 he moved to Lincoln County, Mo., where he now resides on a good farm. The mother was born in Montgomery County, Ky., in 1829, and was brought to Missouri when an infant. In 1830 her parents moved to Lincoln County, and here she met and married Mr. Shaw in 1850. She was the daughter of Gen. David Stewart, who represented Lincoln County in the Legislature of 1846. In 1860 Mr. Shaw was elected judge of the county court, and served until he refused to take the iron-clad oath. In 1872 he was chosen collector, being the first to hold that position after the office of sheriff was divided. He served two years and then retired to farm life. In politics Mr. Shaw has always been Democratic, and he and wife are members of the Christian Church. Their family consisted of eight children, Jesse J. being the fourth child. He was born December 6, 1857, in Lincoln County, Mo., and was reared on a farm. He attended the district school, the Troy High School and the State University. He then taught school three years, clerked in a store, and in 1881 he came into the county clerk's office as deputy and served until 1886, when he was chosen county clerk, receiving the largest majority of any man in the county running for an official position. Since 1881 he has been clerk of the probate court. In 1884 he married Miss Annie M. McKay, a native of Lincoln County and a member of the Christian Church. Mr. Shaw is a Democrat in politics, is Past Master of the A. O. U. W., is Master of the Troy Lodge of the A. F. & A. M., and is also a member of the Chapter.

Peachy G. Shelton, farmer, is the son of Abraham C. and

Mary L. (Claiborne) Shelton, both natives of Virginia, he of Pittsylvania County and she from near Richmond. To their marriage were born seven children, only two of whom are now living. The mother died at the age of thirty-five, and in 1837 the father, with his four sons, moved to Lincoln County, Mo., and located on a farm. He had prepared himself for the legal profession and followed the same for many years in Virginia, but failing health caused him to abandon it. He was a Whig, and died in 1840. The mother was a member of the Episcopal Church. The youngest child but one, Peachy G. Shelton, was born in Pittsylvania County, Va., September 20, 1832, and came to this county in 1837. He was reared on a farm and his education was acquired at the old subscription schools of long ago. After the death of his father he was cared for by his uncle, and after attaining his majority he engaged in agricultural pursuits. In 1853 he married Miss Susannah C. Shelton, also a native of the same county. To this marriage four children were born, two now living—Willie C., wife of Charles Martin, attorney of Troy, and Robert S., a rising young man. In 1858 Mr. Shelton was elected sheriff of Lincoln County and held this position one term. In 1874 he was elected collector and re-elected in 1876. In 1882 he was again called to that office and re-elected in 1884. Besides this he has been deputy collector for about three years. He is a Democrat in his political principles, is a member of the Masonic fraternity and a member of the A. O. U. W. He has been a resident of Lincoln County for fifty-one years, and is an excellent citizen.

Capt. Aylett M. Shults, of Moscow Mills, was born in Flint Hill, Rappahannock County, Va., in the year 1835, and is the sixth of thirteen children, all but one of whom lived to be grown, born to the marriage of Thompson Shults and Axe Anna Nicol, who were born in 1803 and 1806, respectively, in Virginia. They located in Indiana about 1835, and in 1853 came to Lincoln County, where they spent the remainder of their days, dying in 1879 and 1885. Their ancestors were supposed to be German. Capt. Aylett M. Shults began keeping a nursery near Moscow Mills in 1860 on his father's farm, but in 1867 removed to his present location, and although beginning the nursery business on a small scale at that time, has now about forty acres which he devotes to raising all kinds of nursery products. He began this work without any experience, but by industry and good business management has been quite successful. His home farm consists of 200 acres, and with his other farm his total amount of land is about 600 acres. He has a very handsome residence, which is nicely and comfortably furnished. In 1865 he was commissioned by Gov. Fletcher as captain of Company H, Sixty-fourth Missouri State Militia. He had previously served as corporal. Lucy Vertrese became his wife in 1864. She was born in Illinois, and is a daughter of Isaac and Rebecca Vertrese, who were formerly of Kentucky, and by them was brought to Lincoln County when quite small. Mr. and Mrs. Shults became the parents of eleven children, nine of whom are living: Clara E., Henry Thompson, Isaac F., Aylett A., Albert J., Lucy M., James L. C., Mary A. E., and John William. Mr. Shults is a Democrat, and he and wife are faithful and consistent members of the Christian Church. On one of Mr. Shults' farms are the celebrated sulphur and mineral springs, one-half mile west of Moscow Mills.

Charles Shumate, junior member of the firm of Kabler & Shumate, was born in St. Louis County, Mo., September 26, 1846, being the son of Rev. W. D. Shumate, of the Methodist Episcopal Church South. The father was born in Culpeper County, Va., and there married Miss Susan Quisenberry, whose grandfather came to St. Louis County, Mo., about 1844, and kept the Fee Fee post-office and the stage stand on the St. Charles and St. Louis route. The parents of our subject came about the same time. The father was engaged in his ministerial duties all his life, and in connection with this followed farming. At one time he traveled as an agent of a colonization society through this country. The mother died in 1848, and afterward the father married again, and lived until 1869. To the first union were born three children, the second child being Charles Shumate. He received his education in the common schools and at Des Peres, and at Henderson & Stewart's Commercial College at St. Louis. He then returned to the farm, and engaged in tilling the soil in St. Louis County until 1876, when he moved to Lincoln

County, and purchased a farm one and one-half miles south of Troy. In 1886 he moved to Troy, and one year later he became a member of the present firm. In 1865 he married Miss Cornelia H. McHaney, who was born in Tennessee, but who was reared in this county. Six children were born to this marriage, three sons and three daughters. The eldest son, Albert, is a graduate of the California State Normal School, and is corresponding agent for the Singer Sewing Machine Company. The second son, James W., is salesman in a dry goods store in Eugene City, Oregon. The youngest son, Thomas D., is in a wholesale drug store at San Jose, Cal. As a business man Mr. Shumate has been quite successful. He is a member of the I. O. O. F., and is strongly Democratic in his political views.

James M. Sitton was born in Lincoln County, Tenn., in 1811, and is a son of William and Anna (Gray) Sitton, who were born in South Carolina and Tennessee, respectively. They were married in Smith County, of the latter State, and lived in Lincoln County until 1819, when they removed to Missouri, locating near Auburn. The mother died in 1844, and the father about seven years after. He was of Scotch-Irish descent, and was a captain in the War of 1812, and was at the battle of New Orleans. James M. Sitton is the sixth of sixteen children, fifteen of whom lived to be grown, but only three are now living, and distinctly remembers the hardships the family had to endure after coming to Missouri. His education was received from Judge James Wilson, who received his pay in labor from the farmers. He was married in 1833 to Matilda, a daughter of Clifford Gray, a native of Smith County, Tenn., and six children were born to their union, only two of whom are now living: Lucy, wife of William Doty, and John R. During 1846–48 Mr. Sitton lived in Dubuque County, Iowa, and in 1861–62 in California, mining lead in Iowa, and gold in California; with these exceptions he has lived in Lincoln County for nearly thirty years, and is the owner of 118 acres of land. He has been a life-long Democrat, and his first presidential vote was cast for Jackson. Mrs. Sitton is a member of the Baptist Church.

John W. Skurlock. Among the prosperous farmers of Lincoln County may be mentioned the subject of this biography.

He is a native of the county, and was born January 1, 1849, and owing to the death of his parents, when he was very young, he was reared by an uncle, David Barley, who gave him plenty of work to do, but few educational advantages. On attaining his eighteenth year he began working for wages, and continued until 1869, when he was united in marriage to Mary E. Bryant, a native of Lincoln County, and their union was blessed in the birth of five children, two of whom are living: Joseph W. and Maggie O. Mr. Skurlock began farming soon after his marriage, and by proper management and industry is the possessor of 360 acres of land. He deals quite extensively in stock, and is accounted one of the honest farmers of the county. His parents were William and Chaney (Barley) Skurlock, who were early settlers of Missouri. The former died about 1851, and the latter about 1856.

Abbott W. Slaughter, M. D., of Whiteside, was born in Westport, Mo., December 1, 1860, his parents being Alfred and Laura (Abbott) Slaughter, natives of Virginia, where they attained their growth and were married. The father was well educated, and came to Missouri in 1858. He was principal of the Wellington High School, Missouri, for five years; of the Lexington High School, nine years; Prairie Home Institute, Cooper County, Mo., eleven years; McCune College, Louisiana, Mo., and is now president of Blandville Institute, Kentucky, where both live. Four children were born to this union, two sons and two daughters. Abbott W. Slaughter was educated at Prairie Home Institute and at McCune College, graduating in 1880. He then studied medicine under Drs. Ayers and Dreyfus, of Louisiana, Mo., for three years and then took a course of lectures at St. Louis Medical College, graduating from that institution in 1884. He then located at Silex, and moved to Whiteside in November, 1887. In 1886 he was married to Miss Ruth Reeds. To this union one child, Alfred, was born. Dr. Slaughter is a rising young physician, and justly deserves the patronage with which he has been met. In December, 1887, he opened a neat drug store at Whiteside. He is a Democrat in his political views, is a Mason, a K. of H., and he and wife are members of the Missionary Baptist Church.

Jacob F. Srote. Among the early settlers of Pike County,

Mo., may be mentioned Jacob F. and Elizabeth (Willhoit) Srote, both of whom were born in 1808, the former in Kentucky, and the latter in Virginia. They were married in the latter State, whither the mother had come in 1810, and there resided until 1838, at which time they took up their residence in Missouri. The father was a Democrat, and died in 1877. The mother still lives, and resides with her children. Although eighty years of age she has never seen a railroad car. She is the mother of five children, and Jacob F. Srote, whose name heads this sketch, is her youngest child. He was born in Pike County, Mo., December 27, 1842, and assisted his father on the farm until twenty-one years of age, at which time he began tilling the soil on his own responsibility. In 1869 he married Alice Haislip, who was also born in Lincoln County, May 6, 1849. Their union has resulted in the birth of two children: William E. and Lester E. Both parents are members of the Missionary Baptist Church, and he is a Democrat. He owns 143 acres of land, having made the most of it since he came to Lincoln County. During the war he served in the militia, and belongs to the A. O. U. W.

F. C. Stoker was born in St. Louis County, Mo., on the 23d of September, 1863, and is a son of Fritz and Mary Stoker, who were born in Germany. After reaching manhood and womanhood they came to America and located in Missouri, and still reside in Lincoln County on a farm. In their family were five children, of whom F. C. Stoker is the fourth. He spent his boyhood days on his father's farm, but received meager educational advantages. When about seventeen years of age he began working at the blacksmith and wagon-maker's trade, and in 1884 came to Olney, where he has a fine business. He usually has two assistants and sometimes more. Mr. Stoker never served an apprenticeship at his trade, but notwithstanding this is a fine workman, and has a commodious and convenient workshop of three rooms, one for blacksmithing, one for wood work, and the third for a paint shop. He supports the principles of the Republican party, and he and wife, Harriet (Davis) Stoker, whom he married in 1884, are members of the Missionary Baptist Church. They have two children—one son and one daughter.

Capt. Joseph Story was born in 1822, and is the son of Joseph and Ruth (Davidson) Story, who were born, reared and spent their lives in New Jersey. The father died about 1833, and his father, Joseph Story, was of Scotch origin and was a Revolutionary soldier. The mother died in 1864. Capt. Joseph Story was the fourth of seven children, and was educated in the common schools. When about thirteen years of age he went with a cousin to Illinois, where he made his home until 1846, at which time he joined Company I, First Illinois Volunteers, and served under Gen. Taylor in the Mexican War. After the close of the war he returned to Illinois, and in 1849 was married in Jersey County to Abigail B., daughter of Basil Griggs, by whom she became the mother of seven children, six living: John G., Joseph, James P., Filmore, Capitola (wife of J. E. Witcher) and Mary A. (wife of Lafayette Pendleton). After coming to Adair County, Mo., in 1855, he resided here until 1863, when he returned to Illinois, but located permanently in Lincoln County, Mo., in 1875. He owns a good farm of 276 acres, and is well fixed financially. In July, 1861, he organized Company B, Twenty-first Missouri Volunteer Infantry, and commanded the same until July, 1862, when he resigned on account of disability. He participated in the battle of Shiloh, and since the war has been a stanch Republican in politics. Previous to that time he was a Whig. Mr. Story is an enterprising farmer and a good citizen.

Jefferson Sullenger, a leading farmer of Lincoln County, is the youngest of seven children born to John and Lucinda (Berry) Sullenger, who were natives of Virginia and Kentucky, respectively, the former having been born in 1789. They were married in the latter State, and soon after moved to Henry County, Ky., and in 1852 to Lincoln County, Mo. The father was a house carpenter, but also carried on farming with the assistance of his sons. He was a life-long Democrat and died in 1872, followed by his wife two years later. Jefferson Sullenger was born in Henry County, Ky., November 29, 1834, but came with his parents to Missouri and worked on the farm and attended the old subscription schools, where he received but a limited education. When the late war broke out he went to Kentucky and volunteered in the Confederate Army, but not being supplied with guns the regiment disbanded, and every man was told to get south of the Federal lines. Just at this time he received a letter from his father asking him to come home and take charge of the farm. He did so, and began rearing and shipping stock. He soon purchased a farm, and now has a fine lot of land consisting of 700 acres, all of which he has acquired since he was thirty years of age. His marriage with Mrs. Mary S. (Moore) Frank was celebrated November 21, 1883. She was born in Indiana, July 22, 1843. She, as well as Mr. Sullenger, is a member of the Cumberland Presbyterian Church, and he has always been a Democrat, and is a Chapter Mason.

Eugene L. Sydnor, D. D. S., was born in Troy, Lincoln, Co., Mo., January 24, 1853, and is the son of William and Elizabeth J. (Crews) Sydnor, both natives of Virginia, he born in 1808 and she in 1818. After marriage they lived in their native State until 1835, when they moved to Troy, Mo., and passed the balance of their days there. The father was a first-class business man, and was a trader by occupation, and a Democrat in politics. He died in 1856. Their family consisted of four children, three of whom are living, one son and two daughters. Eugene L. Sydnor was reared and educated in Troy. At the age of nineteen he began learning the dental trade, and in 1871 he entered the St. Louis Medical College, took two courses of medical lectures and a complete course in dental surgery, graduating in 1873. He then located in St. Louis, and after practicing for eighteen months moved to Troy, where he has met with well deserved success, and has received a liberal share of the patronage. In 1886 he married Miss Hettie R. Robinson, a native of Lincoln County, who bore him one son, who is now deceased. The Doctor has followed his profession in Troy for fifteen years, and the class of work he does speaks for his ability as a dentist. He is a member of the Christian Church, is a member of the A. O. U. W., and he is a Democrat in politics. Mrs. Sydnor is a member of the Methodist Episcopal Church.

Josiah M. Terrell, merchant at Auburn, Mo., was born in the "Old Dominion," May 20, 1840, and is one of eight children born to Lindsey L. and Mary (Smith) Terrell, who were also born in Virginia. They and six children are still living there. The other two are in Lincoln County, Mo. Josiah M. was reared on his father's farm and had good educational advantages. In 1861 he enlisted in Company G, Thirtieth Virginia Infantry, C. S. A., and served until the close of the war. He was in a number of engagements, and while scouting near Howlet was captured and held a prisoner for eight months at Point Lookout, Md. After his return home he taught school for some time and then turned his attention to stock trading. After his marriage to Leonora E. Luck, which occurred May 24, 1868, he started for the West in 1869, visiting Tennessee, Mississippi and Arkansas. The following year he reached Lincoln County, Mo., where he has ever since resided. After farming for three years he began merchandising in connection with the same, following the latter business in Burr Oak, Whiteside and Auburn. He began business in the latter place in February, 1888. He owns 450 acres of land, well stocked. All his property has been acquired since the war. He and wife belong to the Missionary Baptist Church, and he is a supporter of Democratic principles. He and wife became the parents of four children, but only one now lives, Emory, eight years old.

Martin G. Thompson is of Irish descent, and is the youngest of nine children born to John and Mary (Wilkinson) Thompson, both natives of Kentucky, born in 1784, and died in 1864 and 1858, respectively. They were married in Warren County, Ky., in 1804, and located first in Missouri in 1828, and in Lincoln County in 1830. In 1831 the father built the house in which his son, Martin G., now lives. He was tobacco inspector while in Kentucky, but his usual occupation was farming. Martin G. was born in Warren County, Ky., in 1828, and in 1857 was married to Timandra Powers, and by her became the father of eleven children; Gentry, Lou (wife of John Bradley), Elmer, Cyrus, Charley, Houston, David and Vollie are those living. Mr. Thompson was in the merchandise business from 1856 to 1868, but since then has lived on the old homestead, which consists of 230 acres. Besides this he has forty acres in another tract. He was previously a Whig in politics, but since the war has been a Democrat. He and three children are members of the Methodist Church, and his wife and three other children are members of the Baptist Church. Mrs. Thompson's parents, Edward and

Mary Powers, were born in Virginia in 1796 and 1799, respectively, and were reared in Kentucky. They became residents of Lincoln County, Mo., in 1830, and there spent the remainder of their days.

William Thomas Thurmond, editor and proprietor of the Troy *Herald*, was born in Prairieville, Pike Co., Mo., June 23, 1839, and is a son of George W. and Frances A. (Shaw) Thurmond, both of whom were born in Virginia. The father's birth occurred in 1815, in Nelson County. When about sixteen years of age he came to Missouri with his parents, and located in Pike County, where he was for several years a farmer and dealer in tobacco. He also for many years manufactured tobacco in Prairieville, Louisiana and St. Louis, Mo., and before the war was mayor of Louisiana for several years, and was for some time county judge. He was also president of the St. Louis Tobacco Association. His family consisted of three children, two of whom are living, Prof. C. M. B. Thurmond and William Thomas. After the mother's death, which occurred in St. Louis in 1846, Mr. Thurmond returned to Pike County, and in 1847 married Frances A. M. Appleberry, by whom he had five children who lived to be grown. He was a Democrat in politics, and died in 1885. William T. was educated in the High School of Louisiana and at Bethany College, West Virginia, graduating from the latter institution in 1860. After working at the tobacco business until 1865 he went to Memphis, Tenn., where he was engaged in the wholesale tobacco business until 1870, shortly after which time he turned his attention to teaching. In 1873 he and his brother took charge of the Christian Institute, and organized the public and high school in Troy, inducing the directors to rent that year and buy the building and grounds the next. They ran it very successfully for three sessions, giving a pronounced impulse to higher education in the county. In 1876 he purchased one-half interest in the Troy *Herald*, and two years later became sole proprietor. August 10, 1874, he married Harriet E. Moore, a daughter of Fountain Moore, one of the early settlers of Lincoln County. She was born April 10, 1852, and was educated in the Convent of the Sacred Heart at St. Charles, Mo. Seven children were born to them, but only three are living. Mrs.

Thurmond died December 22, 1887. She was a faithful wife and mother, and was an earnest and devoted member of the Catholic Church.

George S. Townsend, one of the proprietors of the Troy *Free Press*, was born near Fulton, Mo., November 11, 1859, and is a son of Eli and Margaret C. (Kelly) Townsend, who were born in Bradford, England, and Utica, N. Y., respectively. The father came to America when a young man, and located at Utica, N. Y., where he and Miss Kelly met and married. They afterward moved to Fulton, where the father engaged in business. He is present mayor of Fulton, which position he has held for a number of years. He and wife are members of the Presbyterian Church, and he is a Republican in his political views. They became the parents of seven children. George S. Townsend was educated in the public schools, and at the age of seventeen years entered a printing office at Fulton, where he worked until 1880, at which time he became foreman of the Troy *Free Press*, and later local editor. In February, 1888, he became one of the firm. He is a supporter of Democratic principles and is a Royal Arch Mason.

Ephraim Trail is a native of Lincoln County, Mo., born in 1834, and is a son of John Rollins and Rachel (Cannon) Trail, who were born in Kentucky and Tennessee, respectively. The father came to Missouri at an early day, and settled in the woods near New Hope, being one of the pioneer farmers of the county. His wife died about 1880. Ephraim is the seventh of twelve children, three now living: J. W., of Colorado; Thomas B., of Vernon County, Mo., and Ephraim, whose name heads this sketch. The latter was educated in the old log school-house and at home. He lived with his parents until twenty-one years of age, and after working for his brother, J. W., for some time went to Kentucky, and was overseer of a plantation in that State for eleven years. After living in Colorado for some time he located in Vernon County, where he was engaged for about nine years in farming and stock raising. He has lived in Lincoln County three years, where he has 126 acres of good land near New Hope. Kate Wilson became his wife in 1887. She is a member of the Baptist Church, and is a daughter of Robert and Diana

Wilson. Mr. Trail votes the Democratic ticket, and his first presidential vote was cast for Buchanan in 1856.

Benjamin Milton Vance, farmer, stock raiser, and a native of Lincoln County, Mo., was born May 7, 1829, and is the ninth of twelve children born to Benjamin and Margaret (Lindsay) Vance, who were born in Virginia and Kentucky in 1780 and 1790, and died in Missouri in 1848 and 1843, respectively. The father moved to Kentucky in 1810, was married the following year, and in 1827 came to Lincoln County, where he became an extensive and prosperous farmer. His father, Samuel Vance, was born in Scotland, and when a young man came to the United States, locating in Virginia, where he married an Irish lady. He was a colonel in the French and Indian Wars under Washington. Benjamin Milton Vance was educated in the primitive log schoolhouses of Lincoln County, but in 1849 emigrated to Wisconsin, and engaged in the mercantile business, and in 1850 went to California in quest of gold, and spent four years in the gold region of that State. He then returned to Wisconsin, and soon after to Lincoln County, where he now resides. He is owner of the old Vance homestead, which contains 700 acres of fine land; is a Democrat and a demitted Mason. In May, 1855, he was married to Virginia A., daughter of Francis and Malinda Harvey, whose sketch appears in another part of this work. By this union two children were born, Charles C., who died March 2, 1858, and Frannie M., wife of Prof. W. J. Seaman. They are all members of the Baptist Church.

Dr. James A. Ward, of Troy, Lincoln Co., Mo., the subject of this sketch, is the son of John and Rebekah (Perkins) Ward, his mother being a sister of Walton Perkins, deceased, whose sketch is to be found in another part of this history. Both parents were born in Lincoln County, N. C., his father in 1795, and his mother in 1798. They were married when very young, and in 1818 moved to Lincoln County, Mo., the country then being new and almost unbroken. His father was a farmer all his life, and in politics a Democrat. His mother, in early life, joined the Methodist Episcopal Church, but afterward united with the Primitive Baptist, of which she was a consistent member for about thirty-five years. Eleven children were born to this union, ten reaching years of maturity. In 1840 the father died, leaving a family of small children, and but little property; but the mother, with characteristic determination, reared this family to be respectable and useful citizens. She died in her eighty-second year at the home of her son, Dr. James A. Ward, by whom she was well cared for. Dr. Ward was the fifth child born to his parents, his birth occurring in Lincoln County, Mo., July 20, 1826. His early educational advantages were almost wholly wanting. After reaching years of maturity, however, he educated himself. From the age of fourteen to seventeen years, his health being bad, he was sent by his mother to West Tennessee, where he resided with a friend for nearly a year, and having recovered his health returned to his home in Missouri. He went to Wisconsin in 1845, where he followed mining, clerking, etc., returned to Troy, Mo., in 1849, and engaged as a clerk in a dry goods store, for a year or so, and then embarked in the dry goods business for himself; but being unsuccessful, he accepted a position as deputy clerk for both county and circuit courts, which position he held for over two years. He was married September 10, 1851, to Miss Virginia Hamilton, a native of Lincoln County, Mo. To this union were born two sons and a daughter. Mr. Ward commenced the study of medicine in 1853, at the same time filling the positions of deputy county and circuit clerk; attended his first course of medical lectures at the St. Louis Medical College in 1855-56; practiced medicine for a time in the interval, and graduated from that institution in 1860, and since then he has enjoyed a good practice at Troy. In 1857 he was appointed clerk of the county court, by Gov. Jackson, to fill a vacancy caused by the death of N. H. Merriwether, and held the office until after the next general election, a period of about one year. During the late war he held the office of post surgeon at Troy for most of the time, and was for some time professor of chemistry in the Troy Christian Institute. In 1868 the Doctor lost his first wife, and four years later married Miss Sarah C. Worsham, also a native of Troy. He, as well as his present wife, is a member of the Presbyterian Church, as was also his first. He is a Democrat in politics, a Mason, a member of the State Medical Association, and one of the oldest practicing physicians in this part of the State.

Alfred Weeks is the youngest of seven children, and was born in Shelby County, Ky., October 29, 1833, the son of Alfred and Clarissa (Dowdle) Weeks, who were born in Virginia and died in Kentucky and Missouri, in 1833 and 1879, respectively. The father was a teamster by occupation, and a Whig in politics. In 1851 the widow and her children came to Lincoln County, and settled near Auburn on a farm. Owing to his father's early death Alfred received but little schooling, but aided his mother on the farm. At the age of nineteen years he began the battle of life for himself and followed carpentering for about a year, but not liking the work he returned to farming and has since continued that occupation, and is now the owner of 240 acres of valuable land. He has been a hard working man all his life, and as a result has met with good success. In 1855 he was married to Martha E. Mounce, who was born in St. Louis County, Mo., February 27, 1838, and became the mother of ten children, eight of whom are living. Mr. and Mrs. Weeks are members of the Cumberland Presbyterian Church. Mrs. Weeks' parents were Henry H. and Edith (Davidson) Mounce, who were natives of Kentucky and Virginia, respectively. They were married in St. Louis County, Mo., and came to Lincoln County in 1844. They were the parents of three children. The mother died in 1840, and the father married Louranie Sitton, who bore him two children. After her death he married Ann E. Downing, and by her is the father of eight children. He was a Democrat, and died in 1880.

Henry Wehrmann is the eldest of seven sons, and was born in Lippe Detmoldt, Germany, April 25, 1837, where his parents, Christian and Caroline (Drunert) Wehrmann, were also born, the former in 1796 and the latter in 1816. The father was a well-to-do farmer in the old country, and sailed with his family to America in 1848, so that his sons might escape military life. He located in Warren County, Mo., and there spent the remainder of his life, dying in 1860. His widow is still living and resides on the old homestead. They were members of the Methodist Episcopal Church. Henry Wehrmann received a limited education in both English and German, and after remaining at home until 1864 was married to Mina Niehuss, who was born in Hanover, Germany, October 16, 1839. She came to America with her parents when about thirteen years of age, and by Mr. Wehrmann is the mother of three sons and three daughters. Mr. Wehrmann supports the principles of the Republican party, and is one of the successful farmers of the county. He owns over 800 acres of land, the most of which he has made by his own efforts. He and wife belong to the Methodist Episcopal Church.

John C. Wells is a son of Eli and Nancy (Neff) Wells, who were born on the Ohio River in West Virginia, the former in 1797, and the latter in 1803. They made their home in that State throughout life. The father was a farmer and Whig, and died in 1854. His wife died in 1885. John C. Wells is the eldest of their twelve children. He was born November 8, 1823, and his boyhood days were spent in attending school, and assisting his parents on the farm. At the age of twenty-one he left home, and for fifteen years worked on the river, first on flat and keel boats, then as clerk on a steamer, and later as pilot on a steamer, serving in the latter capacity twelve years on the lower Mississippi. In 1851 he married Jane Horne, a native of West Virginia, born September 9, 1827, and by her became the father of five sons and one daughter. Thinking the farm the best place to rear his boys, he located in Lincoln County, where he became the owner of 580 acres of good land. Both he and wife are members of the Old School Presbyterian Church, and he was a Whig in politics while that party was in existence, but since that time has been a Democrat.

Benjamin W. Wheeler, judge of the probate court, was born in Lincoln County, Mo., May 12, 1847, being the son of Otis and Jane F. (Wallace) Wheeler, natives of New Hampshire and Pennsylvania, respectively. The father graduated from the West Point Military Academy in 1821, and rose to the captaincy of a company in the regular army. For about twenty years he was in the regular service. The foes with whom he had to contend were always Indians. While stationed at Jefferson Barracks he married Miss Wallace, who bore him seven children, four sons and three daughters. Resigning he came to Lincoln County, and here turned his attention to farming. He was a Democrat in politics, and died in 1871 at the age of seventy-four years. The mother is now seventy-seven years of age, and is a member of the Presbyterian Church. He was of Scotch-Irish and she of Scotch descent. Their son, Benjamin W., was educated in the common schools, and at Wyman's City University, of St. Louis, where he attended about two years. Soon after he began to read law, and in 1869 was admitted to the bar. Three years later he was chosen prosecuting attorney for Lincoln County, holding the office two years. In 1878 he was elected to his present office, and has held this position successfully ever since. In 1873 he married Mrs. Edna Adams, and to this union were born two children, one son and one daughter. Mr. Wheeler has always been a Democrat in his political views, and is a member of the A. O. U. W. He is a member of the Presbyterian Church, and she of the Christian Church.

William Whiteside, retired farmer and an old and prominent settler of Lincoln County, Mo., was born in Shelby County, Ky., October 10, 1804. He is a son of Isaac Whiteside, who was born in North Carolina, and when a boy started with his older brother to Illinois, but after reaching Shelby County, Ky., Isaac refused to go farther. There he grew to manhood and married Linnie Ellis, a native of that county. Both grandfathers served in the Revolutionary War, and Grandfather Whiteside was a member of the North Carolina Legislature at the time of his death. Both Isaac Whiteside and his wife lived in Kentucky until their respective deaths. William Whiteside is the third of their four children, and when very young began to make his own way in the world, following the occupation of distilling. In 1828 he came to Missouri and located in Lincoln County, where he became the owner of about 1,400 acres of land—the result of his own industry and economy. He was a Whig in politics, but since the war has supported the Democratic party. The town of Whiteside was built on his land and was named in his honor. In 1829 he was married to Eliza A. Robinson, who was born in Shelby County, Ky., in 1810, and died in Missouri in 1856, having borne eleven children. Mr. Whiteside's second wife was Mrs. Sallie A. (Carr) Metcalf, also a native of Shelby County, Ky., born in 1816. She was the mother of six children by her first husband. His son, Isaac, was born in Lincoln County, January 21, 1832, and was educated in the early subscription schools. He was married in 1854 to Mary, daughter of Capt. John and Mary Ann Alloway, who were born in Shelby County, Ky., and came to Lincoln County in 1837, when Mrs. Whiteside was four years of age. Mrs. Whiteside is the mother of five living children: William, John, an attorney; Annie, wife of James W. Powell; Luella and Mary. Since 1856 Mr. Whiteside has lived on the old Capt. Alloway farm, which consists of 440 acres, all of which he has earned by his own endeavors. In the winter of 1861-62 he served six months under Gen. Price, and since the late war has been a Democrat in politics. He has been a member of the Masonic fraternity for twenty years (New Hope Lodge No. 199), and he and wife have been consistent members of the Baptist Church for forty years. His son Eugene, who died in March, 1880, at the age of twenty-one years, was a licensed Baptist minister with a bright future before him. He was preparing to enter William Jewell College at the time of his death.

George W. Whiteside, farmer, stock raiser, and a native of Lincoln County, was born December 12, 1843, and is the son of William and Eliza (Robertson) Whiteside. His early education was obtained under many difficulties, and when quite small he was compelled to walk three miles to school. He made his parents' house his home until 1864, when he enlisted in Shelby's brigade, under Sterling Price, and served until the close of the war, when he went to Mexico, and after a residence there of eighteen months went to California, where he herded sheep and farmed. In 1868 he returned home via the Isthmus of Panama and New York, and since then has been a successful agriculturist of Lincoln County, where he has a fine farm of 315 acres. His wife, who was formerly Mildred A. Baskett and a daughter of Judge H. N. Baskett, was born in Lincoln County, September 29, 1847. They were married in 1870 and became the parents of six children, four sons and two daughters. They worship in the Missionary Baptist Church, and Mr. Whiteside belongs to the Knights of Honor fraternity.

John F. Whiteside was born near Whiteside, Mo., June 26, 1849, and is a son of William and Eliza (Robertson) Whiteside. [See sketch of George W. Whiteside.] John F. was reared on his father's farm, but owing to ill health in boyhood attended school somewhat irregularly, though as his health gradually improved he attended school after becoming grown. He has made farming his chief calling through life, and has a fertile and well improved farm of 315 acres. In 1873 he was married to Ruth C. Metcalf, a native of St. Charles County, who died in 1882, having borne three daughters. Two years after her death Mr. Whiteside married Mrs. Susan F. Mendleton, a sister of his first wife. He and wife are members of the Missionary Baptist Church, and he is a supporter of Democratic principles and is a member of the Knights of Honor fraternity.

James C. Wilkinson was born near Elsberry, Mo., in 1846. His parents, Joseph and Gabrilla (Watts) Wilkinson, were born in Tennessee (he in 1818 and she in 1816), and became early residents of Missouri, where they were married in 1844. The father died near Elsberry in 1867, and the mother in 1880. Mr. Wilkinson's father, familiarly known as "Uncle Jimmy Wilkinson," was a soldier in the War of 1812, and was one of the early and prominent settlers of Lincoln County; he died about 1856. His wife died only a few years ago. James C. Wilkinson was the elder of two brothers, and was educated in the common schools, remaining at home until 1866, when he was married to Nancy Elizabeth, daughter of Robert T. and Julia Elsberry, whose sketch appears in this volume. Mr. and Mrs. Wilkinson have eight children: Joseph R., Bellezora, Udora, John M., Gabrilla A., James A., Laura Viola and Hettie Temperance. Immediately after his marriage Mr. Wilkinson went in debt for a piece of timber land, but has been very successful in the management of his business affairs, and is now the owner of 248 acres of fertile and well cultivated land. He was in the mercantile business for some time at Elsberry, in partnership with Mr. Elsberry, the firm being known as Elsberry & Wilkinson, and was afterward partner in the erection of the flouring-mill at that place. Since then he has devoted his attention to farming and trading. In November, 1887, a fine large residence and contents, the accumulations of almost a life-time, were consumed by fire. Mr. Wilkinson is a very public-spirited man, and in his political views is a Democrat. He belongs to the A. O. U. W. and the Triple Alliance, and he, wife and two daughters are members of the Baptist Church. [Since the above sketch was written, Mr. Wilkinson was taken sick on the 20th day of July, 1888, with abscess of the brain, and notwithstanding the efforts and skill of the best medical aid, after four weeks of terrible suffering, he died August 11, following.]

Robert S. Williams (deceased) was born near Pittsburgh, Penn., in 1811, and there grew to manhood on a farm. He married Isabella Seville, daughter of John and Isabella (Gale) Saville. Her father was born near Manchester, England, and was of Spanish descent. Her mother was born in London, and was of thorough English stock. Mrs. Williams was born in Manchester, England, October 23, 1820, and when six years of age came with her parents to America, locating in Philadelphia, where her mother ran a large millinery establishment. In 1838 her parents moved near Pittsburgh, Penn., and there died at the age of seventy-five and eighty-two, respectively. After marriage Mr. Williams settled upon a farm, and for about sixteen years kept a public house. In 1868 they moved to Lincoln County, Mo., purchased a farm, and here he followed agricultural pursuits, being considered one of the neatest farmers in the county. He was a man upright in his dealings, one beloved at home, and esteemed by all who knew him. He was of the Episcopal faith, as is also his wife. He was Democratic in his political views, and, although a man who never sought office, he was twice elected to the position of county auditor. He was well educated and fond of reading. He died in 1881. His widow still lives, and is well provided for. To their marriage were born three children, two now living: Charles, and Maria, who is the wife of William Noel, of Southwest Missouri. Charles, the only son, was born August 16, 1848, in Alleghany County, Penn., where he grew up and secured a good common school education. In 1867 he moved to Lincoln County, Mo., and has made the same his home ever since. In 1879 he married Miss Addie W. Tuttle, daughter of Rev. J. H. Tuttle. By her one child was born, who is now deceased. She, too, passed away in 1886. Mr. Williams is a Democrat in politics, and is a highly respected citizen. He owns a farm of 277 acres, of which about 160 acres are under cultivation. June 24, 1888, he married Miss Sarah E. Crigger, of Lincoln County.

John C. Williams, merchant and farmer, is a son of Nathaniel and Nancy (Cross) Williams, who were born in Kentucky and Virginia, respectively. They were married in the latter State, and about 1820 came to Missouri, locating in Lincoln County, where they spent the remainder of their lives. He died at the age of sixty-one years, and she when sixty-three years old. Both were members of the Regular Baptist Church, and he was a Whig in politics and a farmer by occupation. John C. Williams is the second of their ten children, and was born in Logan County, Ky., May 29, 1818, but was reared on a farm in Mo., and educated in the old subscription schools. After attaining his majority he learned the cabinet-maker's trade, and also manufactured furniture, pieces of which he still has in his house. In addition to this he carried on farming, and in 1845 was married to Margaret Cox, a daughter of John B. Cox. She was born in Lincoln County, and became the mother of nine children. She died in 1870, and three years later he married Margaret L. Kimler, a daughter of Daniel Kimler. She was born in Loudoun County, Va., October 1, 1825. In 1850 Mr. Williams located on his present farm of 240 acres, and in addition to farming follows merchandising. He engaged in the latter business in 1877 at Corso, and when the post-office was established at that place he became its postmaster. Since the death of the Whig party he has been a Democrat. He has been a resident of the county for about sixty-seven years, and is one of its highly respected citizens.

Romulus Williams is a son of Alexander H. and Lydia A. (Sanford) Williams. He was born in Lincoln County about one mile from where he now lives December 20, 1831. He was reared on a farm, and at the age of six years started to school, riding a distance of five miles. After remaining with his father until he attained his majority he began farming for himself, and in 1853 located on the farm where he now lives. He was married at that date to Margaret Ellis, a daughter of Duncan Ellis. She was born in Kentucky September 19, 1836, and when a small girl came with her parents to Lincoln County. She died January 27, 1873, leaving three sons and six daughters. She was a consistent member of the Missionary Baptist Church, and a faithful wife and mother. Mr. Williams has a fine farm of 170 acres, the most of which he has made by industry and good management. Previous to the war he was a Whig in politics, but since that time has been a Democrat.

Benjamin R. Williams, farmer and stock raiser, is a son of Alexander H. and Ann (Robinson) Williams, and was born in Union Township, Lincoln County Mo., September 21, 1850. He spent the happy and healthful life of a farmer's boy, and was educated in the district schools and at Auburn. He made his home with his parents until September 17, 1867, when he was united in marriage to Margaret E. Mounce, a daughter of Henry H. and Ann E. (Downing) Mounce. She was born in Lincoln County, her birth occurring August 18, 1852. She and Mr. Williams became the parents of four children, three sons and one daughter. Three of the children are living: Walter E. (a telegraph operator), Alexander H. and Benjamin. Soon after marriage Mr. Williams settled on a farm, and is now the owner of 400 acres of land. Both he and wife are members of the Cumberland Presbyterian Church, and he is a Democrat in his political views, and a worthy and honored citizen.

James M. Wilson is a son of John and Mary (Miller) Wilson, who were born in Mecklenburg County, N. C., but were reared in Lincoln County, Va. There they were married and lived until 1818, when they came to Lincoln County, Mo., and settled on the farm where their son, James M., now lives. The father was a wagon-maker by trade, and took an active part in the war of 1812. He was always a Democrat in politics and died in his eighty-fifth year. The mother lived to be seventy-two years of age. Only two of their four children are living, the younger being James M., who was born March 19, 1822, within half a mile of where he now lives. Margaret Hill, who was born in Mecklenburg County, Va., January 14, 1823, became his wife in 1841 and the mother of his twelve children, seven of whom are living. His wife died in 1876 and since that time Mr. Wilson has remained a widower. He is a member of the Presbyterian Church, and in 1875 was appointed tobacco inspector for the city of St. Louis. He has been quite extensively engaged in the manufacture of tobacco, but has given most of his attention to farming. He owns 335 acres of land and has assisted his children to a start in life. He upholds the principles of the Democratic party.

John F. Wilson, county surveyor, was born near Lexington, Va., on the 4th of April, 1823. His father, James Wilson, was born in Ireland, and when but six years of age was brought to the United States and was reared in Virginia, where he married Miss Ann McCowen, who died in 1831, leaving five children. James Wilson then married a Miss Anderson. He was a farmer and distiller by occupation and in his political views was a Whig. His death occurred in 1855. John F. Wilson is the eldest of his father's family and was educated in the high school near home. His favorite study was mathematics, which he pursued as far as trigonometry. He became a resident of St. Louis County, Mo. in 1846, and he there farmed and acted as justice of the peace. In 1847 Elizabeth D. Lasley became his wife. She was born in the "Old Dominion," and was brought by her parents to Missouri when three years of age. They came to Lincoln County in 1855, and here the mother died in 1875. The following year Mrs. Attillia (Copher) McCulloch became his wife. His first union resulted in the birth of four sons and two daughters, and to the last union one daughter was born. Mr. Wilson affiliates with the Democratic party, and in 1872 was chosen county surveyor, which position he has filled continuously to the present time. He and wife are members of the Christian Church, and he is a Mason and a prosperous farmer of the county, owning at the present time 160 acres of land.

Thomas C. Wilson, of the firm of T. C. Wilson & Co., was born in Lincoln County, Mo., April 12, 1851, and is the son of Alexander K. and Alzira (Gibson) Wilson. The father was born in South Carolina in 1813, and at the age of five was brought to Lincoln County by his parents, who were born, reared and married in Ireland. They immigrated to America about 1806. The mother of Thomas C. was born in Lincoln County, Mo., in 1816, and her parents were natives of South Carolina. When a young man Alexander learned the blacksmith's trade, at which he worked the principal part of his life. He was justice of the peace for many years, and judge of the county court for six years. For several years he was a director of the St. Louis & Hannibal Railroad. In politics he was a Whig, and after the war he espoused the principles of the Republican party. He died in 1886, and his wife in 1888. Thomas C. was the fifth of eight children. He was educated in the common schools and in the State University, from which he graduated in 1874, having made a specialty of civil engineering, which he followed for some time, on the railroad. In 1881 he drifted into the business. In 1886 the present company was formed, and he became a partner. During the year 1887 they got out about 400,000 ties. In 1885 he married Miss Ann Perkins, daughter of H. W. Perkins. She was born in Troy April 15, 1862, and to her marriage were born two children, a son and a daughter. The son is deceased, but the daughter, Hazel, is now living. Politically Mr. Wilson is a Republican. He has made this county his home all his life, and is a good business man and a competent engineer. He was selected as a delegate to the National Republican Convention at Chicago, from the Seventh District, as alternate, and was nominated by his party for representative of Lincoln County in 1888. Mr. Wilson, his parents, Mrs. Wilson and her parents, all were born in the month of April, a rather singular coincidence.

Judge G. G. Wilson, farmer and stock raiser, of Lincoln County, and a native of the same, was born in 1836, and is the eldest of seven children born to Roth and Diana (Gibson) Wilson, who were born in South Carolina and Tennessee in 1808 and 1814, respectively. Roth Wilson moved to St. Louis with his father, David Wilson, in 1818, and came to Lincoln County in 1820. Here he died in 1887. He was a farmer and blacksmith, and was one of the pioneer settlers of the county. Judge Wilson, whose name heads this biography, attended the early subscription schools of Missouri, and has spent his entire life on a farm. He now owns 320 acres of land, which he has earned by his own industry and economy, and, besides being an experienced farmer, is an excellent surveyor. In 1859 he was elected county surveyor, and was again elected in 1865. In 1878 he was elected judge of the county court, and was re-elected in 1880, and in 1882 was chosen presiding judge, to which position he was re-elected in 1886. He is a Democrat in his political views, and cast his first presidential vote for Buchanan in 1856. His marriage to Jane Finley took place in 1871, and their union has resulted in the birth of three children: Anna, Martha and Robert. Mrs. Wilson is a daughter of Gilmore Finley, formerly of Kentucky, but an early settler of Lincoln County.

Thomas W. Withrow, saddler and harness maker at Troy, is the son of Jacob H. and Ann (Wright) Withrow. The father was born in Pennsylvania, and was of Scotch-Irish descent. The mother was born not far from Lexington, Ky. In his youth the father learned the harness-maker's trade, came to Troy in 1836 and opened a shop. Here he married in 1839, and settled in Troy. He died at the age of fifty-five, but the mother is still living, is sixty-six years old and does her own work. The mother is an Old School Baptist, and her father was a preacher of that faith. Thomas W. Withrow was the eldest of ten children, four now living. He was born in Troy, March 20, 1840, and received a common school education. At the age of nine he began doing odd jobs in his father's shop, and ever since has been working at the business. In 1866 his father took him in as partner, and after the father's death he became sole proprietor. In 1866 he married Miss Abiah F. Merriwether, a native of Lincoln County, who bore him five children, one son and four daughters. Mr. Withrow is a stanch Democrat, as was his father before him. He is a member of the I. O. O. F., and in connection with his harness business is interested in agricultural pursuits.

Hart B. Wommack, M. D., of Millwood, is the son of Richard and Elizabeth (Hammond) Wommack. The father was born in Halifax County, Va., in 1804, and when two years old was taken to Tennessee. In 1823 he came with his mother to Lincoln County, and two years later he married Miss Cynthia Smiley, who bore him three children. After her death he married, in 1831, Mrs. Elizabeth Gilmore, *nee* Hammond, and by her became the father of seven children, two sons and five daughters. She was a native of Kentucky but came to this State in early womanhood, and had one child by a previous marriage. She died in her sixty-fifth year. The father then chose for his third wife Mrs. Fanny Morris. He was a man of superior ability, and one of influence in his county. He was chosen to represent Lincoln County in the Legislature during the following years: 1848, 1856, 1858, 1862 and 1866, served as sheriff four terms, and as assessor two terms. He died in his seventy-sixth year. His son, Hart B., was born in Lincoln County, January 7, 1844, and received his literary education at the academy at Troy, Mo. Having studied medicine for three years under Drs. Bartlett and Griffith, of Louisiana, Mo., he entered the Missouri Medical College at St. Louis, from which institution he graduated in 1865. He then came to Millwood where he has practiced since. In 1866 he married Miss Tillie E. Whitmore, of St. Charles County, who lived about two years. In 1870 he married Elza Dyer, a native of Lincoln County, Mo., and a daughter of George I. Dyer. This union resulted in the birth of seven children, three sons and four daughters. He and wife are members of the Catholic Church, as was also his first wife. He is a Democrat in politics, and in connection with his practice he is interested in farming and is the owner of 388 acres. He belongs to the Catholic Knights of America, and is a member of the A. O. U. W. The Doctor has been practicing medicine in this community for twenty-three years, and has had very liberal patronage and satisfactory success.

Brice H. Wommack, farmer and stock raiser, of Lincoln County, Mo., and a native of the same, was born December 4, 1851, and is a son of Richard and Elizabeth (Hammond) Wommack. He was educated in the common schools and at Troy, and taught one term of school, but the confinement of such a life did not agree with him, and he engaged in farming. He has been very successful in this calling and owns about 600 acres of valuable land. He is a Democrat in his political views, and he and wife are worthy members of the Christian Church. In 1873 he married Hannah H., daughter of Francis B. Clare. She was born in Lincoln County, September 5, 1856, and is the mother of three children—Elizabeth, Richard F. and Roy C.

Shapleigh R. Woolfolk, one of the oldest residents of Troy now living, is the son of John A. and Elizabeth (Ross) Woolfolk, both natives of Kentucky. When young both came to Missouri, were married here in St. Charles County, and soon after moved to Lincoln County. The father was an extensive contractor and builder, being one of the contractors of the Lunatic Asylum at

Fulton, and the Christian College at Canton. He was an old line Whig in politics, and he and wife were both zealous workers in the Presbyterian Church. Their family consisted of twelve children, Shapleigh being the second. He was born June 23, 1825, was reared on a farm and educated in the log school-house of early times and at Troy. At the age of fourteen he began clerking in his father's store, and after reaching years of discretion he took an interest in his father's store and ran it for several years. In 1866 he was elected sheriff and collector, holding the same until 1870. Previous to this he was county treasurer about four or five years. For about five years he has been connected with D. Dubach & Co., lumber firm. In 1855 he married Miss Susan C. Bragg, a native of Virginia. The fruit of this union was four children, three now living, and all daughters. In connection with the lumber business Mr. Woolfolk is also interested in farming. In politics he was a Whig before the war and a Democrat afterward. Both he and wife are members of the Presbyterian Church, he being an elder of the same.

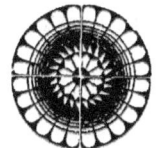

INDEX
Lincoln County History

Abernathy, James R. 361
Agricultural and Mechanical Fair Assoc. 328
Agricultural and Mechanical Society, 328
Allen, Benjamin 220, 234, 263, 458
Allen, Edwin, 221
Anderson, Major 225
Art Exhibition of 1885, 493
Attorneys, listing of early 354
Averell, John 220

-B-

Bailey, David 219, 234, 261, 264, 277, 318
Bailey, Samuel 219
Barce, John 238
Barker, Lemon 237
Barker, William 237
Bates, Edward (in Lincoln's cabinet) 363, 365
Bear Hunts, 255
Beck, James 238
Biographies 499-637
Black Hawk, 214, 215, 220, 221, 226, 286
Blanton, Thompson, 271. 319, 458
Boone, Daniel 219, 291
Boone, Nathan 219, 231
Bowles, James 220
Britton, John 238
Burnes, George 221
Burnes, James 221, 234
Burr Oak Lodge 778, IOOF, 414

-C-

Callaway, James 219, 228, 229, 232, 368, 431
Cave on Wilson farm, 209, 264, 317
Chambers, John 238
Clark's Fort, 218, 226
Christmas frolics, 258
Cholera epidemic, 448
Churches, 473 to 493
Civil Action, first 352
Civil War, 392-405
Clark's Fort, 218, 226
Clark, Major Christopher 215, 218, 227, 228, 230, 252, 259, 264, 281, 317

Clark's Fort, 218, 226
Climate in County 328
Cochran, Andrew 237
Cocke, Burt J. 233
Collard, Elijah 229, 235, 263, 264, 331, 339
Collard, Joseph 229, 235
Constables, township 263
Cornick, Tully R. 230
Cottle, Benjamin 431
Cottle, Deacon Joseph 218, 229, 233
Cottle, Ira 233, 234, 269, 317
Cox, Jesse 232
Cox, Meredith 237, 317
County Court, first 266, 249
County Court, 2nd session 271
County Court, session speeded by impending birth 271
County officials, first 261
County officials, listing and biographies to 1888, 331
County seat, donation for 265
County seat, first change 267
Cox, Jesse 232
Cox, Meredith 237, 317
Crenshaw, Joel 220
Craig, Capt. 222
Crops in County, 324-325

-D-

Daniels, Nancy 234, 249
Dixon, Frederick (Indian scout) 216, 220, 224, 234
Downing, Ezekiel 234, 236
Dramshops, 353
Draper, Daniel 236, 237, 458
Drownings at Moscow, 419
Durgee, Chauncey 221, 224
Durgee, Roswell 220, 234

-E-

East, Thomas 237
Edwards, Judge Wm. 358
Elections, first in County 263, 343
Entertainment, early 254
Ewing, John 221, 223, 233, 234, 263, 269
Ewing, Wm. 223, 234, 235

-F-

Fagg, Judge Thomas 357
Farm Census of 1880, 327
Ferry, first license 276

Fire in the outhouse, 446
Floods, early 205

Foreigners, first naturalization 353
Fort Howard 217, 219, 227, 234
Freise, Francis 225

-G-

Game hunting 256
G.A.R. 422, 453
Gibson, James 236
Gibson, Samuel 236, 263
Gilliland, John 236
Gladney, Samuel 237
Groshong, Jacob 232, 317
Groshong, Jeremial 226, 232
Groshong, Samuel 226, 457

-H-

Hammond, Slade 236
Hammond, Thomas 236
Harpole, Peter 227
Hemmersmeyer, Mrs. Henry 233
Highways, early 274
Homicide and suicide, 387
Hoss, Charles 237
House raising 244
Howard, Benjamin 219
Howdeshell, Jos. 236
Howell, Samuel 237, 241, 242, 254
Hudson, Isaac 238
Hudson, John 236
Hughes, Judge Elliott 349
Hunt, Judge Ezra 269
Hunter, John 235, 237
Hunter, Joseph 235

-I-

Indian treaties, 284
Ingram, Jarot, 236

-J-

Jail, 1840 construction 278
Jameson, George W. 235, 236, 237
Jameson, Major Robert 235, 263
Judicial organization 346
Justices of the peace, first 263

-K-

Keightley, Abraham 225
Keller, Anthony 231
Kempler, Daniel 236
Kennedy, Armstrong 237
Keokuck, Chief of the Foxes 215
Killam, David 234
Killing of Henry Turner, 386

-L-

Lamaster, David 224
Land Survey of 1819, 291
Lewis, James S. 236

Lincoln County Settlers to Texas, 252-253
Lindsey, John 216, 220, 234
"Link-horn" County 260
Local Option 494
Lynn, Wm. 225

-M-

McCormick, Wm. 222
McCoy, Jos. Jr. 227
McCoy, Jos. Sr. 227, 236
McHugh, children massacred 216
McHugh, Wm. 216, 220, 233
McKee. Judge Archibald 360
McLane, Alexander 233, 234
McLane, John 221
McNair, David 228
McNair, John 219, 224, 228
McNair, Robert 219, 220, 228, 235, 236
Marriages, 1st in county 245
Meracle, David 236
Mill, 1st water-powered, 233
Miller, Wm. 236
Monroe, "Father" Andrew 272
Moore, Fountain 237
Mounds and mound builders, 212-213
Mudd, Dr. 214, 215, 267, 420
Mudd, Judge 490
Murders 362-386
Musters, description of first 388

-N-

Natural Bridge and cave 209, 210
New Spain, 388
Null, Jacob 229, 235
Null, John 229, 235, 249

-O-

Old Settlers Institute 423
Old Settlers reunions 247, 251
Olney Institute 423
O'Neal family massacre 223, 235
Owens, James 236

-P-

Palmer, Burton (surveyor) 363
Paris family, 229
Parker, Francis 269
Parker, Howard S. 361
Peers, Valentine 232
Perkins, Walton 236, 254, 255
Petit jury, 1st 352
Pioneer cabins, 243
Pioneer weddings, 244
Poor Farm and asylum, 278
Porter, David 235
Porter, James 236

Post offices and postmasters in 1888, 456
Pottery 209
Presidential vote of 1884, 344
Probate court, 1st 350
Proctor, Gen. 220
Public buildings, 1st 277
Public lands, 292
Public spring in Troy, 205
Pugh, Peter 226, 228

-R-

Railroad bonds, 295
Railroads thru county, 294
Railroad ties, 414
Rector, Noah 238
Riffle, Francis 220, 233
Riffle, John 234
Riggs, Jonathan 219, 226, 227, 229, 266, 269, 431
Riley, James 236
Robbins, J. R. 431, 432
Robinson, Judge Elijah 359

-S-

Sac Indians, chiefs 217
School districts, 1st 461
Schools for colored children, 471
School population of 1887, 472
School tax, 1st 459
Silver bracelets excavated, 212
Sitton, Lawrence 236, 363
Sitton, Sheriff Wm. 362
Slave burned at the stake, 365
Slaveholders, lists 319, 320, 321
Slave burned at the stake, 365
Slicker War, 389
Smith, Hans 363
Spanish grants 287, 293
Stephens, Stephen 237
Stock law of 1887, 329
Stonebreaker, Capt. 217
Stouts Fort, 218

-T-

Taxable property in 1870, 1880, 1888   322-323
Taxes, 1st county 316
Taxpayers in 1821 (heads of pioneer families), 239
Taylor, President 219
Teachers, early 457
Temperance Benevolent Association 443
Timber, Indians burning 207
Todd, David 260
Towns in County--Location and Description
    Alexandria 205
    Auburn 406
    Brevator 406
    Briscoe 406
    Cap-au-Gris 407

Chain of Rocks 407
　　Chantilla 408
　　Elsberry 409
　　Falmouth 413
　　Foley 413
　　Hurricane 415
　　Jonesville 415
　　Louisville 415
　　Millwood 419
　　Monroe 416
　　Moscow 417
　　New Hope 421
　　New Salem 421
　　Olney 422
　　Owen 426
　　Silex 427
　　Sterling 428
　　Troy 428
　　Truxton 451
Townships, 1st changes 281, 350
Trail, Aunt Sallie 236
Troy fire of 1887, 446
Troy newspapers 449
Troy, prices in 1840, 433
Troy schools 450
Troy, 1873 business directory 438
Troy Lodge 34 AF and AM 439
Troy Lodge 68, IOOF 441
Truxton seminary 452

-U-

Uptegrove, Wm. 238

-V-

Vivion, Thacker 236, 253, 263, 317

-W-

War of 1812
　　Volunteers 219
　　Forts 218
　　Attacks 220
　　Fight near Ft. Howard 221
Watts, Henry 238, 272
Watts, William 256
Wehde, Capt. 234
Wells, Jeptha 249, 360
Wells, Judge Carty 356, 363
Wells, Joseph 421, 422
White, Isaac 228
Williams, Alambe 229, 235, 238
Williams, Ben R. 238
Williams, Job 229, 235
Williams, Mrs. Frances 249
Wills, 1st probated 351
Wilson, James 236
Wilson, John 237
Wine production 326

Winfield Milling Co., 454
Wing, Frederick 231, 236
Wolf bounties, 257
Woods' Fort (at Troy) 218, 229, 235, 430
Woods, James 233, 263
Woods, Martin 233
Woods, Zaddock 218, 229, 233, 255, 263, 430, 431

-X-

-Y-

Young, William 360

-Z-

Zumwalt, Adam 214

www.ingramcontent.com/pod-product-compliance
Lightning Source LLC
Chambersburg PA
CBHW020635300426
44112CB00007B/119